ROYAL ROMANCES

TITILLATING TALES OF PASSION
AND POWER IN THE PALACES OF EUROPE

LESLIE CARROLL

AUTHOR OF *NOTORIOUS ROYAL MARRIAGES* AND *ROYAL PAINS*

Roy

"For those who enjoy reading about th learn more about the darker side of va enjoyable, quick read."

— *Booklist*

"If you love history and you love scandal, give *Royal Pains* a go. Between shaking your head at some of the antics and feeling glad Ivan the Terrible never picked you to be his Czarina of the Week, you'll learn the odd bit of history. Or you could watch the non–Moogles and Googles shows on the History Channel, but those are few and far between. Stick with Leslie Carroll; her bank account and history majors everywhere will thank you." —Book Slut Gwen

"This installment in Leslie Carroll's 'Royal' series is as thought-provoking as the first two." —Historical-Fiction.com

Notoriou∫ Royal Marriage∫

"For those who tackled Hilary Mantel's *Wolf Hall*, and can't get enough of the scandal surrounding Henry VIII's wives, [*Notorious Royal Marriages* is] the perfect companion book." —*The New Yorker*

"Carroll writes with verve and wit about the passionate—and occasionally perilous—events that occur when royals wed. . . . Carroll's fascinating account of nine centuries of royal marriages is an irresistible combination of *People* magazine and the History Channel." —*Chicago Tribune* (5 stars)

"Sex! Intrigue! Scandal! Carroll's newest offering chronicles well-known matrimonial pairings among European royals during the last nine hundred years. With a breezy and lively narrative, she gives the dirt on a parade of often mismatched couples." —*The Historical Novels Review*

"Carroll is a sharp and amusing writer. . . . You'll be entertained like a tabloid would entertain you, but you'll also learn as much as you would in a European studies course in college . . . a perfect marriage of a book!" —Examiner.com (Pittsburgh)

Royal Affair∫

"Carroll . . . has a true talent for weaving fascinating narratives. Her entertaining writing style makes this one book you do not want to put down. Entertaining, impeccably researched, and extremely well written, it will appeal to all readers with an interest in British history." —*Library Journal*

"There are lots [of] royal romps cataloged in this entertaining, enormously readable book." —*Las Vegas Review-Journal*

"Carroll offers . . . insight behind the closed doors of the last thousand years of England's busiest bed-hopping and head-lopping kings and queens."—Book Fetish

"This book is a historical work, but because of Leslie Carroll's strong writing and her own personal voice, it comes off like a delicious novel."
—Examiner.com (Pittsburgh)

Royal ROMANCES

TITILLATING TALES
OF PASSION AND POWER
IN THE PALACES OF EUROPE

LESLIE CARROLL

 NEW AMERICAN LIBRARY

NEW AMERICAN LIBRARY
Published by New American Library, a division of
Penguin Group (USA) Inc., 375 Hudson Street,
New York, New York 10014, USA
Penguin Group (Canada), 90 Eglinton Avenue East, Suite 700, Toronto,
Ontario M4P 2Y3, Canada (a division of Pearson Penguin Canada Inc.)
Penguin Books Ltd., 80 Strand, London WC2R 0RL, England
Penguin Ireland, 25 St. Stephen's Green, Dublin 2,
Ireland (a division of Penguin Books Ltd.)
Penguin Group (Australia), 250 Camberwell Road, Camberwell, Victoria 3124,
Australia (a division of Pearson Australia Group Pty. Ltd.)
Penguin Books India Pvt. Ltd., 11 Community Centre, Panchsheel Park,
New Delhi - 110 017, India
Penguin Group (NZ), 67 Apollo Drive, Rosedale, Auckland 0632,
New Zealand (a division of Pearson New Zealand Ltd.)
Penguin Books (South Africa) (Pty.) Ltd., 24 Sturdee Avenue,
Rosebank, Johannesburg 2196, South Africa

Penguin Books Ltd., Registered Offices:
80 Strand, London WC2R 0RL, England

First published by New American Library,
a division of Penguin Group (USA) Inc.

First Printing, November 2012
10 9 8 7 6 5 4 3

LIBRARY OF CONGRESS CATALOGING-IN-PUBLICATION DATA:

Carroll, Leslie, 1959–
    Royal romances: titillating tales of passion and power in the palaces of Europe/Leslie
Carroll.
      p. cm.
    Includes bibliographical references.
    ISBN 978-0-451-23808-5
    1. Europe—Kings and rulers—Paramours.   2. Queens—Europe—Paramours.
3. Favorites, Royal—Europe.   I. Title.
    D107.C294 2012
    940.09'9—dc23   2012007790

Set in Sabon
Designed by Patrice Sheridan

Printed in the United States of America

For my late grandparents
Carroll and Norma Carroll,

❖

whose unflagging love and support inspired me to take their
name professionally, and who introduced me to the glamour
and magic of Europe's royal courts;
and to Lazarus and (the wisest woman in the world) Sylvia
Goldsmith, whose English roots continue to inspire me to
rediscover my own, even as I wonder whether I may be
distantly related to the Duchess of Cambridge.
I grew up with the best of role models: my grandparents'
lengthy and happy marriages taught me to believe in
romance and the concept of an enduring love.

Contents

CAROLINE MATHILDE

1751–1775

Queen of Denmark: 1766–1772

AND

Johann Friedrich Struensee (1737–1772)
227

MARIE ANTOINETTE

1755–1793

Queen of France: 1774–1792

AND

Count Axel von Fersen (1755–1810)
255

NAPOLEON BONAPARTE

1769–1821

As Napoleon I, Emperor of the French, from
1804–1814
and for 3 months in the spring of 1815

AND

Marie Walewska (1786–1817)
297

LUDWIG I OF BAVARIA

1786–1868

Ruled: 1825–1848

AND

Lola Montez (1821–1861)
327

"... my heart is loath to remain even one hour without love."

—Catherine II of Russia (Catherine the Great),
February 21, 1774

ROYAL ROMANCES

Foreword

ro·mance \rō-'man(t)s; rə; 'rō\
n.
1.
    a. A love affair.
    b. Ardent emotional attachment or involvement between people; love.
    c. A strong, sometimes short-lived attachment, fascination, or enthusiasm for something.
2. A mysterious or fascinating quality or appeal, as of something adventurous, heroic, or strangely beautiful.

ro·manced, ro·mancing, ro·manc·es
v. tr. Informal
1. To make love to; court or woo.
2. To have a love affair with.

In fairy tales, royal romances are those happily-ever-afters that involve an unmarried pair of lovers, big dresses, shimmering jewels, and nights of untold ecstasy, although you won't find that last bit in any of the Disney adaptations.

Real-life royal romances, however, are somewhat different: same gowns and jewels, same nights of fevered passion—but rarely enjoyed with one's own spouse. Indeed, many of the royals featured in the fourteen romances profiled in this volume fell in love *with someone else* after they were already married to their consort or to the reigning monarch. In this book, there are a couple of exceptions: Louis XV of France and Russia's Catherine the Great were widowed at the time of their respective liaisons with the comtesse du Barry and Grigory Potemkin. Rare indeed is the marital love match, such as the union of George VI and Elizabeth Bowes Lyon, the parents of Queen Elizabeth II (and featured in the 2010 film *The King's Speech*), and that of the Duke and Duchess of Cambridge, Prince William of Wales and the former Catherine Middleton.

One of the romances profiled here was a great *affaire de coeur* that may have crossed the line into the realm of the physical. The nature of their relationship remains hotly debated, with many historians insisting that it was no more than a chaste and pure, unconsummated passion in the grand tradition of medieval chivalry. Scholars can agree on one point, however, which is that Axel von Fersen more than once risked his life to save Marie Antoinette's.

At the other end of the sexual spectrum, some of the monarchs whose romances fill these pages were serial debauchers, the Bourbon kings Louis XIV and his great-grandson Louis XV being legendarily priapic. Louis XV even took his pleasure with nubile young girls in a mansion kept strictly for their own amusement known as the Parc-aux-Cerfs. But few of these bed warmers had the staying power of a Madame de Maintenon or a Pompadour. For that, a royal mistress needed brains and talents that could be plied beyond the bedchamber. She had to amuse the king, she could never appear tired or bored in his presence, and she had to be a true partner in every way—a meeting of minds and hearts, bodies and souls.

In a world where marriages were arranged for political and dynastic reasons, the lover in a true royal romance is the person the sovereign or consort would likely have selected as a spouse, had he or she been permitted the choice. Yet in one rare instance, the relationship between Louis XIV and the marquise de Maintenon resulted in a marriage, albeit a morganatic one—a legal union where the lover remained uncrowned and any children would have no rights of succession. It is also believed by many historians that Catherine the Great clandestinely wed Potemkin.

Several of the paramours in *Royal Romances* were perceived as the powers behind their respective lovers' thrones. Agnès Sorel was a beautiful blond medieval life coach, less famous than Joan of Arc, but more effective in spurring Charles VII to victory over the English.

Diane de Poitiers cosigned state documents with Henri II. Madame de Montespan was nicknamed "the real queen of France." And to be a "Pompadour" referred to a royal mistress who appeared to be running the country. Caroline Mathilde was the youngest sister of George III of England, dispatched to Denmark at the age of fifteen to wed a king who was madder than her brother ever would be. She eventually embarked on a torrid romance with a commoner, her husband's physician; the pair of them seized the reins of power and overhauled the kingdom. And the overweening influence of the tempestuous dancer Lola Montez toppled the monarchy of Ludwig I of Bavaria.

As for the two marriages profiled toward the end of the book, Elizabeth Bowes Lyon, who became queen of England in the wake of a constitutional crisis and boosted British morale during the kingdom's darkest hours of the twentieth century, was far more than a mere consort. She was her husband's full partner and an indispensable and indefatigable helpmeet. Prince William's wife, Catherine, Duchess of Cambridge, with her beauty, elegance, and charm, in addition to her education, appears to have been cast in the same mold.

The lovers, mistresses, and wives in these pages are graced with a combination of qualities that rendered them utterly irresistible to their royal paramours. The romances are of the passionate, heart-stopping, I-can't-live-without-you/you-are-the-air-I-breathe variety. However, the adulterous liaisons caused no end of heartbreak to the third wheel in the relationship—the straying sovereign's spouse. The queen was invariably left embarrassed by the public role played by the royal favorite and by her husband's passion for her. Queens were traditionally expected to produce an heir to the throne and to remain quiet, pious, and philanthropic, and to stay out of the limelight. But Catherine de Medici, in particular, was one consort who was pathetically in love with her husband, Henri II. She was deeply humiliated by his outsize devotion to his much older *maîtresse en titre*, or official mistress (a formal role at court that the French invented), the cool blond Diane de Poitiers.

Sometimes, what was good for the gander was good for the goose—or so the goose thought, until she got cooked! Sophia

Dorothea of Celle was the wife of George Ludwig of Hanover, the future George I of England. He was enjoying two simultaneous affairs, so Sophia Dorothea indulged in a lurid romance of her own with a dashing Swedish mercenary, Philipp Christoph von Königsmark. Things did not end happily for either of them.

But many of the royal romances featured in this book infuriated, upset, mortified, and disgruntled more than the sovereign's consort. From Potemkin to Lola Montez, and several others in between, including the bewitching (literally, perhaps) Athénaïs de Montespan and Mesdames de Pompadour and du Barry, these lovers captivated their royal paramours to such an extent that the power they wielded, over both sovereign and kingdom, became immense. And from the monarchs' ministers and courtiers to their relatives to his subjects and the country's often hypocritical clerics came the hue and cry that the royal favorite's influence with the ruler was the ruination of the nation. Sex as a weapon was never perceived as more dangerous, or more alluring.

But there is also something to be said for the maternal "Don't worry, darling; I'll never let you down" kind of love as well, for that, too, has its appeal. Henri II, who never knew a mother's affection, fell passionately in love with Diane de Poitiers, a woman nearly twenty years his senior. The marquise de Maintenon had a few years on the Sun King, and, although she was hardly old enough to be his mother, had a maturing influence on him. Potemkin was a decade younger than the libidinous Empress of all the Russias. And Elizabeth Bowes Lyon, though five years younger than the Duke of York, the future George VI, was a steadying influence on her spouse, who had never wished to assume the throne.

Catherine Elizabeth Middleton's marriage on April 29, 2011, to the dashing Prince William was of historical significance; she was the first true commoner (one not of noble birth and aristocratic lineage) to wed an heir to the English throne since Anne Hyde clandestinely married the Duke of York in 1660. The story of William and Kate is a genuine royal romance for the twenty-first century, a modern fairy tale absent cynicism and brimming with hope for the future, where the girl gets her prince and becomes a fully respected partner in his life. She shops for her own big dresses, sometimes on the High Street with discount coupons, and even wears them more than once, just like the rest of us.

As for the shimmering jewels . . . well, one day the duchess will have access to the rather glamorous collection in the Tower of London. The pomp and circumstance connected with centuries of tradition does have certain undeniable advantages.

CHARLES VII

1403–1461

RULED FRANCE: 1422–1461

$\mathcal{A}$t the time, some people believed it had taken a miracle to spur Charles VII to his destiny, but the real impetus may have come not from the illiterate virgin Joan of Arc who heard heavenly voices, but from his beautiful and pragmatic paramour.

Charles was the fifth son born to the clinically insane Charles VI of the royal House of Valois and his wife and queen, the flirtatious Isabeau of Bavaria. When they wed in 1385, Charles's father was seventeen and his mother was in her fourteenth year. After all four of his older brothers died young, Charles became dauphin, the heir to the throne of France, which at the time was one of several regions located within the country as we now know it. But inheriting the crown would hardly be a pro forma matter of waiting for his father to die.

On St. Crispin's Day, October 25, 1415, after exhorting his troops to surge once more into the breach, England's Henry V achieved a massive victory at Agincourt, littering the battlefield with the flower of French chivalry and claiming the title of king of France. To cement his claim, Henry V wed Catherine of Valois, the daughter of the mad Charles VI.

Catherine's brother, the future Charles VII, faced threats from within France's borders as well. Not long after he inherited the title of dauphin, in May 1418 he was compelled to flee Paris when his cousin, the Duke of Burgundy, invaded the city with his personal army. Charles planned a reconciliation with the duke the following year, meeting him on September 10, 1419, on the bridge at Montereau. Whether at Charles's instigation or not, his men murdered the duke. Rather than securing his power, the murder forced Charles to flee once again, this time to the city of Bourges.

The succession of the French throne continued to remain in doubt. By the 1420 Treaty of Troyes, it was agreed that upon the death of the dauphin's father, crazy Charles VI, Henry V's son Henry VI would be recognized as the king of France. However, the kingdom would be ruled by the boy's uncle, the Duke of Bedford, as his regent.

The following year, the dauphin's paternity was called into question, when it was alleged that he was the by-blow of one of his mother's numerous extramarital affairs. Fearing for his life after his parents' repudiation of his legitimacy, Charles headed south, receiving sanctuary from his cousin Louis II of Anjou and his wife, Yolande of Aragon. In April 1422, the nineteen-year-old Charles married their eldest daughter, Marie.

While Marie was judged to be a brunette beauty, it's difficult to conjecture, from contemporary portraiture, whether Charles was considered handsome. He has the high, plucked forehead that was deemed most attractive, but his nose has a Jimmy Durante aspect to it. The court painter Jean Fouquet's portrait of him, circa 1445–1450, when Charles was in his forties, depicts a world-weary man with a woeful countenance.

Meanwhile, back in Paris in 1422, little Henry VI's regent had taken up residence and was respected by the French. But the dauphin Charles, whom the English and their allies, the northern French Burgundians, had tauntingly nicknamed *le Roitelet de Bourges* (the Kinglet of Bourges), wanted what was rightfully his. He began amassing an army.

Charles VI died on October 21, 1422, and the dauphin began referring to himself as Charles VII, king of France, although it was the English boy-king Henry VI who was recognized as the sovereign, according to the documents registered on November 19 with the Parlement of Paris, the capital's judicial body. Charles remained uncrowned, and he would have to fight for the right to sit on the throne of the Valois kings.

Five years later, the English had Orléans under siege, and things were not looking good for Charles. But on February 24, 1429, a peasant girl from the village of Domrémy in the province of Lorraine arrived in Chinon, riding a bony horse. Her name was Jehane, daughter of Jacques d'Arc, Jack the Archer. She insisted that the Holy Virgin and saints Catherine and Marguerite had revealed her destiny to her: to deliver Orléans and conduct Charles under his own banner to be crowned at Reims Cathedral, the traditional site for French coronations.

Willing to believe in miracles, Charles's superstitious troops were roused by the girl known to history as Joan of Arc. With Joan and the saints behind them, their war was transformed into a crusade, and the French trounced the Burgundian-English enemy forces. The Maid of Orléans, also known as *la Pucelle* (the virgin), did indeed escort Charles to Reims, where he was crowned. But in 1430, Joan was wounded in battle and was delivered into the hands of the English. Convinced that a French victory had to have been the devil's work, they tried, convicted, and burned Joan as a witch, and her eight-month influence over Charles VII literally went up in smoke.

But then the Grim Reaper dealt him a winning hand. First, Charles's mother, who had repudiated him and instead sided with the Burgundians, died. By the Treaty of Arras, in 1435, Philip the Good, Duke of Burgundy (son of the duke that Charles had murdered back in 1419), recognized Charles VII as king of France. The death of the Duke of Bedford, one week before the Congress of Arras concluded, left the English with no regent to rule France in Henry's name. And with no representative in Paris to uphold the authority of the absent king of England, the French turned to their hometown *homme*— Charles VII—and were willing to accept his restoration.

On November 12, 1437, Charles spent the night at the abbey of Saint-Denis, and on the following day he was formally received in the chapel as king of France.

Having finally gained the crown for himself after thirteen years of tussling with the English regent for the throne, Charles VII buckled down to the business of governing. But he would not prove to be one of France's finest monarchs. His two greatest legacies to France thus far had been the creation of the kingdom's first standing army, and the establishment in 1432 of the University of Poitiers. Charles spent the latter part of his reign quarreling with his oldest son, Louis, who wanted a role in the government. Louis plotted against his own father and detested Charles's mistress Agnès Sorel. The king banished Louis to a region known as the Dauphiné in 1446, and the two men never spoke to each other again.

In 1458, a sore on Charles's leg grew infected, and he developed a raging fever. In one of the longest death scenes in history, the king's illness persisted for nearly thirty months. During the last days of his life, a jaw infection led to an abscess in his mouth that prevented him from ingesting any food or water because he could not swallow it. Charles VII died on July 22, 1461, at the age of fifty-eight. He was buried at Saint-Denis, the traditional resting place for the kings of France.

CHARLES VII AND
AGNÈS SOREL (1409–1449)

Charles's April 1422 marriage to the seventeen-year-old Marie of Anjou brought more adherents to his campaign for his father's crown than he could ever have imagined. The girl's family had connections. The inhabitants of Brittany, Touraine, Lorraine, and southern France became pro-Charles. And after he claimed the throne upon the death of his father that October, aware that maintaining allies was even more important than gaining them, the clever new queen personally worked on her relatives the way savvy socialites used to spin their Rolodexes.

Marie was everything Charles could want from a wife. She bore a dauphin, the future Louis XI (as well as thirteen other children, seven of whom lived to adulthood), she was deeply devoted to him, and she was passionately in love with him. Best of all, like all good medieval wives, she was submissive to his will, never uttering a word of remonstrance (this no doubt came in handy when he took a mistress). Instead she averred, "He is my lord; he has a right to guide all my actions, and I have none."

Unfortunately for Marie, her love, devotion, and humility weren't enough.

The court of Charles VII and Marie of Anjou typified the age of chivalry, with colorful pageants and jousting tournaments, gallant knights on their brave steeds, ladies fair in their towering hennins with fluttering silk veils, and, of course, the poetry of the troubadours, of whom the queen's brother René was one of the finest and most famous. Within the retinue of René's wife, Isabelle of Lorraine, was a maid of honor named Agnès Sorel.

The original spelling of her surname was Soreau. Born in 1409, Agnès, who had entered Isabelle's service when she was quite young, was the daughter of Jean Soreau, Lord of Codun, squire of the comte de Clermont. Her mother, Catherine de Maignelais, came from an aristocratic family in Touraine.

It's difficult to judge the portraiture of the fifteenth century against our contemporary standards of beauty. But Olivier de la Marche, who lived at the court of Burgundy around 1444, described Agnès Sorel as "one of the most beautiful women I have ever seen, and by this beauty she had a great influence on the realm of France."

Indeed, by any account, Agnès Sorel was thought to be a stunner in her day. Her forehead was extremely high, making her hairline appear almost bald, which at the time was considered a hallmark of beauty. Her blue eyes, long lashes, and sultry lids, then, as now, were favorable assets. Her mouth was small and her nose was judged the perfect shape by her peers, which likely means it was aquiline. Her neck and shoulders were perfectly symmetrical and fashionably pale. Jean Fouquet's painting *Virgin and Child Surrounded by Angels*, circa 1449, for which Agnès is supposed to have modeled, shows one exposed, snowy breast that is absolutely perfect in its roundness. The viewer can almost feel its weight, and become curious to touch it. The portrait therefore becomes erotic, more the image of a royal mistress and her russet-haired love child than the Madonna gazing at the infant deity. Is the child representing the Baby Jesus really one of the three illegitimate daughters that Agnès Sorel bore the king?

Charles VII met Agnès in 1424, at one of the lowest points in his life. In the years after his father's death, although he was recognized as king in parts of France, the English (and the rest of the French) still acknowledged Henry VI as their sovereign. Charles had been fighting to regain his entire kingdom. His several military companies had met with hammering defeats. His Scots forces had been scattered at the Battle of Verneuil in Normandy on August 17.

Charles and Agnès became lovers, but her relationship with the king was far more than amatory. She became both coach and head cheerleader, personally responsible for spurring him to victory. And according to the courtier Olivier de la Marche, Agnès "brought to the King young men-at-arms and noble comrades by whom the King was well served."

Contemporary chronicles as well as sixteenth-century texts refer to an interesting incident that may have occurred at the court of Bourges. An astrologer had announced to the assembled lords and ladies that the Lady of Fromenteau, Agnès Sorel, would be loved by a great king. Agnès then dropped into a profound curtsy before Charles. "[S]he asked permission to withdraw to the Court of England, for it was that King whom this prediction referred to, since the King of France was going to lose his Crown, and the King of England to place it on his head."

If the story is true (although Victor Duruy's *A Short History of France* relegates it to the realm of legend), Charles was so taken aback by Agnès's remark that he immediately pulled himself out of his funk. Charles's chronicler, Brantôme, says that the king "began to weep, and then taking courage, and quitting his hunting and his gardens, he acted so as to drive the English from his kingdom by his bravery and courage."

Some historians may take the level of Agnès's influence on Charles VII with a large dose of salt, but she did manage to wean him from the cadre of chieftains he'd run with in his youth—the council of roustabouts who had consistently given him bad advice and who had led him into one military defeat after another. With Agnès in his corner—whether it was due to the self-confidence that comes from loving and being loved, or as a result of the appropriate martial and financial connections that Charles gained by their romance, or because of a lot of both—he started winning.

Agnès acted as a go-between in the negotiations to heal the rift between Charles VII and the House of Burgundy, as his murder of the Duke of Burgundy a few years earlier hadn't exactly endeared him to his vassals there. She also helped repair the breach with his vassals in Anjou and Brittany. Interestingly, the primary diplomat in this summit was another woman: Agnès's employer, Charles's sister-in-law Isabelle, the Duchess of Lorraine.

Known for her gentle spirit, Agnès possessed "eloquence . . . so much beyond that of other women that she was looked upon as a prodigy." It was Agnès who purportedly convinced the Burgundians to absolve Charles of all responsibility for the duke's death by falsely pinning the murder solely on his evil advisers. As Philip, the present Duke of Burgundy, was angry because the English were reneging on certain terms of their treaties, he was primed to switch allegiances and support Charles. Although Agnès unceasingly inspired the king with "the thought of France's restoration," according to the fifteenth-century monastic chronicler Jean Chartier, Charles could not have recaptured Paris from the English without the might of the Duke of Burgundy behind him.

But Charles needed money as well to finance his war.

It's almost axiomatic for a royal mistress to be fond of luxury, and Agnès was no different. Also typical of French royal mistresses, she set the fashions at court. Even when the queen was in mourning (seven of her fourteen children died young), Agnès and the rest of the ladies displayed such deep décolletage that their nipples and breasts were exposed. Charles liked the vogue so much that he scoffed when others were scandalized.

Another of Agnès's passions—jewelry—ended up benefiting her royal lover as well. Her friend the goldsmith Jean Coeur amassed such a fortune in the luxury goods business importing fine textiles and cutting gemstones (he was the first to cut the diamond in Western Europe; they had previously been uncut and unpolished) that he became the royal treasurer. Encouraged and protected by Agnès against his numerous detractors, who were envious that someone who was not an aristocrat should possess such great wealth, Jean Coeur personally financed Charles's military campaign against the English.

In November 1437, when Charles was hailed at Saint-Denis as the king of France, the people of Paris couldn't help but notice the beautifully dressed woman dripping in furs and gold and precious stones who accompanied the queen as she rode into the city on a horse as richly caparisoned as Her Majesty. The whispers began; it was Agnès Sorel—the king's companion—who was so bedecked with diamonds and pearls. Unsurprisingly, the clergy were among her first and most vociferous detractors. She was the new Herodias, a beast of the apocalypse, thundered the bishop of Thérouine.

Upon hearing these insults, Agnès grew anxious. "The Parisians are but villains; if I had known that they would not have done me more honor, I should never have set foot in their city," she told her lover nervously. Agnès could hardly forget that Joan of Arc's persecutors had come from Paris as well. Would she share the fate of *la Pucelle*?

However, the outcry against Agnès's opulence was in some measure justified. The Parisians had endured a particularly severe winter. The Seine had frozen solid, halting all commerce, and as a consequence, poverty had become rampant and people were starving. The famine had sparked outbreaks of contagious diseases. Although by right the festivities for the king's entry into Paris should have been extravagant, the stark contrast between the haves, as exemplified by his mistress, and the have-nots of the spectators was too much for people to bear.

The celebratory events for this grand occasion were a curious mixture of theological and classical entertainments, pageants, and masques, mixed with entirely secular pleasures such as masquerades and balls. And Agnès, whom the king had nicknamed the Queen of Beauty, presided over them all.

Charles adored Agnès because he considered her beautiful both inside and out. According to the contemporary chronicler Jean Chartier, "The love the King bore to Madame Agnès was, as everyone said, owing to her gaiety, her merry and laughing moods, and the purity and polish of her conversation, as well as to the fact that among ladies of fashion and beauty, she was the youngest and fairest ever seen. Besides all this, they said Agnès was very charitable, and gave large and liberal sums in alms, distributing from her own purse large gifts to the poor of the Church."

Agnès eventually got as good as she gave. During the 1440s Charles bestowed upon his Queen of Beauty the Manoir de Beautésur-Marne (the Castle of Beauty), built by his grandfather Charles V, as well as a number of other châteaux. She also received properties upon the births of each of their three illegitimate daughters, Charlotte, Marie, and Jeanne. A generation later, Charlotte's son Louis de Brézé married Diane de Poitiers, who became the most famous royal mistress of the sixteenth century, owing to her affair with Henri II.

In the early months of 1440, Charles's son and heir, the sixteen-year-old dauphin, Louis, participated in an unsuccessful uprising against his father called a *praguerie*, which took its name from the Bohemian dissensions created by the likes of Jan Hus. It was Agnès Sorel who armed the king and rallied supporters to his side. Louis never forgave her, both for aiding her lover, and for befriending his wife, Margaret of Scotland.

Charles let his heir stew for a while, but eventually pardoned him. He had bigger fish to fry, and in this he received Agnès's moral support. Although Paris was in Charles's possession, the English stubbornly refused to leave other regions of France, holding Normandy in the north and Gascony and Guienne in the south. In order for the king to defeat the English once and for all, he had to capture their headquarters, which was at Pontoise. Agnès accompanied her lover to the front in 1441, living at the camp with him. The siege of Pontoise was ultimately victorious for the French.

Queen Marie bore her husband's very public infidelity with characteristic resignation. But a sovereign's legitimate children often have no trouble expressing their open hatred of their parent's lover. Siding with his long-suffering mother, the future Louis XI was no exception. One day in 1444, the twenty-one-year-old heir crossed paths with his father's inamorata and cried, "By our Lord's passion, this woman is the cause of all our misfortunes," and then hauled off and hit Agnès in the face.

After this incident, she quit the court, withdrawing to the Château de Loches in Touraine. However, she would occasionally journey to her other primary residence, the Manoir de Beauté on the Marne River. There the king would secretly visit her, not just for lovers' trysts, but to discuss matters of state as well.

They were wise to meet in secret, because it was not merely Louis' outburst that had led to Agnès's self-imposed exile. Public sentiment was now very much against her because of the extent of her substantial influence with the monarch. Her biggest detractors were those who wished to control Charles instead: the dauphin Louis, the Scottish mercenary nobles, and the captains of his former bands, who had been his allies before Agnès had ever met the king.

Agnès may have left the court, but she did not abandon her lover. In the early days of 1449 she was pregnant with their fourth child when she set out from Chinon in the bleak winter cold to meet him at the front in Jumièges. The forty-year-old royal mistress became ill during the journey and died at six p.m. on February 9, 1449, at the farm of Mesnil, a dependency of the abbey at Jumièges. The abbey records state that "Charles VII had been at Jumièges for six weeks when Agnès Sorel was prostrated by an acute attack of dysentery."

But soon after her death, the belief that she had expired from natural causes was dismissed, replaced by the theory that she had been killed by mercury poisoning, perhaps the victim of a murder. Her friend the jeweler-financier Jean Coeur was at first suspected, although he was never charged, and he does not seem to have had any motive to be rid of her. Agnès had languished for forty days; if she had deliberately been given a fatal dose of poison, wouldn't she have expired a lot sooner?

Agnès Sorel's remains were examined in 2005 by a French forensic scientist, Philippe Charlier, whose tests concluded that mercury poisoning was indeed responsible for her demise. But as mercury was a popular ingredient in cosmetics and it was also used to treat worms, he could not state with any certainty whether she had been murdered.

Although it would have been nice if Charles had elevated his beloved Agnès to the nobility when she was alive to enjoy the perquisites of rank, the king made her a posthumous duchess so that she could receive an appropriately opulent ducal burial. Her body was interred in Loches in the Church of St. Ours.

Charles survived Agnès by a dozen years, dying in 1461. Incapable of fidelity to his poor dishrag of a queen (who would outlive him by more than two years), he took a new paramour—Agnès's cousin, Antoinette de Maignelais.

HENRI II

1519–1559

RULED FRANCE: 1547–1559

$\mathscr{H}$enri needed love from the beginning. He was only six years old when he and his older brother François were sent to the Spanish court as hostages, imprisoned in their father King François I's stead after he was vanquished at the Battle of Pavia in 1525. Upon their departure on March 17, 1526, one of the noblewomen in the French entourage was particularly touched by the sight of brave little Henri. She broke out of the crowd of spectators and took him in her arms, kissing the tearful boy au revoir on the forehead and wishing him Godspeed. For the rest of his life, the child would remember the maternal solicitousness of Diane de Poitiers.

The princes were held in captivity in increasingly squalid conditions for nearly five years while their dad blithely reneged on the terms of the treaty he had forged with Charles of Spain. When the boys were finally sent home to France and had difficulty reacclimating themselves to anything approaching normalcy, François scolded his sons, declaring he had no time for "dreamy, sullen, sleepy children."

On October 28, 1533, just fourteen years old, as part of another deal his father cut with the king of Spain, as well as Henry VIII, and Pope Clement, Henri wed His Holiness's niece, the homely, dumpy, and dusky Catherine de Medici—wealthy, but sullied by the fact that she was not of royal blood. Her family had made its fortune first in trade and then in banking. The couple had a miserable sex life; Catherine did not bear Henri their first child until they had been married for a decade. They eventually had ten children between 1543 and 1555, seven of whom survived to adulthood.

The August 2, 1536, death of the dauphin François made Henri the heir to the throne of France. Upon the death of his father he assumed the crown on his twenty-eighth birthday, March 31, 1547.

Much of Henri's reign was spent in conflict. He fought foreign wars with Austria, in Flanders, and challenged Charles of Spain's sovereignty over Italy. At home he persecuted the French Protestants, the Huguenots, confiscating their property and burning them as heretics.

Although Henri eventually came to respect his wife, the great love of his life was Diane de Poitiers, nearly twenty years his senior. Her elevation to the rank of duchess, let alone *maîtresse en titre*, was wound enough. But Henri's passion for Diane humiliated Catherine de Medici on a deeper level, because the queen was unfortunately very much in love with her husband.

Henri's death was foretold by the prognosticator Nostradamus as well as three other forecasters, who predicted he would meet his end during his forty-first year. Four years before the king's demise Nostradamus had published the prophecy:

The young lion will overcome the old, in
A field of combat in a single fight. He will
Pierce his eyes in a golden cage, two
Wounds in one, he then dies a cruel death.

Like Julius Caesar's wife, Calpurnia, who warned the emperor to stay away from the forum that mid-March morning, Catherine urged Henri not to enter the jousting tournament on June 30, 1559.

But he laid no store by the predictions of astrologers. The contest was just one of many brilliant festivities organized around a double wedding: the marriage of Henri and Catherine's daughter Elisabeth to King Philip II of Spain on June 22 and that of Henri's sister Marguerite to the duc de Savoie, which would take place on July 2.

Henri handily triumphed over his first two opponents. But when he took the field against the third combatant—the captain of his Scots Guard, Gabriel de Montgomery—the king's Master of the Horse warned him that his helmet was not properly fastened. And his opponent had not realized that the metal tip of his lance was missing.

After his second pass, Henri had lifted his visor to mop his brow, but had failed to close the door to his "golden cage" before commencing the third pass. The riders faced off, spurred their mounts, and charged toward each other. De Montgomery's lance struck Henri's gorget, the armorial element that protects the throat, splintering the lance. Because the king's visor had not been secured, a shard of wood pierced him above the right eye, penetrating his skull and exiting through his temple. Another splinter struck him through the throat. The king reeled in pain and shock; swaying from the force of the blow, he dropped his steed's bridle.

Henri was taken from his horse and, according to the bishop of Troyes, "a splinter of a good bigness was removed" from his eye and temple. The renowned doctor from Brussels, Andreas Vesalius, was immediately sent for and was able to remove several splinters of wood and shattered bits of bone from the king's skull. But part of the lance remained embedded in the wound, and the physicians dared not touch it. Henri took ten days to die, finally expiring on July 10, 1559, at the age of forty. He had reigned for twelve years, three months, and eleven days. He was buried in the Valois crypt at Saint-Denis and was succeeded by his frail fifteen-year-old son, François, who was married to the teenage Mary, Queen of Scots.

Henri's queen, Catherine de Medici, became a regent to be reckoned with after Henri's death. She succumbed to pleurisy on January 5, 1589.

HENRI II AND
DIANE DE POITIERS (1499–1566)

Henri became a bridegroom at the age of fourteen, which was not considered particularly young for the era. He was tall for his age, with a muscular, athletic physique, almond-shaped brown eyes, brown hair, a straight nose, and a somewhat olive but clear complexion, perhaps the greatest asset of all for an adolescent boy. Small wonder that his little Medici dumpling of a spouse was immediately smitten. However, the physical attraction was not at all mutual. Catherine had not been warmly welcomed into the French court; her marriage to Henri was purely a matter of political back-scratching. She was short, dark, stout, plain, and a commoner, in a world where willowy, fair-skinned, blue-blooded blondes were the fashion. And Henri had eyes only for the lady who had been assigned to ease Catherine's assimilation into the world of the Valois court. That woman was Catherine's second cousin, who perfectly embodied the era's *belle idéale*—the serenely beautiful Diane de Poitiers.

Educated according to the principles of humanism, Diane was a true Renaissance woman, cultured and literate, well versed in music, Greek, and Latin; her dancing was graceful and her conversation was elegant and witty. An avid huntress, like the Roman goddess who was her namesake, Diane also kept fit and glowing by swimming in cold water every day. To avoid wrinkles, she slept upright against a bolster and concocted her own facial masks from melon juice, young barley, and an egg yolk mixed with ambergris.

Diane's connections to the court reached back to her childhood. In 1524, when she was barely five years old, her father's life was spared at the last possible moment by Henri's father, François I, after Jean de Poitiers had been accused of treason. Diane was born in the south of France in a region known as the Dauphiné, which borders Provence. At the age of fifteen, she was married to a man some forty years her senior, Louis de Brézé, seigneur d'Anet, who happened, appropriately enough, to be the royal Master of the Hunt. Louis was the grandson of King Charles VII—his mother, Charlotte, was the king's oldest daughter by his *maîtresse en titre* Agnès Sorel. However, Charlotte's disastrous marriage to Jacques de Brézé ended in a double murder when he came home one day to discover his wife (who, according to trial witnesses, was "moved by an inordinate lechery") in bed with his Master of Hounds. Jacques immediately drew his sword and ran the pair of them through—one hundred times.

By the time Henri was old enough to know Diane, she was a lady-in-waiting to the queen. She had also given Louis de Brézé, now governor and Sénéchal of Normandy, two daughters: Françoise (who was only a year older than Henri), and Louise, who was two years younger.

The first scandal to enmesh Henri and Diane ensued when he was just a boy, during the March 1531 joust to honor the marriage of Henri's father to his second wife, Eléanore, a princess of Portugal. The theme was a Spanish chivalric legend, the story of twelve-year-old Amadis, which hit bone-close to the prince, who was a few weeks shy of his own twelfth birthday. The plot revolves around the two young sons of the King of Wales exiled to a strange land and enslaved by a magician. The princeling falls in love with a lady fair and a fairy grants them eternal youth.

At a tournament, the knights traditionally lower their lances in front of the object of their admiration so that she can tie her favor—her silken scarf—to the tip, and her knight then sallies forth into the combat wearing her colors. It was naturally expected in the grand tradition of courtly love that the new queen would be judged "*la belle parmi les belles*"—the beauty among the beauties. It was Henri's first tournament and he was cast in the role of the hero, Amadis. But instead of lowering his lance before the auburn-haired Eléanore of Portugal, or even his father's buxom and vivacious blond mistress, Anne de Pisseleu d'Heilly (who believed she deserved the honor, and privately expected it), Henri, perhaps wishing to publicly acknowledge the woman who had shown him kindness on the saddest day of his life, halted before the thirty-year-old Diane de Poitiers, Grande Sénéchale of Normandy. He dipped his lance and, in a reedy voice not yet matured by adolescence, boldly offered his protection as her gallant knight if she would favor him with her green and white colors that day.

The crowd didn't know whether to be shocked or charmed. Anne d'Heilly was steamed and made a dramatic exit from the wooden stands, drawing even more attention to her rejection. From then on she regarded Diane de Poitiers as her enemy and spared no opportunity to attack her beautiful rival. A couple of years later, long before their romance began, the fourteen-year-old Henri energetically defended Diane from Anne d'Heilly's slanderous allegations that "the Wrinkled One," as the royal mistress called Diane (who was only nine years her senior), maintained her youthful looks by practicing witchcraft—a serious charge in the sixteenth century.

By the time Henri became a bridegroom in 1533, the tall and slender comtesse de Brézé had already been widowed for two years. Diane had added the widow's symbol, an upended torch, to her coat of arms, with the motto *Qui me alit me extingit*—"He who inflames me has the power to extinguish me." It was a family symbol, but the semierotic phrase would prove prophetic.

Black and white were the official colors of mourning in France, and the Sénéchale, as Diane was also known, decided that they flattered her pale complexion and strawberry blond hair so well that she retained them. Black and white became her signature, and from then on she wore nothing else and decorated her rooms at court as well as her great gift from Henri (upon his accession to the throne), the Château d'Anet, exclusively in those two hues. Diana was not only the Roman goddess of the hunt; she was the goddess of the moon, and black and white also represented the dark and light sides of the celestial sphere.

From the outset, Henri made no secret of his attraction and devotion to Diane de Poitiers, and Catherine de Medici endeavored to compete with her kinswoman for his affection. But the new bride was soon compelled to acknowledge that this elegant older woman in the prime of her beauty had utterly bewitched her husband.

In 1537, while Henri was on a military campaign in Piedmont, he impregnated a commoner named Filippa Duci, which was all it took to convince him that the fertility issues he and Catherine had been suffering in the four years since their wedding were his wife's fault. Filippa bore a daughter, and Henri named her Diane, after the Sénéchale, to whom he gave the child to be raised alongside her own two girls. Because of the infant's name, and the fact that the comtesse de Brézé was parenting her, rumors abounded that little Diane de France was really the bastard daughter of Diane de Poitiers and Henri. By now he had moved up a notch in the line of succession and was the dauphin, owing to the death in August 1536 of his older brother.

Although it is possible that Diane and Henri consummated their romance as early as the end of 1536 or the start of 1537, it's more

likely that the liaison didn't blossom into a full-blown sexual relationship until 1538, after Henri returned from the front. The
eighteen-year-old had come back more confident and mature of mind
and body (not to mention a dad). An erotic poem that Diane, then
thirty-seven, wrote soon after Henri's return to France refers to her
having submitted, "quivering and trembling . . . [to] a boy, fresh,
ready, young," so she may indeed have kept him waiting and wanting
until then.

Henri and Diane's is one of the greatest romances in royal history.
Until she slept with Henri, the Sénéchale's sexual experience had
been limited to a successful seventeen-year marriage with a man
forty years her senior, a man she'd wed at fifteen, when he was old
enough to have been her grandfather. With Henri she was experiencing passion for the first time in her life, but enjoying relations with a
man young enough to be her son.

One clue that their affair became carnal in 1538 is that Henri
began to dress only in Diane's colors—black and white. He also
adopted the crescent moon as his emblem, and created a mono-
grammed device with their initials as entwined as their limbs must
have been every night. Emblazoned beneath the moon, Henri's motto
became an erotic double entendre: *Cum plena est, emula solis*—
"When full, she equals the sun." Portraits of Diane, including nudes
depicting her as Diana, goddess of the hunt, were hung everywhere.
Desperately in unrequited love with her husband, the unhappy Catherine de Medici had no choice but to accept the ubiquitous HD insignias and the new decor with dignified silence, tamping down her
bitterness and humiliation. There was nothing she could say, because
until she gave Henri a child, she could be sent home to Florence at
any time, repudiated for barrenness.

A plot to put aside Catherine had already been set in motion by
François I's scheming blond mistress, Anne de Pisseleu d'Heilly. Anne
wished to topple her rival courtesan, Diane de Poitiers, by finding
Henri a new bride—one he would actually desire. But Catherine had
an unlikely ally: her second cousin Diane. It was in Diane's interest as
well that her lover retain his homely little wife; otherwise she, too, ran
the risk of being cast aside. So she became the couple's sex therapist.

Meanwhile, Catherine availed herself of every known remedy in an effort to become fertile: wearing a girdle under her gowns that was made by a witch (soaked in she-donkey's milk and bearing charms such as the middle finger of a fetus); sporting an amulet about her neck containing the ashes of a giant frog; ingesting myrrh pills and mare's urine; and slathering herself with poultices of cow's dung and ground stag antlers. But as things transpired, part of their conception problem may have been Henri's. Referred to in several diplomatic dispatches, he suffered from a mild deformity of the penis, a downward curvature known as chordee or hypospadias. Evidently, Catherine's real medical issue was an inverted uterus, and some scholars have hypothesized that had Henri's penis been straight, she would have had far less trouble conceiving.

Henri was an adventurous lover with Diane but never attempted anything too exotic with his wife. Diane advised Catherine to jettison all the quack remedies, and instead (in concordance with the royal physicians), she suggested a number of sexual positions to the royal couple that would facilitate successful intercourse, including making love *à levrette*—which we might call doggie style, a *levrette* being a greyhound.

Not only did the gossip regarding Henri and Catherine's embarrassing sex life spread through the French court, but foreign ambassadors provided the intelligence to their employers. It humiliated Catherine all the more that the whole world seemed to know that Henri's mistress "at night urges [him] to that couch to which no desire draws him."

By reminding Henri of Catherine's many fine qualities of character as well as encouraging him to become more acrobatic in his spouse's boudoir, Diane was able to thwart Anne d'Heilly's scheme to supplant the dauphine, thereby maintaining her *own* place in Henri's affections and bed. Diane would get Henri all hot and bothered and then send him upstairs to his wife's bedchamber to perform his conjugal duty.

Catherine reveled in each visit, but for Henri it was purely an obligation. He could not even bear to look his Medici bride in the face while they made love, and when he finished he would return to his mistress's slender arms. It was a body slam to Catherine's ego. What did Diane de Poitiers have that she didn't? Catherine's curiosity got the better of her when she hired an Italian carpenter to drill a pair of holes in her floor so she could spy on Henri and his paramour. What she saw sickened her: "a beautiful, fair woman, fresh and half undressed, was caressing her lover in a hundred ways, who was doing the same to her." They were all over Diane's furniture, and on the floor, made more comfortable and sensuous by her velvet rug puddled about them. Brokenhearted, Catherine admitted to her friend the duchesse de Montpensier that Henri had "never used her so well."

In any event, Diane's advice proved fruitful and Catherine bore children. To Catherine's displeasure, Henri thanked his lover for her successful sex counseling by giving her a role in the raising of his children. Diane's cousin Jean d'Humières was awarded the governorship of the nursery, and Diane appropriated Catherine's private nicknames for the royal children. To the future queen, even in her maternal triumph, nothing remained entirely hers; her husband's mistress was not only in *his* bedroom, but in their children's sphere as well. At least she was qualified. Diane, who had successfully raised two daughters of her own, in addition to Henri's illegitimate Diane de France, would eventually be placed in charge of the education of Henri and Catherine's offspring, which she managed until 1551.

On March 31, 1547, Henri became king of France upon the death of his father. After a lavish procession in which he passed beneath a trio of triumphal arches, one of which bore the motto he and Diane devised as their own, *Donec totum impleat orbem*—"Until it fills the whole world"—Henri was crowned at Reims on July 26. His black velvet doublet and coronation robes were embroidered not with the traditional lilies of France but with Diane's insignias in countless seed pearls: her quivers, bows and arrows, her entwined crescent moons, and their initials—an H and double D. From then on, these would become Henri's kingly symbols, a public acknowledgment of his liaison with his moon goddess, openly, if not defiantly, bringing their romance into the sunlight. Not only the king's garments and his horses' caparisons, but each royal property would eventually become emblazoned and embellished everywhere one looked with their combined ciphers and insignias.

As queens of France were merely consorts and were not crowned beside their husbands, the very pregnant and opulently gowned Catherine was no more than an honored spectator at Henri's coronation. But she was outshone by the even more resplendently attired Diane de Poitiers, whose fair hair was adorned with a diamond crescent that to the eye of every beholder looked like a crown. The new queen did not even spend her husband's coronation night celebrating privately with him. According to the Italian ambassador, after the banquet, the king "went to find the Sénéchale."

As soon as the crown was on his head, Henri showered Diane, whom he called "madame," or *ma dame* ("my lady," in the high-flown chivalric sense), with jewels, real estate, and revenues, many of which his father had previously given to *his maîtresse en titre*, Anne d'Heilly. Among Diane's new perquisites was a percentage of income from a tax imposed on every church bell in France. This unusual love token prompted the poet Rabelais to bawdily quip that the monarch had hung the bells of his kingdom about the neck of his mare.

Rabelais realized that Diane was Henri's paramour in the fullest sense, but there were some at court who still didn't believe it, unwilling to wrap their brains around the idea that such a young, virile man had any sexual desire for a woman twenty or so years his senior. Ambassador Lorenzo Contarini, in his dispatches to the Vatican in 1547 (after the pair had been lovers for nearly ten years), wrote that the French king displayed a "real tenderness" toward Diane de Poitiers, "but it is not thought that there is anything lascivious about it, but that this affection is like that between a mother and son." It's a testament to the lovers' discretion that they managed to fool at least some of the people some of the time.

However, not every ambassador was so taken in, and the paramours weren't always so tactful. At the outset of Henri's reign he created an intimate circle of loyal nobles, which excluded his queen, but included his official mistress. The imperial ambassador Jean de Saint-Mauris, whose boss was the Holy Roman Emperor and king of Spain, Charles V (the same monarch who had held Henri a prisoner when he was a boy), was exceptionally disparaging of both the king and his mistress. Saint-Mauris wrote of this relationship:

"After dinner [his midday meal] he visits [Diane] and when he has reported to her details of all the matters he has discussed in the morning meetings, he sits on her lap and plays the guitar to her, frequently asking [his Grand Master of the Household, the duc de Montmorency] whether she had not preserved her beauty, occasionally caressing her breasts and looking at her face, like a man dominated by his infatuation. . . . The king has many good qualities, and I would hope much more of him if he were not so foolish as to allow himself to be led as he is . . . none may dare to remonstrate with the king in case he offends [Diane], fearing that the king will tell her, since he loves her so much. . . . He continues to yield himself more and more to her yoke and has become entirely her subject and slave."

Evidently Diane's signature perfume, a lightly peppered scent, acted as an aphrodisiac for Henri. Privacy was scarce during this era, and in the presence of trusted attendants and advisers (and the occasional ambassador), the lovers felt comfortable getting blatantly physical. Signor Alvarotti, the Venetian ambassador, wrote in 1549 that on one occasion when Diane and Henri began to indulge in some heavy foreplay, the king caressed her with such abandon that the bed collapsed and Diane cried, "Sire, do not jump on my bed so violently or you will break it."

It would not have been unusual for Diane's serving women to remain in the chamber during their mistress's lovemaking, but in their presence she never entirely disrobed, for according to them, "one never saw her with hanging breasts as she was always wearing a bustier." From Catherine's two spy holes in the floor, however, she managed to see everything.

Two men loyal to Catherine de Medici, the duc de Nemours and Gaspard de Saulx-Tavannes, offered to disfigure Henri's *maîtresse en titre*, either by cutting off Diane's nose or by throwing vitriol, or acid, in her face—whichever method Catherine preferred. The queen declined their offer. Her motto was *"Odiate et aspetate"*—"Hate and wait." She favored endurance over violence, but her fortitude was not superhuman.

Even for the official entry into Lyon on September 23, 1548, a city filled with Italian émigrés, especially financiers—the world from which Catherine de Medici had emerged—Henri entered with Diane de Poitiers at his side on the first day of festivities. They were greeted everywhere by the good citizens of Lyon with the HD insignia and metaphorical tributes to Diane in poetry and theatrical spectacles, as though *she* were the queen of France. So as not to forfeit the king's favor, the Lyonnais had decorated the entire city in black and white. Catherine was publicly mortified and never forgot the city's slight.

Her entrance into the city did not take place until the following day at dusk, when the light was too dim to see the procession. Her detractors insisted that the scheduling was Henri's idea "so that her ugliness should pass unnoticed." The Lyonnais had scrambled to replace all of the black and white buntings and banners with green ones, Catherine's signature color, and rewrote the tributes in her honor. That day, Catherine was covered *cap-à-pie* in diamonds, lest no one forget who was the real queen. Diane rode behind her in the cavalcade. But when Henri formally greeted the dignitaries of Lyon he kissed his own hand and then touched his lips to Diane's hand before kissing the hand of his queen. The city's movers and shakers were appalled and embarrassed.

At Lyon, on October 8, 1548, Henri granted Diane the title of duchesse de Valentinois. This elevation placed her on a par with princes of the blood, because in France, dukedoms were reserved for members of the blood royal. Henri also had a gold medal struck with Diane's profile on it. The motto on the obverse read, *"Omnium Victorem Vici"*—"I conquered him who conquered all." As a further insult to Catherine, Henri announced that Diane would henceforth be one of her ladies-in-waiting.

Henri placed so much trust in his *maîtresse en titre* that they generated and signed government documents in tandem; the king would begin a letter, and Diane might finish it. And at the bottom, the signature would read *HenriDiane*. With Diane's encouragement Henri enacted sumptuary laws that restricted expenditures for lavish entertainments and other displays of wealth; the court was drastically reduced and the number of attendants slashed. These new strictures even affected the queen, who would be limited to only four ladies-in-waiting, all of whom were to be "serious and honest," the latter word usually taken to mean chaste or conjugally faithful. Among this quartet, however, was Diane de Poitiers, the king's regular bedfellow and by that definition the most "dishonest" woman at court.

One of the few times Catherine allowed her temper to get the better of her was in 1547, when Henri bestowed the Château de Chenonceau upon Diane, for the queen had always coveted this beautiful jewel box of a castle on the Cher River. That year Henri also had the Château d'Anet built for his mistress on the site of her late husband's property near Dreux. Far removed from the center of court life, Anet became the couple's love nest, a safe haven where they could escape for idyllic quality time, creating an alternate reality of domestic bliss.

In August of 1548, the five-year-old Mary, Queen of Scots, arrived in France, ostensibly at Henri's invitation. In reality she'd come at the behest of her powerful Guise uncles, whose sister Marie de Guise, the dowager queen of Scotland, was Mary's mother. The charming auburn-haired child was contracted to wed the dauphin of France. In accordance with tradition, she would be raised in her future husband's court until both children came of age and could be wed. Among Mary's entourage was her thirty-five-year-old governess, the gorgeous redheaded Lady Fleming.

In 1550, Diane broke her leg in a riding accident and quit the court for several months to convalesce. Her departure allowed Henri more time with his queen and children, and Catherine rejoiced in her rival's absence. But her husband could not remain faithful for two seconds, embarking on a Highland fling with Lady Fleming. Catherine played the role of wronged and outraged wife to the hilt, but privately reveled that Diane de Poitiers had been displaced from her husband's affections.

Upon her return to court, Diane's discovery of Henri's infidelity marked the only time she completely lost her legendary equanimity. She waited outside Lady Fleming's door for the king to emerge with France's Constable and Grand Master of the Household, Anne de Montmorency—a man whose career she had advanced and supported for years. Diane accused Montmorency of betraying her by facilitating Henri's affair with Lady Fleming. Henri tried to shuffle and shamble his way out of his massive indiscretion, but Diane asked him what the powerful Guise family might think if they were to learn that their niece, little Mary, Queen of Scots, was being raised by a cheap harlot? They might even scotch their girl's marriage to the dauphin, on the assumption that the child suffered from malevolent influences!

Fearful of forfeiting the crown's vital friendship with the Guise family, with his tail meekly between his legs, Henri returned to Anet with Diane, where the couple reconciled.

But the king did not abruptly end his liaison with Mary Fleming. She became pregnant, then flaunted her swelling belly, ostentatiously announcing to all and sundry that the king was her lover. With this wee bit of grandstanding she managed to transform the court's two greatest adversaries into a pair of allies, as Catherine and Diane joined forces to oust her. But Henri ennobled their bastard son as the duc d'Angoulême, and the boy was raised alongside the king's legitimate offspring. He grew up to become Grand Prior of France, notable for his particular viciousness during the St. Bartholomew's Day massacre of the Huguenots in 1572. He was killed in a duel in 1586.

Henri also fathered another royal bastard in 1558 by a married woman named Nicole de Savigny, but this affair did not become a cause célèbre and was quickly forgiven and forgotten. The king did not legitimize this son, who was also named Henri; the boy's surname was that of Nicole's cuckolded spouse, Monsieur Saint-Rémy. A descendant of this royal liaison, Jeanne de Lamotte-Valois, would make Marie Antoinette's life hell in the mid-1780s.

In 1551, the court noticed that the king was paying marked attention to Catherine and he had begun to rely on her political advice. By then she had given him six children. Diane was now fifty-one years old, perhaps no longer as interested in maintaining the sexual element of their romance. In an effort to demonstrate her attachment to both members of the royal couple, when Catherine came down with scarlet fever in 1552, Diane, behaving like a true cousin, nursed her kinswoman back to health.

That year, when Henri was thirty-three, Lorenzo Contarini, now the Venetian ambassador, furnished posterity with a detailed description of the French sovereign and his daily habits, including Henri's avid fitness regimen.

[He is] tall, well-built, with black hair and lively eyes, an attractive head, large nose, normal mouth, and a beard as long as the width of two fingers, and altogether he has one of the most gracious figures and a real air of majesty. He has a very robust complexion, which is helped a lot by his physical exercises, such that every day, from two hours after lunch until evening he spends his time playing tennis or ball or [in] archery. . . . He also enjoys hunting all animals . . . especially the deer, which he does two or three times a week. . . . He is extraordinarily good at swordsmanship and horsemanship . . . an excellent fighter. . . . His body is very healthy, it is only his teeth which sometimes cause him pain and he suffers from nothing except occasional migraines, for which he takes pills. He is very fit and muscular, but if he does not take care and watch his food, he could easily gain weight. His appearance is a little melancholic by nature but also shows great majesty and kindness. . . . He eats and drinks moderately. After his audience, he retires with a small group to Madame de Valentinois' bedroom, where he stays for about an hour before leaving to play pall-mall, or tennis or other exercises. After dining in public, he visits the queen where he joins a large group of the court's ladies and gentlemen and chats to them for about an hour.

. . . He is never angry when something goes wrong, except sometimes when hunting, and he never uses violent words. . . . [H]e is very chaste in matters of the flesh [meaning, one supposes, that he was devoted solely to one lover?], and he conducts his affairs in such a way that no one can discuss them very much, which was not the case with king François [Henri's father].

Contarini added:

But the person who without a doubt is the most loved by the king is Madame de Valentinois. She is a lady of fifty-two . . . [who] came into the hands of this king while he was still dauphin. He has loved her a great deal and loves her still. She is his *mistress*, old as she is. It is true to say that, although she has never worn face paints, and perhaps because of the minute care that she takes, she is far from looking her age. She is a lady of intelligence who has always been the king's inspiration.

Then Contarini summed up Catherine's reaction to her husband's grand passion:

> Since the beginning of the new reign, the Queen could no longer bear to see such love and favor being bestowed by the king on the duchess, but upon the king's urgent entreaties she resigned herself to endure the situation with patience. The Queen even frequents the duchess, who, for her part, serves the Queen well, and often it is she who *exhorts him to sleep with his wife*.

In 1558, Henri signed a peace treaty with Spain ceding France's Italian possessions to either the Duke of Mantua or the Duke of Florence. Catherine, a native of northern Italy, was understandably livid. According to the terms of this Treaty of Câteau-Cambrésis, their eldest daughter would be given to king Philip of Spain in marriage. Philip had been a widower since the November 17, 1558, death of his first wife, Mary, the elder daughter of Henry VIII. Mary was scarcely cold in the ground when Philip negotiated a new alliance, but despite the prestige brought by her daughter Elisabeth (to be renamed Isabel de la Paz—Isabel of the Peace) becoming queen of Spain, Catherine was furious with the terms of the treaty. She blamed the unfavorable provisions for France on Diane's malevolent influence upon Henri.

One day when Diane entered the queen's presence, Catherine happened to be reading a book, and the duchesse inquired as to its subject.

"I am reading *The Chronicles of France*, and I find that in every era there was a time when the affairs of Kings have been governed by whores," Catherine replied.

The unpopular Treaty of Câteau-Cambrésis was fully ratified during the first week of April in 1559. With one stroke of the quill, France was compelled to return all of the territories she had won during the past sixty-five years, the reigns of the last four kings. Henri could now direct his attention to pressing domestic concerns, the largest of which was the issue of, in his words, the "Protestant vermin" overrunning his realm.

During this time, he also remained unfaithful to Catherine, and more frequently strayed from the bed of the fifty-eight-year-old *maî-*

tresse en titre as well, enjoying brief, casual liaisons. Diane turned an elegant blind eye to these infidelities. Catherine, too, was less unnerved by them than she was by Diane's impenetrable influence upon her husband. Although Henri and Diane remained passionately devoted to each other, the sexual element of their relationship may have ended by 1558, if a phrase in a letter of Henri's, dated August 10 of that year, offers any clue to the nature of their romance at the time. Despite any of his present, relatively meaningless flings, in that letter the king urged Diane never to forget the one who always had and always would love her.

The queen refused to allow her husband's *maîtresse en titre* to come anywhere near the king after his horrific jousting accident on June 30, 1559. Although Henri called Diane's name and asked to see her several times during the final ten days of his life, Catherine willfully denied his request. The lovers never got to say good-bye. Ironically, the mortal wound had been dealt by Gabriel de Montgomery, the son of a former admirer of Diane de Poitiers who had always hoped to wed her.

On July 8, Henri slipped into a coma. Diane received a messenger from the queen demanding the return of the crown jewels. "Is the king dead?" asked the duchesse de Valentinois. When the messenger shook his head, Diane refused to hand over the treasure. "So long as there remains a breath of life in him, I wish my enemies to know I do not fear them," she said firmly. "As yet there is no one who can command me. I am still of good courage. But when he is dead, I do not want to live after him; and all the bitterness that one could wish me will be but sweetness beside my great loss." So many years his senior, Diane had genuinely believed she'd be the first to go.

Henri died on July 10 from septicemia. The following day, the royal family moved into the Louvre Palace. The Guises, Mary, Queen of Scots's family on her mother's side, appropriated the rooms that had been given to Diane de Poitiers during the late king's lifetime. Throughout her marriage Catherine had been robbed of her husband "by Diane de Poitiers in the sight and knowledge of everyone," as she termed it. Now dowager queen of France, Catherine immediately began redoing the HD ciphers so that Diane's crescent moons more clearly resembled the letter C.

Diane, who was pointedly not invited to her former lover's funeral, returned the jewels that had been crown property. Then the dowager queen dismissed her from court. Diane retired to the countryside, primarily to the Château d'Anet. After the king's death she and Catherine never saw each other again. Diane was also compelled to forfeit another treasure to Catherine: her beloved Château de Chenonceau. She had always wanted to wrest Chenonceau from Diane, and the duchesse de Valentinois could hardly refuse to comply. Catherine was a big admirer of her father-in-law's credo that vengeance was the mark of a feeble king and magnanimity a sign of his strength. She and her son, the new king, François II, could have been a lot crueler to a former royal mistress whose very public romance with the king had humiliated her for every one of the twenty-six years of her marriage.

According to Diane's biographer Princess Michael of Kent, the inscription on her tomb, which Diane herself ordered, reads, "Died 26 April, 1566, aged 66 years, 3 months and 27 days" (which places her birth date on December 31, 1499, three months later than other sources record it). When Diane's remains were disinterred in 2009, French scientists discovered high levels of gold in Diane's hair, evidence perhaps that the drinkable gold she regularly ingested as part of her beauty and fitness regimen may in fact have contributed to her demise. And the sixteenth-century chronicler Pierre de Brantôme referred to the "wash of liquid gold" with which it was rumored Diane bathed each morning.

The duchesse de Valentinois had originally been entombed in a funeral chapel near the Château d'Anet commissioned by her daughter to house her remains. Diane's sepulcher was desecrated during the French Revolution and her bones were tossed into a mass grave (however, in 2008, excavations beneath Diane's memorial revealed bones identified as hers, and her ashes were ultimately returned to the château with great fanfare in May 2010); but her memory had been dishonored centuries before the Jacobins discovered her final resting place.

Catherine de Medici rarely referred to Diane de Poitiers in her correspondence, whether official or personal, but nearly twenty years after the noblewoman's death, the dowager queen of France dispatched some marital advice to her unhappy daughter Margot, queen of Navarre, through the French secretary of state Bellièvre. Catherine confided to her daughter, "If I made good cheer for Madame de Valentinois, it was the king that I was really entertaining, and besides, I always let him know that I was acting sorely against the grain; for never did a woman who loved her husband succeed in loving his harlot; as one cannot call her anything but that, no matter how vulgar the word."

LOUIS XIV

1638–1715

RULED FRANCE: 1643–1715

*K*nown as *le Roi Soleil*, or the Sun King, Louis XIV ascended the throne as the king of France and Navarre in 1643 at the age of four. His parents were Anne of Austria, who was actually a Spanish Hapsburg princess, and the possibly homosexual Louis XIII. Louis XIV, the ultimate French king, was actually a geographic masala: He was in fact only twenty-five percent French. The rest was twenty-five percent German, twenty percent Spanish, and twelve percent Italian, with a smattering of Slavic and Portuguese blood, and perhaps even some Jewish and Moorish ancestry through his Aragonese antecedents.

Because Louis XIV's birth came twenty-three years after his parents had been estranged (although there had been four stillborn babies before him), he was nicknamed *le Dieu-donné*—"the God-given"—as it was a miracle that his mother had managed to conceive with a king who so rarely visited her bed.

Louis' father had intended for the kingdom to be governed by a regency council until his son came of age. But Anne of Austria had her husband's will annulled and became the sole regent, although the governing power of France was entrusted to the prime minister, her purported lover, Cardinal Mazarin.

During Louis' minority, a two-pronged civil war known as the Fronde fractured France. The first wave, the *Fronde Parlementaire* (1648–1649), was a rebellion fomented by France's judicial body, the Parlement. Consisting of aristocrats and ennobled commoners, the members of the Parlement believed themselves the natural defenders of the fundamental laws of the kingdom against what they viewed as the arbitrariness and oppressiveness of the monarchy. The nobility, long exempt from paying taxes, rebelled against Mazarin's attempts to tax them. The second wave, the *Fronde des Princes* (1650–1653), was instigated by the nobility and led by the king's own uncle, the duc d'Orléans. They claimed to be acting in the boy-king's interests, insisting that the regents were ruining the realm. The rebellion gradually fizzled and died, their cause mooted when Louis came of age and was crowned.

In 1661, Cardinal Mazarin passed away and Louis XIV assumed the reins of his own reign. France had been at war on several fronts, and the king harnessed his subjects' desire for peace by consolidating power in the hands of the monarch at the expense of the aristocracy.

When Louis took control of his kingdom, the treasury was on the verge of bankruptcy and his first challenge became fiscal reform. When he chose his ministers, he chose well. Over the course of his spectacularly long reign, under his aegis they also instituted military reforms and modernized the army. The *Grand Ordonnance de Procédure Civile* of 1667, also known as the Code Louis, reformed the kingdom's legal system by unifying the two disparate sets of laws that had been used for centuries depending on whether one lived in the north or the south of the kingdom. The Code Louis became the basis for the Napoleonic Code.

The Sun King brought street lighting and a police force to Paris. He built Les Invalides, then and now a veterans' hospital. He also renovated the Louvre, which, after he officially moved the court to Versailles in 1682, was given over to the public. In 1686, at the instigation of one of his most influential mistresses, Madame de Maintenon (to whom Louis was by then secretly married), he founded the Institut de Saint-Cyr, an academy for impoverished aristocratic girls. Saint-Cyr was the only school for girls in France that was not a convent.

Louis' belief in the divine right of kings led him to turn the monarchy into a centralized state, reducing the power and authority of the feudal nobility. To that end, one of his greatest achievements— politically, socially, and aesthetically—was the transformation of Versailles from a modestly sized hunting lodge into the greatest and most glamorous palace and surrounding landscape in Europe. He developed a rigid system of court etiquette that brought the once feudal (and feuding) aristocrats under his roof and under his thumb, turning them into courtiers, glorified servants who vied for royal preferment and fought over perquisites of rank and the right to perform such menial tasks as handing His Majesty his nightshirt. Having to spend so much time at Versailles prevented the nobles from staying too long at their country estates, where they might conceivably consolidate their feudal power bases and foment rebellion. Manners were ritualistically prescribed, even down to the way one walked, requested admission to a room (you didn't knock, but scratched with your pinkie nail on the wood), or applied your rouge.

The French court became the envy of Europe for its manners and sophistication, and Versailles was its showplace, representing the power and majesty of the monarchy.

In 1660, Louis had married the Infanta of Spain, Maria Theresa, the eldest daughter of King Philip IV. Their marriage was part of the 1659 Treaty of the Pyrenees, which ended a war between France and Spain, and they were first cousins on *both* sides (which may have been one reason that most of their children died young). A loophole in their marriage contract ended up leaving the door open years later for French Bourbon succession in the queen's homeland so that their grandson ended up on the Spanish throne as Philip V.

Louis and Marie-Thérèse (as the queen was known in France) had six children, but only one survived to adulthood, Louis the Grand Dauphin, known as Monseigneur. However, the king managed to sire several healthy children with his many mistresses, among them Louise de la Vallière and Athénaïs de Montespan. He acknowledged seventeen of his royal bastards (he fathered about as many as his English cousin Charles II), and he married them off to legitimate Bourbons.

Louis XIV's largely neglected queen died on July 30, 1683; she had never become terribly proficient at French, and the king had never learned Spanish. It is believed that a couple of months later, on October 10, he secretly married his *maîtresse en titre*, or official mistress, Françoise d'Aubigné, the marquise de Maintenon. Although the marriage was never publicly mentioned, it was an open secret and lasted until Louis' death.

Though her role is probably exaggerated, Madame de Maintenon's influence is considered a major factor in Louis' decision in 1685 to revoke the Edict of Nantes, a law passed by his grandfather Henri IV, which had granted the Huguenots (the French Protestants) religious and political freedom. During the early 1680s the Huguenots suffered institutionalized religious intolerance in France; the revocation of the Edict of Nantes was the bitter icing on a nasty cake.

For the better part of Louis' reign, France became involved in one foreign war after another and her cast of allies shifted with alarming regularity. The control of the Spanish Netherlands (what is now Belgium) was under contention. The succession of the Spanish throne was contested. Louis wanted to press into Austrian Hapsburg terrain wherever possible. And he had an on-again/off-again enmity with England.

Among Louis' primary foreign policy goals was territorial expansion. His explorers ventured beyond Europe's borders, extending French colonialism to North America, Asia, and Africa. Louis Jolliet and Jacques Marquette discovered the Mississippi River in 1673. In 1682, de la Salle followed the route of the Mississippi all the way to the Gulf of Mexico and staked a claim to the Mississippi basin in his sovereign's name—naming it *la Louisiane*. And Louis dispatched Jesuit missionaries to China in an attempt to sunder the Portuguese hegemony there.

Consequently, by the early 1680s, France was the dominant power in the world. The French crown, in the person of Louis XIV, also exerted considerable influence over the Church as well as the aristocracy. He used both ritual and the arts to maintain his control over the kingdom, effectively deifying himself. Representations of the king were ubiquitous, and often allegorical—in painting, sculpture, frescoes, tapestries, and medallions. More than three hundred formal portraits were painted of him, and he commissioned at least twenty statues of himself. The duc de Saint-Simon, a prolific diarist and memoirist in the court of Louis XIV, observed of the king that "There was nothing he liked so much as flattery, or, to put it more plainly, adulation; the coarser and clumsier it was, the more he relished it." And to make sure people revered him, in 1680 the sovereign began to refer to himself as "Louis the Great" on his own coins.

Even Napoleon begrudged Louis XIV his ego trip, calling him "the only king of France worthy of the name."

Add to that the remark made by historian Antonia Fraser that Louis "was as much marked by his industry as by his hedonism." After all, this was the man who was considered so obsessed with sex that he had to make love twice a day.

He fell ill with a gangrenous leg in August 1715 and refused to let the surgeons amputate, although he had braved serious and painful operations in the past. He once underwent an anal operation without anesthesia, and lost part of his jawbone when a dentist used red-hot coal to cauterize an abscess in his mouth.

Aware that he would be succeeded by his five-year-old great-grandson, who would accede to the throne as Louis XV, the old king penned a few words of advice for his little heir. "Do not follow the bad example which I have set you; I have often undertaken war too lightly and have sustained it for vanity. Do not imitate me, but be a peaceful prince, and may you apply yourself principally to the alleviations of the burdens of your subjects."

Louis XV, apart from having a general reluctance to go to war, did not play it safe on the home front, however, taking several mistresses, official and otherwise, and squandering the goodwill of his subjects. But Louis XIV's wars did expand France's borders, adding ten new provinces, creating an empire overseas, and establishing French prominence in Europe. He encouraged the growth of local industry through his patronage of French businesses. And his consolidation of the nobility under Mansart's gently sloping roofs at Versailles reduced the feudal threats of past centuries.

As king of France for seventy-two years, three months, and eighteen days, Louis XIV reigned longer than any European monarch. To put it in perspective, Louis XIV remained king of France while England saw the reign of Charles I, the protectorate of Oliver Cromwell, the Restoration and reigns of Charles II, James II, William and Mary, Anne, and well into the reign of George I.

Louis' sovereignty marked a golden age for literature and architecture. It was the era of Molière, La Fontaine, and Racine, Mansart, Le Brun, and Le Nôtre. And the king wasn't just a patron of the arts; he was a participant. As a devotee of the dance, he often performed in court ballets himself during the early years of his reign.

He died on September 1, 1715, just four days before his seventy-seventh birthday, having lived so long that generations of his heirs predeceased him. A postmortem showed a monstrous abdomen; the king was a man of huge epicurean appetites as well as amorous ones. In the tradition of French monarchs, he was interred in the Basilica of Saint-Denis.

Louis' cult of personality managed to obscure some of the deficits of his reign. While he reduced the fractious nobility to idle courtiers, they weren't taxed, and the treasury sorely needed their money. He was such a genius at propagandizing that he made the crown appear omnipotent, but all the pomp and pageantry obscured the monarchy's weak financial underpinnings, leaving it in a fragile state for his successors and their ministers, who were not skilled enough to govern or to control the aristocracy with as firm a hand.

Louis was indeed the state—although historians believe that the attribution of the phrase *"L'État, c'est moi"* is apocryphal. It is, however, held that on his deathbed, he did declare, *"Je m'en vais, mais l'État demeurera toujours"*—I depart, but the State will always remain.

LOUIS XIV AND
FRANÇOISE-ATHÉNAÏS DE ROCHECHOUART DE MORTEMART, MARQUISE DE MONTESPAN (1641–1707)

For several years, although the Sun King was very much married to a pious and humorless Spanish-born princess with protuberant eyes and black teeth (the product of too much Hapsburg inbreeding), Athénaïs de Montespan was known as "the real queen of France."

Lush and louche, Madame de Montespan possessed an innate sense of confidence, which contributed immensely to her sex appeal as well as her pretensions to entitlement and were (in her view) bred in her DNA; both sides of her family were grander, centuries older, and more aristocratic than the Bourbons. The Rochechouart de Mortemarts looked down their straight, highly attractive noses at the royal family, viewing them as a bunch of parvenus who, by marrying into the merchant class and taking Medici wives, had diluted their blue blood with the stigma of trade.

In 1660, Madame de Montespan made her social debut at the age of twenty. In the glittering salons of Paris's Marais district, she dropped the pedestrian Françoise, preferring her more exotic middle name (pronounced Ah-TEN-Ay-EES), which perfectly suited her nature, for she unquestionably had the ego of a goddess.

Athénaïs's own father was an adulterer; among his numerous lovers was the celebrated courtesan Ninon de Lenclos. His philandering caused her honorable mother, Diane, considerable heartbreak. In 1653, the fifty-something duc de Mortemart abandoned his wife and children for a lover nearly twenty years his junior. Throughout her life Madame de Montespan felt tugged in competing directions. On the one hand there was her father's worldliness and her own ambition to further herself at court; on the other, her mother's piety and the desire to live virtuously. Both were legitimate aspects of her complex personality.

Athénaïs spent her childhood in the medieval castle of Lussac in the countryside of Poitou. At the age of twelve she followed her elder sister Gabrielle into the convent of Ste. Marie des Saintes, which, for a pretty price, educated the daughters of noblemen. There she studied the traditional (and surprisingly well-rounded) curriculum for aristocratic young ladies: sewing and embroidery, dancing, music, history, reading, writing, arithmetic, and geography. She was also taught to act, as it was assumed that all of these girls would be presented at court and would be expected to perform in the king's ballets and masques. Additionally, Athénaïs became a rather good poet; many of the nasty verses that would later circulate through the gilded corridors of the royal châteaux came from her quills. She also learned to cook at Ste. Marie des Saintes, which served her in good stead during her royal romance, because Louis loved to eat and expected his paramours to have equally healthy appetites. Unfortunately for

Athénaïs, corpulence ran in the Rochechouart de Mortemart genes. One of her cousins held the dubious distinction of being the fattest man at court.

The seventeenth century in France was known as the *Grand Siècle*—the Great Century—a flowering of wit and culture, the age of the playwrights Molière, Racine, and Corneille, of the architect Jules-Hardouin Mansart, the landscaper André Le Nôtre, and the composer Jean-Baptiste Lully. But every courtier was expected to be quick on his feet as well, literally a nimble and graceful dancer, but also ready with a quip or a bon mot. Here, too, Athénaïs excelled. Even the duc de Saint-Simon, one of her greatest detractors at court, acknowledged that Madame de Montespan had "the gift of saying things both amusing and singular, always original, and which no one expected, not even she herself as she said them."

Athénaïs's family was known for what they said as well as for how they uttered it—cutting remarks in high, cultivated voices and languid tones that Madame de Montespan's daughters and even her ladies-in-waiting sought to imitate. However, there would come a time when courtiers would fear to walk beneath Athénaïs's windows at Versailles. In the mid-1670s, when she presided over a suite of twenty rooms adjacent to the king's, she delighted in delivering scathing critiques of each passerby for the amusement of her royal audience of one, who stood beside her, eager to hear every clever insult. "Going before the guns," the courtiers called it.

As soon as she was presented at court, her family connections garnered Athénaïs a post as maid of honor to the new queen, Marie-Thérèse. As a courtier she was expected to participate in the ballets and other court diversions. In her maiden appearance she was cast in the ballet *Hercule Amoreux* opposite the Sun King himself. But it took some time before she'd catch his eye as anything other than a dance partner—for in 1661 Louis took his first *maîtresse en titre*, the meek and dewy Louise de La Vallière. Although it seemed that the Grand Monarch had zero interest in her, the ambitious Athénaïs bided her time. Unlike the vapid blond Louise, *she* had sex appeal and knew it.

In 1663, at the age of twenty-two, having spent two seasons in

Paris, Athénaïs became engaged. She was considered old for the era, as aristocratic girls typically wed in their mid-teens. Her fiancé, the marquis de Noirmoutiers, had been selected by her parents. But after the marquis became involved in a duel on the morning of January 21, he was exiled to Portugal, where five years later he died fighting the Spanish.

While Athénaïs was grieving over the banishment of her betrothed she received a condolence call from Louis-Henri de Pardaillan de Gondrin, marquis de Montespan, the brother of the man killed in the duel. He was from Gascony, a region known for producing hotheads, and the stereotype proved true in many cases. Montespan's dark good looks appealed to Athénaïs, and although he had little to bring to a match beyond his family's ancient name, he fell in love with her. On January 28, only a week after the fatal duel, their marriage contract was signed, and they were wed on February 6.

Their union would prove to be a textbook example of the adage, "Marry in haste; repent at leisure."

Montespan's kinsman, the Archbishop of Sens, was a member of the ultraconservative Jansenist sect critical of the king's lifestyle, so not only was he persona non grata at court, but the other members of his family were unwelcome as well. Thus, it fell to Athénaïs to advance the young couple's fortune there. But while his spouse was at court, the marquis de Montespan was busy gambling like mad, amassing debts, and borrowing against her dowry. On one occasion, before Athénaïs was scheduled to dance in a court ballet, she had to schlep him to a lawyer's office in an effort to prevent his arrest for debt. Another time, he had to pawn her pearl earrings to satisfy a creditor.

Finally, Montespan decided that the only way to make a name for himself was to fund a regiment and join the army. It kept him out of town, but landed him even deeper in debt. Perhaps it was a good thing he wasn't around, because seventeenth-century Frenchwomen were not encouraged to bathe during pregnancy, as it was thought to relax the womb. In November 1663, Athénaïs gave birth to a daughter, Marie-Christine. She would bear nine children during the course of her life; only two of them were her husband's.

Upon her marriage, because she was technically no longer a "maid," Athénaïs lost her position as maid of honor to the queen. Consequently, it was imperative to find another post. By February 1664, both she and the king's *maîtresse en titre* Louise de La Vallière (who'd given birth to a royal bastard around the same time as Athénaïs bore her legitimate daughter) were short-listed for Queen Marie-Thérèse's six-woman retinue. In accordance with court etiquette, only two marquises, a duo of duchesses, and a pair of princesses would be selected as ladies-in-waiting. As a marquise, only two of those positions were available to Athénaïs.

By now Athénaïs and Louise had spent four years at court, but Madame de Montespan found herself perennially tamping down her envy of the dull-as-dishwater official mistress, while she had to contend with a spendthrift absentee husband. Nonetheless, scintillating and supremely confident in her assets, Athénaïs decided to use her wits and wiles to supersede Louise in the king's bed, all the while feigning friendship with the insipid girl.

By the summer of 1664, after Montespan had borrowed another fifty-six thousand livres against his wife's dowry to finance another (failed) military venture, Athénaïs was utterly over him. Louis-Henri's success at court depended on hers, but he was squandering her money (including her salary) at the gaming tables in Paris, when she needed those funds to maintain her position. Keeping up appearances was costly. Not only that, there was going to be another mouth to feed. On September 9, she bore a son, Louis-Alexandre, who was given one of his father's lesser titles, that of marquis d'Antin. But the infant would have nothing else to inherit if Monsieur de Montespan didn't give up his gambling.

Other women in similar straits at court took lovers. Her own sister Gabrielle, the very married marquise de Thianges, was one of the king's occasional flings. Yet Athénaïs remained faithful to Louis-Henri. Was it part of her strategy to ensnare the sovereign, on the assumption that making herself available for casual sex was not the way to win him permanently?

Louis XIV noticed her, but his reaction was hardly what she was looking for. "She's desperate to make me fall in love with her," he once remarked to Louise de La Vallière, as they snickered over Madame de Montespan's transparency. "She does what she can, but I don't want her."

But two years later, in 1666, Louis and Athénaïs both lost their mothers. Free from the restraining influence of the formidable Anne of Austria, Louis no longer felt compelled to remain discreet about his affair with Louise de La Vallière. Ironically, under the court's incessant scrutiny, the fragile blonde withered. The great chronicler of the age, Madame de Sevigné, described Louise as "that little violet which hid itself under the grass and was ashamed of being mistress." Not only did it become apparent that she was abundantly lacking in the requisite clever repartee, but she would have to have been made of steel to withstand the perpetual gossip and the constant efforts to undermine her.

And no one tried harder to do so than her dear friend the marquise de Montespan, who by now had become the royal favorite's confidante. In the parlance of the day, Athénaïs was fighting for the king *"avec bec et ongles"* (with beak and talons), but with the subtlety of a hawk observing her prey, waiting for the perfect moment to swoop down and pounce. She also managed to charm her other rival, the queen, with her witty anecdotes about how she was perpetually fending off the advances of rakish courtiers.

Louise gave birth to the king's daughter in October 1666. Only a month later tongues were wagging that the real reason His Majesty so frequently visited her at the Palais de Brion (the charming château was a gift from the king) was to spend time with her glamorous friend. The duc d'Enghien observed, "We are saying at the court that he sighs a little after Mme. de Montespan, and, to tell the truth, she well deserves it, because one could not have more spirit nor more beauty than she has. . . ."

Athénaïs was more than a great beauty of her day; there were some, including the king, who were convinced she was the most gorgeous woman in France. Louis was an exceptionally acquisitive man, and so he doubtless felt the urge to append her to his collection of adornments the same way he might add a brilliant statue, a spectacular fountain, or the *Mona Lisa*. With her spectacular curvaceous figure, enormous china blue eyes, and tumbling honey blond curls that she arranged in a style she called the Hurluberlu (pulled off her forehead and cascading in soft ringlets about her face—a coiffure copied by every woman at court, including the queen), the glorious Madame de Montespan was herself a status symbol.

Yet toward the end of the year Athénaïs declared, "Heaven defend me from becoming the King's mistress, but were such a misfortune to befall me, I should certainly not have the audacity to appear before the Queen!"

Was she being coy, deflecting attention from her true stratagem, or did she really mean it? A ruthless and calculating personality has historically been attributed to Athénaïs, but at the time, that opinion was far from universal. Madame de Caylus, a noblewoman and cousin of the king's secret wife Madame de Maintenon, whose impressions of the court were edited by Voltaire, insisted that "far from being born debauched, the character of Mme. de Montespan was naturally distanced from gallantry [a catchall word for flirtations and affairs], and drawn towards virtue." Regardless of her long-term adulterous relationship, Athénaïs was devout throughout her life, once angrily retorting to a duchess who expressed surprise at her adherence to the Church's prescribed fast days, "What, Madame? Because I commit one sin am I to commit all others?"

Nevertheless, Athénaïs needed to believe that her own fine qualities, rather than any calculated agenda, had won the king's heart. She believed, as did Louise de La Vallière to a point, that the only excuse for adultery was true love.

Louis XIV spent most of his long reign at war, and for several years during the earlier part of his rule, when he decamped for the front he was accompanied by an entourage that included the most important women in his life. In May of 1667 the conflict in question was the War of Devolution in the Spanish Netherlands, now Belgium. Athénaïs and the queen were among the party, both determined to bear the long hours on the road like troupers. But it was the beginning of the end for Louise when, in an uncharacteristic and rather desperate display of bravado, she rode out in great state to greet her royal lover, utterly humiliating her boss, the queen, thereby causing considerable embarrassment to His Majesty. The *maîtresse en titre*'s breach of etiquette became a chasm and Louis began to stray.

Most historians believe that he and Athénaïs became lovers during this military campaign. The story, though it may be apocryphal, goes like this: Athénaïs was staying at the home of friends. Louis disguised himself in the livery of her hostess's servants and surprised Madame de Montespan in her bath—but the king was allegedly more dumbstruck by the sight of the voluptuous marquise than she was by his intrusion. He stood rooted to the floor, transfixed by her beauty. It fell to her to dispel the tension, which she purportedly did by dropping her towel.

A new age was about to dawn. Their royal romance would span the most successful and dazzling years of the Sun King's reign, earning the era the nickname *l'Âge Montespan*.

People at court began to notice a change in the winds when the guard at the door to the king's apartments was removed, and it was remarked that Louis seemed to be spending an inordinate amount of time in there. Athénaïs started to neglect her customary responsibilities as lady-in-waiting to Her Majesty, and her roommate was suddenly making herself scarce in advance of the visits the marquise would receive from Louis—in disguise. When the queen inquired what was keeping him from her bed till four a.m., he muttered something about being busy with military dispatches. It was all quite risky, in addition to being risqué. Louis' new liaison was being conducted right under his wife's nose, as well as that of Louise, who still held the position of *maîtresse en titre*.

After the sovereign returned to Paris from the battlefield, courtiers had noticed his swagger; he'd grown more confident around women. Athénaïs had changed, too. She was no longer just another very pretty woman at court who was also smart and pious. Her glorious conquest had hardened her, as though inside and out she had been coated with a veneer of shellac. Victorious in love, she became imperious, capricious, and coquettish. Or were people seeing only what they wanted to see, attributing a different color to her usual behavior, now that she was in the throes of a royal romance? Was it Athénaïs who had changed, or the courtiers' point of view?

Perhaps they condemned her for being brazen about her royal liaison, rather than diffident, like the "violet" Louise de La Vallière. Madame de Montespan was not embarrassed about her doubly adulterous affair, and she enthusiastically enjoyed sex in an era when women typically considered *"commerce"*—intercourse—to be anything from an inconvenience to an annoyance to an outright burden. And Louis was a man of large appetites. He had a libido like JFK and "needed" to make love to Athénaïs three times a day, so hot and impatient for her that often he began to disrobe before her attendants had quit the room. Her ardor equaled his, and in this, as well as in their massive egos and desire for public acknowledgment of their grandeur, they were perfectly matched.

The foundation of their love was clearly physical. And they were both sensualists, sharing a passion for spicy food, heady perfumes (particularly jasmine), and tactile textiles.

Soon, the marquise found herself criticized for turning the king libertine, but he had been raising petticoats with impunity long before their liaison began. It was true, however, that he seemed in thrall to her. "Her tears moved him, not because she was pained, but because he found her beautiful in tears," it was said. What made Athénaïs different was that she took the time to study her royal lover's amatory habits as well as his preferences outside the boudoir, and assiduously strove to please and excite him.

And yet, as heady as the first flush of the love affair was, the king was still sleeping with Louise de La Vallière. Madame de Montespan had much to consider. Was she just an entertaining diversion during Louise's pregnancy? Could she maintain the monarch's affection for the long haul? And what would be the ultimate fate of her rival? Louise, still *maîtresse en titre*, bore her fourth royal bastard during the autumn of 1667, and, as with her three previous children, this infant (a boy who was immediately made comte de Vermandois) was smuggled out of the court on the day of his birth.

In July of 1668, Louis hosted a Grand Divertissement, an opulent outdoor spectacle, ostensibly to celebrate a peace treaty, but in truth intended to impress Athénaïs. The hedonistic theme of the event, hardly martial, was *Les Fêtes de l'Amour et Bacchus*. Louise was seated beside the king as *maîtresse declarée*, and the queen hosted her own table. But Louis had eyes only for Athénaïs, who was laughing up a storm with her friends, including Françoise Scarron, the attractive, intellectual widow of a poet and playwright as famous for his crippled form as for his satirical wit.

The pyrotechnics at the Grand Divertissement—the waterfalls and fireworks, cascades, and candles—demonstrated Louis' dominance of the elements. As three thousand guests danced the night away, dazzled by the aura and brightness of the handsome young king, the monarchy was being mythologized. The sun was his emblem, and he adopted the god of light and music, the healer and the civilizer, as his avatar. Although dreary Marie-Thérèse was the crowned queen of France, it was glittering Athena, as ambitious for power and splendor as her lover, who would truly reign beside her gleaming Apollo.

At the time, however, adultery was a criminal offense in France. A guilty woman could be immured in a convent for life—although a man suffered no similar punishment. It was simply assumed he would literally go to hell. The king's other mistresses had all been unwed, and when His Majesty was the only cheater in the relationship, most people, even among the clergy (several of whom also had female lovers), tiptoed around the subject. But Louis' liaison with Madame de Montespan created a scandal not merely because he already had a *maîtresse en titre*, but because Athénaïs was married as well. A double adultery was a sin of considerable magnitude, indefensible even for a king.

Two key players who remained unaware of this new romance were the queen and the marquis de Montespan, who in 1667 was off fighting near the Spanish border while his wife was pleasuring the king at another battlefront in Flanders. His Majesty dispatched a notice that vastly overpraised the marquis' modest military efforts, but Louis-Henri's sizable vanity didn't permit him to think anything unusual was amiss. "The king claims to be very satisfied with the bravery and bearing which you have shown in this encounter and His Majesty will give proof of this when he has occasion," de Montespan was informed. To celebrate whatever this good fortune might be, the marquis disguised himself as one of his own cavalrymen and kidnapped a local serving girl. Her family eventually located her and demanded that the bailiff imprison her for her own safety, whereupon de Montespan provoked a fight with the bailiff. He left the wench in the frontier town of Perpignan with twenty pistoles as a parting gift and returned to Paris and his old habits, once again borrowing a good deal of money. He was surprised to find that his wife had moved across the Seine to lodgings on the Right Bank, but Athénaïs quickly explained that the new digs were closer to the queen and a shorter commute to work.

In debt now to the tune of forty-eight thousand livres, the marquis rejoined his regiment so he could remain a step ahead of his creditors. He left Athénaïs with a power of attorney over his affairs and didn't return until the end of the summer.

Meanwhile, Louise de La Vallière was playing the "beard" in the king's affair with Athénaïs, for as far as the queen knew, *she* was still his *maîtresse déclarée*, and the marquise de Montespan no more than another witty lady-in-waiting. At first the scenario had been humiliating for Louise, because the sovereign had to pass through her rooms at Versailles to reach those of Athénaïs. But by this time Louis had long since tired of Louise and rarely made love to her anymore—which makes one wonder how both inamoratas felt about the whole arrangement. In 1667, the king made Louise duchesse de Vaujours as a consolation prize. Meanwhile, His Majesty's grand passion, whom he supposedly made love to three times a day, had to remain clandestine.

In September 1668, Athénaïs realized she was pregnant. Obviously it was not her husband's child, as the marquis had been away at war for far too many months for the conception to be fudged. However, Louis-Henri could still legally claim the child as his own, ruining its opportunities for a life of great wealth and privilege. Athénaïs panicked. The marquis knew nothing yet. She *almost* considered sequestering herself and begging Louise, of all people, to pretend the baby was *hers*.

If ever there was a time to make the proverbial pitcher of lemonade out of a bag of lemons it was now, and the oh-so-fashionable Athénaïs was the perfect woman to do it. After all, she had already popularized her Hurluberlu hairstyle with every woman at court. She invented a loose-fitting chiffon gown called a *battante*, a style ironically dubbed *l'Innocente*. Soon all the ladies were dressing *à l'Innocente*.

Louis anonymously rented a house near the Tuileries for her lying-in, but insisted on being present at the birth. Legend has it that the accoucheur, or male midwife, was compelled to perform his duty blindfolded the entire time. When he insisted on something to eat, followed by a glass of wine to wash it down before commencing, he demanded it be fetched by the young man (unbeknownst to him, his sovereign in disguise) who was hovering by the bedcurtains, ordering the anxious father-to-be about as though he were a lackey. "Have patience; I can't do everything at once," muttered the agitated monarch, clearly unused to waiting on anyone.

The arrangement was such a clandestine one, it's possible that the gender of Athénaïs's infant was not formally recorded (historians presume the baby to have been a girl, Louise-Françoise, who died at the age of three; Athénaïs would give her second daughter by the king the same name). Nor were the proud parents permitted the luxury of cooing over their illicit bundle of joy. The baby was probably spirited away by Mademoiselle des Oeillets, one of the marquise's maids.

Nevertheless, the news of the royal romance was eventually leaked. Athénaïs's father, the rakish duc de Mortemart, was delighted by it, as was, rather shockingly, her father-in-law, who exclaimed, "Praise the Lord! Here is Fortune knocking on my door at last!"

His son, however, wasn't about to take his wife's lying-in lying down. Although the older Montespan took the pragmatic view, he wasn't the one being cuckolded by the king. The marquis made an embarrassing nuisance of himself by rampaging all over Paris, loudly denouncing His Majesty as another King David (a biblical reference to his adulterous affair with Bathsheba) and a vile seducer. Evidently Montespan's own kidnapping of lowly serving wenches near the Spanish border didn't count.

To the marquis' astonishment, his tirades were scoffed at. Among the French aristocracy of the seventeenth century, marriages were made purely for financial gain, adulterous affairs were de rigueur, and spouses who were in love with each other were mocked for their sentimentality. Most people wondered why he didn't behave like the traditional *mari complaisant*, and just put up and shut up, taking his wife's infidelity to the bank like every other husband anointed by the king with a set of cuckold's horns. Who knows—he could end up with a dukedom and wealth beyond his imagination. He was deeply in debt; he certainly could have used the bailout. To be fair, at the time the marquis was making a nuisance of himself, the public didn't know Athénaïs was carrying the king's bastard. But Montespan didn't want a dukedom. Besides, the title would benefit his wife even more. It would grant her the "right of the *tabouret*," permission to sit upon a stool in the sovereign's presence, when lesser mortals, and nobles, had to stand. So he was determined to punish her by refusing any offer of a dukedom for the rest of his life, and no matter how powerful Athénaïs became at court, Versailles' rigid etiquette would deny her a privilege that even poor discarded Louise de La Vallière enjoyed.

Not only did the marquis de Montespan perversely trumpet his cuckoldry; he wanted all of France to know about it, which he achieved by ostentatiously affixing a pair of stag antlers to his coach.

Things progressed from the merely embarrassing to the genuinely frightening when the marquis began to stalk his wife. She had sought refuge in the home of Julie de Montausier, whose elderly mother was a celebrated hostess of one of Paris's poshest salons. After Louis-Henri finally located Athénaïs, he went berserk. On more than one occasion he broke into the marquise's bedroom at night and ransacked it; at other times he would lie in wait for her there and beat her up. Then he would boast of his intentions to visit the skankiest brothels in Paris, with the near-certainty of contracting syphilis, which he would pass on to the king by raping Athénaïs and transmitting the disease to her. One night the marquis de Montespan broke down the door and assaulted Athénaïs. Screaming for help, she clung to Julie de Montausier. Fortunately, the servants rushed in and were able to prevent her violation.

Surprisingly, the ostensibly omnipotent king was legally powerless to intervene in what was considered a domestic dispute between spouses. There was no law against a man beating, or abducting, or even raping his own wife. It was a delicate predicament for Louis. He could assign a team of bodyguards to protect his paramour, but he had to tread cautiously so as not to alert the queen to his love affair.

Athénaïs's royal romance sent the marquis de Montespan over the edge, but his embarrassing—and violent—behavior was hardly the way to regain her affection and fidelity. The glue that at first cemented their marriage was sexual attraction, but the relationship quickly soured when he revealed himself to be an inveterate gambler and wastrel, squandering her dowry, and philandering with various women of low birth.

Finally, for Athénaïs's safety, her lover did something that *was* within his power: He issued a *lettre de cachet*, a notice of imprisonment without trial at the king's behest. Traditionally, the monarch did not need to specify a reason for issuing a *lettre de cachet*, but this time Louis enlightened his prisoner. Behaving as though Montespan had merely leveled a professional complaint against the crown, the king sentenced the marquis because he had dared to challenge His Majesty's choice of the duc de Montausier as the dauphin's governor or tutor.

After a week of exceptionally unpleasant confinement, Monsieur de Montespan revoked the power of attorney he had made in Athénaïs's favor. A few days later he was released on the proviso that he remain in exile on his country estate.

Perhaps the marquis might have gone quietly if he had been paid off, but his reaction to his wife's affair was so vitriolic that no remuneration was forthcoming. He fired a parting shot at Athénaïs in the only other way he could legally do so, by taking their three-year-old son Louis-Alexandre back to Gascony, where his mother was already caring for their daughter. Madame de Montespan was not allowed to see Louis-Alexandre again until he was fourteen. The loss of her legitimate offspring was the first casualty of Athénaïs's liaison with the king.

At his country estate in Bonnefont just north of the Spanish border, the marquis declared that his "dear and beloved spouse" was dead, due to "coquetry and ambition," and staged a mock funeral for her at the village church, complete with a church service and a coffin.

It was trendy in seventeenth-century France for posh ladies to consult *devinesses*, or fortune-tellers, and "sorcerers," from whom they would purchase aphrodisiac powders or love potions. Athénaïs visited two of the popular ones, Lesage and Mariette, whose emporia lay in the slums of Saint-Denis, to purchase a concoction that would permanently net her the king, and allow her to replace Louise de La Vallière as his *maîtresse en titre*. The abbé Mariette recited some mumbo jumbo over her head and gave the marquise a packet of powder (possibly Spanish fly, which in small doses would rev up Louis' heartbeat). Since he routinely took emetic "purges" for his bowels, the other powder would pass undetected. The king's doctor turned a blind eye to Athénaïs's secret administration of aphrodisiacs, figuring that whatever was in the "love potions" was fairly harmless, and certainly no worse than whatever *he* was prescribing for His Majesty. But there would come a time when her little excursions to the local witches wouldn't be deemed so innocuous, and the marquise would wish she hadn't established such a well-known pattern of visiting sorcerers and clandestinely feeding their products to the king.

After the 1668 Grand Divertissement, thirty thousand workmen had been brought in to transform the existing structure of Versailles into the masterpiece of Louis' vision. *"Versailles, c'est moi,"* he declared, and it would be a palace with no rival on earth. It was not completed until 1682, when it became the French court's permanent residence. In 1670, the king built a pleasure palace for Athénaïs on the grounds of Versailles, located on the site of a razed village. Known as the Porcelain Trianon, this series of miniature pavilions dedicated to their love was covered with fragile blue-and-white Delft tiles and surrounded by lush gardens that bloomed with their favorite fragrant blossoms: tuberoses, Spanish jasmine, anemones, and orange trees.

That year, Athénaïs instituted proceedings for a legal separation from her husband on the grounds of "cruelty and improvidence." She also requested permission to live apart from her spouse, known as "separation of bed and board," and demanded the return of her dowry (which for the most part remained unpaid, although the sums had been pledged to the marquis' numerous creditors).

Although Louise had *still* not been dethroned, in practice, Athénaïs was now Louis' *maîtresse en titre,* and he was clearly head over heels in love with her, whether genuinely so or chemically induced. She was conspicuously at his side at a lavish fête hosted by his cousin the prince de Condé in Chantilly, and that spring, when the court toured the towns in the Spanish Netherlands (Flanders) conquered by the French. Writing of that excursion years later, during the reign of Louis XV, Voltaire observed, "It was to Mme. de Montespan that all the court paid homage, all honors were for her save those reserved by tradition and protocol for the Queen."

Yet Marie-Thérèse, astonishingly, had yet to deduce what was hiding in plain sight and what everyone else in France seemed well aware of. Under the assumption that Athénaïs was merely her attendant, she had nothing but smiles for her, while she remained openly rude to Louise de La Vallière, the acknowledged *maîtresse declarée*.

Even the German mercenaries they encountered during Louis' hail-the-conquering-hero tour seemed to know what Her Majesty did not, and had no such difficulties expressing their views. When Athénaïs accompanied the king during a review of his German troops she was greeted with cries of *"König's Hure, Hure!"*—the king's whore.

Where others might have pitched a fit, Madame de Montespan accepted the epithet with good humor and grace, archly informing her lover, "Since I had the German translated, I find they are very naïve to call things by their proper names."

As long as the other "whore," Louise, remained in the picture, Athénaïs could never be confident of the king's love; she certainly didn't have a hundred percent of it. While the two women pretended to cordiality, genuine friendship was impossible. Nicknamed "the Dew" and "the Torrent" by the witty memoirist Madame de Sevigné, on one occasion they argued over possession of a costly pot of rouge that Louise refused to lend to Athénaïs. The king himself was compelled to referee the quarrel, and the duchesse de Vaujours would surrender the cosmetic only if Louis would agree to honor the women equally. As a result, Louise became pregnant and Athénaïs became angry. The child was probably miscarried or stillborn, because no further mention of it exists, and Madame de Montespan grew even wearier of Louise's maddening tenacity.

Louis XIV had a pattern of extramarital affairs: His current *maîtresse en titre* would introduce him, in a manner of speaking, to the new one. Louise and Athénaïs had begun as bosom friends (or so Louise had thought). In later years, it would be Athénaïs who would introduce the king to Madame de Maintenon. Yet not only did the monarch juggle simultaneous mistresses; he also enjoyed "meaningless" quickie trysts with additional paramours—ladies who were well-known to his more permanent lovers. For example, Athénaïs's older sister, Gabrielle, Madame de Thianges, scratched the king's itch on occasion. Louis would also tumble one of Athénaïs's lady's maids if the urge struck. These dalliances, even with her own sister, didn't seem to bother Madame de Montespan, because she knew the king was not emotionally involved with any of these minor conquests. His attachment to Louise de La Vallière, on the other hand, remained a source of consternation.

The birth of Athénaïs's first royal bastard, her purported daughter, in 1669 was followed a year later by the arrival of a son, the duc du Maine. It was imperative that these infants, smuggled out of the palace as soon as they were born, were raised by a discreet, trustworthy person who could be relied upon to care for them in relative secrecy. Even if her role as Louis' mistress (not to mention her job as lady-in-waiting to the queen) had permitted her the time, Madame de Montespan could not have openly cared for her illegitimate children, because they were born with the taint of their parents' double adultery. Louise's royal by-blows were adopted by Madame Colbert, the wife of the king's Pooh-Bah of ministers, but as she'd met the king when she was a virgin of sixteen and had never wed, she didn't have a husband to make trouble. Athénaïs and the king had to keep the existence of their offspring a secret, or the marquis de Montespan might perversely try to claim them as his own blood.

As governess for their rapidly increasing royal brood Athénaïs recommended the widow Scarron, a pious woman of impeccable moral rectitude who was also a friend from her days at the Hôtel d'Albret, one of the fashionable salons in the Marais. Françoise Scarron was housed with Athénaïs's children (and a couple of others, including her own niece, so that things wouldn't seem too suspicious), in an anonymous-looking building in the Marais district. So seriously did Françoise take her role as gatekeeper that she often did the laborers' jobs to prevent strangers from traipsing in and getting a glimpse of the kids. Few babysitters would suffer *that* much for their young charges!

But in 1672, after the birth of Athénaïs's third royal bastard, the comte de Vexin, it became clear that a better system had to be devised. The king purchased a charming townhome across the Seine in the rue de Vaugirard near the Luxembourg Gardens, where Françoise Scarron could live quite retired from society and care for the royal children she was growing to love. In 1673 and 1674 Athénaïs bore the king two more daughters, Mademoiselle de Nantes and Mademoiselle de Tours, respectively.

Over the years, Athénaïs lost a number of her children. Not only did her husband remove their legitimate offspring to his family's seat in Gascony, but their daughter Marie-Christine passed away before reaching her teens. Athénaïs's firstborn child by the king died in her third year at the house in the rue de Vaugirard; the little comte de Vexin would die at the age of eleven in 1683; and Mademoiselle de Tours was only six when she perished. By that time, the semiroyal children were all openly acknowledged and living at court, but proximity could never lessen the pain of parting.

As a mother, however, Madame de Montespan found herself in a terrible bind. For years she was deprived of the ability to see her children very often, or even to acknowledge their existence, ironically to protect them from her lawful husband. Were Montespan to claim them as his own, it would damage their brilliant futures as the offspring, even illegitimate, of the king of France. The children, too young to be aware of the societal rules and behind-the-scenes machinations, saw only that their *maman* was an absentee, and consequently directed their devotion toward their governess.

Unsurprisingly, this dynamic engendered countless spats and a good deal of tension. Athénaïs and Madame Scarron, although they were ostensibly friends, and the widow needed her job, often disagreed on child-rearing methods. The *maman* would arrive for a visit with sweet treats in an effort to overcompensate for rarely getting to see her children, while the nanny was the firm but benevolent disciplinarian who supplied the tots with routine and stability.

In time a new form of tension developed between the women; they became rivals for the king's attention and his love. The quietly virtuous and somewhat sanctimonious Madame Scarron made Athénaïs feel guilty about her lifestyle. "In God's name, do not make any of your great eyes at me," la Montespan once snapped at the governess, when she'd paid a call on the nursery, pregnant with another of the king's by-blows.

Athénaïs was jealous of the way her children had bonded with their caregiver. Even worse, soon their father was spending more time than usual in the nursery. The king adored his children by Athénaïs, but Madame Scarron, whom at first he had found to be a bluestocking and a prig, had begun to grow on him. He enjoyed her intelligent conversation, but what had changed his mind about her was that she loved and cared for his kids as if they had been her own.

On September 7, 1673, by issuance of letters patent, a legal instrument formally issued by a sovereign conferring a title or grant upon a designee, Louis XIV formally legitimized his children by Athénaïs de Montespan. It was a risky move, because her husband could contest it, but Louis had already declared legitimate his offspring by Louise de La Vallière, and he could do no less for his beloved Athénaïs. This act, more than any other expression of favor he had shown the marquise, demonstrated to the court that Athénaïs was now his *maîtresse en titre* after spending six years as an also-ran beside Louise. But His Majesty had to dig deep for a legal precedent that would allow him to legitimize the children without naming their mother (the specter of the marquis de Montespan galloping in from Gascony was an omnipresent fear, and the adulterous sin in which the *légitimés* were conceived was even more problematic).

The ceremony dripped with irony. To avoid the mention of Madame de Montespan, even though everyone knew the children were hers, the wording of the letters patent was spectacularly oblique. Louise was undoubtedly humiliated to have been selected as one of the godparents, yet did she hide a triumphant smile at the memory of the letters patent legitimizing her own royal bastards, which referred to "our well-beloved Louise de La Vallière"?

In 1674, Madame Scarron's arrival at court with Athénaïs's children, where they would all be housed from then on, created additional conflict, as the former official mistress and the current one competed for the attention of the king, who was finding the nanny ever more intriguing. "The Dew and the Torrent are bound close together by the need for concealment, and every day they keep company with Fire and Ice [Louis and Françoise Scarron]. This cannot continue long without an explosion," wrote Madame de Sevigné.

That year, recognizing that His Majesty had romantically moved on for good, Louise decided to leave the court—and her children—

forever. Atoning for her sins, she took the veil, becoming a Carmelite nun.

With her longtime rival safely behind the high walls of a convent, Athénaïs was overjoyed to finally take her place in the sun as Louis' *maîtresse en titre*. Her formal separation from the marquis de Montespan was finally adjudicated in 1674 as well, but he continued to contest it, journeying to Paris for the hearing. His presence unnerved the monarch as well as his estranged wife, and the hotheaded Gascon did indeed make things as uncomfortable as possible for Athénaïs. He demanded reimbursement for the entirety of her dowry, despite the fact that her father didn't have the funds in a lump sum, and in any case the marquis was hardly entitled to it, as he had squandered the dowry (in loans against it) at the gambling tables. If anyone had a claim to Athénaïs's dowry, it was her husband's creditors.

The case before the bar got ugly. Athénaïs availed herself of the king's counsel as an attorney, and he did all he could to demonstrate Montespan's pattern of cruelty against her. Louis-Henri's lawyer was, of course, bent on proving that *his* client was the injured party. Witnesses for both sides were called, and final judgment was passed by a panel of magistrates on July 7, 1674. The vote was overwhelmingly in Athénaïs's favor. It would seem like a no-brainer, since her lover was the king, but the court relied upon all the evidence presented. Her husband had stalked her, physically attacked and beaten her, and dissipated her money; all that, as well as his own pattern of disorderly conduct and adultery, contributed to their verdict.

The marquis de Montespan was ordered to reimburse Athénaïs for her dowry money that he had already spent (some sixty thousand livres). Plus he had to pay her four thousand livres in annual alimony, in addition to settling any debts she'd amassed during the course of their marriage. He was also banned from coming anywhere near her, the equivalent of a modern-day order of protection, a separate document that he was served with on July 16, 1674.

The contents of the marquis' household in Paris were appraised at a grand total of only 985 livres. Essentially, he lacked the proverbial pot to pee in. Upon learning just how destitute her estranged husband had become, Athénaïs took pity on him and insisted, through her attorneys, that it had never been her intention to ruin "the house of the said Seigneur her husband nor to prejudice his children." She directed that her alimony payments be used for their care and education instead, and postponed her claim for the restitution of the sixty thousand livres of her dowry that he'd breezed through at the gaming tables. And since her royal lover was exceedingly generous to her, she decided to pay it forward, electing to discharge ninety thousand livres of the marquis de Montespan's debts.

For the next few years, Athénaïs was the uncontested beauty at court, her voluptuous golden splendor the feminine equivalent of the sovereign's. While Louis was busy turning the kingdom into the most envied spot on the globe, achieving his desire of making everyone want to emulate French fashions, cuisine, and culture; wear their perfume; and practice their etiquette, Madame de Montespan herself was the ultimate advertisement, named "the most splendid ornament of this splendid century."

Madame de Maintenon's cousin, Madame de Caylus, wrote of Athénaïs, "Her mettle, her spirit, her beauty which surpassed everything seen at the court, flattered the pride of the King, who showed her off like a treasure. He was proud of his mistress, and even when he was unfaithful to her he returned quickly because she was more gratifying to his vanity."

During Athénaïs's bad moods, she would accuse Louis of loving her only because she was a trophy who enhanced his *gloire* and made such a spectacular accoutrement. What Louis did find so sexy about her, in addition to her looks, was her self-confidence and self-esteem. This ultimate egoist was also excited by her apparent refusal to be intimidated by him, owing to her ingrained certainty that her ancient Rochechouart de Mortemart genes trumped his nouveau Bourbon blood any day of the week. Their relationship was singular for a megalomaniac monarch and his lover: She felt completely at ease bantering with him, and even scolding him, always treating His Majesty as a social equal. During the dozen years that their passion blazed, Athénaïs loved Louis the man as much as she loved Louis the king, and never behaved as though she were in awe of his title.

During the span of their romance Louis founded the Académie des Sciences (1666), the Académie Royale de Musique (1669), and the

Académie d'Architecture (1671). He and Athénaïs shared a love of high culture (she promoted the work of Molière, Racine, and La Fontaine), as well as a mania for extravagance. Beginning in 1674, by the time her royal bastards were acknowledged and her husband was legally out of her famously coiffed hair, Madame de Montespan became the ultimate material girl. Her rather snarky nickname at court, purportedly bestowed by the quick-tongued Madame de Sevigné, was "Quanto," after the popular Italian card game *Quanto-va*, meaning "How much?" because it was common knowledge that Athénaïs always wanted more.

Louis wasn't generous when it came to gifts of jewelry, and Athénaïs had always made a point of refusing gems, perhaps so she would not appear *too* greedy. But both of them finagled a way around the traditional man-gives-his-mistress-jewelry issue in an intriguing way. Louis instructed his finance minister to prepare a casket of gems that Madame de Montespan could "borrow," drawing up a laundry list of earrings and necklaces of diamonds and pearls, the latter even more prized than the former in seventeenth-century France. The pearls Louis specified to be set aside for Athénaïs were larger than those owned by the queen.

Typical of all *maîtresses en titre*, Madame de Montespan used her position to further her family's interests. Her father was made governor of Paris and the Île-de-France, and her morbidly obese brother, the marquis de Vivonne, was made Captain General of His Majesty's Galleys in charge of the Mediterranean Fleet; vice admiral of the Levant; viceroy of Sicily; and governor of Brie and Champagne, an amusing sinecure for a gourmand. In every one of his offices, Vivonne, who was embarrassed about being the recipient of nepotism, served the crown with distinction.

Although he didn't shower Athénaïs with jewels, Louis made up for it with real estate. In 1665 he purchased an estate at Clagny and hired the same architect and landscaper who were redoing Versailles, Jules-Hardouin Mansart and André Le Nôtre. Clagny took twelve hundred men and more than two million livres to build. It was so opulent, even the queen wished to see it. More than a century before Marie Antoinette's *hameau de la reine* at the Petit Trianon, Madame de Montespan had a working farm designed with faux rusticity.

In 1670, the blue-and-white-tiled Porcelain Trianon near Versailles was completed. The boudoir, named the Chambre des Amours, boasted an enormous mirrored bed festooned with silver and gold lace, tasseled fringe, gold-and-silver braid, a gilded canopy, and flounced curtains. The Sun King delighted in abundance and excess and found Athénaïs's ripe sensuality, even during her numerous pregnancies, to be exceptionally erotic.

The grandly theatrical style known as Baroque was the order of the day, but Athénaïs's taste was not only excessive; it was downright eccentric. She kept barnyard animals, including pigs and goats, in her rooms at the royal châteaux. To amuse Louis, she owned a silver-filigreed carriage designed to be pulled by white mice, and a full-size one that would be drawn by the pet bears she kept in the menagerie at Versailles.

It was around this time that Primi Visconti, an Italian count who chronicled the Sun King's reign, bestowed upon Athénaïs the nickname "the real queen of France." Foreign ambassadors gave her presents when they came to court as though she were *le Roi Soleil*'s "second wife." And the duc de Saint-Simon described her salon as "the center of court life—the center of pleasures, of fortunes, of hopes, the terror of ministers."

Royal mistresses were often surmised to be the powers behind the throne, but in many cases their influence was far less than envious courtiers and ministers believed. Such was the case with Athénaïs, who astutely realized that her role was to amuse the king rather than advise him. Madame de Caylus was of the opinion that she "had an ambition to govern and made her authority felt," but in truth, Louis never permitted his mistresses to have any such sway. "[T]ime given up to love affairs must never be allowed to prejudice affairs of state," he wrote in his memoirs. "And if we yield our heart, we must never yield our mind or will. We must maintain a rigorous distinction between a lover's tenderness and a sovereign's resolution . . . and we must make sure that the beauty who is the source of our delight never takes the liberty of interfering in political affairs."

Madame de Montespan's networking consisted of arranging brilliant matches for the *légitimés*, and creating a coterie of supporters among the courtiers so that people would look to her for favors.

But pride goeth before a fall, as the old adage goes, and in 1675, Athénaïs discovered that she had some powerful enemies at court. On April 11, when she went to make her Easter confession, not only did the priest, Père Lécuyer, deny her the sacrament, but he lambasted her through the grille. "Is that the Mme. de Montespan who scandalizes the whole of France? Well, Madame, cease your scandals and come and throw yourself at the feet of Jesus Christ!"

The local priest also refused to hear her confession, which meant that she could not receive Holy Communion at Easter Mass, a devastating blow to any devout Catholic. The king himself went to the court cleric, Bishop Jacques Bossuet, to arbitrate the matter, but received a rebuke and a lecture on the perils of adultery instead. The bishop so terrorized Louis that he ultimately agreed to dump his mistress.

His decision, predictably, did not sit well with Athénaïs, who flew into a rage, closeted herself in her boudoir for two days, and allegedly shredded the bed linens with her teeth in her sleep.

But there was more to the story. Bishop Bossuet had been coached by the babysitter. He had become close friends with the pious Madame Scarron, who had taken it upon herself to save the king's soul by turning Louis away from his mistress and sending him back into the arms of his lonely queen, even though she owed her position at court to Madame de Montespan. By this time, Françoise Scarron was so sick of arguing with Athénaïs over the upbringing of the *légitimés* that she was ready to leave the court. Nothing substantive remained of the women's friendship, and the only reason the governess could be persuaded to remain was the prospect of persuading His Majesty to embark on a straight and narrow path to heaven. Consequently, in 1675 a plot was hatched to frighten Louis into abandoning Athénaïs de Montespan.

At Lent, Père Louis Bourdaloue preached—for the third time—his forceful sermon against adultery, condemning the monarch's practice of it and encouraging him to set an example for his subjects by returning to a pious life.

Then, at Easter, when Athénaïs was twice refused absolution by the confessors at Versailles, Bishop Bossuet managed to convince the superstitious king that God's hand was at work and that he should break with her. However, Louis couldn't abandon his mistress cold turkey. After all, he was used to making love with her three times a day, and he was a man of routines.

"I do not require, Sire, that you should extinguish in a single moment a flame so violent, but, Sire, try, little by little, to diminish it; beware of entertaining it," Bossuet advised.

The clergy came down harshly on the genuinely pious Athénaïs because they couldn't do so on the king of France. He was never refused communion; on the other hand, he wasn't hypocritical enough to attend confession. And yet the marquise sincerely wished to repent and continually struggled between her devotion to her religion and her devotion to the king.

After emerging from her two-day tantrum, Athénaïs accused Bishop Bossuet of using Louis' soul as a political football and a path to controlling the king himself. But the cleric held his ground. Increasingly desperate to hang on to her lover and her position, Madame de Montespan began to forfeit her dignity and her kindness. She tried to smear Bossuet's reputation, but could find no dirt to dig up. Then she tried to bribe him with the promise of a cardinal's hat, but the bishop could not be bought with a biretta.

Tongues wagged at court about the favorite's failure to corrupt Bishop Bossuet. Athénaïs went to Clagny to regroup her thoughts, which gave rise to further gossip. Mademoiselle de Scudéry exulted, "The King and Mme. de Montespan have left one another, loving one another more than life, purely on a principle of religion. It is said that she will return to court without being lodged there, never seeing the King except in the presence of the Queen."

Meanwhile, Louis kept to himself, rarely visiting Athénaïs, and allowing Bossuet to lecture him daily on his religious obligations. Torn between love and duty, the king requested a final meeting with Madame de Montespan, after promising to lead a blameless life from then on, but the bishop scolded him, saying that good Christians avoided temptation. Bossuet ultimately relented and the estranged lovers met in a glass room, where courtiers handpicked for their piety could observe their movements.

"Their conversations were long and sad," reported Madame de

Caylus. Nonetheless, the courtiers were placing bets that the enforced separation would be only temporary.

Bishop Bossuet stressed to the king, "Sire, you must know that you cannot be truly converted unless you work to remove from your heart not only the sin, but the cause of it," compelling Louis to stamp out all traces of love for Athénaïs. Even crueler, Bossuet sent a copy of his lecture to the marquise at Clagny, a sermon insisting that if His Majesty returned to the arms of his *maîtresse en titre*, it would bring about France's ruin.

That summer Louis set off on a military campaign, but absence from Athénaïs only made his heart grow fonder. He ordered his finance minister, Jean-Baptiste Colbert, to purchase as many orange trees for the marquise as she liked, a coded love message, owing to their mutual appreciation for them. Colbert spent nearly twenty-three thousand livres on orange trees for Clagny in the summer of 1675 alone. In July, the king returned from the successful siege of Maastricht determined to see his beloved.

Some at court were defending the couple, insisting there was no reason they couldn't reunite as *friends*. Madame de Caylus agreed. "Madame de Montespan ought to be there because of her birth and her duties; she can live as a Christian as well there as anywhere else."

Athénaïs's apartments at Versailles were aired out and dusted in preparation for her arrival after she had endured a year of separation from her lover. In a triumph of the devil-you-know principle, Louis' ministers recognized that it was better for the king to return to her arms than to watch him surrender his soul to the bishop and his cadre of *dévots*. Yet Athénaïs's victory was somewhat hollow; the king assured his family, and the court, that he intended to honor the vows he had made before heading off to the war in Holland— meaning that he would no longer visit her bed. He greeted Athénaïs civilly upon her return to Versailles and would see her only in the company of others, falling back on the stringent dictates of the court etiquette he had devised himself in order to avoid anything beyond a cool cordiality in her presence. His face betrayed not a glimmer of acknowledgment of their years of passion and shared intimacy.

Madame de Montespan had no alternative but to bite back her

bitterness. Regardless of their personal history, and the fact that they were the parents of five children together, it would have been a gross transgression of protocol for her to question the king's behavior toward her.

In 1675, Madame de Sevigné wrote, "Everybody thinks that the King is no longer in love, and that Mme. de Montespan is torn between the consequences that might follow the return of his favors . . . and the fear that he might turn elsewhere."

Yet even though they were no longer lovers at that point in time, she remained his *maîtresse en titre*. And Athénaïs was keen to remind the court that her social status remained unchanged, even if her sexual one appeared to be in limbo.

In the spring of 1676, Louis set off for the front again, and Athénaïs, exhausted emotionally and physically from the months-long campaign against her royal romance and her own character, took the spa cure at the town of Bourbon, the Bath or Baden Baden of its time and place. In July, when the pair first saw each other again at the queen's reception at Saint-Germain, Louis practically launched himself into her arms. The *dévots* managed to keep them apart that night, and Françoise Scarron volunteered to chaperone Athénaïs during the following day's visit to Versailles. Louis then announced his decision to call upon the marquise at Clagny, whereupon the clucking *dévots* assembled a cluster of high-minded ladies to accompany him.

At Clagny, the king strode over to greet Athénaïs and the pair enjoyed a quiet tête-à-tête by a window. When Louis began to lecture the marquise, she interrupted him, saying, "It's useless to read me a sermon," then murmuring, "I understand my time is over." They both began to weep, although Athénaïs never cried in public. "You are mad," she added softly.

"Yes, I am mad, since I still love you," Louis replied.

The couple then bowed to the entourage of *dévots* and disappeared into Athénaïs's bedchamber—proof, if anyone still needed it, that the king's immortal soul was no match for the marquise's corporeal splendor. Madame de Sevigné observed, "Joy has returned and all jealous airs have vanished." The monarch had never seemed more in love, and their renewed passion silenced the warring factions at court. The king had made his choice, and further remonstrance would not only be futile, but might backfire on the dissidents.

Reclaiming her role in all aspects, Athénaïs was now referred to as *maîtresse regnante*, and she celebrated the renewal of her royal romance with lavish fêtes. The poor crowned queen, Marie-Thérèse, wasn't regnant at all, literally, socially, or in people's hearts; most courtiers acknowledged that they preferred to be entertained by "the real queen."

After Louis' passion for Athénaïs triumphed over his fear of God, or at least over the fire and brimstone of his preachers, she grew more vain than ever, trumpeting her victory, and the assets that helped gain it, through fashion. Her first influence on the court had been the curly Hurluberlu hairstyle in the 1660s, followed by the loose-fitting *"l'Innocente"* gowns. In the mid-1670s she ushered in a third era of high fashion with highly decorated garments in costly, opulent textiles. Lace, gold embroidery, and shimmering fabrics became the rage; she popularized flounces known as *falboas* that ornamented the low, boat-necked bodices, as well as *transparents*—translucent fabrics embroidered with velvet or lace worn to dramatic effect over a black skirt. Athénaïs also introduced the informal *déshabillé*, similar to the *robe battante* that had disguised her early illegitimate pregnancies. Because this new style was easy to remove, it was considered "racy" in a court that was beginning to equate a woman's moral character with how tightly she was corseted. "Loose" women wore loose gowns. In 1682 when Versailles finally became the permanent residence of the French court, in the monarch's private bedroom a portrait of Athénaïs in one of her *déshabillé* gowns was inserted into the canopy of Louis' solid silver bed.

While Athénaïs was never afraid of the king, she remained afraid of losing him, particularly after such a close call as the year of estrangement brought about by the sermons of Bishop Bossuet. Although her temper often got the better of her, she had schooled herself to suppress her jealousy over the other women who would fling themselves at the king—from the ambitious mothers who would push their nubile daughters under his Roman nose to the canonesses who should have been leading celibate lives. Louis remained emotionally faithful to Madame de Montespan, although he indulged in numerous flings, treating his casual conquests "like post horses that one mounts but one time, and that one never sees again," in the words of the marquis de Saint-Geran.

At her end, Athénaïs went on the offensive, making sure that her entourage was comprised of homely and virtuous women. But in 1676, when she was pregnant with her sixth child by the king, giving birth to Mademoiselle de Blois on April 4, 1677, an interloper slipped through the cracks. Such was the scandal made by the beautiful Madame Isabelle de Ludres that Athénaïs and Madame Scarron patched up their differences and presented a united front against her.

On September 11, 1676, Madame de Sevigné wrote, "Everyone thinks that Quanto's star is paling. There are tears, genuine grief, affected gaiety, sulks; in short, all has an end. . . . Some tremble, others rejoice. . . . In a word, we are on the verge of a crisis, say the most clear-sighted."

But Madame de Ludres proved too conniving for her own good. Louis did not appreciate her faking a pregnancy in an attempt to gain supremacy over Madame de Montespan, or behaving as though she had already superseded her as the *maîtresse en titre*, when he had given her zero indication that the position would ever be hers. He publicly snubbed la Ludres, equivalent to the kiss of death, and of course the rest of the court followed suit.

Madame de Sevigné was hard-pressed to conceal her surprise when, after his torrid fling with Isabelle de Ludres, the king seemed more in love with Athénaïs than ever, showering her with diamonds, by cleverly circumventing their mutual rules not to give or accept gifts of jewelry. Louis would organize lotteries for prizes of jewelry, ornamental trinkets, or items of chinoiserie and—*quelle surprise*—Madame de Montespan always seemed to win!

While the queen had only a single page to manage her train, in 1678 at the zenith of *l'Âge Montespan*, when the *maîtresse déclarée* "stood forth in the full blaze of her shameless glory" (in the words of her 1936 biographer Gonzague Truc), her train was carried by no less grand a personage than the duc de Noailles. "This whore will kill me," Her Majesty was once overheard to remark. The cost of Athénaïs's extravagant entourage far exceeded her annual salary of six thousand livres as a lady-in-waiting to Marie-Thérèse, so Louis gave her a hundred and fifty thousand for child care and the education of their brood. (She gave birth to the last of their seven children, the comte de Toulouse, in 1678). And for her personal expenses, he permitted her to draw upon the privy purse.

In 1679, after bearing a total of nine children for two men, the thirty-seven-year-old Athénaïs was beginning to lose her looks. Late nights at the gaming tables (cards and games of chance had become all the rage at court) and the stress relief she had sought from the bottle had taken their toll as well. Having fought a lifelong battle against weight gain (no thanks to Louis' large appetite and his desire for epicurean companionship, as well as her own genetic predisposition to corpulence, in addition to all the pregnancies), she was growing stout. Meanwhile, her sober rival, the royal bastards' childless nanny, Françoise Scarron (elevated now to the title of Madame de Maintenon), despite being three years older than the king, remained fresher than the proverbial month of May.

Louis and Madame de Montespan had not been lovers since the birth of the comte de Toulouse the previous year, and as the year 1679 progressed, she became increasingly panicked over the inordinate number of hours he spent closeted with Madame de Maintenon. Rumors spread through the halls of Versailles. "We are talking of changes in love at court. Time will make things clear," wrote one courtier.

To distract the king's attention from Françoise, Athénaïs made the fatal error of directing his interest to a gorgeous blond newcomer, the eighteen-year-old Mademoiselle Marie Angélique de Scorailles de Roussille, Demoiselle de Fontanges. She even had flawless teeth. *"Belle comme une ange,"* people said about her. "As beautiful as an angel—but as dumb as a basket."

La Montespan assumed that la Fontanges—more than twenty years younger than Louis, and the same age as his heir, the dauphin—would be just another flash in the royal pan, like Madame de Ludres. But she woefully miscalculated. First, the forty-year-old monarch gave the new object of his admiration a suite of pearl jewelry, the usual precursor to his intentions to bed her and make her his mistress. And after only two months at court, Mademoiselle de

Fontanges succumbed. Athénaïs acted complacent at first, biding her time. It was several months before she learned that Louis' new liaison was serious and realized that after all their years of passion, plus seven children, she had been cast aside.

In March 1679, Madame de Maintenon wrote to a friend, "Mme. de Montespan complains of her last *accouchement*, she says that this girl [la Fontanges] has caused her to lose the King's heart; she blames me, as if I hadn't told her often to have no more children. . . . I pity Mme. de Montespan at the same time as I blame her: what would she be if she knew all her misfortunes? She is far from believing the King unfaithful, she accuses him only of coldness. We don't dare to tell her of this new passion."

Although Athénaïs had not been dethroned from her position as *maîtresse en titre*, the entertainments and diversions at court were now held for the amusement of Mademoiselle de Fontanges. And to la Montespan's mortification, the middle-aged Louis began dressing like a young gallant again, his garments trimmed in ribbons and lace. The fickle court rushed to curry favor with the new favorite, and regarded Athénaïs like yesterday's fish. Even the poets whose writing her patronage had helped popularize and enrich dashed over to superpraise the king's new inamorata.

Just as her star had been on the ascent during the wane of Louise de La Vallière's, Madame de Montespan now played the role of the fading, unwanted beauty to the rising Angélique de Fontanges. Hurt and betrayed, she let her temper get the better of her, but the hypocritical bishops had no interest in her rants, for the king's affair with his unmarried teenage mistress was untainted by the stain of a double adultery.

Athénaïs became increasingly desperate to rid the court of her new rival. First she tried to compete with Angélique in the piety department, sitting beside her in church as the pair of mistresses clutched their rosaries and rolled their eyes heavenward. Then she denied all knowledge (though the story may be apocryphal, it's a good one) of how her pet bears "accidentally escaped" from the royal menagerie and utterly destroyed la Fontanges' apartment at Versailles. Ultimately, and least creatively of all, Athénaïs tried to befriend her naive but supremely arrogant rival.

She began to joke with Madame de Maintenon (with whom Louis still preferred to privately converse more than he enjoyed anyone else's company) that His Majesty had three lovers: Fontanges in his bed, herself in name, and Maintenon in his heart. But lovely and young as she was, Angélique could not hold the king after all, unable to match Athénaïs's cleverness or Françoise's charm. According to the astute Madame de Caylus, "The King never cared for anything but her face, and was even ashamed when she spoke before others. One grows accustomed to beauty but not to stupidity, especially when one has lived with a person of the wit and character of Madame de Montespan."

At the end of 1679, Mademoiselle de Fontanges gave birth to the king's son, but the infant died right away. Grief, illness, and childbirth caused her to lose her celebrated looks with alarming rapidity. She became clingy and whiny, and Louis tired of her, pensioning her off with a gift of eighty thousand livres and a duchesse's *tabouret*, the usual consolation prize for castoff mistresses. At the age of twenty, she died of a pulmonary abscess on June 28, 1681.

Death had eliminated another rival, and Athénaïs hoped to win back the king's affections. But something far more insidious than a pretty young newcomer was about to destroy her hopes.

Back in 1668, two of the charlatans she had patronized for "love potions," Monsieur Lesage and the abbé Mariette, were convicted on charges of sorcery. The case was not made public at the time.

The people of pre-Enlightenment seventeenth-century France were often as superstitious as they were religious. Faith in scientific experiments had yet to take hold. Posh aristocrats who never missed a Mass would still visit Parisian soothsayers; it was the chic thing to do, in tandem with praying to the requisite saint for a remedy.

One of the most popular sorceresses of the age was Catherine Monvoisin, known as La Voisin. A practitioner of black magic as well as an abortionist, she enjoyed a booming business from rich, often sexually frustrated female clients, earning enough to purchase a villa on the outskirts of the capital. Her own lovers were noblemen, and she conducted her hocus-pocus in a hundred-thousand-livre purple velvet emperor's robe tooled with gold leather embellishments.

In 1679, La Voisin became the prime suspect in a police investigation regarding a series of mysterious deaths and illnesses among the aristocracy. Known as "The Affair of the Poisons," the scandal became internationally renowned, exposing the corruption of some of the highest members of the nobility, and most specifically targeting Madame de Montespan.

Athénaïs had hastily left the court on March 15, her departure attributed to a quarrel with Mademoiselle de Fontanges. Two days later, although the events were not connected, Louis chartered a special court specifically to handle all the poisoning cases. Called *la chambre d'arsenal*, it was better known as *la chambre d'ardente* (the burning chamber), a reference to the inquisitional courts of the sixteenth century. Presiding over the proceedings was Paris's chief of police, Gabriel Nicolas de La Reynie. It was a literal witch hunt; in the three years of the *chambre d'ardente*'s existence, 194 people were arrested and 104 of them were sentenced. Of those, 36 were executed, 4 sent to the galleys, 34 banished or fined, and the remaining 30 were acquitted.

During La Voisin's trial, Athénaïs's name was raised numerous times, and her family members were accused of purchasing "love potions." Lesage testified that Athénaïs plotted to poison Mademoiselle de Fontanges. But even under torture, La Voisin herself never named Madame de Montespan, and although she went to the flames kicking and screaming and hurling epithets against the crown, she still never implicated the king's *maîtresse en titre*.

But after her death, Catherine Monvoisin's daughter Marie, who had psychological and emotional issues that were exacerbated by imprisonment and torture, told one elaborate tale after another, directly accusing Athénaïs of using her mother's love powders on the king. She also accused the marquise of conspiring to murder Angélique de Fontanges, and alleged that she participated in Black Masses in order to gain the Devil's cooperation in maintaining the monarch's love. Marie Monvoisin also claimed that Madame de Montespan was so jealous at having been thrown over for Mademoiselle de Fontanges that she schemed to kill the king with a poison-soaked petition that was to have been delivered by La Voisin and another poisoner, who would each be paid a whopping hundred thousand ecus for their participation.

With regard to the Black Masses, which allegedly took place in 1667 or 1668, Marie accused Athénaïs of using her naked body as an altar, while a chalice containing the blood of three or four newborn babies mixed with wine rested upon her belly. During the trial, the priest who conducted these inverted Masses quoted verbatim the incantation the marquise had requested him to chant, which any sane person should have known was an absolute fabrication on his part. It asked "that the Queen should be sterile and that the King should leave her table and her bed for me" and "that the King should leave La Vallière and look at her no more, and that, the Queen being repudiated, I can marry the King."

The queen was, of course, *not* sterile—she had already given birth numerous times, and her son, the fat and healthy dauphin, was poised to inherit his father's kingdom. Louise de La Vallière had quit the court for a convent in 1664, three years before the first Black Masses purportedly took place. And Madame de Montespan, a noblewoman with so many years at court, would certainly know that a king could put aside his queen only for reasons of infertility. Besides, Louis could never have wed Athénaïs anyway; not only was her husband still very much alive, but in 1667 the Montespans had not yet been legally separated. The only one who believed all of the charges leveled against any of the witches' customers, including Madame de Montespan, was the police chief, the incorruptible La Reynie.

Despite flinging her name into the mud, none of the witches on trial were able to prove that they had actually seen the *maîtresse déclarée* at any of these events they described. The ambitious war minister, Louvois, intent on bringing Athénaïs down, tampered with witnesses, and admitted years later, in 1682, that the sorcerer Lesage, whom he had bribed, "could never have said a word of truth" with regard to Madame de Montespan's connection with *l'affaire des poisons*.

The woman who may actually have participated in these gothic rituals was Athénaïs's lady-in-waiting, Claude de Vin des Oeillets, a tall brunette who carried on a clandestine affair with the king and even bore him a love child while her employer was still his *maîtresse en titre*. A woman of Claude's physical description is mentioned several times in the witches' testimony. It was Claude who had more need than la Montespan of magic love philters, as she yearned to replace Athénaïs as *maîtresse declarée* and to have the king recognize their royal bastard. And it was Claude who in 1675 brought her lover, an Englishman, to see La Voisin and Lesage to discuss assassinating Louis by giving poisons to Madame de Montespan, who would unwittingly pass them on to the king.

It took a clear head and a dear friend to sort things out for Louis, who didn't otherwise know what to believe. His trusted finance minister, Jean-Baptiste Colbert, whose wife was governess to the king's two youngest children by Athénaïs, and who was also a close friend of her family, sent La Reynie's file to an expert criminologist. The lawyer analyzed Madame de Montespan's motives, as well as Catherine Monvoisin's. Colbert then presented the facts to His Majesty.

"Could there be a witness more reliable or a better judge of the falsity of all this calumny than the King himself? His Majesty knows in what sort of a way Mme. de Montespan has lived with himself, he has witnessed all her behavior, all her proceedings at all times and on all occasions, and a mind as clear-sighted and penetrating as Your Majesty's has never noticed anything which could attach to Mme. de Montespan even the least of these suspicions. . . . Such things are inconceivable, and His Majesty, who knows Mme. de Montespan to the very depths of her soul, could never persuade himself that she could have been capable of such abominations."

Not only did Colbert manage to convince Louis of Athénaïs's innocence, but after a scene of tears and reproaches between the lovers, in 1680 the king appointed her superintendent of the queen's household, the highest-ranking position for a female at court. And she remained at court for another eleven years. Moreover, Louis gave her a gift of fifty thousand livres after the poisons investigation was suspended.

In 1681, Athénaïs and the king appeared at a ball for their daughter Mademoiselle de Nantes, and that year their two youngest children, Mademoiselle de Blois and the comte de Toulouse, were legitimized. It was a banner year in another way as well. Louis personally burned the documents pertaining to Athénaïs's involvement in *l'affaire des poisons*. But he was never again able to fully trust, or to love, Madame de Montespan. Her reputation was forever tarnished, not only to her paramour, but to posterity.

The scandal had achieved one of the intentions of its perpetrators: By 1680, the relationship between Louis XIV and Athénaïs had dipped to an all-time low. That spring they engaged in an embarrassing public quarrel because she was wearing a very strong perfume. Did he think that she was deliberately trying to make him ill? They had another spat after the king refused to take supper in her rooms, his custom for years. From then on, he would dine with her only in the presence of the court.

However, Louis ordered La Reynie to keep all documentation with regard to Athénaïs in a dossier separate from his investigation of everyone else. The king also suspended the *chambre d'ardente* on October 1, 1680, because he thought the investigations could not continue without further damage to la Montespan's character. La Reynie remained convinced of her guilt; her royal lover not so much. The sordid testimony of the witches and the possibility that infants were slaughtered at her behest for Black Masses was too much for Louis to bear.

On the romantic front, Louis was clearly moving on. On June 5, 1680, Madame de Sevigné wrote that a new favorite was gaining traction. "The credit of Madame de Maintenon still continues. . . . She goes to visit him every day; and their conversations are of a length which give rise to numberless conjectures." Four days later she wrote, "Mme. de Maintenon's favor is constantly increasing, while that of Mme. de Montespan is visibly declining." In a popular joke at court, as the marquises pass each other on a staircase, Madame de Maintenon quips to la Montespan, "What, are you going down, madame? I am going up."

Horribly jealous of her former friend and her children's onetime nanny, Athénaïs became desperate to destroy Françoise's pristine reputation, in an effort to displace her from Louis' affections. She insinuated that the widow Scarron had dabbled in lesbianism with the famous courtesan Ninon de Lenclos back in their salon days in the Marais. When no one believed it, or cared, Athénaïs tried to dangle her sister, Gabrielle, in front of the king, in order to tempt him away from Françoise.

By 1681, Louis spent only a few moments a day with la Montespan, whiling away the entire evening with Madame de Maintenon. Athénaïs's oldest *légitimé*, the crippled duc du Maine, also preferred his beloved governess, the woman who had schlepped him across Europe and back in the search to cure his wonky spine and short leg, over the glib and glittering mother who had spent the better part of his childhood in the company of the king.

And yet, it was during a mission on behalf of the young duc du Maine's inheritance in September 1681 that Madame de Montespan learned of the death of her six-year-old daughter, Mademoiselle de Tours. As she was en route to Bourbon at the time, her errand kept her from attending the little girl's funeral.

The queen died on July 30, 1683. Athénaïs was disgusted at the flippant reaction of both the king and his new inamorata, Madame de Maintenon. True, Louis had never been in love with his wife, but she'd been a good woman who'd never given him cause for complaint. And even if he might be in the throes of a new romance, the couple could at least show a little respect and humility! Hers weren't crocodile tears; the marquise de Montespan was geniunely appalled that people were making jokes about the deceased sovereign, and that no one had gone to see the poor woman's body interred. Moreover, now that there was no queen, what would become of the position Louis had created for the marquise as superintendent of Marie-Thérèse's household?

"Madame de Montespan wept a lot," said Maintenon's cousin, Madame de Caylus. "Perhaps she was afraid she'd be sent back to her husband." There was talk around the court of getting the monarch remarried as soon as possible, but not to the mother of his brood of *légitimés*. For starters, the marquis de Montespan was still alive, which immediately disqualified Athénaïs.

Ironically, she found herself in concord with her old enemy, Bishop Bossuet, agreeing to help His Majesty find a new wife. "Without that, so well do I know him, he will make a bad marriage sooner than none."

And yet, after the king secretly wed Madame de Maintenon in the autumn of 1683 in a morganatic marriage (meaning that she would not have the title or rank of queen), Athénaïs could never be contented with the scenario. How could Louis prefer the frigid, self-righteous Françoise to her own sensual brilliance? "And what should I call Madame de Maintenon?" she demanded. "That goose girl, that arse-wipe!" Following one of her infamous tantrums she took to her bed for several days, pleading a migraine.

Although Louis continued to visit Madame de Montespan's rooms at Versailles, he annexed her twenty-room apartment for his own use and relocated her to the exotic Appartement des Bains directly below his own, renovating the Turkish-style baths where the couple used to enjoy sensuous romps. After so many years of living by the king's side, Athénaïs was being placed beneath him, a sad metaphor that was not lost on her. "The real queen" had been displaced by the secret one. Yet Madame de Montespan remained the reigning "favorite," and nothing could erase her status as the mother of Louis' legitimized children. As another consolation prize, he gave her the estate of Clagny for their offspring to inherit after her death.

One of the most controversial decisions of Louis' reign was to marry his *légitimés* into the royal family. Twelve-year-old Mademoiselle de Nantes was wed to the grandson of the Grand Condé in 1685. The following year, plump and pretty Mademoiselle de Blois married Philippe, duc de Chartres, the son of Louis' brother Monsieur and his second wife, Liselotte, the Princess Palatine—much to Liselotte's disgust. She wrote to her aunt Sophia, electress of Hanover, "Even if the Duc du Maine were not the child of a double adultery but a true prince, I would not like him for a son-in-law, nor his sister for a daughter-in-law, for he is dreadfully ugly and lame and has other bad qualities to boot, stingy as the devil and without kindness. His sister, it is true, is rather kind. . . . But most of all . . . they are . . . the children of the most wicked and desperate woman on earth . . . whenever I see these bastards, my blood boils over."

Madame de Montespan wasn't even invited to her youngest daughter's wedding; she read about the event in the *Mercure Galant*, the popular gossip magazine. But it was the ultimate snub to later be told that Mademoiselle de Blois would be placed with a tutor and that Louis intended to bring their youngest child, the comte de Toulouse, to the front with him. With her last two children taken from her, Athénaïs no longer felt necessary at court. Her pride wounded, she requested the king's permission to retire to a convent. He called her bluff, at which point she backpedaled and admitted that she had no intention of making a permanent exit from court. She went to Clagny instead, and her ungrateful eldest son, the duc du Maine, who was going to move into her apartments at Versailles, helped her pack—by cruelly tossing her furniture and other possessions out of the windows. Eventually the cowardly and arrogant duc would even deprive his mother of Clagny, demanding it as a wedding gift, despite the fact that Louis had promised it to her for life.

In 1691, on March 15, Athénaïs did make her genuine departure from court, remarking to her old enemy Bishop Bossuet that he could finally deliver her eulogy. "*Yes*, Madame la Marquise," Bossuet agreed. "The King no longer loves you, you are as good as dead."

Athénaïs returned to court only for a few important events: the birth of her first grandchild in 1692, and his first communion in 1698. She saw her children, except for the duc du Maine, fairly frequently and was reunited with the marquis d'Antin, her son by the marquis de Montespan.

Since 1676, Madame de Montespan had been involved in the Filles de Saint-Joseph, nuns who devoted themselves to educating indigent orphan girls. Her generosity to them had always been magnanimous, and her penitence after she retired from court was just as grand and public as the rest of her life had been. She spent money as extravagantly as ever, but disbursed it philanthropically.

Athénaïs devoted her final years to charitable deeds, setting up a hospital at Oiron. It was there, toward the end of her life, that she began to wear hair shirts, as well as steel belts and bracelets with iron spikes, beneath her sumptuously hued gowns. She pared down her rich diet to the simplest foods, and exchanged her fine linen sheets and soft petticoats for coarse fabrics in order to mortify her delicate flesh. She developed a horror of being alone and a fear of dying, certain that no amount of atonement could erase her sin of double adultery and send her to heaven.

On the night of May 22, 1707, she suffered a fainting fit at the spa town of Bourbon. In the absence of a physician, her attendants, thinking they were helping, dosed her with enough emetic to choke a horse. She vomited sixty-three times. After rallying briefly, she gave her confession, and last rites were administered on May 26.

At three a.m. on May 27, Madame de Montespan died at the age of sixty-five. As a result of family squabbles over where her body would be laid to rest, she was not interred until August 4. After a torchlight procession, she was buried with generations of Roche-chouart de Mortemarts in the Church of the Cordeliers. According to the duc de Saint-Simon, "The poor of the province, on whom she had rained alms, mourned for her bitterly, as did vast numbers of other people who had benefited by her generosity."

Athénaïs's memory would not be soon forgotten while her DNA lived on. Through her youngest daughter, Mademoiselle de Blois, who had wed the duc de Chartres, la Montespan's triple-great-grandson became king of France, the country's only constitutional monarch. Athénaïs's great-great-grandson Louis-Philippe d'Orléans (who famously changed his name to Philippe Égalité during the French Revolution and voted for his cousin Louis XVI's execution) married her great-granddaughter (through the line of her youngest son, the comte de Toulouse). Their child, born in 1773, became King Louis Philippe, a direct descendant on both sides of Madame de Montespan and Louis XIV.

King Louis Philippe married a cousin, one of Marie Antoinette's nieces. They had ten children, and through *their* various marriages Athénaïs's genes eventually made their way into the royal houses of Spain, Portugal, Belgium, Württemberg, Luxembourg, Bulgaria, and Italy.

On hearing of Athénaïs's death, her longtime frenemy Madame de Maintenon hid herself in the cabinet of her *chaise percée* (in other words, she locked herself in the bathroom) and privately sobbed her heart out. But la Montespan's royal lover of nearly twenty years shed not a single tear. Louis XIV retired to his rooms after a hunt without removing his boots, announcing that he wished to be alone. For hours his footsteps were heard pacing the parquet.

Finally, the duchesse de Bourgogne dared to ask why he displayed no emotion over the loss of a woman who had meant so much to him for so long. Evidently, his statute of limitations on mourning had expired sixteen years earlier. "When she retired, I thought never to see her again, so from then on she was dead to me," the king replied.

LOUIS XIV AND
FRANÇOISE D'AUBIGNÉ, MADAME SCARRON, MARQUISE DE MAINTENON (1635–1719)

It's an old cliché—the wife worrying that her husband will have an affair with the babysitter. But what if the man happens to be the king of France? And it's not his wife who's tied herself in knots over his crush on the too-intriguing governess of their numerous offspring, but his official *mistress*?

Such was the uncomfortable love triangle between Louis XIV, the voluptuous and fecund Athénaïs de Montespan, and Françoise Scarron, the sexually frigid but tenderhearted nanny of their brood.

The future Madame de Maintenon, Françoise d'Aubigné was born in Niort prison, near Poitiers, where her father, Constant, had been jailed for conspiring against Cardinal Richelieu. It was not Constant's first run-in with the law; he had previously been incarcerated for rape and abduction and had murdered his first wife by stabbing her multiple times after catching her in flagrante delicto. Françoise's mother, Jeanne de Cardhillac, was the sixteen-year-old jailer's daughter.

Françoise was baptized a Catholic but as a little girl she was sent to live with her father's Huguenot sister at the family's charming country Château de Mursay. She was eight and a half years old when her family embarked for the "Isles of America," or what we now call the Lesser Antilles. There, Constant was set to assume the governorship of one of the minor islands, but eventually ended up on Martinique instead. Françoise became so ill on the voyage that she was mistaken for dead. Her shrouded body was about to be tossed overboard when her mother bent over to give her a farewell kiss. Madame d'Aubigné noticed some tiny sign of movement and the child was fortuitously taken down below. The ship's bishop presciently remarked, "Ah, Madame, one does not come back from such a distance for nothing."

In 1647 the family returned to France, but Constant died that

August, en route to Turkey to rebuild his fortune. An ambitious baronne who was friendly with her mother enrolled Françoise in a convent school in an effort to restore her Catholic roots and ingratiate
herself with the queen mother. Mademoiselle d'Aubigné hated the
experience and from then on had "issues" with convents, although
she agreed to give Catholicism a second chance.

When Françoise was sixteen, the baronne brought her to Paris,
introducing her to the world of the fashionable salons of the Marais
district. There she hobnobbed with the clever minds and the great
beauties of the day, including the notorious courtesan Ninon de Lenclos and the stunning marquise de Montespan, who reached out and
befriended her. In 1660, Athénaïs and Françoise stood side by side on
a balcony as the handsome Louis XIV made his entrance into Paris
with his Spanish bride.

The teenage Françoise appeared sober, serious, and modest, although she would later tell people who had pegged her as a prude
that it was all a persona, carefully crafted not for God but for love of
her reputation. While her masses of shiny, ink dark hair were univer-
sally admired, and her heart-shaped face was considered attractive,
her mouth was thought too small and her chin a trifle plump. In this
age of paper-white beauties, her complexion, owing to all her years
in the islands, was too dark for most French tastes, earning her the
nickname *la belle Indienne.* According to the contemporary writer
Madeleine de Scudéry, her best feature was "the most beautiful eyes
in the world . . . brilliant, soft, passionate, and full of intelligence. . . .
A soft melancholy" pervaded Françoise's personality; "her gaze was
gentle and it was slightly sad."

"I was what you call a good little girl," she told her best friend,
Madame de Glapion, when Françoise was herself middle-aged. She
was always obedient and eager to please. "That was my weakness."
She never complained of her family's hardships, even though her widowed mother and siblings were so impoverished that she and her
younger brother had been compelled to troll the almshouses of Paris
three times a week, begging for scraps of bread. "[I]t was my good
name that I cared about," she insisted.

Frequenting the posh salons of Paris in her mid-teens, Françoise,
badly dressed, shy, and melancholy, met the depressive poet and

playwright Paul Scarron. He was one of the great wits of the age; at his famous salon, the guests were as vibrant as the yellow wallpaper, but he was often in such financial straits that they were expected to bring their own food, wine, and firewood. It was popularly held that Scarron owed his misshapen and paralytic condition—his body was bent like the letter Z—to a prank he had played at the age of twenty-seven during Carnival. Having tarred and feathered himself as a joke, he was ultimately set upon by an angry mob and had no alternative but to leap into a freezing river to escape them. His malady developed gradually, leaving his mind unaffected, as his body grew plagued with acute rheumatoid arthritis.

The pair began an epistolary courtship when Françoise was only fifteen. Scarron, who was twenty-five years older, was quite the flirt. In 1652, he offered the pretty, intelligent teenager two options that would relieve her poverty and uncertainty: He would fund her retreat into a convent (annual bed and board were as expensive as any private school tuition) or she could become his wife, though it would certainly be an unconventional marriage. Monsieur Scarron assured her that he would not claim the rights of a husband (in other words, he would not expect her to have sex with him).

Although Françoise was pious, she enjoyed the world of the salons, loved fine clothes and intoxicating perfumes (when she could afford them), and adored Paris. So she selected the lesser of the two evils. Her mother gave her consent to the match on February 19, 1652, and the contract was signed on April 4.

The union was fodder for the gossips. "At the time of his marriage he couldn't move anything but his tongue, and one hand," said his friend Jean de Segrais. The priest who officiated at the wedding wondered aloud how the marriage would be consummated. "That is between Madame and myself," the playwright snapped.

Despite his boast to initiate his teenage bride into as many *sottises* as possible (the word literally means "foolishness," but he was obliquely referring to sexual experimentation as well as other hijinks), it was Françoise who tamed the libertine Scarron, transforming his salon from bawdy to elegant. In time she would work the same magic with the libidinous king of France.

Eight years later, on October 6, 1660, Paul Scarron died, and his widow emerged with an utter dislike, if not a dread, of sex. Much later, she would refer to herself in a letter to her younger brother Charles as "a woman who has never been married," leading one to conclude that her union with Scarron was never consummated in any traditional sense.

Until he'd written a scathing satire against her cohort Cardinal Mazarin, Scarron had been the Honorable Invalid to the Queen, the recipient of a five-hundred-livre annual royal pension. As his widow, Françoise applied to get his pension reinstated.

But Anne of Austria claimed to have forgotten the amount, and a quick-thinking courtier advised Her Majesty that it had been two thousand livres. Consequently, and quite serendipitously, Madame Scarron ended up with a comfortable income.

After Athénaïs de Montespan bore the king their first child together, Françoise was approached by a mutual friend, Bonne de Pons. A discreet and modest woman was needed to care for the increasing number of royal bastards, and Françoise filled the job description to perfection. The widow Scarron hesitated. She did not approve of her old pal's doubly adulterous liaison and had no desire to condone it by agreeing to be the secret nanny of her illegitimate children. Françoise discussed the job offer with her confessor, who equivocated: If the children were merely the offspring of the king's whore, then he agreed that even though Françoise needed the salary, she should decline the employment. But if the father of Athénaïs's kids was the king, then she would be passing up the opportunity to raise and influence them. Afer all, if her *sovereign* needed her, then she could justify accepting the gig. However, if this was indeed the case, her confessor recommended that Madame Scarron insist Louis XIV himself make the offer of employment.

The king sardonically nicknamed her *votre belle esprit*—"learned lady." It was only as he came to know her by visiting his children with increasing frequency that his opinion began to soften. "The King did not like me at first. For a long time he had an aversion for me. He was afraid of me as a pedant, thinking that I was austere and cared only for things sublime," she confessed many years later.

Françoise was compelled to shuttle between the house in the Marais district where she secretly cared for the royal bastards of

Louis and Athénaïs and her own home in the same neighborhood. Madame Scarron remained socially ambitious, enjoyed the intellectual atmosphere of the salons, and hoped not to have to abandon her lifestyle entirely, forced to remain hidden from view with precious little adult companionship or stimulating conversation. Taking the act of suffering for her job to an extreme, she had herself bled before any event where she might be questioned about her activities because she had a tendency to blush when she lied.

Madame Scarron was a born teacher and took delight in shaping the minds of the young, whether the subject was religion, manners, or culture. But in an age that didn't sentimentalize a woman's relationships with children (whether they were her own or in her care), Françoise was an exception. Despite the fact that, as she once sorrowfully admitted, her own mother never kissed her when she was a girl, she loved all children, although she never bore any of her own. She grew especially fond of the king's first son by Athénaïs, the crippled duc du Maine. He in turn considered her his true *maman*, for she was the woman who raised him, taking him from Antwerp to the Pyrenees in search of cures for his gamey leg and twisted spine.

After Madame de Montespan gave birth to the king's third child in 1672, Louis purchased an unprepossessing house for his children at 25 rue de Vaugirard on the Rive Gauche, near the Palais de Luxembourg, across the river from the prying eyes of the courtiers who frequented the salons of the Marais. There Madame Scarron, visited by only a few trustworthy friends, looked after the expanding passel of royal bastards, augmented by a couple of other children, one of whom was her own relation, in order to stave off the whiff of scandal. The king himself, in disguise, would pop in unannounced, and become utterly charmed to find his children's nanny with one kid on her knee, another in her lap, one in a cradle, and one hanging lovingly about her, while she read aloud to them. Over time, his opinion of the governess changed. "She knows how to love . . . one would be very happy to be loved by her," he mused one day.

In 1674 and 1675, Athénaïs bore the king two more daughters. By this time, their illegitimate children's existence had been leaked by one of the ladies of the court who'd confided it to her lover. As the gossip spread, the identity of the children's governess was revealed.

No sooner was Madame Scarron outed than she and her semiroyal charges were moved to rooms within Madame de Montespan's apartments in the palace of Saint-Germain. Françoise suddenly became an important person, and the toadies came hopping, under the assumption that she had some influence with the monarch.

Yet Madame Scarron had no sway and even less ego. Even at court she dressed simply, preferring discreet jewelry, and gowns in her favorite shades of blue and green, constructed of expensive textiles, but with little in the way of embellishments.

The proximity of the governess to the children's mother led to no end of quarrels. By this time tensions between the two women ran high. Madame de Montespan was envious of Françoise's close relationship with her offspring, and of the time the king passed in their company. They argued frequently about methods of child rearing. One day, after a violent quarrel, Athénaïs complained to the king about Madame Scarron. The *gouvernante* retaliated by considering quitting not only her job, but the court, and becoming a nun instead, vowing, "I swear that I suffer a good deal by remaining in a state where I will have such experiences every day, and it would be kind to me to let me have my freedom. . . . I cannot understand that it is God's will that I suffer Mme. de Montespan. She is incapable of friendship . . . she speaks of me as she likes to the King, and causes me to lose esteem. . . . I do not dare to speak to him directly because she would never forgive me, and even if I could all I owe her would prevent my talking against her."

Anxious that her lover was becoming too intrigued by the babysitter, Madame de Montespan tried to marry her off to another hunchback, the odiferous and notoriously dishonest duc de Brancas. The union would elevate the widow Scarron to a status that was technically higher than Athénaïs's, as a duchesse would have the "right of the *tabouret*" and could sit in the presence of the king, a perquisite forbidden to a mere marquise. Aware that la Montespan was up to something, Françoise had no interest in being fobbed off on one of the ugliest and most unpleasant men at court and refused to entertain the match.

The king thrived on the competitive dynamic between the two most important women in his life (neither of whom was the queen).

But Madame Scarron didn't desire him in the same way his mistress did. Around 1675, she began to make it her purpose to save his soul—which she, and the ultraconservative coterie of religious *dévots*, intended to do by detaching him from his lover. One wonders whether Françoise would have embarked upon her crusade if Athénaïs had been nicer to her and had not consistently endeavored to undermine her credibility by criticizing her job performance to the king.

In January 1675, Louis created Madame Scarron the marquise de Maintenon, although she would never permanently reside at the eponymous château, and during the course of her hectic life at court could manage only a few flying visits. Courtiers began to notice how much time the king spent with the woman he had nicknamed "*Votre Solidité*" for her pragmatism and her grounded, no-nonsense approach to everything. They didn't doubt a burgeoning affair of the heart, although no one could have predicted how important the marquise would become to him. Besides, at the time not only was Louis madly in lust with the nubile, blond Angélique de Fontanges, but Françoise's employer, Madame de Montespan, remained firmly in possession of the title of *maîtresse declarée*.

Their contemporary, the abbé de Choisy, provides numerous reasons the Sun King basked in la Maintenon's glow. "She had looked after the education of M. le duc du Maine which had given her a thousand occasions to show what she could do, her wit, her judgment, her straightforwardness, her piety and all the other natural virtues which do not always win hearts as fast as beauty, but which settle their conquests on a much sounder, indeed almost indestructible, base. She was no longer very young but her eyes were so alive, so brilliant, and there was such sparkling wit in her expression when she spoke, that it was difficult to see her often without feeling an inclination for her. The King, accustomed since his childhood to being surrounded with women, was delighted to find one who only spoke about virtue; he did not fear that people would say she ruled him; he had seen that she was undemanding and incapable of abusing her close connection with him."

In 1679, the rivalry between Mesdames de Maintenon and de Montespan flared up again over the children. And in 1680, after the dim-witted Madame de Fontanges' pregnancy was tragically terminated, it was the marquise de Maintenon whom the king turned to for solace and companionship. Although he usually gravitated to smart, quick-witted women (la Fontanges being an exception), Madame de Maintenon's background was so humble that people assumed she received all of her elevations and perquisites because of some sexual service she rendered him. In truth, it was because he loved her, even if the nature of his ardor was not necessarily physical; it was her innate decency that so attracted him. By this point Madame de Maintenon was enjoying her tenure as second *dame d'atour* (mistress of the robes) to the dauphine. She became more determined than ever to save Louis' soul by persuading him to return to his conjugal duties to the queen, which naturally pleased Marie-Thérèse immensely. The marquise freely admitted her role in encouraging the king to break with his mistresses, first Athénaïs, and then Angélique, because the adulterous liaisons were sinful.

By 1681, however, Madame de Sevigné was punning that the king's favorite was indeed no longer Athénaïs de Montespan, but the governess, whom she had nicknamed "Madame de Maintenant." If the widow Scarron wasn't necessarily "Mrs. Right," she was "Mrs. Right Now."

The courtiers didn't understand the attraction. The Italian count Primi Visconti wrote:

No one knew what to believe of it, because she was old: some saw her as the confidante of the King, others as a procuress, others as a skillful person to whom the King was dictating his memoirs of his reign. It is certain that with regard to the change in her clothes and manners, no one could explain what had taken place. Many were of the opinion that there are men who are drawn much more towards older women than to younger ones.

Although the courtiers were setting her up as a rival to Madame de Montespan, in August 1682, Madame de Maintenon insisted, "People are saying that I want to put myself in her place. They don't understand my distance from these sorts of *commerce* [sex] nor the distance which I want to inspire in the King."

Soon after she wrote those words, however, Françoise may have become Louis' mistress. Her most recent biographer, Veronica Buckley, suggests the pair consummated their romance as early as 1675, the same year Madame Scarron was made marquise de Maintenon. Additionally, Buckley posits that the newly minted marquise was also distracting the king from Madame de Montespan's alluring embraces with intellectually unthreatening young girls, but that contention seems so antithetical to Françoise's morals and is equally difficult to justify given everything else we know about her character: her piety, her purity, and her distaste not only for sex, but for hypocrisy. Buckley also believes that the marquise de Maintenon and the king resumed their physical relationship in 1680, as Françoise reclaimed him from the ailing Angélique de Fontanges. This would date their reunion to three years before the queen died, again incongruously violating everything the marquise held herself up to be: the poster girl for decency and morality. Moreover, in 1681 Madame de Sevigné reported the delight and gratitude of Marie-Thérèse, who saw the marquise as her personal savior, exclaiming, "God has raised up Mme. de Maintenon to bring me back to the heart of the King!"

So, *if* the marquise *did* agree to sleep with Louis even as early as the summer of 1682, she must have begrudgingly submitted herself to the king's will for the higher good. But she also must have been gritting her teeth and thinking of the kingdom of heaven, justifying the adultery and the betrayal of her new bosom buddy, the queen, by telling herself that if she didn't warm his bed, the role would soon be filled by someone else, someone frivolous whose motives were focused not on the care and feeding of the sovereign's soul, but of her own purse.

Nevertheless, it seems hard to swallow the idea that Madame de Maintenon was openly and actively campaigning to restore the king to the arms of his neglected wife while she herself was his mistress. It seems much more plausible to believe that the marquise won the king's affection through her kindness to his children and her conversation. She was a terrific listener who never demanded anything from him, and her rooms provided a nonjudgmental place for him to relax. Had she succumbed to any sexual seduction while the queen was still alive, she would have (a) become one of the moral hypocrites she deplored, and (b) lost the king's affection, because her discomfort with *"commerce"* would have been abundantly apparent. It is doubtful that Louis would have tolerated for very long a lover who was a lousy lay—not after so many years in the arms of the sexually liberated Athénaïs, who had taken the time to learn his pleasure both in and out of bed and devoted herself to his physical satisfaction.

Another point of view regarding Madame de Maintenon's influence on the king comes from Monsieur Lavallée, one of her chief supporters:

> People saw with dismay that this Prince had not yet abandoned the irregularities of his youth, that he was becoming more and more the slave of his pleasures, and that he was advancing towards a disgraceful old age, in which his own glory and that of his country would be tarnished. . . . [T]he King was not only the head of the state, but its very soul; he was the country incarnate . . . the lieutenant of God on earth. . . . Out of this slough Mme. de Maintenon drew Louis XIV; she brought him back to his duties, to the assiduous care of his realm, to the good example which he owed his subjects; she dissipated the clouds of pride which enveloped him, and made him descend from Olympus to inspire him with Christian sentiments of repentance, of moderation, of tenderness . . . and, above all, of humility.

On July 30, 1683, at the age of forty-five, the queen died a few days after an abscess under her arm was so horrifically mistreated by the court physicians that they effectively killed her. Finally, the field was open for the forty-four-year-old king to remarry. He had no political need for an international alliance, and in any event, there were few appropriate candidates.

According to the abbé de Choisy, "Mme. de Maintenon pleased him greatly. Her gentle, insinuating wit promised him an agreeable intercourse capable of regenerating him after the cares of royalty. Her person was still engaging and her age prevented her from having children. To which we may add that Louis was sincerely desirous of leading a regular life."

The marquise de Maintenon accompanied him to Fontainebleau shortly after the queen's death. According to Françoise's secretary, Mademoiselle d'Aumale, "During this visit her favor grew greater than ever. The King, unable to do without her, had her lodged in the Queen's apartment, the counsels were held in her room, and he did the greater part of his work there and consulted her often about it."

The marquise de Maintenon's cousin Madame de Caylus contended that at this time the king endeavored to persuade Françoise to become his *maîtresse en titre*. But she refused to be Louis' harlot, even in the absence of a wife, and was willing to risk banishment from court for her principles. This belief, supported by Madame de Maintenon's twentieth-century biographer Maud Cruttwell, completely negates Victoria Buckley's theory that Louis and la Maintenon became lovers not only while his wife was alive, but while he was also still sleeping with other women.

The marquise grew anxious about her future and started moping about Fontainebleau in tears, complaining of headaches and suffering from attacks of the vapors. Would the king of France actually wed the widow of a paralyzed poet, a woman who'd been born in a prison, and who had been the governess of his children?

And what about Louis? He'd been lovelessly married to Marie-Thérèse for twenty-three years, in perpetual conflict between duty and desire. If he now espoused a woman he was attracted to, he wouldn't be tempted to stray, and could honor his newly found faith as well. As the writer Alphonse de Lamartine put it, "An attachment to Mme. de Maintenon seemed almost the same thing as an attachment to virtue itself."

Yet to marry a commoner would violate the natural order of the world as Louis knew it. He dared not make his commitment public.

Madame de Maintenon held out for marriage. Cruttwell posits that, somewhat displeased by her all-or-nothing terms, the king laid out a major ground rule of his own. He demanded that their union had to be discreet. Not desirous of power and glory in the manner of Athénaïs de Montespan, the marquise de Maintenon accepted the offer of a secret, morganatic marriage. Only a few days after joining the king at Fontainebleau in the wake of the queen's death she wrote to her ambitious and grasping brother, cautioning him to cancel his immediate plans to visit her, with the cryptic "It does not suit me to have any intercourse with you and the reason is so favorable and so glorious that you should feel nothing but joy."

Was this a hint that Louis had informed her of his intention to make her Mrs. Despotic King of France? Even so, Françoise would always remain a marquise. As such, the rigid court etiquette forbade her from being seated in her husband's presence, and compelled her instead to take her place behind the least important duchesse at court. Louis also awarded her no increase to her pension. Cruttwell believes that this was a punishment for her insistence on making their liaison legal. The Sun King also permitted Maintenon's position at court, and in his personal life, to be forever misunderstood—the object of endless speculation, gossip, innuendo, and rumor that persists to this day, in the absence of a marriage certificate.

And yet, Madame de Maintenon was never heard to complain. She remained the epitome of tact and discretion, two of the reasons Louis loved her. Instead, she spoke with gratitude at what she referred to as her elevation. "I am so glorified in this world for the good intentions God has given me that I am fearful of being humiliated and confounded in the next," she wrote to Madame de Brinon, her headmistress at Saint-Cyr.

According to the duc de Saint-Simon, "Some time after the King's return from Fontainebleau, in the middle of the winter which followed the queen's death, a thing took place which posterity will have difficulty in believing, yet which is perfectly true and proven. The Monarch and la Maintenon were married in the presence of Harlay Archbishop of Paris, as Diocesan, and of Louvois, both of whom had, it is said, extracted an oath from the King that he would never make it public."

For the rest of her life Madame de Maintenon refused to confirm that she had ever married the king of France. But most historians believe that the secret wedding ceremony took place in the middle of the night of October 9–10, officiated by the archbishop of Paris, François de Harlay de Champvallon, the king's confessor Père La Chaise, as curate of Versailles, or both men. One source suggests that the clerics wore green vestments, which would date the wedding to a weekday between Pentecost and the first Sunday in Advent. The only additional witnesses to the ceremony may have been Louis' *valet de chambre*; Madame de Maintenon's relative the marquis de Montchevreuil; and the war minister, the marquis de Louvois, who had done everything in his power to persuade the king from the "indignity" of marrying Françoise—and she knew it.

According to Louis' sister-in-law Liselotte, the Princess Palatine, addressed by her formal title, Madame, most people at court believed that Françoise had married the king, although in the absence of an official announcement Liselotte didn't award the assumption much credence. With her cynic's eye and famous German bluntness (she detested la Maintenon and frequently referred to her as *die alte Zott*—"the old trollop"—as well as *la vieille sorcière*—the old witch—and *ordure*—shit), she offered a left-handed compliment about the royal romance. "If they were married their love would hardly be as strong as it is. But perhaps secrecy adds a spice not enjoyed by people in official wedlock." And yet Madame conceded that His Majesty had never felt "such passion for any mistress as he does for this one," which almost strains credulity, as Louis' lust for the marquise de Montespan was so intense that he was known to make love to her three times a day during the height of *their* romance.

The Sun King's subjects found his new love match a big yawn. It lacked the cachet of a grand political alliance and the excitement that a new foreign bride would bring to the kingdom, or the sex appeal of another extramarital affair with a glamorous beauty such as Athénaïs de Montespan. Few could understand what Louis saw in Madame de Maintenon, a middle-aged prude three years his senior. An unflattering ditty made the rounds soon after it was apparent that they were a couple, referring to his sin of concubinage with the sexy Madame de Montespan, adding snarkily that with the frigid Maintenon, Louis was doing his "penance."

In 1684, Madame de Sevigné wrote to her daughter, "The situation of Madame de Maintenon is unique in the world. Never has there been such a one and never will be again."

Two years later, in 1686, the subject of did-they-or-didn't-they still held the public interest. And yet a bawdy ditty feigning disinterest in the matter compared Madame de Maintenon both to the virtuous Roman wife Lucrece and to the notorious French courtesan, their contemporary Ninon de Lenclos (with whom it was inventively rumored that during her late teens or early twenties Maintenon had engaged in a lesbian tryst).

Although nothing was ever stated aloud, there were a number of big hints that Louis and Françoise had made their liaison legal. For starters, she retained her virtue with the Catholic Church and the pope; although she and the king were both widowed, neither was accused of living in sin. Regardless of whether Louis' subjects were kept in the dark, if the king of France had entered into a morganatic marriage, His Holiness would have had to have been informed. Historian Antonia Fraser believes that the pontiff knew of the union by 1685. If Madame de Maintenon had merely remained Louis' mistress, the papacy would hardly have been as respectful of them. Another clue to the legality of their relationship is that by 1692, Madame de Maintenon was visiting closed convents, the sole prerogative of the queen of France. Soldiers, too, relied upon her, writing from the front to the "Protectress of the Realm," for her aid in securing warm clothes—as well as their salaries. Throughout the 1690s, she never appeared at the great state functions, although she sat in the queen's place at daily Mass and received the dauphin and the princes of the blood seated in an armchair while they remained standing in her presence. The king conversed with her bareheaded, a mark of tremendous respect. In fact, it became the subject of an international scandal during an extravagant spectacle he staged in 1698 at Compiègne, ostensibly to induct his oldest grandson, the sixteen-year-old duc de Bourgogne, into the arts of war. Louis spoke to no one but Madame de Maintenon, casually resting his chapeau on the roof of her glass-enclosed sedan chair while he leaned down to address her in the presence of thousands of spectators.

According to her confessor, God had placed "the salvation of a great king" in her hands. "You are his refuge, remember that your room is the domestic Church where the king retires." But Madame de Maintenon was not quite the zealous religious influence on the king that her detractors, such as the king's sister-in-law, Liselotte, and the duc de Saint-Simon, depict. By the death of the queen in 1683, the middle-aged Louis was no longer the libidinous lothario of earlier years. The marquise de Maintenon's sobriety had tamed him to an extent, but age and illness slowed him down as well. In 1686, he had a painful boil on his thigh cauterized, suffered a horrific case of gout in his left foot, and was operated on for an anal fistula.

That same year, Madame de Maintenon embarked upon her greatest legacy. She married her piety, her love of children, and her passion for teaching by inaugurating the Foundation of Saint-Louis at Saint-Cyr, a school for the free education of the daughters of impoverished gentry. Saint-Cyr accepted girls from grade school through twenty, separated into four divisions by age. It began as an academy where the arts and humanities were combined with religious instruction and pragmatic lessons in the womanly arts. However, over time, after criticism that her girls were becoming too vain and worldly for their own good by performing in plays and falling in love with the sound of applause, Saint-Cyr morphed into the sort of rigid convent school that Françoise had herself detested as a child.

Having married well into their forties, Madame de Maintenon and Louis had no children of their own, but they treated the king's grandniece Marie-Adélaïde of Savoy as if she were their darling pet. Marie-Adélaïde came to the Bourbon court just shy of her eleventh birthday, and wed Louis' eldest grandson, the duc de Bourgogne, at the age of twelve. She was dandled on the Sun King's knee, educated at Saint-Cyr, and essentially could do no wrong, eventually becoming spoiled to the point of dissipation, a star that burned white-hot and flamed out before she reached the age of thirty.

The monarch and marquise had one major dispute throughout the course of their lengthy relationship. As Saint-Cyr began to metamorphose from finishing school to convent in terms of its outlook and curriculum, Madame de Maintenon had hired a headmistress who was a follower of François Fénelon, a theologian perceived as fanatical. The marquise herself became something of an adherent to Fénelon's ecstatic religious "Quietist" beliefs and persuaded the king to engage him as tutor to the duc de Bourgogne. For two years she managed to keep it from Louis that through Fénelon, the radical beliefs of Quietism had pervaded not only Saint-Cyr but the court.

When the sovereign discovered Madame de Maintenon's betrayal, he froze her out of his life for two years, refusing to visit her rooms or even to speak to her. On the occasions when their eyes met, she received a glower of rage for daring to poison the mind of the future king of France by introducing a heretic into their midst. Luckily, the hotheaded little duc had no interest in his governor's sermonizing, and so Fénelon's extremism made no dent. But the marquise lived every day in fear of banishment, and after the popular Bishop Bossuet published a treatise mocking Fénelon and his adherents, Françoise became so devastated by the courtiers' snickering reaction that she fell gravely ill.

Witness to her deterioration, one of the court priests, Godet Desmarets, implored Louis to pardon the marquise; his cruelty was genuinely killing her. "Give back your confidence to this admirable companion, full of God's grace, of tenderness and devotion to Your Majesty. I know her heart to the core and will guarantee that it is impossible to love more tenderly or respectfully than she loves you. She would never have deceived you had she not herself been deceived."

The king was ultimately moved by Desmarets' letter and immediately went to Françoise's rooms, where he found her weeping. "*Eh, bien*, Madame, must we see you die over this affair?" he said.

And that was it. She was forgiven.

Although Madame de Maintenon viewed the stewardship of Saint-Cyr as a full-time vocation, she remained the sovereign's chief confidante. "When the King returns from hunting, he comes to my room; the door is shut and nobody is allowed to enter," she told her dear friend Madame de Glapion. The marquise "listened to all his cares and woes," and was literally the shoulder that Louis secretly wept upon.

But well into her seventies, she told her confessor that her greatest affliction was the king's *pénibles*—burdensome—sexual demands, an aspect of her wifely duties that had not ceased with old age. Madame de Maintenon had always described her visits to the royal bed as "slavery and martyrdom," enduring them as stoically as she did her severe bouts of rheumatism, accepting the king's insistence on throwing all the windows wide-open, even in the dead of winter.

But after listening to her kvetch about the septuagenarian Louis' sexual demands, the cleric reminded Françoise of her conjugal obligations. "It is at the same time an act of patience, of submission, of justice and of charity."

She never got much rest out of bed, either. Back in 1691, she had written to her confessor, "Pray God to give me strength to support the pleasures of the court." And at the age of sixty-nine in 1704, ailing with rheumatic aches and pains, she couldn't go to sleep when she wanted to, because at the French court the sovereigns conducted not only their toilettes but affairs of state from their bedchambers, and her rooms were always crowded with men on official business. That November she described herself as "sick and old," and the following May, still ailing (and unaware that she'd have another fourteen years to live), she wrote, "The life we live here [at court] kills me. I am no longer made for this world."

After the death of Louis' beloved twenty-six-year-old grandniece, the dissipated Marie-Adélaïde of Savoy, who was dauphine of France when she succumbed to measles in 1712, the king spent increasingly more time with Madame de Maintenon. He dined with her each midday and remained in her rooms all afternoon, returning again for the evening concerts organized to distract him from his grief and stress. As the years progressed he had become so dependent upon her that he could not bear to forgo her companionship for even a day, but his peripatetic lifestyle was hard on her. At the age of seventy-seven, her body racked with painful rheumatism, she was still jouncing about in coaches, *chaise-à-porteurs* (sedan chairs), and barges as she traveled from one royal château to another.

Her secretary, Mademoiselle d'Aumale, observed, "I have seen her sometimes, weary, unhappy, anxious and suffering, entertain the King for three or four hours and when he left her room at ten o'clock at night and they drew the curtains of her bed, she said to me, 'I am dead of exhaustion.'"

In 1714, Madame de Maintenon crowed over the remarkable physical prowess of her elderly royal spouse. "The King's health is a miracle every day renewed. Yesterday he fired thirty-four shots and killed thirty-two pheasants. Strength, eyesight, skill, nothing is diminished."

But she could hardly say the same for herself. "My sight is nearly gone, my hearing still worse. No one understands what I say because my pronunciation has gone with my teeth; my memory begins to fail; I no longer remember names and confuse them all the time."

The following year, however, the king's much-vaunted health began to suffer. He never recovered from the strain of the multiyear War of the Spanish Succession (1701–1714) or the grief of the sudden loss of all of his heirs but one (the toddler who would reign as Louis XV) from a measles epidemic. He spent many afternoons in Françoise's rooms weeping uncontrollably. By then he was able to enjoy his favorite pastime of hunting only from a wheelchair. He had very few teeth left; part of his jaw had been removed years earlier. Even his hearty appetite had dwindled. On August 9, what his physicians mistook for sciatica turned out to be gangrene.

During the summer of 1715, aware that he was dying, Louis XIV began putting his life in order. His demise took on a somber, elegiac quality, "the saddest and most poignant spectacle that one could witness in this life," his sister-in-law, Liselotte, observed. On the day after it was confirmed that his leg had become gangrenous he shared the first of four farewells with Madame de Maintenon. They jested of her three years' seniority, as the king remarked that his only regret was in leaving her but that odds were they'd meet again fairly soon. The marquise returned to Saint-Cyr, but was called back when the king's health took a turn for the worse. "[H]e asked me to forgive him for not having been kind enough to me and that he had not made me happy, but that he had always loved and esteemed me. He wept, and then asked if anyone was in the room. I said, 'No.' He said, 'But even if they saw me weep no one would be surprised.' I went away that I might not agitate him."

The third time the couple said farewell, Louis fretted about her future. As she'd never been a gold-digging royal mistress, she'd not amassed any wealth. On top of that, she'd always been a philanthropist, and much of what she had was funneled to Saint-Cyr. "What will become of you, for you have nothing?" he reminded her.

"I *am* nothing," Madame de Maintenon replied. "Think only of God," she added, and departed.

The last time the marquise saw her husband, "[H]e said, seeing me still by his bedside, 'I admire your friendship and courage to be still near me at such a time.'"

The dying Sun King gave Madame de Maintenon a rosary from his private keepsake pouch, telling her the gift was intended to be a *souvenir*—the French word for a remembrance—and not a relic. The marquise despaired of her ability to contain her grief in his presence, but she managed to wait until she returned to Saint-Cyr, apologizing to the schoolgirls for weeping in front of them.

Louis conferred with his nephew, the duc d'Orléans, the future regent of his successor, to receive his assurance that the marquise would not become destitute, remarking, "She only gave me good advice. She was useful in every way, but above all for my salvation."

On August 30, 1715, the king and his secret wife shared a final good-bye, after her confessor informed Madame de Maintenon, "You can go, you are no longer necessary to him." She was not at his side at the very end, for which she would later be criticized. But at that time a sovereign's deathbed was considered the milieu of clerics, not of courtiers, or even the monarch's family.

Louis XIV died on Sunday, September 1, 1715, and was buried at Saint-Denis on October 28. In choosing Madame de Maintenon as a companion, after his "perilous season" of passions, as Père Massillon referred to the king's libidinous earlier years during his funeral oration, the monarch was influenced by the mature, wise sort of woman his mother, Anne of Austria, had been, even though Françoise d'Aubigné was not born into rank and privilege. Louis was always fascinated by good women, and if men in their forties marry their mothers, he had done so with the former widow Scarron.

In the pocket of the sovereign's waistcoat when he died was a miniature of Madame de Maintenon depicted as Saint Frances of Rome. When he painted the full-length canvas, the portraitist Pierre Mignard had requested Louis' permission to drape the marquise in ermine, by law a perquisite reserved for kings and queens. "Certainly Saint Frances deserves ermine!" the king had declared, which some took as another hint that Madame de Maintenon was in fact his wife.

The marquise was at Saint-Cyr when she learned of Louis' death. Her former correspondence secretary, Marie-Jeanne d'Aumale, paid her a visit on September 1 to tell her that everyone had gone to the chapel to pray. The marquise immediately understood what that meant and burst into tears. As the days passed she received letters of condolence on her "special loss" from duchesses and bishops, cardinals and courtiers, and from foreign dignitaries, including the queen of Poland. Still she staunchly refused to either confirm or deny her marriage to the Grand Monarch. As one of her biographers wrote, if "a child or simple person" asked her about it, her stock reply was, "Who told you that?"

Pressed by Mademoiselle d'Aumale to pen her memoirs, Madame de Maintenon demurred, insisting that her life was the work of God. As for her twenty-six-year relationship with Louis XIV, "It has been a miracle when I think that I was born impatient and that the King never perceived it, though often I was at the end of my force and ready to throw up everything. . . . Sometimes I was angry when the King would not grant me what I asked. . . . Sometimes I felt outraged and ready to leave the Court. God only knows what I suffered. But when the King came to my room he saw nothing of it. I was in a good humor, thought of nothing but amusing him and detaching him from women, which I could never have done if I had not been good-tempered and equable. If he had not found his pleasure with me he would have sought it with others. . . ."

With the aid of Mademoiselle d'Aumale, the marquise burned every letter she ever received from the king. "We will leave as little as possible about myself," she averred. "Now I can never prove that I have been in favor with the King and that he did me the honor to write to me."

Madame de Maintenon spent the rest of her life in seclusion at Saint-Cyr, aging gracefully and dying with scarcely a gray hair on April 15, 1719, at the age of eighty-three. Her passing went largely unremarked except by her old nemesis, Liselotte, who wrote, "I just learned that . . . *die alte Schump ist verreckt*," employing a rude phrase one might use to describe the horrible death of an old animal.

In 1794, during the French Revolution, as Saint-Cyr was being transformed into a military hospital, workers in the chapel came across Madame de Maintenon's tomb. Seeing the name, they broke the coffin to bits and tied a rope around the perfectly preserved corpse, intending to drag it through the courtyard to unceremoniously set it ablaze. Mercifully, the young officer in charge had a conscience and a sense of history. He tossed the vitriolic mob a fistful of coins and exhorted them to get drunk, suggesting they could burn the body the following day. While the workers were gone, a grave was dug in an obscure corner of Saint-Cyr's garden and the mutilated corpse of the secret queen of France was relaid to rest.

But not for long. In 1805, the school became a military academy and the marquise's remains were ordered to be exhumed and desecrated by General Duteuil, who referred to her as "the fanatic who caused the revocation of the Edict of Nantes," erroneously ascribing far too much influence to her regarding Louis XIV's persecution of the Protestants. Madame de Maintenon's remains were tossed into an old packing case and shoved in a corner of the bursary, where the students, aware of its contents, over time appropriated the marquise's bones as relics. After thirty years, all but the largest bones had disappeared.

In 1836, the academy's commanding officer alerted the authorities to the scandal and received permission to erect a monument to la Maintenon in what had been Saint-Cyr's chapel. During its construction, the workers fortuitously found remnants of the marquise's original coffin and black burial gown, as well as some of the embalming spices, the heel of one shoe, and a small ebony cross. These relics were placed in an oaken coffin with the few remaining bones and buried under a black marble cross with the simple inscription, HERE LIES MADAME DE MAINTENON, with the years of her birth and death.

Unfortunately, she was not to rest peacefully. The marquise's marble sarcophagus was reduced to rubble when Saint-Cyr was damaged by German bombs in World War II during the summer of 1944. The exposed bones were removed to Versailles and reinterred there. In April 1969, 250 years after Madame de Maintenon's death, her remains were transported once again to Saint-Cyr, where they received a sixth, and final, burial.

Sophia Dorothea of Celle

1666–1726

Hereditary princess of Hanover (1682–1694)

When Sophia Dorothea of Celle learned that she would be compelled to wed her unattractive and obnoxious twenty-two-year-old first cousin George Ludwig, son of the Duke of Brunswick-Lüneburg (a duchy in Hanover), she pitched a fit and declared, "I will not marry the pig snout!"

But the dark-haired, doe-eyed sixteen-year-old had little choice in the matter. Sophia Dorothea was the legitimized love child of the duke of the tiny neighboring duchy of Celle and his luscious mistress Eléanore Desmier d'Olbreuse. Her father, George William, had been the heir to the prestigious duchy of Hanover, but it came with strings attached: the mannish bluestocking of a bride that his father had preselected for him, Princess Sophia, daughter of the Palatine king of Bohemia.

So George William cut a deal with his younger brother, Ernst Augustus. If Ernst Augustus would agree to wed Sophia instead, George William would cede him his rights to inherit Hanover and promise never to marry anyone else. Ernst Augustus accepted this arrangement, but Sophia, who had been in love with George William, was furious at being foisted off on his brother. And her jealousy of the woman George William preferred instead never abated.

The daughter of a marquis, Eléanore Desmier d'Olbreuse hailed from a French Huguenot family that had been forced into hiding during the reign of Henri III. She endured a terrifying childhood, always one step ahead of the persecuting Catholics, and had witnessed firsthand the burning of heretical Protestants, the fires fanned by the incendiary sermons of the Jesuit Père Bourdaloue. Her family ultimately settled in Breda in Holland, where they were taken under the wing of another refugee, the princess of Tarente. It was there that the penniless young Eléanore met George William of Brunswick-Lüneburg and the pair fell in love.

However, because George William had pledged never to wed another as part of the jettisoning of Sophia of Bohemia, he could not offer Eléanore anything more than a morganatic marriage. From her vantage, it was better than being his mistress, but it voided any rights their future offspring might have. Still, the princess of Tarente encouraged the twenty-six-year-old Eléanore to accept George William's offer. She loved him, she had nothing to bring to the match herself, and she wasn't getting any younger.

The morganatic marriage was celebrated in September 1665, and little Sophia Dorothea, for all intents and purposes illegitimate, was born the following year. It was not until 1676, when she was ten years old, and her uncle Ernst Augustus and her aunt Sophia had plenty of boys to inherit their duchy (meaning that her parents no longer posed a dynastic threat), that they begrudgingly permitted the marriage of George William and Eléanore to be fully legitimized. This action retroactively removed the stain of bastardy from their daughter, but some people would never let Sophia Dorothea forget her roots.

She grew up to resemble Walt Disney's Snow White, with fair skin, luscious dark hair, and pouty red lips. And she enjoyed an idyllic childhood in Celle, living in a castle straight out of an illustrated fairy tale. Celle was full of sylvan woods and groves and charming cottages with thatched roofs. One can practically imagine her romping with spotted fawns, fluffy bunnies, and chirping bluebirds.

By the time Sophia Dorothea reached her mid-teens, her father and his brother Ernst Augustus had become determined to eventually unite their separate Hanoverian duchies by wedding Sophia Dorothea to the oldest son of Ernst Augustus and Sophia. In that way, *their* eldest son (the fathers were thinking *way* ahead) would one day inherit the entire duchy of Hanover, and become a powerful player on the Central European stage.

A good deal of baggage accompanied the match between Sophia Dorothea of Celle and George Ludwig of Brunswick-Lüneburg.

The prospective mothers-in-law still detested each other. Sophia, a Machiavellian termagant, remained jealous of the sweet-tempered Eléanore, whom she had always considered to be a nobody from nowhere, an impoverished refugee who had bewitched the man *she* should have married with her dark good looks and her grace on the dance floor.

The marriage was doomed even before the vows were taken on November 22, 1682. George Ludwig couldn't get past the fact that his gorgeous wife had been born a bastard, and Sophia Dorothea couldn't get past the fact that her husband was just a bastard, period. He was fond of two things, neither of which included her: war and ugly women. In fact, he took not one but two hideous mistresses. One of them, the married and morbidly obese Sophia Charlotte von Kielmannsegg, was purported to be the daughter of his *father's* mistress, most likely making her George Ludwig's half sister. George Ludwig's other inamorata, Ehrengard Melusine von der Schulenberg, who was as tall, angular, and bone-thin as Sophia Charlotte was roly-poly, had been one of his mother's ladies-in-waiting.

In between George Ludwig's martial campaigns and his extra-marital affairs, he and Sophia engaged in domestic altercations of the sort that involved physical violence and flying crockery. Nonetheless, somehow they managed to produce two children: in 1683 a son, George Augustus, who would grow up to be George II of England, and in 1687 a daughter, also named Sophia Dorothea, who would become the mother of Frederick the Great.

But after six years of marriage, Sophia Dorothea, Hereditary Princess of Hanover, had had enough of her husband's infidelities, as well as having her complaints about them shrugged off by both her parents and his. By that time she had done her duty as a royal spouse by producing an heir, and she decided to reward herself by commencing her own romance, heedless of the consequences. She was graceful and lively, with a stunning figure, even after giving birth to two children. She was quick-witted and clever, accomplished in all the womanly arts—music and singing, needlework and dance. She loved to have a grand old time. She deserved to be loved.

Unfortunately, no one else except her paramour, Philipp Christoph, Count von Königsmark, thought so. Sophia Dorothea's royal romance cost her absolutely everything she held dear. Although her behavior had certainly contributed to her downfall, the punishment hardly fit the crime, especially when her husband remained free to cat about with his own pair of mistresses.

The Hereditary Princess lost her freedom. In 1694, Sophia Dorothea was divorced from her husband by mutual consent. But then she was banished from Hanover. However, a simple exile wasn't enough for her vindictive in-laws. At the age of twenty-eight, Sophia Dorothea was incarcerated within the moated castle at Ahlden, where she remained until her death, thirty-two years later.

As she grew old and lonely at Ahlden, her ex-husband went on to become king of England. Queen Anne had died without issue in 1714, and by Great Britain's 1701 Act of Settlement, the crown had to pass to her nearest Protestant relation. That would have been George Ludwig's mother, the duchess Sophia, who was a granddaughter of the first Stuart king, James I. But Sophia had passed away just weeks before Anne did, making George Ludwig, elector of Hanover, the next British monarch. Dropping his middle name, he became George I and thus began the dynasty of England's House of Hanover that would rule until the death of Queen Victoria in 1901.

Consequently, as Sophia Dorothea remained behind the moated walls of Castle Ahlden, there was no queen of England during the reign of George I. He never remarried. Instead, his Hanoverian mistresses, primarily Melusine, acted as his hostesses.

On November 13, 1726, at the age of sixty, Sophia Dorothea died of a fever as a complication of liver failure and an accumulation of sixty gallstones. In her extremis she had scrawled a letter to George, cursing him from the grave. At the news of her death, the court of Hanover went into mourning, but George sent word to Germany that no one was to wear black, and he celebrated her demise by attending the London theater that night.

George destroyed her will, in which she had left all her property to their children, appropriating it for himself, and commanded all of her personal effects at Ahlden to be burned. He still despised Sophia Dorothea so much that he refused to allow her coffin to be interred, and it sat around in a dank chamber for two months until his mistress, the superstitious Melusine, claimed to see the princess's unfettered spirit flying about in the guise of a bird. Finally, George commanded Sophia Dorothea's body to be buried in the family crypt at Celle.

On June 19, 1727, George was making one of his return visits to Hanover when he received a mail delivery. Upon reading his late wife's ghostly missive he turned pale, recalling the prediction made decades earlier by a fortune-teller: that if he were in any way responsible for his wife's demise, he would expire within the year. Collapsing with the words, *"C'est fait de moi"*—I am done for—he was dead within three days.

The new king of England (and elector of Hanover), George and Sophia Dorothea's son, ordered Hanover's records unsealed. He discovered 1,399 pages of love letters (representing only a fraction of those exchanged) between his mother and Count von Königsmark. George II opposed the ill treatment and emotional torture his father had inflicted upon his mother. Had Sophia Dorothea not predeceased her husband, her son would likely have liberated her from Ahlden and installed her as the dowager queen of England.

In any event, the Georgian apple didn't fall far from the paternal tree. George II also took mistresses, although at first he did his best to respect the feelings of his wife by not flaunting his liaisons.

Few mourned the passing of George I, but Sophia Dorothea's grave became a cult destination. Visitors still leave floral tributes and pity the soul who endured such a weighty punishment for her royal romance.

SOPHIA DOROTHEA OF CELLE AND PHILIPP CHRISTOPH VON KÖNIGSMARK (1665–1694)

On March 1, 1688, a sophisticated Swedish mercenary, Philipp Christoph, Count von Westerwyk and Steghorn as well as Count von Königsmark, swaggered into Hanover's Leine Palace. He made a low bow to the twenty-one-year-old, chestnut-haired, cherry-lipped Sophia Dorothea and inquired, "Does Your Serene Highness remember that I was her page at the Court of Celle?" She was metaphorically swept off her feet.

Flooded with nostalgia for her lost and happy youth, Sophia Dorothea said nothing. But she smiled. They had indeed met before—years earlier, at her father's court, where the count's father, a war hero, had brought him for military training. Back then, the sixteen-year-old Philipp and fifteen-year-old Sophia Dorothea had enjoyed a puppy-love crush. The steamiest it had gotten at the time was when the pair spelled the words "forget me not" in the condensation on the palace's 383 windows.

The Duke of Hanover, Ernst Augustus, offered the twenty-two-year-old count a job as a colonel of the guard, which landed him in the third rank of court hierarchy. Sophia Dorothea's young brothers-in-law thought he was a totally cool guy—a soldier-courtier-adventurer who had traveled the world! With ample opportunity to excel in his two favorite skills—fighting and flirting—Königsmark was in his element, the very embodiment of a seventeenth-century gallant.

Soon after his arrival at court, he and Sophia Dorothea excited both admiration and envy at a costume ball. She was gowned as Flora, the goddess of spring. Königsmark was the ultimate Rosenkavalier in a suit of pink-and-silver brocade. All eyes were upon them as they danced the minuet, and, save one opinion, everyone was charmed by their elegance. What a lovely couple they made, with their clouds of dark hair, delicate features, and divine grace on the parquet. The lone dissenter was the blowsy Clara Elisabeth von Meysenburg, Baroness von Platen, the mistress of Sophia Dorothea's father-in-law, the Duke of Hanover.

Count von Königsmark remained in Hanover for two years. While there is no evidence to indicate that he and Sophia Dorothea were doing anything more serious than flirting, it was clear that they were captivated by each other. The count wrote romantic letters to Sophia Dorothea recalling their shared childhood memories—his having promised as a youth to serve her, body and soul, reminding her about all those moist "forget me nots" on the frosty window-panes. Königsmark had never forgotten Sophia Dorothea, and he wanted to be her hero, avenging the cruel mistreatment she suffered at her philandering husband's hands. With characteristic reckless-ness, he wrote about challenging George Ludwig to a duel.

The count's military appointment afforded the would-be lovers the proximity required to act upon their desires. But Sophia Doro-thea was fearful of violating her marriage vows and tried to keep her old crush at arm's length. And Baroness von Platen, monstrous in every way, coveted the dashing Swedish mercenary and detested So-phia Dorothea for having ensnared his fancy.

It was easy to understand what women saw in Count Philipp Christoph von Königsmark. His dark curly wig framed the face of a true sensualist. His manners were courtly and refined, which, for a career military man, was saying something. And his international reputation as a lothario may have been something of a titillation as well.

Baroness von Platen seduced Königsmark, even though it was a bit like shooting fish in a barrel, for the rakish Swede was ambitious—and the baroness, being the Duke of Hanover's lover as well, had in-side access to the corridors of power. But Königsmark's true, albeit unrequited, passion was Sophia Dorothea. Denied the woman he re-ally wanted and unable to evade the clutches of the one he didn't, he was trapped in a romantic purgatory. In order to escape it, in January 1690 the count asked to join the expedition to the Pelopponese, under the leadership of the duke's twenty-one-year-old son, Charles.

Around this time, Sophia Dorothea and her handsome mercenary began to correspond. Königsmark became ill in the Balkans and, in a letter from April 1690, begged Sophia Dorothea to cure him by sending a few encouraging lines. "I am on the verge of death now, and the only thing that can save me is a word from the incomparable princess." He declared himself her slave.

The campaign was a disaster. The Hanoverians, including the young prince, were sliced to ribbons by the Turks. Of the eleven thousand men who sallied forth, Königsmark was one of the 130 who returned. By then, he had begun to fall genuinely in love with the princess. Developing an attack of the faithfuls, he dropped the Baroness von Platen cold. She swore to avenge her wounded ego.

After Königsmark decided to devote himself entirely to Sophia

Dorothea, the pair embarked on a full-blown romance, complete with clandestine trysts and secret signals. For example, a letter from Königsmark to Sophia Dorothea written in December 1692, reads, "I am shaved. I look fine, and one could sing 'The knight is a conqueror.' We will recognize each other by the usual signal, I shall whistle 'The Spanish Follies' [an aria by Corelli] from a distance."

They employed a loyal confidante, the count's sister Aurora, as a go-between. Every morning from Celle, the princess would entrust her precious correspondence to a faithful postilion or lackey, or to a traveler who had no idea he was carrying such incendiary material. Copious numbers of passionate letters were exchanged, nearly fourteen hundred of which still survive. The lovers wrote in code, ascribing nicknames or numbers to the principal players. But the correspondence was eventually intercepted by Baroness von Platen's spies, who had little difficulty decoding the cipher. Sophia Dorothea's mother, the Duchess of Celle, was "the Pedagogue," whose sage advice was never heeded; her father was "the Scold." George Ludwig, Sophia Dorothea's husband, was "the Reformer." Baroness von Platen was "the Fat Girl." Königsmark was "Thyrsis," a shepherd out of classical poetry, and Sophia Dorothea called herself the "Clumsy Heart," which encapsulated her naive, reckless abandon. Another encryption technique the lovers used was the insertion of a prearranged group of letters before each syllable, similar to Pig Latin.

As a brief overview, insofar as historians have been able to piece together, their epistolary romance began with a note from Königsmark to Sophia Dorothea dated July 1, 1690, and ended at the close of 1693. Not all of the letters that have survived are dated. The correspondence began with a respectful tone, but after the affair was consummated, the tenor became much more florid. Both count and princess wrote as if they were characters from an epic romance of the era. Their early letters were sealed with the image of a heart on an altar lit by a ray of sunlight, emblazoned with the motto "Nothing impure can set me on fire." But the later letters threw purity to the four winds, with a new, highly suggestive motto on the seal that read, *"Cosi fosse il vostro dentro il mio"*—"Thus might yours be inside mine"—accompanied by the image of two hearts, one enclosed inside the other.

Rarely was there a more neurotic pair of lovers. Sophia Dorothea's passion became all-consuming, barely sparing a thought for anyone else, even for her two children, the only other people in the world for whom she may have had any affection.

Much of the time, the count was at war, posted to a front, whether near or distant. From her silken boudoir Sophia Dorothea fretted over the firing of every cannonball and fusillade. "Can it be that you think that I love someone other than you?" Königsmark wrote from Berlin on April 23, 1691. "No, I swear to you that after you I will never love again. It will not be very difficult to keep my word, for after having adored you, how could one find another pretty woman? . . . And how could it be that after having loved a Goddess, one could wish to look upon Mortals? No, in truth I have too good taste, and I am not one of those who would like to become a scoundrel. I adore you charming brunette, and I will die with these feelings, if you do not forget me, I swear to you that I will love you all my life. I expect no letters from you because I hope to be soon near you, and my only occupation will then be to show you that I love you madly, and that nothing is dearer to me than your favors. . . ."

Two weeks earlier, the count had told Sophia Dorothea that he had a new roommate: a bear he had trained to tear his heart out if she should prove faithless. No pressure there. Needless to say, the intensity of Königsmark's ardor for Sophia Dorothea was overwhelming. In April or May of 1691, he composed a poem to her, in which he confessed his "own perdition, [b]ecause I have dared to love what I should only have worshiped."

There were two themes that the princess reiterated as she constantly reassured Königsmark of his place in her heart, averring, "I was born to love you." More than once she penned some version of ". . . I have a passion which creates all the pleasure and all the misfortune of my life. It is the only one I can say I have ever felt and it will die with me." One day she wrote, "Without you life would be intolerable and four high walls would give me more pleasure than to remain in the world."

In this, she would eventually get her wish.

Each of the paramours was consumed by jealousy and fear.

Königsmark blamed Sophia Dorothea for his suffering, because he doubted her attachment to him, working himself into a lather at the idea of another man in her box at the theater, or the French ambassador gallantly offering his arm as she descended a staircase. Of course, he had no right to demand or expect her fidelity to him: She was a married woman. Nevertheless, envious even of her husband, Königsmark wrote Sophia Dorothea from his camp during the summer of 1692, "[W]henever I think that you might ever caress anyone but me, my blood curdles in my veins. . . . Oh God, if ever I saw you kiss anyone with as much passion as you have kissed me, and ride astride with the same desire, I never want to see God if it would not drive me mad."

He had no reason to reproach Sophia Dorothea, but saw threats everywhere, asking her to send him a detailed account of her routine every day. She complied, foolishly ignoring the enormous risk posed by revealing such information.

Their romance was conducted against a backdrop of war, including Louis XIV's expansionist incursions into Flanders and Germany. Königsmark fought for members of the allied forces intent on stopping him. The stakes were as high as they could be: life and death, if the lovers were to be discovered. Sophia Dorothea's indiscretion would not be overlooked by either her husband or her in-laws, despite George Ludwig's own infidelity. And the penalty for Königsmark could be dire. Additionally, posted at the front, the count faced the threat of death at the end of each salvo of artillery fire, in the curve of every saber. In one letter, Sophia Dorothea pleaded with her lover, "I beseech you not to expose me in the future to worries like this. Never leave me again, I beg of you, and if it is true that you love me, do yourself a favor and spend the rest of your life with me. How I hate King William [William III of England], who is the cause of all this. He gives me mortal pain by endangering all that I adore."

The night before his men prepared to attack the French at Enghien, Königsmark wrote, "[W]hat makes me a coward is the fear of never seeing you again." Sophia Dorothea replied, "I am charmed by everything you tell me. Rest assured that whatever accident might befall you, you would not be loved the less. My affection is equal to any test, and even if only your head were left, I would always love you to distraction, and would count it a real pleasure to renounce the world in order to live with you wherever you please. However, I am very happy that you came back in one piece. Every bit of you is so handsome and so charming that none of it must be lost. Look after yourself, I beg you."

But Königsmark couldn't restrain his jealousy even when he had no reason to doubt his lover's affection. He seethed when George Ludwig arrived at Halle and evidently spoke of Sophia Dorothea, "[T]elling me of the state you were in, your undress, uncoifed, your hair hanging down loose on your matchless bosom. Oh God, I cannot write for anger!"

It's hard to imagine George Ludwig, who cared nothing for his wife, boasting of her beauty to her lover, let alone to the rest of the officers. Although there is no clear indication that he was aware of Sophia Dorothea's affair (as his mother and his father's mistress were), perhaps it was suggested to him that he might say alluring things about her in the count's presence, in order to gauge his reaction.

Back in Hanover, Sophia Dorothea's mother-in-law was slyly angling for her to betray her affair with the count. The princess was too naive to recognize it, writing to her lover on June 14, 1692, that she "talks about you every time I go for a walk with her . . . I don't know if she does it because of affection for you or to please me. In either case, she speaks of you a lot and I cannot even hear the sound of your name without a surge of emotion which I cannot control. She praises you so highly and with such pleasure that if she were younger I could not help being jealous, for really I think she is fond of you. She could not give me more evidence of it than she does. It even makes me uncomfortable."

While the princess's mother-in-law was giving the young woman enough rope to hang herself, her mother was trying to protect her, but the Duchess of Celle might as well have been spitting into the wind. Worried about her daughter's *tendre* for the Swedish mercenary (and vice versa), Eléanore d'Olbreuse repeatedly cautioned Sophia Dorothea that she was treading into treacherous territory and that Königsmark's ungovernable passion for her might doom them both. But the young woman ignored every warning, listening instead to her paramour, who insisted that the duchess was "the most deceitful woman in the world. She says a thousand nice things and yet she is using her authority to try to ruin me with you."

The lovers had discussed their future, although the count had admitted that his prospects were limited. His huge gambling debts prohibited him from covering himself in military glory at the front in Flanders, because that was where his creditors awaited. On orders from the king of Sweden, Königsmark's estates there were to be confiscated. And he refused to accept any advantageous job offers, because it would mean quitting Hanover, and he had vowed never to leave Sophia Dorothea. When he wrote to say that he had sacrificed everything for her, it was no exaggeration; he was indeed placing their romance ahead of his career and financial stability. But ironically, without either of those two elements, what future could they possibly have on their own? How would he be able to support them?

In addition to pouring his passion onto paper, Königsmark provides a rare glimpse of life at the front. His letters are full of gossip about his fellow officers, anecdotes about the practical jokes they played on one another and getting drunk with his buddies, although he was quick to assure Sophia Dorothea that his inebriation didn't lead to infidelity.

At some point in 1692, several of the lovers' letters were intercepted by operatives working for Baroness von Platen and delivered to her lover, the elector Ernst Augustus, Sophia Dorothea's father-in-law. Until that time Königsmark had been in the duke's good graces. In 1691, for example, he entrusted the count with a diplomatic mission to Hamburg. But after he saw the letters, the duke assigned Königsmark to a Hanoverian regiment that was marching off to fight the French. Although fellow officers were liberally granted leaves of absence, the count's requests to visit Hanover were repeatedly denied.

Stuck at an army camp while Sophia Dorothea glittered at court, surrounded by admirers, the count was consumed with jealousy and doubt, his anxiety exacerbated every time the arrival of a letter he had been expecting was delayed. Every late or missing piece of correspondence filled the lovers with anguish and dread—and with good reason.

At the end of the 1692 campaign, Königsmark reiterated his request for a pass to return to Hanover. After it was denied, he feigned illness and went AWOL, riding to the Leine Palace in disguise and rushing into the arms of his beloved. "What I wouldn't give to hear midnight strike!" he wrote. "Be sure to have smelling salts ready lest my excess of joy cause me to faint. Tonight I shall embrace the most agreeable person in the world and I shall kiss her charming lips. . . . I shall hear you tell me yourself that I matter to you in some way. I shall embrace your knees; my tears will be allowed to run down your incomparable cheeks; my arms will have the satisfaction of embracing the most beautiful body in the world."

But after the magnitude of his desertion sank in, the count presented himself to Marshal Podewils, who was also a sympathetic friend of Sophia Dorothea's parents. However, now that the duke of Hanover had been made an elector, Ernst Augustus had begun to care more about maintaining appearances. Although he did not terminate his own extramarital affairs, nor would he compel his son George Ludwig to do so, someone would have to be scapegoated in order to demonstrate to the Holy Roman Emperor that he was a man of strong moral fiber.

To that end, the marshal had just been assigned the unpleasant task of exiling Königsmark's sister Aurora from Hanover, most likely at the instigation of the conniving Baroness von Platen. Being a tactful woman, Aurora departed the duchy quietly. Sophia Dorothea's letters to Königsmark had passed through Aurora's hands, which was undoubtedly the reason for her banishment. So the princess tapped a new conduit, her lady-in-waiting Eleonore de Knesebeck—who was eventually imprisoned for her supporting role in the royal romance.

But by this point, aware that they were being closely watched, the paramours hardly dared to exchange glances for fear that the electress Sophia or the Baroness von Platen's spies would report it. Consequently, Königsmark was always missing, or misinterpreting, the secret signals from Eleonore de Knesebeck, and when he didn't find an expected letter hidden in his hat, he'd assume he'd been betrayed.

The count knew by now that he had lost favor with his employer, the elector, and feared an assignment that would send him away from Hanover. But in 1693 current events conspired in his favor. Denmark allied herself with Sweden and together they prepared to invade the tiny duchy of Celle, on the pretext that Sophia Dorothea's father had built fortifications on a frontier town. The Danes camped on the banks of the Elbe, and Königsmark was named commander of the troops in charge of preventing them from crossing the river. He was camped at Altenburg, where his letters were written until September of 1693.

On May 19, writing to his "beloved brunette," the count pined, "It is now eight weeks since I left Hanover. I am fasting and live like a Capuchin monk. I don't miss a sermon and I no longer trim my beard. . . . Ah! If I could see those eyes happy to see me die before them. If I could kiss that little place which has given me so much pleasure. . . . At night, your portrait is before my eyes and on my lips and I am no longer a Capuchin. . . ."

By September, Sophia Dorothea was supporting her career soldier's decision to abandon his profession. Königsmark wrote to her on the nineteenth of the month, "You want to know whether I still want to leave the army. I answer that that depends entirely on you, because as I have resolved to be completely yours, heart, body, and soul, you must rule on how I should conduct myself." He was really asking her for money, having confided a couple of months earlier that his estate in Sweden was "rather poor. But I have acquired a much greater treasure and I defy this barbaric king to take it away from me. I have your very dear person and the possession of your heart."

Unfortunately, Sophia's dowry was in the possession of her in-laws, who begrudgingly parceled out just enough for her to live on, and she dared not ask her father for funds. Not only was the duke of Celle entirely unsupportive of their romance, but he needed every thaler he owned to fight the Danes.

Baroness von Platen was also becoming an increasing source of anxiety. Sophia Dorothea urged Königsmark to attend the woman's soirees, as he had done in the past, and to humor the baroness, because if he irritated her too much, she would avenge herself. Her words proved prophetic. At eleven p.m. on the thirtieth of July, the princess wrote Königsmark to confide that she'd had a three-hour conversation with Baroness von Platen, in which the older woman informed her that everyone at court was gossiping because "the life I lead is so retiring" that "they do not think it natural for a woman of my age to renounce everything so completely, and they are seeking the reason for it. I replied that if I had singled out someone and had not treated everyone the same way, people would have a right to complain, but that as I talk to no one everyone should be satisfied and that they were wrong to complain since I treated everyone alike." And yet, after all this time Sophia Dorothea still had no clue that the fox had gotten in among the pigeons, adding, "She spoke several times about you; she is only too pleased to do so. At the end we parted as close friends and never was friendship confirmed by as many pledges as she made."

What elevates this royal affair to the heights of grand opera is that it is a wartime romance, where issues of life and death are at stake. In many cases each letter Count von Königsmark wrote to his beloved princess could have been his last. What plunges the liaison to the depths of melodrama is the scheming presence of Baroness von Platen, overdressed, overweight, and overrouged, so wildly jealous of Sophia Dorothea and so desperately covetous of the Swedish count that one can almost hear her maniacal cackle with every twist of the plot to destroy their love and their lives.

In April 1694, Baroness von Platen convinced Ernst Augustus to exile his daughter-in-law's paramour from Hanover. The elector summoned Königsmark and politely informed him that his services were no longer required.

The Swede left the Hanoverian court and promptly secured a new post as a general in the army of the elector of Saxony. However, one night in Dresden he drank a bit too much punch at an officers' mess party and embarked on a booze-fueled rant about the pathetic antics of the weak Hanoverian elector Ernst Augustus, his pushy lover Baroness von Platen, his podgy, pig-snouted son, the Hereditary Prince George Ludwig, and the prince's skeletal giant of a mistress, Ehrengard Melusine von der Schulenberg. As Ernst Augustus had spies everywhere, word of Königsmark's trash-talking got back to Hanover.

George Ludwig confronted his wife with this story of her lover's indiscretion. Sophia Dorothea immediately countered that it was *his* romance with Melusine that was the real scandal. When she proposed a divorce, it was probably the first time the couple had ever agreed on something. But then George Ludwig began to throttle his wife and yank out her hair. Sophia Dorothea's screams brought the servants running. They saw the Hereditary Prince shove his wife to the floor and swear never to see her again. Unlike his marriage vow, this was a promise George Ludwig would keep. However, he was afraid of doing her too much injury, because of a strange prediction made by a Gypsy fortune-teller years earlier: that if he were in any way responsible for his wife's demise, he would meet his own doom within a year of it.

The parents of the sparring pair had predictable reactions to the news of a possible divorce. Ernst Augustus and his wife, the shrewish duchess Sophia, fearful of losing the annual installments of Sophia Dorothea's dowry, sent their son out of town to clear his head. Sophia Dorothea's father was wholly convinced that his daughter made a better whore than a wife. The Duchess of Celle was the only one who sympathized with the princess's situation, but she was unable to champion her daughter alone.

At the end of June 1694, Königsmark feigned illness and deserted his military post in Dresden, riding hell-for-leather to Hanover, in disguise, to see his beloved Sophia Dorothea. The lovers had conceived the idea of running away together, although the count's spendthrift behavior presented a hitch; he was already deeply in debt. What would they live off of after they fled? Pragmatism was never Sophia Dorothea's strong suit, so they decided to throw caution to the winds, intending to flee to the duchy of Wolfenbüttel on the second of July.

But Baroness von Platen's spies detected Königsmark's disguise. The countess had already hammered the maiden nail into the coffin of Sophia Dorothea's marriage by introducing George Ludwig to his first mistress (her daughter Sophia Charlotte); she remained hell-bent on ruining the princess's extramarital romance as well.

On July 1, Königsmark received a letter from Sophia Dorothea written in pencil, asking him to come to her apartments between eleven p.m. and midnight. The door would be opened to him when he whistled their secret signal, Corelli's "The Spanish Follies."

Sophia Dorothea later asserted that the letter was a forgery, although her lady-in-waiting, Eleonore de Knesebeck, insisted that it was genuine. Surely after so many letters from his beloved, the count would recognize her handwriting. The note was ultimately revealed to be authentic, but Baroness von Platen had known of its contents.

Count von Königsmark had worn borrowed clothes for this rendezvous so that he would be less recognizable. He did not tell his servants where he was going. Königsmark sneaked across the palace gardens, whistled the signal, and Mademoiselle de Knesebeck appeared at the back gate. She conducted him to her mistress's room through a long, dark corridor accessible from either end.

Having been reliably informed by her spies of the mercenary's arrival, Baroness von Platen reported it to Ernst Augustus, who decided to burst in on the lovers, catching them in flagrante delicto. But the countess talked him out of this idea, convincing him that such farcical behavior was conduct unbecoming an elector. She suggested instead that he issue a warrant for Königsmark's arrest and put a handful of halberdiers at her disposal to execute it. As events would bear out, the countess wasn't terribly specific with her pronouns.

Unbeknownst to the duke, Baroness von Platen then plied the guards with alcohol, getting them drunk. She ordered them to wait in the shadows and to seize anyone she instructed them to, swearing them to secrecy upon pain of death by hanging. As the night dragged on, the soldiers dozed off, sleepy with wine and the lateness of the hour. Two women kept a close vigil on the light that shone through the crack at the bottom of the door to Sophia Dorothea's apartments: Baroness von Platen and Eleonore de Knesebeck.

The princess's lady-in-waiting urged the lovers to part before daylight so the count could safely make his getaway in the dark. Although they were reluctant to leave each other's arms, the sexually sated von Königsmark departed her apartment with a light heart, intending to return the following night, when they would make their flight. He crept noiselessly down the long corridor, retracing the steps he had taken to Sophia Dorothea's rooms. But when he reached a door that he had specifically left unbolted and found it locked, he became suspicious. Historians disagree on whether or not he instinctively drew his sword at this point, as some scholars believe he may have been unarmed. Most men, even in a swashbuckling era, might not wear a sword belt to a tryst.

The count was ambushed by the elector's guards, clouted on the head with the flat of a blade. Stunned, he fought back, wounding two of his assailants. In the burgeoning light, the halberdiers recognized the victim as their commander, but, goaded by the countess, they repeatedly stabbed Königsmark with their swords. Baroness von Platen personally avenged his spurning her for Sophia Dorothea by kicking the dying man in the face with the toe of her brocaded slipper.

But then, stung with shock and remorse, she became hysterical and tried to revive him. Unsuccessful, she spun the news of his demise by informing Ernst Augustus that the Swede had forcibly resisted arrest. But what was to be done with his battered corpse, whose blood was leaching into the floorboards where it lay?

With time of the essence before the entire palace awoke and bustled about its business, it is believed that the elector and his mistress hid Count von Königsmark's body within the walls or under the flooring of a small room on the same level of the palace, after first covering it with quicklime to neutralize the stench of decay and hasten decomposition. The official lie was that the count had simply disappeared into the night. After all, the man was a known rake; he probably kept bad company!

The following day Sophia Dorothea awoke filled with optimism and waited breathlessly for her lover. However, she became anxious when she heard rumors that he had been killed in a duel with a Count Lippe. She tried to see the elector, but Baroness von Platen informed her that she and her lady-in-waiting must stay within their apartments. The princess assumed that all would be revealed in the evening, after her son and daughter were brought in to say good night to her. But neither the children nor Königsmark ever came. Instead, the person who arrived to greet her was her dragon of a mother-in-law. The duchess Sophia informed the princess that she was now under house arrest.

Sophia Dorothea's rooms were searched, turning up scores of incriminating billets-doux. As soon as the prime minister of Hanover, who happened to be Baron von Platen, showed them to Sophia Dorothea's father, he all but disowned her. The duchess Sophia and her husband were even more delighted that Duke George William had done nothing to defend his daughter, because it meant that Ernst Augustus could punish her and still keep her lands in Celle and her dowry.

The elector commanded George Ludwig to return home from Berlin, where he was visiting his sister, and dispatched Baron von Platen to cross-examine Sophia Dorothea. She defiantly demanded to know why she was being kept like a criminal.

Baron von Platen stammered something about the possibility of an illegitimate pregnancy, then told the princess that her in-laws knew everything about her romance with Count von Königsmark. "Is he locked up, too?" Sophia Dorothea asked. The prime minister told her that the Swede had died two weeks earlier.

Sophia Dorothea fainted. Baron von Platen coldly stood by. When the princess revived, she exclaimed, "Murderers; they have murdered him. A family of murderers . . . ! Have pity and let me go. I can't stay here any longer."

Under intense interrogation, the princess denied that the romance had been sexual. But the Hanoverian court accepted the admission that there had been any liaison at all as a confession of adultery. It also didn't matter to them that the affaire de coeur had begun well after Sophia Dorothea's children were born, meaning, therefore, that her son and daughter were clearly legitimate. The official statement issued from the Leine Palace was that the Hereditary Princess was formally separating from her husband, "with whom she was no longer on good terms."

"The Princess at first displayed only some coldness towards her husband, but Fräulein von Knesebeck by degrees inspired her with such dislike to him that she begged from her father permission to return to her parents' home. Her father was displeased, and warned the Princess to place confidence in her husband. But her dislike of her husband was so intensified by the machinations of Fräulein von Knesebeck. . . . Her corrupter, Fräulein von Knesebeck, was arrested at the wish of the Duke George William."

There was no mention of adultery in the full formal statement, and little mention of Königsmark, as the Hanoverians did not want the Swedes to come snooping around looking for him. But by now his mysterious disappearance was a hot topic of gossip in every court in Europe.

After her brother's disappearance, Aurora von Königsmark received a sealed packet bearing Sophia Dorothea's coat of arms from the count's secretary, Hildebrand, which had been covertly passed to him by Eleonore de Knesebeck at the behest of her mistress. The parcel bore the words, "To Countess Aurora von Königsmark, to be kept sealed until claimed by the Hereditary Princess. If, however, it is not reclaimed, it is to be burnt without being opened and without its contents being read." The package undoubtedly contained the lovers' correspondence.

Aurora also received several trunks containing her brother's wardrobe and personal effects: two hundred suits and uniforms, forty-seven fur-lined coats, seventy-one sabers, a hundred and two watches, and eighty-seven military decorations.

Unfortunately, Hildebrand had not been able to remove all of his master's papers. A search ordered by the vengeful Baroness von Platen revealed Sophia Dorothea's letters. The secretary had seen Count von Königsmark take great care of a parcel tied with a yellow ribbon and locked in a box. Ironically, if the count had been less of a romantic and had burned these letters, he would have saved his beloved Sophia Dorothea years of anguish.

Baroness von Platen took the letters to the elector, who had them deciphered. As the pair of them read the decoded correspondence, the duke became livid. He might have been able to forgive the adulterous liaison (such affairs were de rigueur in royal courts; after all, his relationship with the Baroness von Platen was doubly adulterous, and his son, Sophia Dorothea's husband, had *two* mistresses). What he couldn't forgive was the lovers' plot to flee to the enemy state of Wolfenbüttel. Adultery might break a commandment, but fleeing into enemy territory with the dowry money that Ernst Augustus believed to be rightfully his, *that* was high treason! The elopement to another state would have raised a number of thorny issues with regard to her dowry, compelling Sophia Dorothea's in-laws to sue for the continued payment of the installments. Money trumps sex every time.

Sophia Dorothea categorically refused to return to her marital home, so George Ludwig sued her for divorce. A religious high court, composed of four churchmen and four laymen, was established to hear the proceedings. Although they knew that the verdict was a foregone conclusion, given the identities of the parties and the families connected with the suit, the men were intent on being fair-minded and impartial, thoroughly reviewing all the documents as though it were any other case.

The duchess of Celle tried to protect her daughter by cautioning her not to consent to everything so willingly. Sophia Dorothea's own lawyer endeavored to impress upon her the immorality of the clause forbidding her to remarry while George Ludwig would be free to do so. But the princess just wanted to get it all over with as quickly as possible, and both dukes—her father-in-law and her father, who had all but disowned her—were duplicitous enough to make her believe that the divorce decree might put an end to her incarceration. Surely Sophia Dorothea could not have imagined that, after consenting to all of the terms of the divorce, she would never be allowed to see her children again.

In her divorce petition, using the royal "we," Sophia Dorothea confirmed the spouses' mutual loathing: "We still adhere to our oft-repeated resolution never to cohabit matrimonially with our husband, and that we desire nothing so much as that separation of marriage requested by our husband may take place."

The court found Sophia Dorothea guilty of "malicious desertion," rather than adultery, so that her in-laws could still collect her dowry, despite the dissolution of her marriage. She and George Ludwig were divorced by decree dated December 28, 1694. By this document Sophia Dorothea also forfeited her title of Hereditary Princess of Hanover. All traces of her existence were expunged from the government documents, and her name was omitted from the Sunday prayers offered for the royal family. To mention her name was anathema.

The twenty-eight-year-old Sophia Dorothea was indeed granted her wish to leave the Leine Palace, but not in the manner she might have hoped for. She lost custody of her children and was banished to the castle of Ahlden, where she was to be immured, along with a tiny retinue (in the employ of Baroness von Platen), for the remainder of her days.

For the first four years of her exile at Ahlden, Sophia Dorothea was denied all visitors or correspondence. But since George Ludwig still feared the fortune-teller's prediction that he would die within a year of his ex-wife's demise if he had any responsibility for it, after the first year of imprisonment Sophia Dorothea was permitted to take local carriage rides, because a doctor warned that being kept solely indoors was endangering her health. After four years, she was finally allowed visitors, but when her son, George, tried to see her, his father punished him. Their daughter, who had wed the tyrannical king of Prussia, was forbidden by her husband to liberate her. For years, Sophia Dorothea dressed up every day and night for the ghost of her lover, who still dwelled in her imagination, as the silhouettes of fashion changed over the thirty-two years of her imprisonment— from 1694 to 1726. But as time went on and she was allowed to mingle with the townsfolk of Ahlden, Sophia Dorothea became their Lady Bountiful, taking an active interest in their welfare.

On the death of the duke of Celle in 1705 and the duchess in 1722, Sophia Dorothea became the richest heiress in Europe, but a lot of good it did her behind the walls of Ahlden. Even a fraction of that fortune would once have allowed her to ride off into the sunset with Count von Königsmark. Now that she had the funds, Sophia Dorothea dreamed of escaping her prison. She had placed a considerable amount of her fortune in a Dutch bank, but she needed a financial adviser. Her daughter, the queen of Prussia, recommended a Count von Bahr, then withdrew her suggestion after hearing some negative reports about him. Sophia Dorothea ignored the warning and, under his name, invested every penny she owned in Holland. Bahr stole it all.

So there was no escape from Ahlden, but as time went on, justice was served in one way or another. Thanks to the aid of a friend, Sophia Dorothea's former lady-in-waiting Eleonore de Knesebeck was able to escape from the fortress of Schwarzfels, where she had been imprisoned for abetting the exchange of the lovers' correspondence.

In 1698, Ernst Augustus died and George Ludwig became the new elector of Hanover. He demanded the immediate dismissal from court of Baroness von Platen. Two years later, as the baroness lay dying of a venereal illness that had left her blind and disfigured for the last six years of her life, she swore she saw Count von Königsmark's ghost, and confessed to her complicity in his murder.

Louis XV

1710–1774

Ruled France: 1715–1774

*F*or the second time in a row the successor to the French throne was little more than a toddler. His father, who had died by the time the child ascended the throne, was Louis, the duc de Bourgogne, and later dauphin of France, although he never lived to wear the crown himself. Louis XV's mother was Marie-Adélaïde of Savoy, the precocious grandniece of Louis XIV and dress-up doll of Madame de Maintenon.

The boy's rakish great-uncle, Philippe II, the duc d'Orléans, served as his regent until 1723, when Louis XV attained his majority. The duc may have been quite the debaucher, but he was a good steward, nearly balancing the budget by 1721, after inheriting a huge debt from Louis XIV in 1715.

Louis XV received a fairly comprehensive education from his tutors. He was a curious, if shy, youth, an avid reader particularly interested in the sciences. Toward the end of his reign he founded departments in physics and mechanics at the Collège de France.

In 1721, at the age of eleven, Louis was betrothed to his three-year-old first cousin, the Infanta of Spain Mariana Victoria, and the following year he was crowned at Reims. In 1723, the king's majority was declared by the Parlement of Paris, the region's judicial body, formally ending the regency. The duc d'Orléans was retained as prime minister until he dropped dead of a massive stroke on December 1. As the years passed, concern arose over the young king's frail health and his ability to produce an heir. By 1725, with the security of the monarchy at stake, France couldn't wait for the Infanta to grow up, so the search began for a more viable bride.

They settled on the twenty-two-year-old impoverished princess of the deposed Polish king Stanislas Leszczyński. The Polish royal family had never intermarried with the French Bourbons, and they could not believe their good fortune. On September 5, 1725, Marie Leszczyńska wed the fifteen-year-old Louis. The marriage proved extremely fruitful. Between August 14, 1727, and July 15, 1737, the queen gave birth to ten children, although there were a few stillbirths and a number of offspring who died young. Unfortunately, only one son survived to adulthood, which left the succession on shaky ground, as France was under Salic law, where only a male heir could accede to the throne.

Still, the young king was perceived to have it all, or so thought the Baron von Pollnitz. In 1732 the visiting German nobleman described the twenty-two-year-old monarch as "one of the handsomest princes in Europe. One can say of Louis XV that he was born without vices, and free of that pride which is usually felt by monarchs. He is friendly with his court, reserved with people he doesn't know, and most particularly with ambassadors; he is more circumspect and secretive than other people his age. His habits, his behavior and his feelings are those of a virtuous man. . . ."

Although Louis was now considered an adult, he did not seem interested in ruling or confident enough to rule alone. His former tutor Cardinal de Fleury played a key role in governing the kingdom, effectively running the shop for seventeen years until his death in 1743 at the age of eighty-nine. On Louis' behalf, Fleury balanced the budget and stabilized the French currency. He freed all political prisoners and relaxed censorship. Also, by the mid-eighteenth century, France had the world's most extensive, state-of-the-art system of roadways, and the growth of the kingdom's merchant marine was encouraged, at the expense of the navy.

By the time Fleury expired, the king was thirty-three years old. He chose not to replace his mentor, opting instead to rule without a prime minister.

At first Louis was happy with his queen, but her devotion to him (and her devotion in general, as she was an exceptionally pious woman) began to grate on him. Like his predecessor, he was evidently incapable of marital fidelity. On the other hand, his queen spent a good deal of time enceinte, and court physicians traditionally forbade sexual intercourse as soon as a consort's pregnancy showed, fearing it was bad for the fetus. This restriction left any king invariably frustrated and with a lot of time on his hands.

The queen was all too aware of her husband's philandering, even complaining to her father about Louis' repeated infidelities. As he worked his way through his first four mistresses, a quartet of siblings (the Mailly-Nesle sisters), she salved her wounded heart in philanthropy and piety. On the other hand, she claimed to endure her husband's lovemaking because it was her duty to submit, so how much fun could the woman have been as a bedfellow? If Marie was looking for ways to chase him from her boudoir, she surely found them, by waking several times a night to complain of the cold, or to look for her lapdog, or to fret about the ghosts that might be haunting the room, which necessitated the presence of a trusted maidservant to sit by the bed and reassuringly hold her hand. Louis was also a libidinous man living in the most licentious of eras. A Catholic, to be sure, but a man of strong passions, who for the sake of his kingdom, like most royals, hadn't the freedom to choose his wife, nor wed for love.

In 1744, eleven years after he took his first lover, Louis decided to personally take command of his army, leaving Versailles to fight the War of the Austrian Succession. His mistress of the moment, the youngest Mailly-Nesle sister, the formidable redheaded duchesse de Châteauroux, insisted on meeting up with him at Metz. But Louis became gravely ill, and it was touch-and-go as to whether he would survive. For safety's sake, so his soul would not go to hell, he had to confess and be shriven. This meant he would have to dismiss his mistress with whom he had been living in adultery. The duchesse would be exiled from court, never to return, although by then it was assumed the king was about to die anyway.

Unfortunately for those who were so eager to get the favorite out of the way, Louis recovered. He deeply regretted the sacrifice of his beloved and didn't forgive those who had compelled him to dismiss her. The incident at Metz changed the king; henceforth he chose temporal solace over the spiritual. He would not make his confession again until thirty years later, when he was clearly at death's door, and even then he delayed the event until the last possible moment.

When he decided to recall the duchesse de Châteauroux to the royal bosom, it was too late. She had only a day or two to gloat before she caught a cold and died. Louis was bereft.

For surviving the illness at Metz, Louis earned the epithet *le Bien-Aimé* (the Well Loved). From 1745 to 1748, his armies made tremendous strides on the continent, triumphantly conquering the land known as the Austrian Netherlands (present-day Belgium), and further cementing his renown.

Yet Louis shocked his subjects in 1748 by deciding in the Treaty of Aix-la-Chapelle to restore his Austrian territorial gains to the Hapsburgs, declaring that he was perfectly content to maintain and cultivate his square field (as he defined France) rather than expand it, averring that he made peace "as a king and not as a merchant." His bold statement even impressed some of his detractors and won him a reputation as the "arbiter of Europe."

Diplomatically, Louis might have been taking the deathbed advice of Louis XIV to heart, but his personal life was a mess. The Well Loved loved too well, and often unwisely, which hastened the demise of his popularity. His personal debauchery, as well as the licentiousness of his court and its extravagance, were harshly criticized in an era of increasing hard times for the poor and the bourgeoisie. His reputation was further and more irreparably tarnished by the costly and unpopular conflict known as the Seven Years' War that was sparked in 1755, when Great Britain violated international law by seizing three hundred French merchant ships. It ended up being fought on two continents from 1756 to 1763.

France lost a good deal of territory in the aftermath of the Seven Years' War. By the Treaty of Paris, concluded in 1763, France handed over to Britain all lands in North America east of the Mississippi, as well as all French territories in India. Spain received France's lands west of the Mississippi.

Public discontent with Louis grew. He was neither an inept nor an incompetent monarch, but he was a vacillator who avoided dealing with anything unpleasant. The excesses of his court were no greater than those of Louis XIV or of his rival monarchs Catherine the Great of Russia or Prussia's Frederick the Great. But the scurrilous propaganda that spread about his powerful mistress Madame de

Pompadour, beginning in the mid-1740s, gave the public a skewed and distorted image of his reign.

Perpetual criticism from the Parlements only inflamed matters. On March 28, 1757, a mentally deranged man named Robert-François Damiens, who had once worked as a menial at the Paris Parlement, attempted to assassinate the king as he walked across the Marble Courtyard of Versailles. Luckily for Louis, it was an exceptionally chilly evening and he was wearing several layers of clothing, so the blade of Damiens' knife did not severely injure him. The king asked that his attacker be imprisoned and not executed, but the Parlement enforced the traditional punishment: an exceptionally medieval torture followed by a gruesome public execution.

Louis was roundly criticized for being too passive, for permitting his ministers, and even his mistresses (or so it was publicly perceived), to push him around. He hated to make decisions for fear of seeming unpopular. And he did nothing to dispel his negative publicity, never fighting back. Three of his mistresses, the duchesse de Châteauroux, and Mesdames de Pompadour and du Barry, imbued him with self-confidence in his capabilities and instincts, and in his own sense of judgment. In the plus column of his reign, Louis recognized that France's real threat on the European continent was not her age-old enemy Austria, but Prussia. To that end, his chief minister, the duc de Choiseul, brokered a historical alliance with the Hapsburgs that paved the way for one of the most famous unions of all times: the marriage of Louis' grandson and heir, Louis Auguste, with the youngest daughter of the Austrian empress Maria Theresa, Archduchess Maria Antonia, who would come to be known as Marie Antoinette. It was a diplomatic coup: A Franco-Austrian alliance would make Prussia think twice about aggressively engaging France.

Toward the end of his reign, Louis finally took control of his own government and disbanded the corrupt and antiprogressive Parlements, whose perpetual refusal to register his taxation orders further mired the treasury in debt. He engaged a workaholic chancellor and a finance minister who didn't care about becoming unpopular and insisted that the nobles and the clergy finally pay their fair share of taxes.

Unfortunately, these reforms all took place in the final months of

Louis XV's life. His successor, the nineteen-year-old Louis XVI, dismissed his competent ministers and recalled the former corrupt Parlement. As a result, all of the fiscal reforms that Louis XV had begun to effect were immediately reversed, causing lasting, irreparable damage to the financial health of France.

The king contracted smallpox in the final week of April 1774. He died on May 10, and his infection-riddled corpse was rushed with little fanfare to Saint-Denis.

His fifty-nine-year reign is the second-longest in French history, surpassed only by his predecessor, Louis XIV. Louis XV had gone from the *Bien-Aimé* to the reviled—no longer loved, but so scorned that his subjects jeered his coffin as it passed.

LOUIS XV AND
JEANNE-ANTOINETTE POISSON,
MARQUISE DE POMPADOUR (1721–1764)

At five years old, Jeanne-Antoinette Poisson, with her bouncing brown curls and perfect oval face, was answering to the nickname "Reinette" (little queen). Four years later the family jest was pegged as her destiny when her mother brought her to visit the celebrated Parisienne seer Madame Lebon.

As an adult, Jeanne-Antoinette would later confide to her good friend François-Marie Arouet (better known as Voltaire) that Madame Lebon's prediction had struck her like a thunderbolt. And at the end of her life, the marquise would remember the fortune-teller in her will, leaving "[s]ix hundred livres to Madame Lebon for having told her at the age of nine that she would one day be the mistress of Louis XV."

Nevertheless, at the time it was made, such a prediction would have seemed like an impossibility. Kings' mistresses came from the nobility, not the bourgeoisie, or middle class, the social strata into which Jeanne-Antoinette had been born. François Poisson (though rumors abounded even then that he was not her biological father, despite his acceptance of her paternity) worked for the Pâris brothers, the quartet of financiers who kept France afloat and provisioned her army with food and munitions.

But in 1726, Poisson was compelled to flee the country, the scapegoat in a scheme to speculate on wheat. His wife received a formal separation from him the following year. While he remained in exile for nearly a decade, Madame Poisson and Jeanne-Antoinette's godfather, the wealthy *fermier général* (tax collector) Charles Le Normant de Tournehem (who was likely one of Madeleine Poisson's lovers), schooled the young bourgeoise for the lofty role Madame Lebon had foretold. They exposed the teenage Jeanne-Antoinette to sophisticated Parisian society and the conversation of the most exclusive salons, and provided her with an expensive education. Private tutors at the top of their professions in the arts taught her music, acting, singing, declamation, and the traditional womanly pursuits. By the time she turned eighteen she had become quite a beauty, slender, taller than average, with an enviably flawless complexion, excellent teeth (another rarity), and eyes of a changeable green-gray-blue color that were already being complimented for their intelligence and depth. She was elegant, poised, cultivated, charming and amusing, and a witty conversationalist.

On March 9, 1741, at the age of nineteen, Jeanne-Antoinette wed her godfather's twenty-four-year-old nephew, Charles-Guillaume Le Normant. Monsieur de Tournehem set the young couple up very nicely, giving them a townhome in Paris and the country estate of Etioles at the edge of the forest of Sénart, not far from the Château de Choisy, which Louis XV had just purchased as a hunting lodge. Consequently, many noblemen began to spend time in the area, and the lovely chatelaine of Etioles, known for her vibrant house parties, did not go unnoticed.

Jeanne-Antoinette's marriage provided her with an entrée to Paris's social elite: libertine clergy, artists, financiers, men of letters, and magistrates of the Parlement.

Madame d'Etioles' first child, a son, was born in December, but died in 1742. On August 10, 1744, she gave birth to a daughter, Alexandrine, who would eventually be placed in a posh convent to derive the benefits of a fine education. By the time Alexandrine was born, Jeanne-Antoinette had become the perfect package for a royal mistress, except for the matter of her low birth.

Fortunately, she had relations in high places. Monsieur de Tournehem played fairy godfather, placing Jeanne-Antoinette in the king's path as often as possible and arranging for his nephew to receive a plum job as a *fermier général* far, far away, his assignments keeping him on the road in Grenoble and Provence. One of Louis' valets, Binet, was a distant relative of Madame d'Etioles; he coached her on where to stand so she might catch the thirty-five-year-old king's eye as he strode through the palace of Versailles. Louis' other valet, Monsieur Lebel, who was one of His Majesty's chief procurers of nubile young girls, had once been a lover of Madame Poisson's. These were not the classiest references, but they stood Jeanne-Antoinette in better stead than most other hopeful aspirants to the king's bedchamber. And a pretty, poised, and sophisticated young lady who was anything but a jaded aristocrat was the perfect tonic for a man who craved diversion.

For by then, Louis XV was bored yellow; everyone at court knew his pallor would grow jaundiced when he was beset with ennui. In 1725, at the age of fifteen, he had married Marie Leszczyńska, a dull Polish princess seven years his senior, and got right down to the business of begetting an heir. It was said he honored her with proofs of his love no fewer than seven times on their wedding night. To the shock of his courtiers, Louis actually fell in love with his bland and pious queen and didn't even consider taking a mistress, convinced by his confessor that if he did so he would be forever consigned to the flames of hell—or at least, he would be if he took a lover before he sired a son.

He didn't stray for a decade, and by the time he was twenty-seven he had ten children to show for it. But Queen Marie couldn't keep pace with the Bourbon libido and was sick of always being pregnant. *Toujours coucher, toujours grosse, toujours accoucher*—always in bed, always pregnant, always giving birth, she would grumble. Finally, she began to invent excuses to keep her randy husband from her bed—Sundays and holy days, for example, were out. Finally, after ten children and too many excuses, in 1738 they ceased sleeping together entirely. Louis became exasperated and turned to the eldest of the five aristocratic Mailly-Nesle sisters. Buxom, homely, and grasping, four of these women in turn became his *maîtresse en titre*, with the last of them, the youngest, prettiest, greediest, and nastiest of the quintet, Marie Anne de Mailly, Madame de Châteauroux, dying in 1744.

The post of *maîtresse déclarée* thus became vacant. The field lay open for Jeanne-Antoinette, Madame d'Etioles, to fulfill her destiny. Wearing a petal-pink gown and driving through the forest of Sénart in a sky blue phaeton, or gowned in baby blue and holding the ribbons of a pastel pink chariot, the young woman with the waist-length ash blond hair, oval face, and doll-like mouth had already caught the king's eye, making sure to accidentally-on-purpose cross paths with his hunting party. And more than the king took notice. As *"la dame en rose"* and *"la petite Etioles,"* she was hardly invisible to the snooty courtiers.

The king's two greatest passions were hunting and women, and by the early weeks of 1745, only one of those itches was being adequately scratched.

By the time they met, Louis was already considered the handsomest man in France. Tall with sparkling black eyes, he had a husky timbre to his voice and a way of looking at people that was described as "caressing." And no less a connoisseur than Casanova described Louis as having "a ravishingly handsome head . . . No painter, even very skillful, could sketch the movement of this monarch's head when he turned to look at someone. One felt compelled to love him instantly. . . . I was certain that Madame de Pompadour had fallen in love with that face."

No one has been able to pinpoint the exact date when the first overtures were made. But by February 25, 1745, at a masquerade to be forever immortalized as the Yew Tree Ball, one of the numerous celebrations in honor of the dauphin's marriage to the Spanish Infanta Maria Theresa Rafaela, the king and the petite bourgeoise were seen dancing all night together—and it was commonly known that His Majesty didn't even like to dance. To preserve his incognito, Louis and eleven of his companions had burst through the doors of the Hall of Mirrors midmasquerade, identically dressed as taffeta-leafed topiaries. But Madame d'Etioles, clad as the goddess Diana, carrying a miniature bow and arrow, with a diamond crescent moon adorning her hair, had already been tipped off as to which tree was His Most Christian Majesty. The king purportedly greeted her with a jolly, "Fair huntress, happy are those who are pierced by your darts; their wounds are mortal."

Before the ball ended, the lady dropped her handkerchief at Louis' feet in a symbolic gesture—a tantalizing dare. The king picked it up and raised it to his lips, then pressed it to his bosom, in full view of his guests. And up rose the murmur, "*Le mouchoir est jeté*"—"The handkerchief is thrown!"

The following evening, after dancing the night away at a public ball in Paris, both incognito in black dominos, they disappeared into a private supper room. After dining, they hailed an unmarked hackney. "Where to?" the king inquired of his new conquest. "Home to mother!" came the reply.

The monarch finally arrived at Versailles, somewhat disheveled, at nine the following morning. Throughout the following week Madame d'Etioles' carriage was seen numerous times on the road between Paris and Versailles as well as in the palace courtyard. With the exception of military campaigns that would take him abroad, Louis XV would not be separated from her for the next two decades.

When Jeanne-Antoinette had wed in 1741, she'd promised her husband, only half in jest, that the only man who could ever induce her to cheat on him would be the king. Ha-ha-ha, Monsieur d'Etioles chuckled, chucking his pretty wife under the chin. But in the winter of 1745, when the royal romance began to blossom, after Charles-Guillaume returned from another distant business trip, it fell to Le Normant de Tournehem to break the news to his nephew. He did so by explaining that "he could no longer count on his wife, that she had such a violent predilection for the King that she could not resist, and that there was no other part for him than to separate from her."

Unfortunately for Jeanne-Antoinette, her spouse was no *mari complaisant*. He fell into a dead faint at the news and, upon his recovery, wrote a sad little letter begging Jeanne-Antoinette to return to him. When she refused, urging him to understand the situation, he took the high road and declined thenceforth either to take her back or to speak with her again. Jeanne-Antoinette committed the faux pas of showing his letter to the king. Louis surprised and somewhat embarrassed her by responding, "Your husband seems to be a very decent sort of man, Madame."

Monsieur d'Etioles' emotional reaction to his wife's royal liaison compelled the king to make a decision about the affair: Was it serious or merely a fling? The king chose to pursue the romance, and Monsieur d'Etioles was subsequently persuaded to accept a formal separation. He remained discreetly out of the way as a *fermier général* in Grenoble for the remainder of Jeanne-Antoinette's life, and she saw to it that he always received any legal or financial aid that he might need.

According to Voltaire, Jeanne-Antoinette "always had a secret presentiment that she would be loved by the king, and . . . she had felt a violent inclination for him. . . . The king noticed her, and often sent her presents of roebucks. Her mother never stopped telling her that she was prettier than any of the king's mistresses, and the *bonhomme* Tournehem often exclaimed: 'One must admit that the daughter of Madame Poisson is a morsel fit for a King.' In short, when she finally held the king in her arms, she told me that she had firmly believed in her destiny, and that she had been proved right."

But the monarch's intimates, his relatives, his ministers, and the courtiers who elevated backbiting, or *médisance*, into an art form would have handily wagered that the new girl in town was no more than the flavor of the month. Charles Philippe d'Albert, the duc de Luynes, observed that everyone had "been speaking of the King's new love affair, and mostly about a Mme d'Etioles, who is young and pretty. . . . They say she has lately been spending much time in *ce pays-ci* [literally "this country," the courtiers' way of referring to the palace of Versailles] and that she is the King's new choice; if that is true, she will probably be just a passing fancy and not a proper mistress."

And that was one of the nicer comments.

Dashed off in both poetry and prose, the nastier diatribes, known as *poissardes* (a snarky reference to Jeanne-Antoinette's maiden name, Poisson, which is also the French word for "fish") began making the rounds. Passed off as the work of Parisian scribblers (and blatantly referring to Jeanne-Antoinette as a "slut" and a "cheap whore" who had brought the court down to her level by turning it into a "slum"), they were more likely the handiwork of jealous ministers and other courtiers who had the advantage of observing firsthand how quickly she rose from obscurity to a position of the utmost influence.

Louis acted utterly unaffected by the derogatory poems and pamphlets. On April 27, the duc de Luynes was compelled to acknowledge, "That which seemed doubtful a little while ago is almost a constant truth; they say that she is madly in love with the King and that this passion is reciprocated." Louis proceeded to install his new paramour in the apartments above his own at Versailles—the former residence of his previous *maîtresse en titre*, Madame de Châteauroux.

But Jeanne-Antoinette's influence had been felt as immediately as late March. Although the king had previously supported painters, sculptors, composers, and architects, he had yet to become a literary patron. Now, thanks to her, Voltaire was awarded an annual pension of two thousand livres. Louis also bestowed upon the playwright, wit, and philosopher the office of Royal Historiographer as well as the much-coveted position of Gentleman of the Bedchamber in Ordinary, one that bore a patent of nobility.

While Louis spent the summer of 1745 on the battlefield as the fifth year of the War of the Austrian Succession raged on, he sent his new inamorata back to her own estate of Etioles for a full Pygmalion-style education. Under the watchful eyes of the marquis de Gontaut-Biron and the jolly, moonfaced abbé Bernis, Jeanne-Antoinette was schooled in the minutiae of the court etiquette laid down by her lover's predecessor Louis XIV, memorizing everything from genealogy to curtsies to forms of address. Having arrived with an aristocrat's usual social prejudices, the cynical Bernis quickly became a fan. "Madame d'Etioles had all the graces, all the freshness and all the gaiety of youth: she danced, sang, played comedy; she lacked no agreeable talent. She liked literature and the arts. She had a lofty soul, sensitive and generous."

Being a jealous lover, the king forbade Jeanne-Antoinette the society of any other men (except relatives) during her summer crash course. Louis missed her terribly, but he acknowledged that she needed the schooling if their love affair had a chance of surviving. As a bourgeoise amid a sea of envious aristocrats who didn't believe she belonged at Versailles in the first place, she couldn't afford the slightest misstep.

Nor could Madame d'Etioles take precedence over the other ladies, or become a *maîtresse en titre* until she was presented at court. For this, she would need her own title.

Louis sent her more than eighty billets-doux from the front, written on drumskins. On the ninth of July she received an important-looking packet sealed with the motto *"Discret et Fidele"* ("Discreet and Faithful"). It was addressed to madame la marquise de Pompadour. He had revived the extinct title for her and purchased the estate of Pompadour in Limousin from the prince de Conti. The packet contained a patent for letters of nobility, circumventing the necessity of having four hundred years of noble blood running through her veins. Her coat of arms depicted a trio of silver towers on an azure ground.

The first hurdle had been surmounted. But now the newly minted marquise needed a sponsor. "Which one of our sluts is to present the woman?" the queen was overheard remarking with uncharacteristic bitchiness.

Finally, the princesse de Conti, whose husband had sold His Majesty the Pompadour estates, was persuaded to stand up for the marquise, but she struck a hard bargain. She demanded that the king discharge her massive gambling debts.

On September 10, Louis returned from the wars, having been victorious at the Battle of Fontenoy. Four days later, his new lover was presented at court to the sovereigns and their daughters, known as Mesdames. Over the grand panniers that made her appear about six feet wide, the marquise de Pompadour wore for this ritual the traditional gown of heavily embroidered black satin with a narrow train and short white muslin sleeves. It contrasted beautifully against her pearlescent complexion. Small white feathers, also customary, adorned her lightly powdered hair.

An eyewitness described her appearance as "[V]ery well-made . . . magnificent skin, superb hands and arms, her eyes more pretty than large but of a fire, a spirituality, a brilliancy I have never seen in any other woman."

To the dismay of the marquise de Pompadour's numerous detractors, her deportment during the presentation, including her three deep curtsies or reverences and her backward exit from the royals' presence, was utterly flawless. And no doubt their chins were on their chests when Her Majesty, making the small talk requisite on such an occasion, evinced no malice, but spoke to the new marquise at some length about an aristocrat of their mutual acquaintance.

Madame de Pompadour was so touched—and surprised—by the queen's solicitousness that she spontaneously, and effusively, promised to do everything in her power to make the queen happy from that moment on. Of course, what truly would have pleased Her Majesty would have been for Madame de Pompadour to quit sleeping with her husband—but that would hardly have delighted the king!

The arrogant courtiers carped that Madame de Pompadour's instant elevation to the aristocracy could not erase the fishy stench of her origins. But they soon realized that they would need to ingratiate themselves with *her* if they wanted the *king's* favor, and so they pasted on smiles as false as their patches.

As she busily set about establishing her own salon, Pompadour also made it her business to take note of all the factions against her and who comprised them. Chief among these were Louis' children (and particularly the dauphin), who referred to her as *"Maman Putain"*—Mother Whore—despite her genuine desire to reunite the squabbling Bourbon spawn with their libidinous father. And not only did the marquise remain respectful of Marie Leszczyńska, but she even convinced *Louis* to be kinder to his wife. Suddenly the queen found herself invited to his hunting lodges and châteaux, where previously she had been persona non grata. Her debts (which were all from philanthropic bequests) were paid, and her apartments, which had become tatty, were lavishly redecorated—all because the woman who was her rival at court had instructed her husband to be nicer to her.

Though the renovations might have been expensive, it cost Louis little to be gracious, for the usually morose king was in a good mood. His ministers and courtiers noticed that for the first time in his life, their sovereign seemed truly happy. He was, in fact, in love. And according to the duc de Croÿ, a Belgian-born observer of life at Louis' court and an admirer of Jeanne-Antoinette's, "Of all the mistresses so far she is the most lovable, and he loves her more than any of the others." The marquise "had the art of bantering" with him, it was noted, which set her apart from her predecessors, the perfect fit for a man who loved to tease. Louis was delighted; his sense of humor had never been appreciated by his previous paramours, and one can never underestimate the importance of shared laughter in a relationship. Warm and tender, Pompadour's personality meshed nearly perfectly with his. When it occasionally didn't, as a consummate actress, "She was, as required, magnificent, imperious, calm, cheeky, mischievous, sensible, curious, attentive," and compassionate to the point of tears, the last a sensibility sorely lacking at the jaded Bourbon court. In short, Louis, so easily bored, suddenly found that his ennui had evanesced. He was convinced that he "would never find a person with whom he could spend such quiet and happy days." Within the monarch's rigidly prescribed schedule, ordained by decades of court etiquette, he contrived to spend as much of the day as possible in her company.

And unlike His Majesty's previous mistresses, Madame de Pompadour belonged to none of the court's little parties or cliques. She had no one in her pocket whom she wished to advance (all that would change in time), and all she wanted to do was please him. To the man who had everything, the marquise bestowed something the king had always craved: a loving, nonjudgmental partnership. Aware that he didn't like to be surrounded by too many new faces, in his *petits cabinets*, his private nest of apartments above the state rooms at Versailles, she established a cozy and intimate atmosphere, a *"petit club très chic, très amusant et très fermé"*—a little club very chic, very amusing, and very exclusive. She introduced him to her own passions, such as gardening and the theater, surrounding him with witty and entertaining people, perpetually buoying the spirits of a powerful man who had a tendency toward shyness, morbidity, and depression. To relieve Louis' boredom, the marquise involved him in her acquisitive mania for redecoration and construction; previously, the only subject that had held his interest had been hunting. Eventually, they would embark on a very expensive mutual hobby—building a number of charming pleasure palaces and pavilions. Another, far less pricy diversion was playing "dress-up." Masquerade balls were a staple of court entertainments, but even in the intimacy of their bedchambers, the monarch rather liked disguises. The marquise, a professionally trained actress, was only too happy to oblige him, costuming herself for his eyes only, as the royal whim might desire—a shepherdess, a sultana, a nymph, or even a nun.

Another of their common interests outside the boudoir might better have been kept within its confines. The king and marquise would read to each other about his courtiers' latest sexcapades or embarrassments. The information came from the king's secret police, whose chief, Nicolas René Berryer, furnished reports to Louis written with the furtive, breathless energy of a peeping Tom in a triple-X double feature. Every week Berryer would deliver his good friend Madame de Pompadour some of the choicest, juiciest, dirtiest gossip—correspondence that was intercepted by the royal postmaster, Robert Jarrelle. The lovers would then get together and pore over their postal porn. The king grew particularly titillated reading about the sexual exploits and perversions of some of his courtiers.

Jean-Louis Soulavie, who published his three-volume history of Louis' reign in 1801, maintained that "The King had so many reasons for believing that [Madame de Pompadour] was essential to his life's happiness that his heart no longer inclined toward the pleasures of fickleness"—which, considering his overactive libido, was saying something.

She was dubbed "the oracle of the Court" and "a well trained odalisque who skillfully managed the superintendence of His Majesty's pleasures" by the comte d'Argenson, who kept a vicious diary of court events. The comte was abundantly cruel to the marquise even when others praised her.

According to the duc de Croÿ, Pompadour "gathered the whole Court into her apartments and almost presided over it . . . the King usually hunted three or four days a week, took suppers, on those days, upstairs in her rooms and spent most of his time there. . . . I found out that the marquise de Pompadour was very powerful and that everyone played court to her, so I arranged to be presented to her. . . . I found her charming, both in looks and character; she was at her toilette and couldn't have been prettier; and full of amusing talents so that the King seemed to love her more than he had the others." Of course, Louis did have boundaries. The duc observed that although ". . . it was believed that in private he told his mistress everything . . . [i]t seemed to me that he spoke very freely with her, as with a mistress whom he loved but from whom he wanted amusement. . . . And she, who behaved beautifully, had much influence, but the King always wanted to be the master, and was firm about that."

Well . . . that changed, too. In small ways, at first. In 1746, the dauphin's wife died of puerperal fever a few days after giving birth and the hunt began for a new bride. That December, the king announced that his heir would wed fifteen-year-old Marie-Josèphe of Saxony (who, after several prospects were discarded, had been head-hunted by the marquise de Pompadour). No time was lost, and on February 9, 1747, the dauphin was remarried. But the lovely *inconnue* who had danced the night away with the king at his son's first wedding was the gatekeeper of the guest list this time around (as well as organizing all the festivities, down to the decor), just to make sure that no lovely masked women got anywhere near her royal lover. Only officers of state were invited to one particular fête, but the marquise insisted on bringing a "plus-one," declaring, "I can be counted as one of the great officers, and so my sister-in-law can be put on the list."

By now the marquise, who had begun to consider the royal family her own (regardless of their feelings on the subject), also controlled the invitations to the king's *soupers*, or private suppers in his *petits cabinets*. Now thoroughly entrenched at Versailles (not to mention the various other royal châteaux, as well as the ones Louis purchased for her), she had her own household staff, which included not only personal maids and valets, liveried in yellow (the Bourbon colors were red and blue), but a librarian to superintend her 3,500-plus volumes bound in red, blue, or yellow Moroccan calfskin and stamped in gold with her coat of arms. These books were not for show. She read for pleasure (718 of them were novels) as well as for self-edification (738 were volumes of history and biography). Her equerry, the chevalier d'Henin, who followed her sedan chair and carried her cloak, came from a distinguished Alsatian family. Her garments and accessories were assiduously chosen to harmonize with or complement the interior decor and colors of her rooms.

Although she had swiftly become one of the most influential people at court, as early as 1747 the marquise de Pompadour was discovering that things could get lonely at the top. That summer, while her royal lover was away at the front, according to the Count von Kaunitz, who would eventually be made Austria's ambassador to France and later chancellor, the marquise "received her courier from the army every day when she lived at Choisy in the absence of the king. Nothing was concluded without her. Her decision upon everything was awaited. She spent whole nights in replying. . . . She hardly saw anyone. This life very quickly bored her. A royal lover causes double anxiety; another could steal his heart. These considerations contributed not a little to the promotion of peace."

But if her schedule was taxing and her role was demanding, Pompadour never let them see her sweat. She always seemed to have plenty of energy to produce a diverting season of plays within the halls of Versailles with her paraprofessional theater troupe, always taking the starring roles (she opened with Molière's *Tartuffe* in January 1747). Her sets were designed by the great painter François Boucher.

Perhaps that was part of her skill, but Madame de Pompadour certainly made it appear effortless. The duc de Croÿ noted that she "mingled in many things, without seeming to do so or appearing occupied: on the contrary, whether naturally or politically, she seemed more occupied with her little comedies or other trifles than the rest. She was very teasing with the King and employed the most delicate flirtatiousness to seduce him. From the beginning she sought to please everyone, in order to provide herself with creatures, above all people of importance. . . . [T]here was almost no favor done without her participation, which brought the whole court to her as if she were Prime Minister: but, in great matters, it is unclear if the King trusted her with everything, as he was born reserved."

Madame de Pompadour saw it as one of her duties to make herself indispensable to her lover. The duc de Croÿ clearly appreciated her efforts, but the marquise also had a number of enemies at court, one of whom, the comte d'Argenson, saw a darker side to this coin. "She besieges the king constantly, shakes him, agitates him, never leaves him by himself for an instant. Before, he used to work for several hours in his office; today he has not a quarter of an hour to himself."

This remark should be taken with a grain of salt, for Louis was at heart an exceptionally lazy man, as a person and as a monarch. If he had a nickname today, he would be the Delegator, happy to relinquish the responsibilities of governance and decision making to his ministers—and to the marquise. Given the assessments of his contemporaries as well as those of numerous historians, it's a fairly safe conjecture that the only things he ever spent several hours doing without interruption were hunting and lovemaking.

Above all else, and despite what any disgruntled courtier or minister believed, it should be remembered that Louis *solicited* his lover's advice, counsel, and companionship. And her primary job description as a *maîtresse en titre* was to keep the king happy, even if it took a toll on her health. And it did. Although she was only twenty-three years old when her royal romance began, Madame de Pompadour endured migraines, ear and eye infections, and heart palpitations. Additionally, she had always suffered from consumptive symptoms and was forever becoming short of breath and coughing up blood. Yet Louis continually demanded her presence and had no patience for weakness (nor could she risk losing her easily bored paramour to a replacement). And so she would rouse herself from her sofa, dab on the rouge and perfume, and make herself look and smell alluring, all smiles and confidence in the presence of a man who demanded perpetual amusement.

The comte de Maurepas, minister of the navy, was Pompadour's greatest detractor. He had made it his business to openly despise each of the king's official mistresses, and his hatred for the marquise's immediate predecessor, the duchesse de Châteauroux, had been so intense that when she died in 1744 after a very brief illness it was rumored that he had poisoned her.

In eighteenth-century France, the pen could be mightier than the sword, and in the right hands a cruel, if witty, epigram was a dangerous weapon. Such was the method Maurepas undertook to undermine the marquise de Pompadour, although he did not admit the authorship of his destructive verses.

Finally, in 1749, when she read a poem referring to the "riffraff" turning the once-elegant court vulgar—followed by an even more direct insult, a pun on her maiden name ("Isn't it from the market that fish comes to us?") the minister's insolence became too much to bear.

Pompadour had long suspected the comte de Maurepas of circulating the scurrilous verses about her, so she paid him a visit and tried to call his bluff. "When will you find out who is writing these songs?" she demanded.

"When I do so, madame, I shall tell the king," the comte replied dryly.

She tried to tamp down her agitation. "Monsieur, you show very little respect for the king's mistresses."

"On the contrary, madame," Maurepas replied, "I have always respected them, whatever kind of people they may be."

The marquise asked Louis to dismiss Maurepas, but for the first time in their relationship, the king denied her something. The two men had a long and storied friendship. Maurepas had served the king since 1715, when he had been made minister of the navy at the age of fourteen.

However, the comte then went too far. He had been present during a supper where Pompadour carried a bouquet of white hyacinth blossoms. Not too long afterward a four-line poem made its way through the corridors of Versailles, obliquely referring to a specific gynecological complaint.

> By your manners noble and frank,
> Iris, you enchant our hearts;
> On our path you spread flowers,
> But they are only flowers of white.

Madame de Pompadour suffered from an embarrassing condition called leucorrhea, which left a smelly white vaginal discharge. (As a side note, Catherine of Aragon had the same condition, which repulsed Henry VIII from her bed.) It was euphemistically known as "white flowers," and it's possible that the marquise developed it during the birth of her daughter. She also had the misfortune to have suffered at least three miscarriages by this time, and her greatest joy would have been to bear the king a child.

The only one who could have written those humiliating lines was the comte de Maurepas. The public revelation of the royal mistress's most intimate details was beyond all bounds of propriety. Still, the comte was shocked when, on April 24, 1749, Louis finally dismissed him with a *lettre de cachet*, exiling him to his country estate of Bourges.

Maurepas's exile sent a clear message to the court that the king now placed the marquise above everyone else. Even at Compiègne, the hunting lodge where the court spent its summers, Madame de Pompadour held her ritualized toilettes as if it were Versailles. On Tuesdays she received ambassadors as she dressed; a guest was doubly honored if she deigned to speak to him or her. But no matter their rank, even princes of the blood had to maintain a respectful distance from her person while she assiduously applied her makeup, including the costly rouge that denoted the highest-ranking women at court.

In advance of this formal ritual the marquise held a *toilette secrète* in her boudoir, which was the most exclusive ticket in town. And yet, it was said that despite all the grandeur her demeanor was always gracious, elegant, and dignified.

Beyond the gilded walls of the insulated court, however, unrest was spreading, and the excesses of the king's mistress formed one of the chief topics of dissent. The Department of *Menu Plaisirs,* or Small Pleasures, which funded her theater troupe and footed the expenses for many of Pompadour's extravagances, was said to be costing the people of France 2.5 million livres a year. The royal household spent 25 million livres annually, nearly one-tenth of the entire treasury's revenue, and a sum higher than the navy's budget. By the autumn of 1749, the kingdom was rife with complaints that the crown's myriad building projects were not for the public good, but for the private pleasure of the sovereign and his mistress—intimate pavilions, zoos, and hermitages constructed on the grounds of every royal château, opulently furnished with luxury items to be seen and enjoyed by only a few pairs of eyes.

This was also the year that Louis made the unprecedented decision to bring the marquise when he went to inspect his fleet at Le Havre.

Publicly flaunting their extramarital affair was bad enough, but people were shocked to see that Madame de Pompadour received all the honors that the municipal authorities would customarily have accorded the queen. When the royal party stopped for the night in Rouen, the queen's chaplain forbade the adulterous couple to stay together under his roof; if the king wished to remain, the marquise de Pompadour would have to find separate lodgings. Refusing to be sundered from his lover, Louis elected to seek other accommodations.

The king shouldered the blame for openly parading his mistress about the country and behaving as though Madame de Pompadour were the queen of France. She was already acting like the uncrowned consort, modeling both her public and private toilettes after those held by Louis XIV's mistress Madame de Montespan. She even took Montespan's former box at the theater and her pew in the royal chapel—a tacit public declaration that she was the next Athénaïs. And now when Pompadour spoke to courtiers, she used the word "us" to refer to herself and the king, a constant reminder that they were an established couple in the manner of spouses.

Before long it was clear, at least at court, that there were two queens of France gliding through the gilded halls of Versailles, but Marie Leszczyńska, although she wore the crown, was not the one who reigned. Louis would ascend the secret staircase to Pompadour's rooms at all hours, unannounced, to converse with her, whether it was to share a confidence or an anecdote. By now he scarcely dared to visit Paris, the perennial cauldron of malaise and discontent, so great was his subjects' disgust with his morals and his governance.

Times were changing—intellectually, socially, and religiously.

Louis, superstitious, yet a serial adulterer, had no intentions of altering his lifestyle. Although he routinely attended Mass, his refusal to take the sacraments led to the widespread view among his subjects that he was an unfit ruler who had tarnished the monarchy with his sinful ways.

Ironically, around the same time, Madame de Pompadour was becoming sexually frigid. Louis "thinks me very cold," she once admitted to Madame Du Hausset, her lady of the bedchamber. "[C]old as *un macreuse*" (a type of cold-blooded game bird), in the king's own words. She once tearfully confided in the sympathetic duchesse de Brancas, "I'm afraid of losing the King's heart by ceasing to be appealing to him. Men, as you know, value certain things enormously and I have the misfortune of having a very cold temperament. I wanted to follow a diet that would warm me up to make up for this failing; and for two days this elixir has been doing me some good, or at least I think it has." To boost her libido, for some time the marquise de Pompadour had been availing herself of every popular aphrodisiac, from celery soup, crayfish, truffles, and drinking chocolate flavored with ambergris, to triple shots of vanilla extract. For the most part they succeeded only in making her sick to her stomach.

Appalled, the duchesse told her the wacky regimen would sooner kill her than transform her into a wanton, and insisted that she swear off the quack remedies. The marquise reiterated what she had told Madame Du Hausset—that she adored the king and wanted to be attractive for him, yet she knew Louis found her to be cold and sexually passive—but "I would sacrifice my life to please him," she averred.

Madame de Pompadour had never been a carnal creature, relying more on her powers of intellect and artistic talent, her art of conversation, and her exceptional skills as a raconteuse. In fact, she found the physical act of lovemaking somewhat uncomfortable, and perhaps even embarrassing, due to her chronic vaginal discharges. Yet she could entertain, amuse, and listen. She could keep a secret. And she had attained her desire to become indispensable to Louis. If she rarely was his bedfellow or paramour these days, she undoubtedly remained his confidante, his sounding board, and minister without portfolio.

"She sells everything, even regiments. The king is increasingly governed by her. . . . She arranges, she decides, she behaves as though the king's ministers were hers . . . more than ever she is the First Minister," grumbled the comte d'Argenson. "The ministers tell her ahead of time whatever they have to say to the King. He himself wants it that way." But Count von Kaunitz, by then the Austrian ambassador, noted that "[S]he has a quality that makes her highly qualified for government; she is capable of impenetrable secrecy. This is how she acquires the King's trust, so much that as soon as something happens, he has the need to tell her every important thing that's been said to him."

In the autumn of 1749 Louis ruffled a lot of feathers at Versailles by moving Madame de Pompadour into a premium ground-floor apartment. These rooms with views of the inner courtyard as well as the flower beds and parterres had been the purview of the king's eldest (and only married) daughter when she visited from her duchy of Parma. They boasted lodgings for the marquise's doctor and lady of the bedchamber, as well as a bathroom, wardrobe room, and two studies. The rumor mill began to churn. Why such a *déménage* from her cozy aerie above the king's own apartments? Was the royal mistress gaining favor or losing it?

The marquise had first captivated Louis in 1745 through her scintillating beauty and charm, and for five years she held him with her talents as a cultivated woman of the world. But as her libido waned she recognized the vital importance of maintaining her position as his *maîtresse en titre*. It was imperative to redefine her role without missing a beat—and she took a huge risk in doing so, for Louis was ruled by his loins. She decided to become the royal best friend.

By the end of 1750, the rumors of a change in the wind were already making their way through the halls and labyrinthine passages of Versailles. The comte d'Argenson, avidly awaiting her fall, crowed, "They say on all sides, those who know her best, that there is hardly any *plaisir d'amour* between her and her Royal lover anymore." Still, the comte had to concede, "Let us assume that passion is no longer the knot of her ascendancy over him. There remains only: habit, which is very powerful in men as gentle and honorable as the King: the superintendence of his amusements and the careful attention to forestall his moments of boredom; and trust, the habit of soothing his heart and soul. It is by these means that she has arrived at governing the affairs of the State. . . ."

To immortalize Louis and Jeanne-Antoinette's Royal Romance 2.0 she commissioned a pair of allegorical marble statues, one of which was titled *Friendship*, in which her likeness appears as a neoclassical nymph, half-clad from the waist up. With her right hand on her bosom and her left one extended in an open gesture to the viewer, the figure offers her heart in a gesture of welcome and sincerity. At the start of their liaison her role model had been the Sun King's famous mistress Madame de Montespan. Now she endeavored to emulate his last great mistress and secret morganatic wife, Madame de Maintenon.

But would friendship be enough to hold *her* Louis? The year 1751 marked Pope Benedict XIV's Jubilee, and in celebration His Holiness was offering a plenary indulgence to anyone who engaged in a certain number of devotional exercises. The pope was also offering Catholics forgiveness for their sins in exchange for contributions to the Church.

The comte d'Argenson wondered whether the king, who hadn't taken the sacrament since 1744, when he thought he was dying, would hop on the holy bandwagon, and if so, would his nemesis the marquise be given her walking papers? "Madame de Pompadour has had some fits of fever. This is what they call Jubilee fever, because the proximity of the Jubilee puts her into a great state of anxiety. . . . If the King decided to return to sincere religious practice, a strict confessor could demand that the marquise be considered as complicit in his adultery and should be publicly sent away."

But the Jubilee came and went and the king remained a sinner, which meant that the marquise retained her job security. But the effort was costing her, both physically and emotionally. "We are so often on the road that I have given up hunting. . . . I need some time to think," she wrote at the end of the year. Ten months later, in October 1752, she wrote, "I have just had a fever for ten days . . . [have been] bled, and have had a terrible headache. . . . I am overcome with visits, with letters, and still have sixty more letters to write." Her life looked glamorous on the surface, but she was beginning to find it drudgery. In yet another letter she lamented, "The life I lead is terrible. I scarcely have a minute of my own: rehearsals and performances, and twice a week a trip. . . . Indispensable and considerable duties . . ." She was only thirty-one-years old.

Madame de Pompadour endeavored to divert the king from the boudoir by involving him in their shared passion of building, but this time she was taking the long view, determined that he should leave France a legacy beyond a few pretty pavilions. She encouraged him to establish the École Militaire, a cadet school for the sons of impoverished noblemen. Her prescience was commendable. In time the École Militaire markedly improved the quality of the French army. Its most notorious graduate was an ambitious, hotheaded Corsican named Napoleon Bonaparte.

Also at his mistress's instigation, Louis decided to patronize the porcelain manufacturers at Sèvres, creating an industry to rival their counterparts in China, and in Saxony, where Meissen ware was made. At the Manufacture Royale, France's finest artists, including François Boucher, were enlisted to create images that could be reproduced on porcelain objects such as plates or vases. Because the items were so costly, the sovereign himself, with his paramour in tow, became shills for the new company. Once a year they transformed Versailles' opulent Hall of Mirrors into a showroom where the thousands of courtiers who made the palace their residence could ogle the latest merchandise, which was all for sale. "At the king's suppers, the marquise says it's unpatriotic not to buy it, as long as one has the money," sneered the comte d'Argenson. Soon, owning a piece of Sèvres became a badge of good taste and refinement.

Taste and refinement, however, would hardly be the phrase one would apply to a parallel venture. By 1753, Madame de Pompadour was dancing as fast as she could to devise divertissements to please the king. The Austrian ambassador Count von Kaunitz noticed that Louis was often rude or cutting to her. "It requires more skill than one might think to feign being madly in love without making oneself ill," he observed.

At 4 rue Saint-Médéric, a modest and unassuming villa in Versailles, nicknamed the Parc-aux-Cerfs, or Stag Park, resided a series of pubescent girls. They had been brought to the house as virgins to ensure that they would be free of venereal disease, and their exclusive role was to carnally entertain Louis XV. They were told that he was a visiting Polish nobleman. If they surmised his true identity, they were not to breathe a word of it or they were summarily dismissed from their horizontal employment. Royal accidents were usually farmed out to strangers. Their mothers were told the children were dead. Sometimes the king would visit a girl at the Parc-aux-Cerfs. Other times she would be conducted to the apartment belonging to

Louis' valet Lebel within the Château de Versailles—ironically situated adjacent to the royal chapel—and left to wait in a room nicknamed *le trébuchet*: "the bird trap."

The marquise de Pompadour has, over the centuries, mistakenly been identified as a pimp or bawd. But she had nothing to do with the Parc-aux-Cerfs. She did not recruit the girls, nor place them in Louis' bed. At best, she was an enabler for tacitly accepting their existence. And once again, she took the long view. "It is his heart I want! All these little girls with no education will not take it from me. I would not be so calm, if I saw some pretty woman of the court or the capital trying to conquer it."

Her own heart would be sorely tested when, in mid-June 1754, her ten-year-old daughter, Alexandrine, fell ill at the convent where she was being educated, and died, most probably of an attack of acute peritonitis. Ten days later, François Poisson expired, overcome with grief at the loss of his beloved granddaughter "FanFan," to whom he had been very close after her *maman* departed for the king's arms.

Devastated that she had been unable to rush to her daughter's side when the end was near, because the king needed her at Choisy, the marquise became inconsolable. But while she grieved she learned that one of her adolescent rivals from the Parc-aux-Cerfs, Mary-Louise O'Murphy, known to the courtiers as "*la belle* Morphise," had given birth to a daughter who was baptized at the end of June. Of all the young girls who pleasured the French king during the era of the Parc-aux-Cerfs, "Morphise" is undoubtedly the most famous, as she is commonly believed to be the nude odalisque depicted derriere up, in a well-known painting by François Boucher.

The loss of Pompadour's own daughter made the anguish all the greater. Yet she dared not permit herself much time to mourn. If she became reclusive she risked being supplanted by the new mother, or by some other nubile beauty. So jealous was the marquise of "Morphise" that when she recognized the girl's features on a painting she had commissioned for the altarpiece at Crécy—in the persona of the Virgin, no less—she ordered the completed canvas to be removed from the church. "Morphise" herself was eventually banished from court when she blew the king's cover by asking him, ostensibly coached by a friend, how he was getting on with his "*vieille cocotte*"—his old flirt—a pointed reference to Pompadour. She was married off to an army officer on November 27, 1755, and walked away from court with a dowry of two hundred thousand livres and an opulent trousseau.

At the end of 1752, the king had made Pompadour a duchesse, which gave her the honors of the *tabouret*, the right to sit on a special low stool in his presence. However, she would always use the title of marquise. But no matter her rank, Madame de Pompadour still had to watch her back. Occasionally one or two of the king's young conquests from the Parc-aux-Cerfs were installed at court and swanned about as the beauties of the day. They threatened her ego, although as yet, none had endangered her position as *maîtresse en titre*. But in 1755, a scheme was set in motion that came within a hair's-breadth of costing her the king.

The plan was concocted by the marquise's purported BFF, the plump comtesse d'Estrades. When she came to Versailles a decade earlier, Jeanne-Antoinette had brought along her cousin Charlotte as a companion so that she would not have to navigate the strange, arcane world of the Bourbon court alone. Charlotte d'Estrades was also born a bourgeoise, but had wed into the minor nobility. Somewhere along the line the ambitious, jowl-faced comtesse grew tired of being the perennial sidekick and took a lover—none other than one of Pompadour's greatest enemies at court, the comte d'Argenson. Madame d'Estrades was equally ambitious for her paramour; she wanted to see him become Louis' Chief Minister. However, Pompadour, who not only detested d'Argenson but had considerable influence in all government appointments, was in the way. Therefore, the marquise had to be eliminated and supplanted by another *maîtresse declarée*. Their candidate was another of Madame d'Estrades's cousins, the married, empty-headed, eighteen-year-old comtesse de Choiseul-Romanet.

The scheming pair of lovers tried to dangle their pretty bait under Louis' nose and were making some progress. He was certainly attracted. But the little comtesse had been coached not to succumb without conditions: His Majesty had to dismiss Madame de Pompadour forever. While Louis' loins burned for her, so to speak, he couldn't bring himself to jettison a decade-long liaison for a night of passion. Pompadour, meanwhile, had to pretend she didn't know what was going on, as she privately agonized over her future, which seemed to be spiraling out of her control.

One night at Fontainebleau, the king twisted his ankle on a staircase that conveniently led to the teenage comtesse's bedchamber. Louis hobbled into the room, one thing led to another, and it appeared as though the grand bargain was about to be sealed.

The marquise fretted anxiously in her rooms, consoled by her friend the marquis de Gontaut. Also staying at Fontainebleau, purely by chance, was another member of the Choiseul family, Gontaut's brother-in-law, the redheaded, pug-nosed comte de Stainville.

When the young comtesse burst forth from her bedroom, somewhat disheveled, clutching a letter and crying, "He loves me! It is done!" and asked her relations what to do next, the cunning comte de Stainville took it upon himself to counsel his kinswoman. He convinced her to hand over the king's hastily written letter promising to dismiss the marquise and allow him to keep it overnight so he could mull over their course of action. The birdbrained girl complied, and Stainville immediately brought the letter to Madame de Pompadour—who marched straight to her royal lover and confronted him with his own promissory note.

A scene of tears and recriminations followed—after all they'd been through together, how dared the king be so craven that he not tell her to her own face that she was to be dismissed! The bottom line, however, was that Louis XV prized discretion above all else. He was livid that his tootsie was running all over Fontainebleau bragging about her conquest. Within twenty-four hours the comtesse de Choiseul-Romanet and her husband were exiled from court. Pregnant, either in her first trimester at the time of her banishment or as a result of her tryst with His Majesty, the comtesse died in childbirth.

Unfortunately, the two concocters of the scheme to replace the marquise remained firmly entrenched there. But Madame de Pompadour wished to reward the man who had exploded the plot. Louis wanted to banish the comte de Stainville merely for being a member of the Choiseul family, but the marquise suggested that he make him an ambassador instead. The king named Stainville his envoy to the Holy See in Rome. The appointment marked the beginning of a lifelong professional friendship between Madame de Pompadour and the comte—who would eventually be made duc de Choiseul and ambassador to the Austrian court, instrumental in brokering the 1770 marriage between the empress's youngest daughter, Marie Antoinette, and Louis' grandson and heir, the dauphin Louis Auguste. In time, Choiseul would become Louis' chief minister and foreign minister, the most powerful man in his government, until he was toppled by the monarch's last *maîtresse en titre*, his enemy Madame du Barry.

The Choiseul-Romanet incident made it all the more apparent to the marquise de Pompadour that *she* should be the one controlling the access to the king's bedchamber. At least she could vet his visitors first to ensure that they lacked an ulterior motive or were not the tool of another's political agenda.

In January 1756, she wrote, "Except for the happiness of being with the King, which assuredly makes up for everything else, all the rest is nothing but nastiness and platitudes, in a word, all the worst of which we poor humans are capable."

A sea change had taken place in her personality after the death of her daughter in 1754. The marquise's profound depression not only affected her willingness or ability to eat and sleep, but it had forever altered her relationship with the king. She had turned to God and, in an effort to demonstrate her chastity to Him, had the connecting staircase between her apartments and Louis' bricked up. She also gave up her famous theatrical performances, stopped eating meat on Fridays and Saturdays, began reading religious books, and no longer received the court at her toilette—although she did not go so far as to forswear rouge.

In 1756, it completely shocked the court when in February the king appointed her the thirteenth (there were customarily twelve) supernumerary *dame du palais de la Reine*, a lady-in-waiting to the queen, considered one of the highest honors at court. The halls buzzed with backstairs gossip. How could the pious Marie Leszczyńska countenance her husband's whore in her household? But the queen knew that her rival had not warmed the king's bed for quite some time, and sanctioned the appointment, and Madame de Pompadour took her job seriously.

Primarily from personal motives, the marquise decided to take sides in a religious dispute between two factions, the Jesuits, who had long been the court confessors, and the Jansenists, a conservative sect of Holy Roller types favored by the powerful members of France's judicial bodies, the Parlements. A tug-of-war between Church and State and Crown grew hideous, with innocent believers being denied last rites and a Christian burial if they had confessed to a Jansenist priest. Madame de Pompadour had never been particularly religious, but decided to support the Church position (pro-Jesuit/anti-Jansenist) in the hope that as a fallen woman she would once again be received into the bosom of the Church. Her confessor, Père de Sacy, advised her to write to her husband, from whom she had received a formal decree of separation soon after she became the king's mistress, and to plead for a reconciliation, as she might be granted redemption if she returned to her marriage. But Monsieur d'Etioles had a happy life and a new family of his own with his longtime mistress and didn't want her back. Charles-Guillaume wrote a polite thanks-but-no-thanks letter (coached, it was rumored, by Louis' cousin, the prince de Soubise). Well, if la Pompadour wasn't sleeping with the king, nor was there any possibility of resuming relations with her husband, and as she had no desire to enter any other relationship, from her perspective it was as if the slate had been wiped clean. And with Rome now satisfied that she was undesired, and would therefore remain celibate for the rest of her days, Madame de Pompadour could begin to pave the path to heaven.

Or so she thought. Her confessor was not so progressive. Evidently, the Church position was, Once a slut, always a slut, and there was no wiggle room for repentance after all. From this contretemps with her confessor and her rancor against those of his Jesuit bent who would continue to damn her stems the inflated (and incorrect) claim that Madame de Pompadour was responsible for Louis' campaign from 1761 to 1764 to expel the Jesuits.

She was powerful, though, and she approached her zenith in the late 1750s. "Mademoiselle Poisson, dame Le Normand [sic], marquise de Pompadour, was in fact the Prime Minister of the state," wrote Voltaire.

On May 1, 1756, thanks to some clever buttering up of the marquise by the Empress Maria Theresa's diplomatic envoys, the First

Treaty of Versailles was signed. It obligated France and Austria, who had been enemies for the past 950 years, to aid each other in a time of war, except in case of a conflict between France and her other age-old nemesis, England. This pact, a baby primarily birthed by Pompadour and Choiseul on the French side, would pave the way for the marriage fourteen years later between Marie Antoinette and Louis' eldest grandson. At the time, France believed the First Treaty of Versailles was merely a defensive strategy. Little did they know that war was about to break out between Maria Theresa and the king of Prussia over a region called Silesia, and that France would be dragged into a lengthy, expensive, and unpopular foreign conflict. Fought between 1756 and 1763 on several fronts, the Seven Years' War would even cost France her North American colonies. Voltaire quipped that "a few acres of snow" (Canada) weren't such a great loss, but Louis' subjects were both livid and disgusted.

Pompadour would forever shoulder the blame, and what was perceived as her malignant political influence on the king would eventually cost him any public relations credit he had amassed during his reign. The only sympathy Louis elicited during the Seven Years' War came at a high price, and nearly cost him his relationship with the marquise as well.

On January 5, 1757, angry about the high taxes levied on the already overburdened poor in order to fund the war, a deranged and disgruntled unemployed manservant named Robert-François Damiens stabbed the king with the short blade of his penknife while Louis stood in the courtyard of Versailles awaiting his carriage. Piercing his layers of outerwear, the blade plunged three inches into the king's skin, and he was convinced he was bleeding to death. The royal family rushed to his side, and in the event that he was about to expire, his mistress was banned from his presence. For eleven agonizing days Louis—who was behaving like a hypochondriac, as he was told that he could be on the mend and dancing within the day if he wished it—neither visited the marquise nor sent for her to attend his bedside. But finally, on January 16 (other biographers put the date at January 13, only eight days after the incident), having had enough of his relatives and the toadying courtiers who seemed to count the minutes to Pompadour's dismissal, he borrowed a cloak from her friend Madame de Brancas and went upstairs to the marquise's apartments, where he remained for several hours.

When Louis returned, he was in much jollier spirits than he had been in weeks, and everyone was compelled to acknowledge that it was because he had just enjoyed a fabulous chat with his confidante and best friend. The sycophantic courtiers turned on a sou and scuttled back to Madame de Pompadour's salon to curry favor with her. "She was the god in the Opera who came down in the machine to calm all anxieties," observed her pal the duc de Choiseul. "She showed pleasure in seeing him, did not reproach him for his silence; she put him at his ease; he was most relieved to find peace instead of a storm of reproaches and from this moment he took up the same habit of going once a day to see her and telling her everything he knew."

And within twenty-four hours the detestable comte d'Argenson, mastermind of the 1755 plot to replace her with the comtesse de Choiseul-Romanet, found himself stripped of all of his ministerial offices and banished to his provincial estate—a fate worse than death for a French courtier of the day.

Contrary to public opinion, it was Louis who determined government policy, not Madame de Pompadour, but she did often help him implement it, and he took her opinions and suggestions into account in the matter of appointing ministers and even military commanders—which led to disaster when he placed a crony of hers, the prince de Soubise (though also his cousin), in command of one of his armies during the Seven Years' War. Soubise managed to snatch defeat from the jaws of victory, and the marquise was roundly criticized for pressuring the king to appoint him. Rumors continued to spread that the king was weak and ineffectual, guided—or misguided—into a gory sort of glory by his mistress, whose vain head had been turned by the clever empress of Austria.

Understandably, the marquise became stressed out by the disastrous situation in central Europe. She was plagued with health issues: headaches, sore eyes, coughs and colds, and innumerable sleepless nights. For a brief period after Damiens' attack, Louis had tried to tamp down his overactive libido, as his multiple liaisons with pubescent girls repelled his subjects even more than his long-term affair with the elegant marquise, but his effort didn't last long. Soon he was turning ever more frequently to his adolescent concubines from the Parc-aux-Cerfs. In the aftermath of Damiens' gruesome execution on March 28, 1757, the king had grown even gloomier than usual, and the marquise used the occasion as a teachable moment to enlighten him on the climate that produced the would-be assassin.

In 1759, the king became smitten by a raven-haired, statuesque twenty-year-old named Anne Coupier, who went by the name Mademoiselle de Romans. That year, Louis also impregnated Marguerite Sainte-Hainault, one of the girls from the town house in the rue Saint-Médéric. She bore the king a daughter in 1760, the same year the king got seventeen-year-old Lucie d'Estaing with child. Madame de Pompadour, now pushing forty, took more than a passing interest in these fertile royal paramours, but there was never a question that the king's by-blows would be legitimized or even be taken to reside in the palace. In 1761, Mademoiselle de Romans became pregnant, and Louis began to flaunt his luscious brunette everywhere. The son she bore him on January 13, 1762, was baptized Louis-Aimé de Bourbon, and for the first time, Pompadour worried. Would the king legitimize him? He obviously recognized the boy as his own.

Unable to suppress her curiosity, one day the marquise and the mistress of her household rode out to the Bois de Boulogne, aware that the new mother had a habit of brazenly breast-feeding her bastard in the park. To disguise her features, Madame de Pompadour held a handkerchief to her face and pretended to have a toothache in order to get close to the nursing mother and glimpse her longtime lover's child—the infant she would have dearly loved to have given him herself.

Louis' liaison with the bourgeois Mademoiselle de Romans made Pompadour appreciate all the more the precariousness of her position after so many years. Perhaps being the king's most trusted confidante was no longer enough. More than anything, she wished to stay at court, but what remained between her and Louis seemed a mere shadow of their former romance.

Luckily for the marquise, motherhood had transformed Mademoiselle de Romans into a transparent gold digger, and Louis soon tired of her. He moved on to a less demanding chit, enjoying an even briefer flirtation with a woman from an even lower class.

The maréchale de Mirepoix, one of Pompadour's friends at court, summed up the king's attraction to the marquise long after the passion waned and Louis had turned to younger, nubile, and more willing girls to warm his bed. These adolescents could never know his mind. "He's used to you, he doesn't have to explain himself when he's with you. If you disappeared and somebody younger and more beautiful were suddenly to be found in your place I dare say he wouldn't give you another thought, but he'll never be bothered to make a change himself. Princes, above all people, are creatures of habit."

In the spring of 1761, plagued with migraines, fevers, and failing eyesight, the marquise de Pompadour began to retire from society. By the time the Seven Years' War was concluded in 1763, she rarely ventured upstairs to visit Louis, who now entertained his young conquests in his *petits appartements* above the state rooms, despite the specially constructed "flying chair" that servants drew up the stairs on pulleys because she frequently grew too winded to climb them. It was almost as painful to acknowledge that she was no longer a part of that milieu.

Although she was only forty-two years old, by the summer of 1763, Madame de Pompadour had been ailing for some time. She was in constant pain; her legs were swollen and her limbs ached, she suffered from shortness of breath, and she had no appetite. Years of micromanaging her royal lover had worn the marquise out, physically as well as emotionally. Her unique role, with its demands of state, of courtesanry, and of intrigue, was all-encompassing and debilitating. Over the year, her condition steadily worsened.

The marquise de La Ferté-Imbault, a frenemy who had disdained to socialize with Jeanne-Antoinette even before the start of her illustrious royal liaison, described their meeting at the beginning of 1764, when she deigned to call on the favorite of two decades:

"I found her beautiful and grave. She seemed in good health, though she complained of insomnia, bad digestion and shortness of breath whenever she had to climb stairs. . . . She then went on to tell me, with the warmth and feeling of an actress who is good at playing her part, how distressed she was by the deplorable state of the kingdom, the parlement's rebellion and the things going on up there (pointing to the King's apartment, with tears in her eyes). She assured me that her staying with the King was a great token of her affection for him; that she would have been a thousand times happier living alone and quietly at Ménars, but that the King would not know what to do if she left him; and in opening her heart to me—which, she said, she could open to no one—she depicted her torments for me with an eloquence and energy that I had never seen in her before. . . . In sum, she seemed demented and raving, and I never heard a more convincing sermon proving the misfortunes tied to ambition; and at the same time, I saw her in turn so miserable, so insolent, so violently agitated and so uncomfortable with her supreme power that I came away from her, after an hour of conversation, struck by the thought that she had no refuge left but death."

On February 29, 1764, while the marquise was at Choisy with Louis, she was felled by an excruciating headache. Louis wrote to his son-in-law, "I am as much worried as ever; I must tell you that I am not very hopeful of a real cure, and even feel that the end may be near. A debt of nearly twenty years, and an unshakable friendship!" Seven days later she rallied, but then she developed a putrid fever and pneumonia. The king rarely quit her bedside. "At Court, Mme. de Pompadour's illness stopped everything," observed the duc de Croÿ.

She was at death's door on March 10. The very fact that she remained at Versailles in such a condition was a huge violation of etiquette, as only monarchs and members of the immediate royal family could die in a royal palace. Yet the marquise held on to life for several more weeks. On Wednesday, April 11, she asked to receive last rites. Louis delayed as long as possible, aware that she was dying; he knew that once she was shriven, they would never be allowed to see each other again. On Friday the thirteenth the marquise couldn't breathe. Yet in her final hours, the pious, self-righteous dauphin who had never liked her found a kind word to spare for the woman he had called *Maman Putain*. "She is dying with a courage rare in either sex," he told the bishop of Verdun. "Every time she breathes, she believes it to be for the last time. It is one of the most painful ways to die and one of the cruelest one can imagine. . . ."

Madame de Pompadour received extreme unction in the middle of the night on April 14. On Palm Sunday, April 15, after adding a codicil to her 1757 will and refusing any assistance from her ladies-in-waiting, insisting that she didn't have long to live, she noticed the *curé* of the Madeleine, who until then had not quit her bedside, about to quietly depart.

"*Un moment, monsieur le curé*; we will go together," she murmured. And scarcely a few breaths later, at seven p.m., Madame de Pompadour expired, age forty-two and four months.

Her servants discreetly covered her body with a sheet and quickly conveyed it to the Hôtel des Réservoirs, as it was already a gross violation of court etiquette for her corpse to remain within Versailles. Although he received the story secondhand, Jean-Nicolas Dufort, the comte de Cheverny, one of the king's minor household officials, described the scene: "The duchesse de Praslin told me: 'I saw two men pass by carrying a stretcher. When they came closer (they passed right under my window) I saw that it was the body of a woman covered only with so thin a sheet that the shapes of the head, the breasts, the belly and the legs were clearly visible. I sent to ask: it was the body of that poor woman who, according to the strict rule that no dead person can remain in the Palace, was being carried to her house.'"

Most poignant of all was that the man who was first her lover and then her closest friend and confidant for two decades was not permitted to attend her funeral or openly mourn her, because their liaison had been illicit and adulterous. According to Dufort, who witnessed the king observing the departure of the marquise's funeral cortege on April 17, "It was six o'clock at night . . . and a dreadful storm was raging. The king took [his valet] Champlost by the arm; when he arrived at the mirrored door of the *cabinet intime* which gives out onto the balcony facing the avenue, he told him to close the entrance door and went with him out onto the balcony. He kept absolutely silent, saw the carriage drive into the avenue and, in spite of the bad weather and the rain, which he appeared not to feel, he kept looking at it until it went out of sight. He then came back into the room. Two large tears were still running down his cheeks, and he said to Champlost only these few words: 'These are the only respects I can pay her.'"

Madame de Pompadour's hearse was drawn by twelve horses

caparisoned in black-and-silver silk. Following them on foot were a hundred priests, two dozen children, forty-two liveried servants, and seventy-two beggars (the last group wearing respectable garments, which they were expected to return after the funeral). But the wind whipped their hats from their heads, blowing them irretrievably into the ditches along the sides of the road. "The Marquise has bad weather for her journey," her royal lover was said to have murmured sadly.

It was the dead of night before the cortege reached the Convent of the Capucines, where Madame de Pompadour was laid beside the body of her daughter.

At Versailles, the woman who had for nearly twenty years influenced France's art, culture, and politics, as well as its most powerful and illustrious resident, was either genuinely mourned or not given a second thought, depending on whom one asked. "No one talks anymore of the person who has just died, as though she had never existed," wrote the queen to a friend only five days after Pompadour's death.

The words of the duc de Croÿ, always a Pompadour devotee, contradict those of Her Majesty. "In general she was missed, being a good person and doing only good to most who came to her . . . and she had never done any harm, except when forced, but so many misfortunes had befallen France during her life, and so many extravagances!"

The nasty epigrams that made the rounds of the Paris coffeehouses were predictably cruel.

Here lies one who was twenty years a virgin,
Eight years a whore and ten years a pimp.

And then it was the philosophers' turn to weigh in. Denis Diderot asked, "[W]hat remains of that woman who exhausted us of men and money, left us without honor and without energy and who has overturned the political system of Europe? The Treaty of Versailles, which will last while it is possible. The Cupid of Bouchardon which one will admire forever, some stones engraved by Guay which will astonish the antique dealers to come, a good little painting by Van

Loo which one will regard from time to time, and a handful of ashes."

It's a portrait of a remarkably influential woman for any era, however unflattering Diderot intended it to be, and an unvarnished view of one of the most powerful royal mistresses who ever lived. Madame de Pompadour's extravagances were said to have cost Louis XV 36 million livres (in comparison, the Seven Years' War cost the crown 1,350 million livres), but each of the marquise's houses was constructed on royal property, and all of them reverted to the crown upon her death. Tragically, most of these châteaux and the priceless treasures they contained were destroyed during the Revolution.

Madame de Pompadour carefully cultivated the image of a woman of refinement and discernment, a tastemaker whose personal sensibilities influenced art, culture, architecture, and interior design for two decades. This most influential of royal mistresses paired with the most libidinous of lovers was physically and emotionally cool and did not enjoy sex. Yet remarkably, she held him for twenty years, in some measure because she remained trustworthy and discreet. Despite some close calls in his bed, no one else supplanted Madame de Pompadour in Louis' affections.

From his self-imposed exile in Switzerland, Voltaire eulogized, "It is indeed ridiculous that an old scribbler is still alive, and that a beautiful woman should die at forty while in the midst of the most dazzling career in the world. . . . I believe . . . that the king is experiencing a great loss; he was loved for himself by a soul born sincere who had *justesse dans son esprit et de la justice dans son coeur* [sound judgment and sure instinct]. One does not meet with this every day. . . ."

LOUIS XV AND
JEANNE BÉCU, COMTESSE DU BARRY (1743–1793)

Madame de Pompadour died on April 15, 1764, and although she went to her grave as Louis' *maîtresse en titre*, she had not warmed his bed for a decade. He was a man of large appetites, and he was lonely. Not only was he unsatisfied sexually, but after her death he missed the Pompadour's vivacious companionship. Escorted to him by his faithful valet and sometime-pimp Lebel, the beauties from the Parc-aux-Cerfs scratched the temporary itch, but the king was craving a more permanent relationship, and none of the girls had the talents to keep him amused. It takes a certain amount of cultivation and skill to be more than just a professional courtesan and to become a be-loved mistress. A woman must understand how to stimulate far more than a man's nether regions, particularly when her client is a king.

Jeanne Bécu had literally been groomed for the position. But she was not schooled by her mother, Anne Bécu, a lowly seamstress. Nor did she receive her tutelage from her purported father, a monk, Jean-Baptiste Gomard, who went by the ironic name of Frère Ange (Brother Angel). Jeanne's Pygmalion was a scoundrel and renowned pimp named Jean-Baptiste du Barry. He was a man well-known not only to the Paris police but among society as "the Roué." Du Barry transformed the seamstress's illegitimate daughter into, as he termed it, *"un vrai morceau du roi"*—a morsel fit for the king. But the phrase had a frank sexual connotation as well, *morceau* also being a syn-onym for "piece," as in piece of ass.

Jeanne had enjoyed quite a checkered career before she crossed paths with the Roué. Her mother, who was also somewhat free with her favors, managed to liberate herself from the garrison town of Vaucouleurs in Lorraine by seducing Monsieur Dumonceaux, the visiting postmaster of Paris. She became pregnant and followed him back to the capital, with Jeanne in tow. At first they stayed with Anne's sister Hélène, who was the housekeeper to the king's librarian. Then Anne and Jeanne moved in with Anne's lover, and—to her shock—his mistress Francesca, a notorious Italian demimon-daine who went by the name of Madame Frédérique.

Anne was taken on as a cook, and Madame Frédérique, who loved children, indulged the five-year-old Jeanne, giving the child the run of her lavishly appointed apartments. The provincial child with the wide blue eyes and masses of blond hair had never seeen such luxuries—perfume bottles, gilded beds and hand mirrors, abundant jewels, and sumptuous gowns in the latest fashions. Madame Frédé-rique played dress-up with Jeanne as if she were a little doll. She taught the child how to dance, while Monsieur Dumonceaux, an amateur artist, painted her as a nymph.

Anne got out of Dumonceaux's kitchen by wedding a pockmarked valet named Nicolas Rançon. Dumonceaux supplemented Rançon's income by giving him a plum assignment to the army detachment in Corsica.

Little Jeanne was placed in the convent of St. Aure in the heart of Paris. St. Aure was a school for "at risk" girls of modest means where they could learn a trade—a good way to avoid the paths of temptation. Jeanne spent nine years there, leaving at the age of fifteen with a fairly comprehensive education.

To keep her out of trouble, her aunt Hélène arranged for Jeanne to apprentice to a hairdresser. It seemed like a good idea at the time, but her employer, Monsieur Lametz, was so smitten with her that in short order they became lovers. When his mother showed up, she accused Anne Bécu of prostituting her underage daughter. Anne sued Madame Lametz for defamation of character, and Jeanne's first love affair ended in tears. It also resulted in the birth of a daughter, Marie Josephine, nicknamed Betsi, who was raised in a convent, passed off as the daughter of Jeanne's stepfather, Nicolas Rançon. Many years later, when lowly Jeanne Bécu was warming the bed of the king, Betsi would be married off to a marquis.

In 1761, her brief career in coiffures at an abrupt end, eighteen-year-old Jeanne spent several months as a lady's maid for Madame de la Garde, the wealthy widow of a provincial finance minister. But when madame found out that her voluptuous domestic was sleeping with *both* of her married sons (and had clumsily fended off the advances of one of their wives), Jeanne was promptly sacked.

She had much better luck at her next job. In the spring of 1762, she became a grisette, or shopgirl, at Paris's most exclusive fashion house, À la Toilette, owned by Monsieur Labille. There she regularly crossed paths with Labille's posh clientele, which included both aristocrats and demimondaines, and was surrounded day in and day out by the finest textiles, ribbons, and laces.

The Prince de Ligne, a bon vivant of the era, described "the charms of the little grisette who worked at Labille's, a girl who was tall, well made and ravishingly blonde with a wide forehead, lovely eyes with dark lashes, a small oval face with a delicate complexion marked by two little beauty spots, which only made her the more *piquante*, a mouth to which laughter came easily and a bosom so perfect as to defy comparison."

Working among luxury goods every day, Jeanne coveted such items for herself and had no qualms about doing what it took to secure them. Soon she was retailing more than ribbons and bonnets. She developed a discerning eye and knew what type of man would pay the most for her favors. Working her way up the social food chain, she rented herself to merchants, bankers, and financiers, and soon became well-known to the local police (although as Mademoiselle de Vaubernier). Police records of 1782 describe Jeanne as "a pretty little grisette ready to accept whatever came her way—in short, a kept woman living with various men to whom she was not married, but in no sense a prostitute or a *raccrocheuse* guilty of soliciting in the streets."

That report would put the lie to the rumors that dogged Madame du Barry during her royal romance, namely that she had been a whore in the house of the notorious procuress Madame Gourdan. But Jeanne was indeed in the game for the material gain. Her heart had been broken by the coiffeur Monsieur Lametz. Now she just wanted to amass as many worldly goods as she could by casting the right sort of glances with her notorious *yeux fripons*—her mischievous, or roguish, eyes.

In 1763, at the unveiling of an equestrian statue to celebrate the inauguration of a public square named in the king's honor, Jeanne's vivacity attracted the attention of another spectator, one who always had an eye out for a fresh and pretty face and a pulchritudinous form. Jean-Baptiste du Barry (who styled himself as a comte, though he certainly did not behave like a member of the aristocracy) had noticed Jeanne at Labille's shop, and recognized in her the answer to his greatest ambition. He had started out with more quotidian aspirations, but when his plan of becoming a foreign diplomat didn't pan out, he turned to his fallback talents of debauchery and cardsharping. In time he developed a niche for himself, specializing in finding the perfect girl for his friends at court. His ultimate goal was to place one of his protégées in the king's bed, but for obvious reasons, Madame de Pompadour had been hell-bent on thwarting it.

In the weeks following the unveiling of Louis' statue, Jean du Barry, having decided that Jeanne Bécu was the girl he'd been waiting for all his life, arranged with her mother and stepfather for her to move in with him. It was understood that she would be his mistress, and Jeanne does not seem to have put up much of a fuss. On Jean du Barry's arm, she would always be impeccably gowned, coiffed, and jeweled, and would gain entrée into the world of sophisticated demi-mondaines and their aristocratic lovers—the sort of education she never could have gotten at St. Aure. She already possessed all the requisite natural talents of a courtesan: She knew how to amuse, flatter, and cajole; she could bestow her body while withholding her heart. With Jean du Barry, she had plenty of opportunities to observe how the nobility carried themselves: how they dressed, moved, and spoke—and not only *how* they spoke, but what they spoke *of*. In eighteenth-century Parisian salons, conversation was both an art and a skill.

Jean-Baptiste du Barry's activities were well-known to the Parisian police force. "When he begins to weary of a woman he invariably sells her off. But it must be admitted that he is a connoisseur and his merchandise is eminently salable," read one report.

Sure enough, the comte du Barry also retailed Jeanne to other men, and she did not protest. On the contrary, every experience was a teachable moment, and every client was another contact, another potential friend. One of them, the sixty-seven-year-old duc de Richelieu, a crony of the king's, would become a lifelong champion. At the age of twenty Jeanne became the duc's lover as part of a business transaction. She was his fee (plus fifty gold louis) for securing a position at court for du Barry's fourteen-year-old son, Adolphe.

From 1765 to 1766, Jeanne rented her own house in the rue de la Jussienne, setting up shop as a courtesan in order to afford her lavish lifestyle. Alternately calling herself Mademoiselle de Vaubernier, Mademoiselle Beauvarnier, and Mademoiselle l'Ange (an ironic nod, perhaps, to her alleged father, the so-called Frère Ange), she entertained poets and courtiers, ministers and other influential men of the day so that she could learn how to converse with them. Jean du Barry had found a diamond in the rough. He realized he might have only one shot to dangle her tantalizingly before the king; he couldn't risk blowing it. It was four years from the time they had serendipitously met on the Place Louis XV until du Barry deemed Jeanne ready to present to the king.

She was first dispatched to Versailles on an errand that would appear innocuous enough: pleading a matter before the powerful duc de Choiseul, who held several ministerial offices simultaneously. In the spring of 1768, Mademoiselle de Vaubernier, dressed like a country lass in a beribboned straw hat and a simple muslin gown that revealed her famous décolletage, entered the duc's office with a sob story. Choiseul was unimpressed by her looks and her tale of woe (that she'd given all of her money to an army contractor in charge of supplies for Corsica and now needed help collecting it). He fobbed her off on an underling, but Jeanne remained undeterred and requested a second meeting a few days later. The subsequent meeting didn't go well either. Jeanne made the mistake of mentioning du Barry's name, and Choiseul quickly curtailed the interview, suspecting that her real motives in coming to see him were to ask him for money or to seduce him.

It was a matter of being in exactly the right place at the right time for the wrong reasons. Or not. After all, du Barry's intention had always been for Jeanne to catch the king—and hold him. As she was headed out of the palace she locked eyes with His Majesty as he strode through the Hall of Mirrors on his way to Mass. She gave Louis one of her dazzling smiles and he was smitten for life.

Soon he was making inquiries about the luscious blonde. He had to meet her, to possess her. To the Roué, Jean du Barry, it must have felt like shooting fish in a barrel.

The queen of France died on June 24, 1768. That same week, Jeanne Bécu, alias Mademoiselle de Vaubernier, a.k.a. Mademoiselle l'Ange of the rue de la Jussienne, spent her first night in the king's arms. The following morning, so the story goes, Louis cornered the randy old duc de Richelieu and told him, "I am delighted with your Jeanne. She is the only woman in France who has managed to make me forget that I am sixty." (He was fifty-eight).

So delighted was His Majesty with his new toy that he kvelled about Jeanne's remarkable talents to anyone who would listen. When he marveled about some of her amatory skills to the duc d'Ayen, the duc bluntly replied, "That, Sire, is because you have never been to a brothel."

There was, however, a slight hitch: the brothel aspect of the whole business. Louis had been given a whitewashed version of Jeanne's background. Although she had never been a prostitute (despite the propaganda the duc de Choiseul would eventually, and anonymously, disseminate against her), she had certainly been around the block more than a few times. In any event, Jeanne had been both euphemistically and erroneously represented to the king as a married woman who had dallied with a few powerful men here and there, primarily in the world of finance, but otherwise she was a lady of sound repute—in other words, she was no better or worse than most wives of the eighteenth-century French bourgeoisie.

Except that Jeanne was no one's wife, nor ever had been. Although her married name had been presented as "du Barry," it was common knowledge, as gossip was currency at Versailles, that comte Jean du Barry already had a wife living back in Languedoc, so he could not be this mythical husband of the king's new inamorata.

Louis' ever-faithful valet Lebel, who summoned Jeanne to Versailles for her royal trysts and guided her up the secret stairs to the king's bedchamber with extreme frequency, began to realize that she was no passing infatuation. It was therefore becoming hard to conceal her past from his boss. Sooner or later Louis was bound to find out the truth for himself. The more often she visited the palace, the greater the risk of her being recognized by the courtiers who frequented du Barry's home as well as Jeanne's salon in the rue de la Jussienne, some of whom may even have been her lovers.

Louis was so serious about Jeanne that he talked of installing her as his *maîtresse en titre* and shuttering the Parc-aux-Cerfs, as he no longer had the need for an on-call seraglio. It was Pompadour all over again—and then some. At least the marquise, although a bourgeoise, had enjoyed a more or less respectable background. And Jeanne, too, had the problem of not being a member of the titled aristocracy with a coat of arms dating back to the year 1400.

Lebel decided to set the record straight before things got completely out of hand, so he confided Jeanne's sexual résumé to the king. But he received a somewhat unexpected reaction. Anger, yes; Lebel had anticipated that. But Louis was not feeling duped or betrayed. He was livid that such aspersions should be cast upon this lovely and winsome woman, this fine specimen of femininity! How dared Lebel malign her so? But, just in case it was all true, Louis instructed his valet to begin making the necessary arrangements to recast his new mistress as a reputable woman. Lebel was so shocked that he dropped dead a few weeks later.

Jeanne's former lover the duc de Richelieu assumed control of the project. The first step was to get Jeanne married for real. Conveniently, Jean-Baptiste du Barry had a brother languishing in Languedoc named Guillaume, fat, paunchy, and provincial—but unwed. Guillaume was summoned from the du Barrys' hometown of Lévignac and instructed to show up for a proper church wedding that autumn, well advised that his wife would never warm his bed.

In the interim, Jeanne remained in a twilight zone of respectability. She was unmarried, but not as yet Louis' formal mistress. Oh, how times had changed since the Sun King's reign! Where Louis XIV had been vilified for choosing married mistresses, what irony— and hypocrisy—now attended the era of his successor. The new, un-wed paramour of Louis *le Bien-Aimé*, a man who was now a widower, had to get herself legally hitched to a man she'd never met, didn't love, and would never sleep with or see again, just so her adul-terous romance with the sovereign could be formally recognized at a court hidebound by arcane etiquette. In the interim, Jeanne could not socialize at court with the other women, regardless of her relation-ship with the king.

During the summer of 1768, while the court frolicked at Com-piègne, one of Louis' favorite hunting lodges, although she swanned about in sumptuous gowns and rode in lavish carriages, Jeanne found herself particularly lonely. She was desired by her lover and sover-eign, but unwanted by everyone else. She had no friends and had, in fact, through no fault of her own, made one very powerful enemy who would spend the rest of his career endeavoring to destroy her.

The duc de Choiseul was informed by a colleague "that there was a certain Madame du Barry at Compiègne with whom the king was said to have fallen in love and who was nothing but a prostitute kept by du Barry, who was now planning to marry her off to a brother with no other part to play than to give her his name and disappear at the earliest opportunity." Choiseul was appalled that the young woman who had come to his office had risen so far so fast. After hearing the rumors that the king intended to make this soi-disant Madame du Barry his next *maîtresse en titre*, he just couldn't wrap his brain around the fact that "such a mediocrity could ever become a successor to the brilliant marquise."

Choiseul didn't even know Jeanne, apart from the encounters in his office, where, it was true, she had been trying to wheedle something out of him, and her presence at Versailles had indeed been an excuse to accidentally-on-purpose bump into the king. But there was a backstory to the duc's words. He had first met the marquise de Pompadour when he was the comte de Stainville and had leveraged a serendipitous event into an opportunity to obtain the appreciation of both the king and the marquise. A grateful Pompadour had arranged for the comte to be made a foreign ambassador, jump-starting what would become an illustrious diplomatic career. So as far as Choiseul was concerned, no one could be as fabulous as Pompadour.

Another reason that the duc was disinclined to give Madame du Barry the benefit of the doubt (though it was true that she never had the intellectual gifts nor the cultural sophistication of the marquise) was that his sister, the duchesse de Gramont, had designs on becoming Louis' next *maîtresse en titre*. She had even thrown herself at the king while Madame de Pompadour was dying, and had been rebuffed. Undeterred, Madame de Gramont kept trying, with the same negative result. She kept hoping that the king would come around, but the moment he spied Madame du Barry on the Ambassadors' Staircase at Versailles, it was game over. From then on the duchesse de Gramont was determined to detest Madame du Barry, and pressured her brother to do so as well.

Choiseul was also livid to discover that, thanks to all the spies and gossips pervading the palace of Versailles, the foreign courts had already gotten wind of the king's infatuation with a trollop of low birth. But Jeanne's past, present, and future were rapidly becoming sanitized so that she could become Louis' *maîtresse en titre*.

Guillaume du Barry was made "Gouverneur de Lévignac," which was almost a joke, since the place was about the size of a postage stamp, populated mostly by livestock. Jeanne was henceforth known as the comtesse du Barry, even though it was Jean du Barry, Guillaume's younger brother, who'd been passing himself off as a comte, while Guillaume was styled as a chevalier.

Jeanne's coat of arms, however, was pure invention, having been cribbed from the Irish Barrymore family. Louis' minions had even co-opted the Barrymore motto, *"Boutez en avant"*—"Push forward." These armorial accoutrements were then blended with the thoroughly fictitious "Gomard" coat of arms, purportedly belonging to Anne Bécu, who, of course, had never wed the monk who'd fathered Jeanne.

Signed on July 23, 1768, the marriage contract itself contained so many fictions it's amazing that it was legal, but it bore the king's imprimatur. It shaved three years off Jeanne's age, making her only twenty-two. The document listed her father, "Jean-Jacques Gomard de Vaubernier," as "deceased," although the lecherous Brother Angel was not only a priest at the Church of Saint-Eustache, which was right in the neighborhood where Jeanne lived, but was in attendance at the ceremony, passing himself off as the bride's uncle. Being the nearest and dearest of kin to the king's mistress came with its perqs, and Frère Ange landed in clover, boasting that Louis had made him a royal almoner, although his claim may have been no more than hot air. Jeanne's mother, Anne, and her stepfather, Nicolas Rançon, were also present for the shotgun wedding on September 1. By then, they, too, had reinvented themselves as the posh Monsieur and Madame de Montrabé.

Painfully aware that he was no more than a prop at his own wedding ceremony, Guillaume du Barry got drunk on brandy prior to the ceremony. But he was heartily thanked for playing and given a lovely parting gift: a handsome pension of five thousand livres. To everyone's chagrin, Guillaume stuck around Paris for a few weeks after his wedding. He found himself a buxom blond mistress (the exact physical type as Jeanne Bécu) named Mademoiselle Lemoine and brought her back to Lévignac, where they raised a family.

But at least two people who were present at Madame du Barry's wedding left the ceremony deliriously happy. Jean-Baptise du Barry, the groom's baby brother, had reached the apogee of his ambition. And within an hour of the "I dos," the bride was being driven about in a carriage emblazoned with the false heraldry and flaunting her new status as the king's paramour.

Many of Louis' courtiers were disgusted. But they had to admit that the king's vigor and vim had returned. Madame du Barry's presence, her luminosity, her vivacity, her kindness, and her myriad amorous talents, had lifted him from the doldrums. The duc de Croÿ, a Belgian nobleman who spent a good deal of time at the French court, observed that Louis "is more in love than he has ever been. He seems to be rejuvenated and I have never seen him in better spirits, extremely good-humored and far more outgoing than he has ever been."

Jean du Barry sent for his sister Claire Françoise, known as "Chon," to accompany Jeanne at court so she would have at least one friend there. Chon fit the stereotype of the gorgeous girl's plain-but-amusing sidekick. Ironically, her clever wit, in a world where such an attribute was as great a blessing as beauty, rocketed Chon to the top of many guest lists, where the hosts would ordinarily have shunned her sister-in-law, the king's trollop. Consequently, even the homely Chon never lacked for lovers. And it was she who would have to remind Jeanne to act like a lady at Versailles, and tone down her bawdy humor in public.

During the autumn of 1768, while the court was at Fontainebleau, a number of scurrilous verses were published and disseminated about the king and Madame du Barry. One of them was a parody of an old madrigal with the lyric rewritten to refer to a countess with humble provincial roots who had sexually serviced hairdressers and other tradesmen until she worked her way all the way up to Versailles.

The duc de Choiseul did nothing to stop the attacks. Perhaps it was because (unbeknownst to his boss) he had financed them. The king's reaction to the defamatory verses was to insist that they surely didn't depict his modest darling, she of the soft, almost baby-talking speech. The comtesse du Barry's little-girl lisp was well-known. Had she perfected it as a courtesan, and then used it to seduce and soothe a sovereign, or was it the natural timbre of her voice?

Louis not only loved Jeanne's voice; he thought the sun rose and set in her smile, and he couldn't stand to be without her. The comtesse du Barry, both voluptuous and nurturing, could delight him with her jade's tricks when he was randy, and smother him with her ample bosom when he needed a hug and someone to soothe him. Louis had already installed her in the tiny apartment (adjacent to the chapel, no less), that had housed his late valet Lebel. She could not be considered his official mistress, because she had yet to be presented at court. But he had to circumvent nearly a hundred years of court etiquette in order to find a loophole, as well as a sponsor who would be willing to overlook the fact that the comtesse was not only not a genuine noblewoman, but had a dodgy ancestry and a checkered past.

Factions had already formed, for and against her. It had not been a tough sell for the duc de Choiseul to enlist the king's three thirty-something unmarried daughters, known as Mesdames, to his side. They had detested the marquise de Pompadour, and du Barry was even more vulgar. Additionally, even though their mother was now dead, it still made them queasy to watch their father, now pushing sixty, making a public fool of himself over a blowsy blonde who was nearly a third his age.

As a brief aside, some scholars disagree about the blowsy part, citing Jeanne's experience among worldy men and women in Jean du Barry's salon and in her own rooms in the rue de la Jussienne, as well as her convent school education. But she was hardly intellectual or cultured, even if she knew which fork or goblet to use, and all of that can coexist with a bawdy wit, depending on the crowd. Several years later, the renowned diplomat Charles Maurice de Talleyrand-Périgord propounded his opinion of the two royal mistresses, although he never knew either of them, but it offers the opposite perspective from the usual way of thinking: "Although Mme de Pompadour was brought up and lived in the financial society of Paris, which was then rather distinguished, she had common manners, vulgar ways of speaking. . . . Madame du Barry . . . although less well brought up, always managed to speak correctly. . . . She liked to talk and had mastered the art of telling stories rather amusingly."

If the comtesse du Barry immediately made detractors of the king's most powerful minister and his trio of backbiting virgin daughters, she found allies in an unlikely quarter, a religious faction at court known as *les dévots* (the devout ones). *Les dévots* had formed as a reaction to Choiseul's support for the Parlements' expulsion of the Jesuits, and they didn't mind looking the other way when it came to Madame du Barry's role at court, hoping that anyone who might *also* be an enemy of the duc wouldn't mind aiding their quest to bring about his downfall.

Oddly, for a man who couldn't spend enough time in Madame du Barry's presence, and therefore couldn't wait for her presentation at court, Louis dithered and delayed. Perhaps, despite his passion for her, he recognized how unsuitable she was for the official role, given the circumstances of her birth and background.

It had also become clear that finding a lady to sponsor her presentation was a difficult sell. The sponsor had to be a woman of quality who had herself been presented at court. And Louis needed someone who didn't know or didn't care about Jeanne's origins or her entirely fictionalized noble credentials. After an exhaustive search, the ambitious duchesse d'Aiguillon, who was eager to see her son replace the duc de Choiseul, located the elderly comtesse de Béarn. The comtesse received a hefty compensation for the sacrifice of her reputation as Madame du Barry's sponsor: Her extensive gambling debts would be discharged by the crown and her two sons would receive military promotions.

So the date was set for Madame du Barry's formal presentation on February 25, 1769. The court was all atwitter in anticipation of the event. The eccentric Sir Horace Walpole, 4th Earl of Orford and a noted English man of letters, who was a frequent correspondent with some of the women of the court of Versailles, wrote, "They say that tomorrow will be the day when a petticoat will perhaps determine the destinies of Europe. . . . But I refuse to believe in all that they say—they may overcome the greatest obstacles and in the end be held up by shame."

Madame de Béarn indeed chickened out, pleading a sprained ankle, which would prevent her from performing the requisite trio of court curtsies, or reverences, required of the presentation ritual. A second delay occurred when the king severely injured his arm after a fall from his horse two days later, entailing several days of convalescence. Louis missed his concubine terribly during this period. As it was Lent, it would have been unseemly for Jeanne to have been hovering about his bedside. Besides, Mesdames had declared themselves his nursemaids, and no one was about to conduct the former grisette into the presence of the princesses.

Jeanne remained at a tasteful distance in her apartment in the rue de la Jussienne, which she had never abandoned, hoping that the elderly duc de Richelieu, her former paramour and current champion, would escort her to the king's rooms. But a summons never came.

Finally Louis recovered, and a new date was set for the comtesse du Barry's presentation, April 22, 1769. There had been so many false starts that the wagering was fierce as to whether it would really take place. The old goat Richelieu was disparaged for getting himself mixed up in the whole sordid business, but most of the gossips had no idea how he'd come to know the luscious Jeanne in the first place.

Madame du Barry's presentation at court, although she was not the only woman to be presented that evening, was nonetheless the event of the year. Even commoners thronged the courtyards, hoping for a glimpse of the king's new love. Soon they grew anxious. She was late. This was unheard-of. Would the newly minted comtesse fail to arrive for her great triumph?

Finally, this eighteenth-century Cinderella courtesan arrived in state, having been outfitted by her fairy godfather, the duc de Richelieu, in a dazzling, and extraordinarily weighty, gown of cloth of silver and cloth of gold, with an enormous train. Her entire ensemble glittered with diamonds. All eyes were upon her, undoubtedly waiting for her to screw up the three deep curtsies, and then to reverse them, walking backward out of the king's presence and kicking her lengthy train out of the way without a misstep. But her detractors were deprived of an opportunity to deride her. And even her sponsor, the old comtesse de Béarn, now fully recovered from her ankle sprain (whether real or dilatory), was impressed. The king was glowing.

Madame de Genlis, who was at Versailles for her aunt's presentation the same day, wrote about the event in her memoirs. Her comments should be taken with a grain of salt, because by that time Madame de Genlis herself had become the mistress of the duc d'Orléans, who in turn had espoused the cause of the revolutionaries.

Nevertheless it provides a colorful, if slightly snarky, portrait of the atmosphere.

> . . . it was the same occasion on which Madame du Barry was presented. It was recognized by everyone present that she was tastefully and splendidly dressed. By daylight her face was a little faded and her complexion spoiled by freckles. But it must be admitted that she looked extremely well at night. We reached the card tables in the evening a few minutes before her. When she entered the room all the ladies who were near the door rushed hurriedly forward in the opposite direction in order to avoid sitting near her. . . . She regarded all this with perfect composure; nothing upset her. When the King appeared at the conclusion of the game, she looked up at him and smiled. The indignation at Versailles was unbounded. Never had there happened anything quite so scandalous, not even the triumph of Madame de Pompadour. It was certainly very strange to see at Court a Madame la Marquise de Pompadour whose husband Monsieur Le Normant d'Étioles was nobody but a tax-farmer, but it was still more terrible to see a woman of the streets presented with pomp to the whole Royal Family. This with many other instances of unparalleled indecency cruelly degraded Royalty, and consequently contributed to bring about the Revolution.

The following day, Madame du Barry attended Mass in the royal chapel, seated in the pew where her powerful predecessor the marquise de Pompadour had warmed the velvet cushions with her panniers; it would be du Barry's pew from then on.

As Louis' *maîtresse en titre*, the comtesse had certain perquisites at court. She could assist at the dauphin's *grand couverts* (the meals taken in public view) as well as the *grand couverts* hosted by Mesdames, and she could sit at the king's card table. Playing cards and various versions of lotto games after dinner was an enormous nightly diversion at the court of Versailles. But despite the privilege of sitting beside, or opposite, her royal lover during endless hands of piquet or rounds of cavagnole, she was roundly shunned and coldly ignored by the courtiers, both male and female, utterly unwelcome in their midst.

She kept a brave face in public and saved her tears for the shoulder of her paramour. Louis sought to console her with real estate, installing the comtesse in a better suite of rooms at Versailles, relocating her from the late *valet de chambre*'s apartment to those that had been occupied by the king's equally dead and exceptionally popular daughter-in-law, the dauphine of France, who had expired from consumption in 1767. Situated directly upstairs from Louis' private apartments, du Barry's new suite was connected to his by a secret staircase. Louis conducted his private life in the intimate rooms of the *petits appartements*. It was where he had his personal library, and where he hosted public gatherings for both friends and frenemies and *petits soupers*, or little suppers, for his most trusted courtiers.

Now that Madame du Barry, as Louis' *maîtresse en titre*, was legitimately able to maintain a constant presence beside him (and he truly despaired of ever spending a moment without her), even the staunchest critics of the romance had to admit, however begrudgingly, that their monarch became radiant by his lover's side. Like a besotted schoolboy, Louis literally couldn't take his eyes off of her. And with all the solicitousness of an ardent boyfriend, he made a point of finding his lonely and outcast love a coterie of sympathetic friends. Wisely, he began with a cadre of courtiers who had skeletons hanging in their own closets. Madame de Mirepoix was a compulsive gambler (for befriending du Barry her debts were discharged by the crown). Madame de Flavacourt had herself warmed Louis' bed. The (married) prince de Condé had his own mistress. And, of course, there was the old duc de Richelieu. Operating on the theory of catching more flies with honey than with vinegar, Louis even invited the duc de Choiseul to the first of the soirees at which Madame du Barry appeared as fresh and glowing and virginal as a Lorrainer milkmaid, angelically, if diaphanously, clad in a youthful white gown, her flaxen tresses dressed with a chaplet of roses. This pastoral manner of dressing was one of the comtesse's signature styles, and she often appeared in a similar costume when she received visitors in her rooms at Versailles.

One of du Barry's guests recounted her appearance on such an occasion. "She was nonchalantly sitting, or rather lying, in a big armchair and wore a white dress with pink garlands which I can never forget. Madame du Barry, one of the prettiest women in a court where beauties were legion, was the most seductive of all because of the perfection of her entire person. Her hair, which she often dressed without powder, was of the most beautiful blond, and so abundant that she hardly knew what to do with it. Her wide open blue eyes had a frank and caressing look. . . . Her nose was adorable, her mouth very small and her skin of a dazzling whiteness."

A dozen years later, Marie Antoinette, then queen, would scandalize France by dressing in the same manner. Anyone who follows fashion knows that what goes around comes around, and both women patronized the same modiste, the entrepreneurial Mademoiselle Rose Bertin. It is therefore entirely possible that the forerunner of Marie Antoinette's [in]famous *"gaulles"* was originally popularized years earlier, when she was still dauphine of France, by none other than her archrival at court!

Jeanne may not have been in love with Louis, but she certainly behaved as though she were, and she most assuredly loved the trappings that came with being his official mistress, including the clout. Like a magpie, she had an affinity for anything that glittered. The knickknacks that cluttered her rooms were made of bronze, marble, and crystal. Her pianoforte was inlaid with Sèvres porcelain tiles and adorned with rococo carvings of gold and bronze. Jewels Louis bestowed upon her in abundance. Among the inventory of her gems were more than 140 large diamonds and some 700 smaller ones, 300 very large pearls, a trio of enormous sapphires, and 7 famous emeralds.

Louis couldn't do enough for the comtesse du Barry. And no expense was spared. He was renovating Madame de Pompadour's rooms at the royal châteaux of Marly and Choisy for her. Loath to have her quit his side, he insisted that she accompany him when he reviewed military maneuvers. Imagine JFK with a gushing Marilyn on his arm, visiting the troops at Fort Bragg. The young officers appeared smitten by their monarch, who, hat in hand, would approach her emblazoned coach to speak to her. As minister of war (among his other offices), Choiseul was mortified to see the king abasing himself, flirting with his mistress when he should have been reviewing his troops. The duc was not alone in believing that Louis was behaving like a doddering old fool.

Yet to Choiseul's chagrin, Madame du Barry seemed to have allies everywhere, even among the officers, which included a du Barry brother and a former client from the rue de la Jussienne. The duc seethed as he watched them treat the *maîtresse en titre* with the same deference they accorded their sovereign.

The vicious lambastes of the comtesse du Barry and the king continued, purportedly funded by Choiseul and his rejected sister the duchesse de Gramont. The *milder* of these slurs referred to the monarch as *un vieux paillard*—an old lecher. From there, the libels became crueler and more inventive. "The rumor is that the young vicomte du Barry [Jean-Baptiste du Barry's young son Adolphe, who had been given a position at court] is imprisoned at Pierre-Encise because he gave the comtesse of the same name a reason to worry about her health, which she has passed on to the king in the same manner" was one such spurious bit of fiction. Another was "The King's attachment for Mme. du Barry comes from the prodigious efforts of which she has rendered him capable thanks to an amber concoction with which she daily perfumes her inside."

And then there were the anti–du Barry poems and songs. Madame de Pompadour had been slandered by anonymously penned snarky verses, and Marie Antoinette would also (eventually) find herself cruelly victimized in them. This one had the audacity and impertinence to address the kingdom in the familiar *"tu"* form.

France, what then is your destiny
To be dominated by a female
Your salvation came from the virgin [Joan of Arc]
You will perish by the whore.

The lampoons and songs hurt Jeanne terribly. What had she done to incur such vitriol? she wondered. Choiseul's nephew, the handsome, rakish duc de Lauzun, had been one of the usual suspects at the rue de la Jussienne. Jean du Barry secretly met with him and informed him that the comtesse had nothing personal against his uncle, but that if Choiseul wanted to play hardball with her, he'd lose, because Louis loved Jeanne far more than he had ever loved Madame de Pompadour.

The warning fell on deaf ears, and the minister's campaign against Madame du Barry continued. Although Choiseul is on record as being unimpressed with Jeanne's looks, finding her only "moderately pretty" the first time she came to see him at Versailles, he had the ulterior agenda of promoting his sister's interests. But some who had no horse in the race remained less than overwhelmed as well. Horace Walpole journeyed from London to Paris to glimpse the royal favorite who was the talk of at least two nations. He saw her in the chapel at Versailles, and was surprised to find her appearance so unprepossessing. "There is nothing bold, assuming, or affected in her manner. She is pretty when you consider her, but so little striking I would never have asked who she was. She was without rouge or powder, almost without having *fait la toilette.*"

Little did Walpole comprehend the work it took to look so effortless. In her mid-twenties at the time, though officially passing for three years younger, the comtesse spent hours at her toilette, arriving late at her lover's supper parties or card games in a diaphanous gown with flowers in her cascading blond tresses, as if she had just stepped out of an allegorical canvas. She favored simply constructed gowns in pastel shades that flattered her coloring and youthful spark. She also turned heads and set tongues wagging with another of her fashion statements, wearing men's clothes to accompany her royal lover when he went riding.

One evening at Compiègne, Louis' favorite hunting lodge, the king dropped a snuffbox. His mistress gracefully sank into a curtsy to retrieve it from where it lay at his feet. The duc de Croÿ heard him murmur to her, "Madame, it is for me to assume that position and for all my life." Can anyone imagine a more romantic declaration? After witnessing that exchange, "She is here to stay," the awestruck duc marveled.

A few weeks later, Louis gave Madame du Barry a villa that had once belonged to the granddaughter of the Sun King. Louveciennes (pronounced "Lucienne") was a much-coveted property. It was small, as far as châteaux went, but it was beautifully situated, and the comtesse would spend a fortune decorating and furnishing it. After the king's death, it would become her home and the repository for her memories and memorabilia.

Luckily for us, the eighteenth century, particularly in France, was a great era for journal writers and epistolary correspondents, leaving us with numerous and voluminous firsthand accounts. One of the duc de Croÿ's journal entries, written in the late autumn of 1769, shows how entrenched at court Madame du Barry had become by then.

> I observe that by degrees more and more people are ready to see the countess. She has been given the 'Cabinet' rooms which formerly belonged to the late Madame la Dauphine, all of which give her the advantage of being treated as a lady of the court. She with everyone else is present at all the entertainments, and one has become accustomed to it. She has gained much, but she appears to have no aptitude for intrigue. She loves dress and to be seen everywhere, without showing any desire to interfere in state affairs. Her manner to the other ladies seems respectful and she never ventures too far.

The comtesse may not (at that stage) have been involved in court intrigues, but she did hold court in her own salon. It was soon clear that those who wanted to gain the king's good graces or be certain of remaining in them made sure to visit the *maîtresse en titre* in her natural habitat at all times of day: as she made her toilette, heard petitions from those who sought her aid (meaning her influence on the king), and hosted her suppers and card parties. Even France's chancellor, the wily Maupeou and the secular abbé Terray, the equally cunning finance minister, paid court to du Barry. The only high-placed courtier who refused to kowtow to her was the duc de Choiseul. By 1769, their mutual disdain was no longer concealed.

Madame du Barry wanted nothing more than to please her lover and, being a kindhearted soul, was inclined to want to help everyone who sought her assistance, or at the very least to lend a sympathetic ear. The ugly side of this coin was that it exposed her to rumors. In due time, she was sexually linked with the ambitious duc d'Aiguillon. It is not likely that either of them would have risked their position at court to dally with each other. Aiguillon's star was on the rise, thanks to the comtesse, so he would not have jeopardized it. Instead, he took as a mistress her sister-in-law, the wily and witty Chon, whom Jeanne often used as a ghostwriter. Chon and the duc became the driving force behind the cabal that would eventually lead to the ouster of d'Aiguillon's rival, the duc de Choiseul.

In the comtesse's sumptuously appointed salon she entertained petitions in an informal way. Obviously she had no legal or formal right to grant anything. Her immense popularity was due not only to her role at court as Louis' mistress, but because she was gaining an ever-increasing reputation for charity and compassion. Those who found themselves in unfortunate situations saw in her an angel who might intercede for them with the authorities, including her lover.

For all the rigid court etiquette (which applied only to the king, the royal family, and the courtiers), Versailles was in fact an oddly democratic palace. What we might consider riffraff had access to Madame du Barry's rooms, because the château was open to the public, as long as the visitors were properly dressed. Men had to be wearing a sword and a hat—and entrepreneurial vendors rented them outside the palace gates.

The comtesse was able to use her position to save lives. She famously became involved with the case of the destitute comte and comtesse de Louesne, who, facing eviction from their château, stood their ground and killed a bailiff and a mounted policeman. For these murders they were sentenced to death by beheading, and even their daughter's entreaties could not induce Louis to clemency.

Madame du Barry then tried her best. She prostrated herself before her lover, yet he remained unmoved. But the comtesse proved just as inflexible, refusing to rise until Louis granted her boon. Finally, with all that was at stake—the outcome of a major judicial decision already in the balance, two lives already lost, and two more perhaps to follow—the king was the first to blink.

Brimming with love, he told his mistress, "Madame, I am delighted that the first favor you should ask of me should be an act of mercy." As a direct consequence of du Barry's plea, Louis spared the lives of the Louesnes, an act that brought many of the nobility who had previously shunned and disdained her flocking to her side. She had obeyed her instincts and at the same time was able to seize an opportunity to turn a nationally notorious situation to her advantage. Had the comtesse du Barry been compassionate, canny, clever, or a combination of all three?

Among other unfortunates whom she interceded for early in her tenure was a mother charged with infanticide because she failed to register the stillbirth of her child, thus saving an already distraught, and innocent, woman from being executed for murder.

If the Louesnes incident was any indication, the king could deny his love nothing. With gifts of real estate and clemency came an allowance. Every month 200,000 livres was paid to her by the court banker. In 1771, two years after she became Louis' *maîtresse en titre*, the sum was raised to 250,000 livres. And yet she always overspent, no matter how much she received. She gave generously to her mother and her aunt, but that wasn't where the lion's share of her money went. Given her passion for fashion, the comtesse was perpetually in debt to her dressmakers—first Madame Sigly, and later Mademoiselle Rose Bertin, the same modiste who would transform Marie Antoinette into a fashionista. Jeanne's dresses cost more than a thousand livres apiece, and were invariably embellished with gemstones and costly lace. One particular bodice was covered entirely with diamonds that had been fashioned into flowers, ribbons, and bows, and cost the king a whopping 450,000 livres. Not content to let the bodice speak for itself, she accessorized it with a diamond necklace of ostentatious proportions. Even in the rococo age, for Madame du Barry, excess was never enough. She was also mad about jewelry. The comtesse was the only woman at court to wear stones of more than one color at a time. Whether such a fashion was considered daring, outré, or vulgar, she didn't seem to care.

Additionally, Madame du Barry's household was so large that it couldn't all be accommodated at the palace of Versailles, and some of her retinue had to be housed in her *hôtel* (the word for a mansion, not a hostelry) in the rue de l'Orangerie in the town. Her former procurer had a difficult time getting his invoices reimbursed as well. Jean-Baptiste du Barry had an understanding with the king (although

Louis hated the unpleasant reminder of Jeanne's provenance) that the gowns, jewels, and carriages the comte had provided for her and had continued to fund before she became the king's property, so to speak, would be repaid.

In mid-May 1770, the youngest archduchess of Austria, Marie Antoinette, came to France to marry Louis' grandson, the shy and shambling dauphin Louis Auguste. Dinner on the day before the wedding was held at the royal hunting lodge of La Muette on the edge of the Bois de Boulogne. The twenty-seven-year-old *maîtresse en titre* dressed with the utmost care for this special event. Her gown was constructed of silver tissue spun with gold, and embellished all over with rubies. Even her detractors had to admit that she was the most beautiful woman in the room. By comparison, despite her freshness and wholesome prettiness, Marie Antoinette was just a charming little girl.

At first the fourteen-year-old dauphine was intrigued by the vibrant Madame du Barry, inquiring of her *dame d'honneur* the comtesse de Noailles what the beautiful woman's role was at court. Taken aback by the question, the head of the dauphine's household diplomatically informed her that the lady's job was "to amuse the king."

"Then I shall be her rival!" the naive and virginal teenager declared, the euphemism utterly lost on her. Yet as soon as she learned that Madame du Barry was the king's *maîtresse en titre*, and that her origins and background were lowly and rather sordid, she refused to countenance the woman, despite repeated entreaties from her mother, Empress Maria Theresa of Austria, to do what it took to please the king, because the Franco-Austrian alliance hung in the balance.

Insisting to her mother that "it is pathetic to see how weak [the king] is with Madame du Barry, who is the silliest and most impertinent creature imaginable," Marie Antoinette stubbornly refused to compromise her morals by speaking even one word to the king's whore. Her recalcitrance blossomed into an international incident. It mushroomed even further when Austria needed France to turn a blind eye to her cooperation with Prussia and Russia in the invasion and partition of Poland, carving up an innocent commonwealth for their own gain.

However, Louis was disinclined to look the other way while his

granddaughter-in-law publicly snubbed his lover. Pulled in two directions, Marie Antoinette was too naive to understand that she was
being used to promote a plethora of secret agendas. Her mother, pious though she was, stood to gain a substantial amount of territory
if her daughter said a few nice words in public to Madame du Barry.
Louis' daughters, Mesdames, who were always intriguing because
they had nothing else to occupy their hours, had been manipulating
the young dauphine ever since she arrived in France, in the guise of
being her mentors. By virtue of her marriage to the dauphin, Marie
Antoinette was now the highest-ranking woman in the kingdom.
This meant that she would soon cultivate her own coterie of courtiers
and ministers keen to gain her favor, as one day she would be queen.
If Mesdames could use her as their tool to snub du Barry, they might
be able to accomplish the fall of the mistress without soiling their
own hands.

It worked for a while. But finally the Austrian ambassador explained to Marie Antoinette why her mother wished her to speak to
Madame du Barry. With great reluctance, the dauphine conceded,
and after an aborted attempt (interrupted by Madame Adélaïde, the
oldest of Louis' daughters) in July 1771, Marie Antoinette finally
spoke to the comtesse on New Year's Day, 1772. *"Il y a bien du
monde aujourd'hui à Versailles"*—"There are a lot of people at Versailles today," she said. Louis heaved a tremendous sigh of relief.
Madame du Barry was exultant. And the crisis was over.

The comtesse won that round, and she also scored another victory against Marie Antoinette. The duc de Choiseul had been one of
the prime architects of her marriage to the dauphin and the Franco-
Austrian alliance; consequently, Marie Antoinette was deeply indebted to him, and it was in her best interests for him to remain at
the head of the government. But Madame du Barry convinced the
king to dismiss Choiseul based upon a number of issues, not least of
which was his dissemination of scurrilous propaganda against her.
She claimed to be aware of documents that proved the duc was trying
to drag France into a conflict with Britain (and Louis had a natural
reticence to go to war) over the Falkland Islands.

The story goes that du Barry herself dictated Louis' letter to his
cousin the king of Spain (with whom France would have been siding

in the Falklands hostilities), informing him that he had no interest in becoming involved in another military conflict. In truth, if the comtesse participated at all in Louis' letter, she had likely memorized something that had been ghostwritten either by Chon or by Jean du Barry, both of whom were renowned for their sophisticated correspondence. The king's letter was sent to Spain on December 23, 1770, and the following day Louis signed a *lettre de cachet* exiling Choiseul to his country estate of Chanteloup and demanding his resignation of the offices of secretary of state and superintendent of the post office.

By the spring of 1771, Louis was more dependent than ever on Madame du Barry. Without her he felt very much alone. He had dismissed Choiseul and suppressed the Parlements, exiling the magistrates and defanging the assembly. The move was so autocratic that his cousins, the princes of the blood, and several ducs refused to appear at the *lit de justice* where Louis, reclining on a throne covered with a purple cloth embellished with fleurs-de-lis, commanded the new Parlement, formed by his chancellor Maupeou, to follow his orders. The highest-ranking men in the land may have protested the event by absenting themselves, but Madame du Barry was right there to support her lover, and many believed that she was behind the king's political vision.

Hapsburg Austria's ambassador to France, the comte de Mercy-Argenteau, was amazed, writing to his sovereign Maria Theresa, "The authority of the countess is such that nothing like it has ever been seen before."

Mercy wasn't quite right, however. Louis refused to allow du Barry to pressure him into appointing her pal the duc d'Aiguillon as Choiseul's replacement. Six months later, however, he capitulated.

Yet even in exile Choiseul remained popular, entertaining all his old friends. And his sister, the duchesse de Gramont, as one of Marie Antoinette's ladies-in-waiting, remained free to spread her jealous vitriol about the royal favorite. Allegedly, she continued to circulate nasty verses about the comtesse containing lies that were as improbable as they were salacious: that Madame du Barry entertained the grand almoner of France and the papal nuncio at a *lever* "as naked as Venus coming out of the sea"; that she asked another cleric to hold her golden chamber pot while she relieved herself; and that she spanked one of her ladies in the king's presence, which greatly amused him. Those who knew the comtesse would have been aware that such conduct was not in keeping with her personality, but her enemies delighted in repeating these anecdotes, and undoubtedly they have contributed to the lasting image of Madame du Barry as bawdy and irreverent.

What she did have was extraordinary input into the lives of the royal family. Louis asked her to coordinate the respective wedding plans of his two younger grandsons, the comtes de Provence and d'Artois, to a pair of homely sisters from Savoy. The boys' mother was long dead by then, so the selection of flowers, music, and other entertainments was awarded to the comtesse. The king's lover made sure that the receptions were as lavish as could be, a deliberate slap to Marie Antoinette, whose wedding to the comtes' oldest brother the dauphin was the greatest spectacle of its kind in generations.

From 1772 to 1773, Madame du Barry was at her zenith, for all intents and purposes the uncrowned queen of France. Louis could deny her nothing, and the lovers scarcely spent time apart. He was very needy, whether it was for sex or a sympathetic ear. Her own bed was an altar to love surrounded by four columns that supported a baldachin entwined with carved garlands of ivy, myrtle, and roses. The comtesse seemed to be the air the king required in order to breathe, and she became afraid to stray too far from her rooms when he was around, in case he might need her. Except when he requested privacy and wanted her all to himself, she was always surrounded by a lavish train that included a Bengali page boy named Zamor, a gift Louis bestowed upon the comtesse when the youth was eleven years old. Madame du Barry was waited on like a queen, and her rooms were a hive of humanity. Thirteen matching upholstered chairs were set out for those who witnessed her *lever*, or morning toilette, as if she were a member of the royal family. Her makeup table was wheeled to the area of the room where the light was the harshest and most unforgiving, and it was there that she would apply her rouge and complete her morning ablutions.

Supplicants and sycophants from all walks of life, from bankers to ministers, sought her out, parking themselves in her antechamber.

Many curried favor in unusual ways: A merchant launched a new ship bearing the cribbed du Barry motto, *Boutez en avant,* on the prow; the king of Sweden sent her a box of perfumed gloves; and Voltaire, who resided in voluntary exile in Switzerland, wrote a poem thanking the comtesse for the two kisses (one for each cheek) she had sent via a visiting friend. Louis was delighted by all these tributes to his mistress, viewing them as encomiums to himself.

In one of his dispatches to Empress Maria Theresa during the autumn of 1773, Comte Mercy wrote, "King Louis is so completely given up to Madame du Barry that he is becoming more and more isolated from his children who can give him neither consolation nor advice, while he can expect no attachment of fidelity from the bizarre kind of people by whom he is surrounded and who are the friends of Madame du Barry."

Louis celebrated his sixty-third birthday in February 1773. Faced with his own mortality, he began to think about the future of his immortal soul. After her father fell for Madame du Barry, the princesse Louise-Marie, Louis' youngest daughter, had quit Versailles and entered the Carmelite convent at Saint-Denis. As Soeur Thérèse-Augustine she had been praying for the salvation of Louis' soul ever since, and now she encouraged him to remarry. Her candidate was the princesse de Lamballe, a young widow less than a third the king's age. Nevertheless, she was beautiful and devout and would make an excellent queen.

Madame du Barry panicked.

But her sister-in-law, Chon, told her to buck up and dry her tears. She reminded the comtesse that her job was to amuse the king, and that the surest way to lose Louis was to be a Debbie Downer. Speaking of which, the princesse de Lamballe always looked like she was on the verge of tears, and in that respect hardly had the requisite temperament to please a man like Louis. Consequently (according to Chon), there was nothing to worry about!

In fact, there was good news on the horizon. The duc de Richelieu reminded Louis that his great-grandfather had contracted a morganatic marriage with Madame de Maintenon, and suggested that he do the same with du Barry. In a morganatic marriage, the wife would not be queen; nor would she have any rights of a queen, and their children would have no rights of succession, but at least Louis in his waning years could make his peace with God. However, there was one major obstacle to this plan: Guillaume du Barry. The comtesse remained very much married.

As if on cue, the chevalier arrived in Paris to remind his estranged wife of that very fact. Guillaume was handsomely paid to turn around and head back to Toulouse, but it didn't solve the problem of finding a bishop who would be willing to divorce the royal mistress. None of them wanted to be responsible for the fact that it would mean Madame du Barry would be queen, even unofficially, should she ever wed the king.

In addition, it was clear that Louis wasn't going to live forever. He was becoming increasingly frail and tired. No one wanted to get on the wrong side of the future monarchs Louis Auguste and Marie Antoinette by appearing to support the ambitions of the comtesse du Barry.

She co-opted the role of the queen anyway at every opportunity. During the marriage celebration of Louis' youngest grandson, the comte d'Artois, to Princess Marie-Thérèse of Savoy in November 1773, it was the party planner who stole the show from the homely bride and even from the vivacious dauphine. The comtesse had booked the most famous performers of the era for the reception, but everyone was looking at *her*. One wedding guest described Madame du Barry as "shining like the sun in a dress of cloth of gold covered in jewels worth over five million *livres* [an exorbitant sum]. She and King Louis appeared to be entirely absorbed in each other, giving each other loving looks, smiling and making signs, His Majesty occasionally pulling a comic face as if by this extraordinary behavior he wanted to prove that, despite all rumors to the contrary, the comtesse du Barry was still the reigning favorite."

Her ego was usually center stage. At Louveciennes, the château that Louis had bestowed upon the comtesse a few years earlier, and into which she had sunk a fortune of his money, the walls were covered with her portraits. She metaphorically bathed in her own praise—verses to her beauty and generosity. "All that she wants is flattery. She can never have enough," Chon du Barry tattled to her lover, the duc d'Aiguillon. Her own beauty was the central theme even at her lavish parties, where, it was rumored, for the voyeuristic delectation of the king, she would import blond peasant girls to pleasure her page boy Zamor—or so said the Austrian ambassador, Comte Mercy. More than her vanity met Mercy's critical eye. In his view, the comtesse's soirees "were carried to such an indecent pitch of luxury as to insult the poverty of the people."

Madame du Barry was indeed living life to the max, and she never dared show her lover her doubts or fears. As his official mistress, part of her job was to play the court jester, to perennially amuse and soothe the royal temper. She could never permit her energy to flag in Louis' presence or she would risk losing him to any number of potential rivals. After all, given his generosity, as well as his reputation as the handsomest man in France, what wouldn't any woman give to warm the bed of the king, if only for a night, even if he weren't as virile as he once was? But by now there were other rivals as well—the influences of his daughters and that of the Catholic Church, in addition to Louis' own tortured conscience about living in sin with her.

The comtesse was equally superstitious. Fond of reading almanacs and horoscopes, in the beginning of 1774 she read in the *Almanach de Liège* that "a great lady of a certain court will play her last role in the coming April." It says much about du Barry's megalomania that she assumed the prediction applied to her. With a sense of foreboding and dread she purchased as many copies of the almanac as she could and had them burned, figuring that if she destroyed the source, it would therefore destroy the prophecy.

Madame du Barry was present during a Holy Week Mass in 1774 when a firebrand preacher, the Abbé de Beauvais, thundered from the pulpit, "In forty days Nineveh will be destroyed." No doubt she recalled the words of the *Almanach de Liège* and shivered at this double dose of unpleasant prognostication. Louis didn't attend confession over Easter that year, once more choosing his mistress over the clerics. But then again, he hadn't confessed in thirty years, ever since the debacle at Metz in 1744 had resulted in the dismissal of his then–*maîtresse en titre*, the duchesse de Châteauroux. Never again, Louis had vowed.

The lovers spent a good deal of time in each other's company that spring, stealing away to the Petit Trianon on the grounds of Versailles for some privacy. Le Petit Trianon was a cozy little villa that Louis had originally commissioned as a gift for Madame de Pompadour, but anyone who has ever dealt with contractors knows that they never finish anything on time. Pompadour was dead before the Petit Trianon was finished, so Louis had bestowed it on Madame du Barry. It boasted some ingenious mechanical contraptions intended to obviate the need for hovering servants, such as a dining table that could rise, fully laden, from the subterranean kitchen.

Still, Louis begrudgingly acknowledged that he wasn't the stud he once had been, admitting to one of the royal physicians, "I am growing old and it is time I reined in the horses." He received the blunt and sobering reply, "Sire, it is not a question of reining them in. It would be better if they were taken out of harness."

During the last week of April 1774, Louis became ill. He had spent the night of April 26 with Madame du Barry at the Petit Trianon and had insisted on going hunting the following day, even though he hadn't felt well. His condition worsened and the royal surgeon determined, "*C'est à Versailles, Sire, qu'il faut être malade*"—"You must be ill at Versailles, Sire." Louis was conveyed to the palace, and on April 28, the telltale pustules of smallpox were detected. Yet no one had the nerve to tell the king the truth about his condition. In any case, he believed he had contracted the disease when he was eighteen and therefore could not die from it. Unfortunately, the doctors had lied to him when he was a teen. His daughters insisted on nursing him 'round the clock. More important, so did Madame du Barry, whose face was her fortune and who also had never been exposed to the disease. She had nothing to gain and everything to lose by remaining by his bedside.

By May 4, it was clear that this was no Metz. This time Louis was dying, and in order for him to be shriven, he would have to dismiss his mistress. He told the comtesse, who was hovering beside him, "From now on I owe myself to God and to my people. Tomorrow you must leave. Tell [the duc] d'Aiguillon to come and see me at ten o'clock in the morning. You will not be forgotten. Everything that is possible will be done for you."

And so they parted forever. Madame du Barry fainted in the doorway of the king's bedchamber and had to be carried to her rooms, where she wept uncontrollably. She had lived at Versailles for five years. The following day she was bundled into a closed carriage for the duc d'Aiguillon's nearby estate of Rueil. Not two hours after her departure Louis asked to see her, but was told that she had quit the palace. "Where has she gone?" he asked hazily.

"To Rueil, Sire," came the reply.

"What, already?" he said forlornly. Eyewitnesses noticed a large tear running down his cheek. "Gone," he murmured, "as we all must go."

Louis lost much of his powers of speech on May 7, and his public confession was made for him by the Grand Almoner of France, Cardinal de la Roche-Aymon. The cardinal also extracted something else from the dying monarch. He blackmailed the superstitious Louis, insisting that the king sign a *lettre de cachet* exiling his mistress to the abbey of Pont-aux-Dames as a prisoner of state. The cardinal must have warned the king that his soul would not enter the pearly gates of heaven unless his mistress's body entered those of a convent.

At the time Louis promised the comtesse on May 4 that she would be well looked after, he never imagined the conversation he'd have the following day with his Chief Minister, the duc d'Aiguillon. Their secret discussion ultimately resulted in the drafting of the documentation that would ignominiously banish Madame du Barry— something the king had never intended to occur.

Louis died on May 10, 1774, and was scarcely mourned by his people, despite a reign of fifty-nine years. As a corpse the Well-Loved was the All-but-Ignored, and his disease-riddled body was swiftly transported with minimal fanfare to Saint-Denis for burial.

Two days later, on May 12, a pair of gendarmes arrived at Rueil to escort a stunned comtesse du Barry to Pont-aux-Dames. Guilty, presumably, of knowing the late king's state secrets, she had no idea that her lover had consigned her to this chilly fate, and for years assumed that the *lettre de cachet* had been among the first orders of business undertaken by the new king, Louis XVI, and his wife, Marie Antoinette, as there had never been any love lost between them. No one had the heart to tell the comtesse the truth for several years. She remained in the convent until May 1775, but the conditions of her release mandated that she remain at least ten leagues away from both Paris and Versailles. Louis XVI did not permit her to return to her beloved Louveciennes until October 1776. The comtesse maintained the château like a shrine to her late royal lover; it was filled with mementos and memorabilia of their liaison.

For the next several years she lived like a grande dame, entertaining friends from the old regime and playing Lady Bountiful for the villagers of Louveciennes. She was rarely at a loss for lovers, all of whom were married. When the French Revolution erupted, the woman who began her life at the very bottom of the social ladder didn't have to think twice with regard to her allegiances. She was a royalist through and through, and deeply sympathized with—and feared for—the plight of the monarchs, even though she had been at odds with them during her tenure as a royal mistress. Madame du Barry allowed her property to be used as a location for secret royalist meetings, sold some of her jewelry, and made other dubious financial transactions, which are believed to have been deliberately roundabout contributions to the royalist coffers. Everything was watched by then, and the movements of a former royal mistress were particularly suspect. More than once, she risked her life to aid those among whom she had spent most of her adult life, even though many of them had never accepted her as one of their own.

Yet time had healed many old wounds. During the 1780s she became the mistress of the (married) duc de Brissac, the mayor of Paris. Women who had snubbed Madame du Barry at Versailles would visit her at Louveciennes and be surprised by her genuineness. She once asked a dinner guest why she had been so detested at court, and received the reply, "There was no hatred but we all wanted to have your place."

Madame du Barry managed to elude the revolutionaries time and time again, but on September 21, 1793, the Committee of Public Safety issued a warrant for her arrest. She was first imprisoned at St. Pélagie, then transferred on December 4 to the Conciergerie, nicknamed "the vestibule of the scaffold." On December 6, she was brought to trial, although she had also been interrogated a few times during her confinement. She was composed and poised during her trial, even shaving eight years off her age, testifying that she was forty-two. But the verdict was a foregone conclusion, and when she was pronounced guilty on December 7, the comtesse fainted in the dock. Hoping to buy her way out from under the blade of the guillotine, she forestalled her execution for a few hours by telling her guards where she had buried countless treasures on the grounds of Louveciennes. They could dig them up and keep them, she proposed, if they would spare her life.

But she was only deluding herself. It was dusk on the afternoon of December 8 by the time she climbed the steps of the scaffold at the Place de la Révolution. She was hysterical, kicking and fighting to save her life with each consecutive tread. "You are going to hurt me! Oh, please don't hurt me!" she exclaimed as she faced the bloodthirsty rabble, and begged the executioner for "one moment more!" But nothing availed. She was beheaded and her body was dumped along with those of countless other victims of the Revolution in the Cimitière de la Madeleine, the same ignominious location where less than three months earlier the headless corpse of her self-proclaimed rival Marie Antoinette had been unceremoniously tossed. Ironically, Madame du Barry, or most of her, ended up reposing among royalty after all.

CATHERINE THE GREAT
(CATHERINE II)

1729–1796

RULED RUSSIA: 1762–1796

Catherine the Great of Russia was not named Catherine, nor was she from Russia. German-born, blond, and blue-eyed Sophie Friederike Auguste was the daughter of Christian Augustus, the prince of Anhalt-Zerbst, and his wife, Johanna Elisabeth, of the duchy of Holstein-Gottorp.

At the age of fourteen Sophie's second cousin, the orphaned Karl Peter Ulrich, Duke of Holstein-Gottorp, was summoned to Russia by his aunt, the childless empress Elizabeth, who named the boy as her heir. Two years later, on New Year's Day, 1744, Sophie was invited to Moscow. Although the journey was billed as a visit to distant relations, it was really an audition for the role of future empress of Russia.

She passed muster with the empress and began a crash course in the Russian language and religion. On June 28, the fifteen-year-old Sophie converted to Russian Orthodoxy in an elaborate ritual and took a new name: Grand Duchess Ekaterina (Catherine) Alexeyevna. A lavish engagement ceremony to her cousin Peter followed. But the more time the young couple spent together, the clearer it became to Catherine that the real prize was not her future husband but her future realm. Peter was not just immature; he was borderline insane, obsessed with his toy soldiers and military procedures. He especially loved drills and ceremonials, and not only compelled Catherine to march about with a rifle but once court-martialed a rat for insubordination. When the time would come to command actual troops, Peter would panic.

The mismatched teens were wed on August 21, 1745. To the dismay of the empress, Peter evinced no interest in consummating the marriage. In 1746, after recovering from an illness, the eighteen-year-old Grand Duke didn't hop into bed; instead, he erected a puppet theater in his rooms and invited the court to attend performances. Evidently, Peter's issues regarding sex were not only a matter of emotional immaturity or psychological unsoundness. He suffered from phimosis, a condition in which the foreskin cannot be fully retracted over the penis, making intercourse, or even an erection, considerably painful. Catherine, however, became convinced that the greater issue was political, certain that factions at court were deliberately keeping the couple apart.

By 1752, Peter and Catherine had been married for seven years with nothing to show for it. The exasperated empress instructed the young couple's respective minders to find each of the heirs a lover to initiate them into the mysteries of sex. The dynasty had to continue. Eventually, they figured things out on their own as well. On September 20, 1754, Catherine finally bore her first child, a son, Paul. Although there were rumors about the boy's paternity, they were put to rest as Paul grew up to resemble his father both temperamentally and physically. Paul would be Catherine's only legitimate child.

Many at court were already aware that Peter would prove to be a disastrous emperor when the time came. Apart from his psychological issues, his politics were dangerous. His hero was Russia's deadliest enemy, Frederick the Great of Prussia, on account of his natty uniforms. While the empress Elizabeth still reigned, the politically astute Catherine quietly began amassing adherents, assuring that she would have the backing to be a coruler. "I shall either perish or reign," Catherine declared.

Elizabeth died on Christmas Day, 1761, and the thirty-four-year-old Peter immediately proved his unsuitability to rule by chasing his aunt's coffin down the road during the somber funeral procession. He established new laws that were an immediate disaster for both church and state, and made it abundantly clear to Catherine that not only had he no intentions of permitting her to reign beside him, but he was looking for a way to cast her aside and replace her with his mistress. He even ordered her arrest and imprisonment, but, through the mutual cousin charged with enforcing Peter's orders, Catherine managed to get the command circumvented.

With her marriage as well as the state of the empire in the balance, Catherine seized control. On June 28, 1762, the elite guards swore allegiance to her. Peter was deposed and imprisoned. He became ill on July 2, and four days later he died under mysterious circumstances while under the ostensible aegis of the Orlov brothers, one of whom, Grigory, was Catherine's lover at the time.

Catherine was crowned empress on September 22. Throughout her thirty-four-year reign she continued to carry out the reforms begun by the popular Peter the Great, modernizing Russia, making her a player on the world stage, and improving the lot of many of her subjects, although the empire's economy continued to depend upon the labor of serfs.

The empress does deserve the epithet "Great," bestowed by her own nobility in the third year of her reign. The "Catherinian era," as her reign is sometimes called, is considered a golden age for Russia—a time of geographical expansion (adding approximately two hundred thousand square miles to the empire), as well as advancements in education, medicine, the arts, and culture. Catherine supported the radical new smallpox vaccination, built hospitals, and founded a medical college and the first foundling home. In 1785, she took up playwriting, and her efforts were produced at the palace, albeit under a pseudonym. Her personal art collection formed the basis for the renowned Hermitage. Many of the treasures had been purchased in early 1771 at a bargain-basement price from the collection of France's disgraced foreign minister, the duc de Choiseul, the architect (with Madame de Pompadour) of Marie Antoinette's marriage to the dauphin of France, and whose ouster was engineered by Louis XV's last *maîtresse en titre*, Madame du Barry. (For more on Choiseul's intrigues, see the chapter on Mesdames de Pompadour and du Barry.)

The final year of Catherine's reign was devoted to making brilliant marriages for her grandchildren and to the dismemberment of Poland, marking the third time since 1772 that Russia, Prussia, and Austria had conspired to carve her apart. As a consequence of this political wheeling and dealing, Stanislas Poniatowski, Catherine's former lover, whom she had recommended in 1764 for the job of king of Poland, found himself unemployed, the hapless poster boy for the slogan "All's fair in love and war."

Catherine was as renowned for her libido as some of her fellow male sovereigns, such as England's Charles II as well as the first, second, and fourth Georges, and France's Bourbon kings Louis XIV and XV. She insisted that she could not be an effective ruler unless her emotional and physical needs were satisfied.

The empress died from a cerebral stroke on November 6, 1796, at the age of sixty-seven. She was succeeded by her son, Paul, from whom she had been estranged for several years. He had long harbored suspicions that his mother played some role in his father's demise. After her death, Paul discovered documents in a lockbox belonging to the empress that incriminated both her and the Orlov brothers. He also found a paper removing him from the succession to the throne, which he surreptitiously consigned to the flames. He then disinterred his disgraced father's body and saw that it was brought to the Winter Palace, where it lay in state beside Catherine's bier, leaving the impression that their inhabitants had been corulers for decades. On December 5, 1796, the two coffins were entombed alongside each other at the Cathedral of Saints Peter and Paul, the traditional resting place for the Romanov dynasty.

Emperor Paul I ruled for only five years. He was assassinated on March 11, 1801. Coincidentally, one of the murderers was Catherine's last lover, Platon Zubov. Perhaps the most indelible mark Paul left upon Russia was a testament to how much he detested his mother: the law of succession establishing male primogeniture and forbidding any female from assuming the throne.

CATHERINE THE GREAT (CATHERINE II) AND GRIGORY POTEMKIN (1739–1791)

On June 28, 1762, Catherine, wife of Emperor Peter III of Russia, stood on the balcony of the Winter Palace in St. Petersburg and staged a coup d'état, with the support of the three separate regiments of elite guards. Aware that it conveyed the message that she was as powerful and competent as a man (and that her tall figure was shown to best advantage in breeches), she was garbed as they were, having borrowed a Preobrazhensky guard's uniform of red and green. Alongside Catherine stood her seven-year-old son, the archduke Paul. Here indeed was Mother Russia.

A young cavalry officer noticed that Catherine had neglected to affix a sword knot to her saber and gave her his own. She thanked him for his gallantry and asked him his name.

Grigory Aleksandrovich Potemkin.

He was born into the petty nobility in the small city of Chizhova near what at the time was the Polish border, and displayed an early aptitude for languages and theology. At the tender age of eleven, he enrolled in the army, a fairly customary practice for boys of his age and social station. Five years later, in 1755, he was selected for the elite Horse Guards unit. He was one of the first students to enroll at the University of Moscow, and won the school's Gold Medal in 1757. Part of the prize was a trip to St. Petersburg later that year.

There, Potemkin received an introduction to the empress Elizabeth, who, after learning that the eighteen-year-old excelled in Greek and theology, recommended that he be promoted to the rank of corporal. But just one taste of the headiness of the imperial court may have turned Potemkin's head, because he suddenly lost all desire to study and ended up getting kicked out of the university. Although he continued to acquit himself admirably in the guards, Potemkin wasted much of his potential with "drinking, gambling, and promiscuous lovemaking," in the words of his twentieth-century biographer George Soloveytchik.

After handing Catherine his own *dragonne*, or sword knot, during the declaration of her coup, the twenty-two-year-old Potemkin spurred his mount to return to his men. But his horse wouldn't budge, as the steed had been trained to ride knee-to-knee in squadron formation and it thought Catherine's horse was his partner. As he struggled with the bridle, Potemkin had no alternative but to converse with the new empress, and the pair shared a laugh over the situation. It was quite a way to get noticed, and his striking looks—his giant physique and brownish auburn mane of hair crowning a large, proud head—ensured that he wouldn't soon be forgotten. Years later, when he was Catherine's coruler, Potemkin told a friend that he was "thrown into the career of honor, wealth and power—all thanks to a fresh horse."

Potemkin, however, was a fine equestrian; he was also a master of the theatrical gesture. It's entirely possible that the young cavalry officer deliberately let his horse delay the proceedings by not returning to formation so that he could press his serendipitous advantage with the equally charismatic empress.

After her successful coup in June 1762, the empress distinguished Potemkin by promoting him to second lieutenant. The following month, after the death of her husband, Peter, Catherine appointed her handsome guardsman a gentleman of the bedchamber, or *Kammerjunker.* For Potemkin's role in assisting the coup, which seems to have been limited to the loan of a sword knot, he also received a gift of eighteen thousand rubles.

Clever and witty, Potemkin could hold court, even when the court wasn't his. His wicked talent for mimicry was discovered at a celebration following Catherine's coronation, when someone dared him to mimic Grigory Orlov, the empress's favorite. In a high-pitched half-German, half-Russian accent that mispronounced some of the Russian words, he insisted that he didn't do impressions. The room fell silent. It was a spot-on impression of Her Imperial Majesty's voice. Luckily for Potemkin, Catherine burst out laughing.

Whenever he would encounter Catherine in one of the hundreds of corridors of the Winter Palace, he would fall to his knees, kiss her hand, and declare that he was passionately in love with her. Because Potemkin was a gentleman of the bedchamber, it was not unusual for the pair to cross paths, but his amorous genuflections were a rash gesture and would have caused quite a scandal had they been observed, especially since the handsome, burly, and jealous Grigory Orlov had been Catherine's lover for several months. While Catherine and Potemkin may have flirted with each other, she loved Orlov and had no intentions of dumping him. Indeed, Grigory Orlov would remain her consort for another decade. On the other hand, Catherine adored being adored. Not only didn't she try to discourage Potemkin's flamboyant posturing; she flirtatiously accepted it.

Later that year Potemkin was sent to Sweden to inform them of Catherine's coup d'état. On his return to the Russian court, he received another promotion, appointed the assistant to the procurator of the Holy Synod. As the procurator was the administrative judge in religious matters, it was a post designed to appeal to Potemkin's passion for theology.

At some point, Potemkin suffered a serious injury, losing the sight in his left eye. No one, from contemporary authors to modern scholars, can pinpoint the date or the circumstances, although they have been able to debunk the myths that sprang up around the mysterious accident. Potemkin was not in a fight with Grigory Orlov, losing the eye to Orlov's fist, a billiards cue, or during a tennis match. It remains popularly held that the wound, however it was received, was mistreated by a quack physician, which led to Potemkin's blindness.

What is certain is that after becoming disfigured and losing half his sight, Potemkin believed he had lost all of his looks. Being more than moderately vain, he fell into a funk and withdrew from society, mortified about his appearance. Throughout his life he made sure that his portraits were painted from the same angle, so as to conceal the defect.

Potemkin stayed away from court for eighteen months. During this time, Catherine sent him messages through anonymous female friends. Years later she admitted that Countess Bruce, her confidante, and the *éprouveuse* who was reputed to road test the empress's lovers (though not Potemkin) for virility, always informed her that Potemkin still loved her.

When he returned to court, he had a bandage swathed about his head like a pirate's bandanna. Over the next few years, Catherine awarded him a number of political and military appointments in which he invariably distinguished himself, including Guardian of Exotic Peoples, Chamberlain, and Major General of the Cavalry.

In November 1770, Potemkin brought the news of Russia's victory over the Turks to St. Petersburg, remaining in the capital several months and dining with the empress many times before returning to his military duties. He was at the front once again in December 1773, participating in the siege of Silistria, but never remained far from Her Imperial Majesty's thoughts. On December 4 she sent Potemkin a supportive note, confirming that he was surrounding himself with "eager, brave, clever and talented people, and so I request that you should not needlessly expose yourself to danger. On reading this letter, you may ask: why was it written? To this I answer: so that you should have confirmation of how I think about you; for towards you I am always well-disposed."

Potemkin chose to interpret the note as a direct summons from the empress to come to court. He returned to St. Petersburg at the beginning of 1774, and expected to be welcomed with open arms. But when he discovered that her lover Vassilchikov still remained entrenched as the royal favorite, he hied off to the Alexander Nevsky monastery and flung himself into one of his alternate passions—religion—growing a beard and ostentatiously adopting the life of a monk. Evidently, his perpetual wailing at the top of his lungs about his unrequited devotion to the empress kept the brothers awake at night, and they couldn't wait to be rid of him.

When word of Potemkin's antics at the monastery made it back to the palace, Catherine dispatched Countess Bruce to inform him that the empress wished him to return to court. He kept the countess waiting while he shaved and changed into his military uniform. Upon his arrival at Tsarskoe Selo at six p.m. on February 4, he was immediately presented to Catherine. They retired to her private apartments, where they remained alone in conversation for an hour. Clearly, they desired each other. But Potemkin was ballsy: He had conditions. Among them, he demanded an immediate promotion to adjutant-general. Catherine was bored to tears with Alexander Vassilchikov, who was good in bed, but that hadn't been enough for some time. She needed excitement, diversion, and intellectual stimulation. Potemkin represented a challenge. And that in itself was erotic.

At the time, Grigory Potemkin was thirty-four years old, a decade younger than the empress, although she was very much considered a woman in her prime. Catherine was fairly tall, and in her youth she'd had an excellent figure, but in middle age she had taken to wearing full gowns with wide sleeves to disguise her increasing embonpoint. She often smiled, and with her pointed chin it lent her a charming, elfin appearance. Although her hair had been blond when she was a girl, it had darkened to a deep chestnut by the time she was in her mid-teens. She powdered it now, and like all Russian aristocrats rouged her cheeks with doll-like circles of color.

Alexander Vassilchikov was pensioned off within days of Potemkin's return to court, and the "Cyclops," as the Orlovs cruelly called him, became the empress's lover. From the start, it was a combustible romance of two like-minded, tempestuous, gargantuan appetites who could never have too much of anything, whether it was power, glory, or love.

On February 18, 1774, after spending a late night with Potemkin, Catherine wrote him a note, fretting, "I exceeded your patience . . . my watch stopped and the time passed so quickly that an hour seemed like a minute." In the early days of their relationship she wrote, "My darling, what nonsense you talked yesterday. . . . The time I spend with you is so happy. We passed four hours together, boredom vanishes and I don't want to part with you. My dear, my friend, I love you so much: you are so handsome, so clever, so jovial, so witty: when I am with you, I attach no importance to the world. I've never been so happy. . . ." She confided to Potemkin that she wished they had commenced their romance a year and a half earlier instead of wasting valuable time being unhappy.

"My darling friend, I fear you might be angry with me," read another note from Catherine to Potemkin. "If not, all the better. Come quickly to my bedroom and prove it."

Catherine sent her new lover infatuated billets-doux, often several times a day, every day, usually written in Russian and sometimes in French, but always peppered with endearments and pet names. Potemkin was her sweetheart, darling, *toton* (French for a child's toy top), *Giaour* (an ethnic slur to denote an infidel, used by Muslims in Turkey), Muscovite, Cossack, and various diminutives of his Christian name, such as Grisha and Grishenka. Given the vast size of her palaces, her ladies-in-waiting and footmen must have received a tremendous cardio workout. Potemkin always saved Catherine's letters to him, some of which contained written replies on the same pages as his letters to her. He kept them in a scruffy wad tied with string, and sometimes stuffed them inside a pocket of his coat so he could reread them. The empress, however, burned his correspondence.

She would typically send him a note when she awoke along the lines of "My dove, good morning. I wish to know whether you slept well and whether you love me as much as I love you." At the end of the evening, she would send another note that could be as short and sweet as "Night, darling, I'm going to bed."

They tended to communicate through written messages rather than face-to-face conversation, even when they were both in the same palace, the way people might e-mail or text each other today. An example of their daily correspondence follows:

P to C: Dear matushka ["mama" or "little mother," a nickname for the empress], I have just arrived but I am so frozen that I cannot even get my teeth warm. First I want to know how you are feeling. Thank you for the three garments and I kiss your feet.

C to P: I rejoice that you are back, my dear. I am well. To get warm: go to the bath; it has been heated today.

C to P, later in the day: My beauty, my darling, whom nothing resembles, I am full of warmth and tenderness for you and you will have my protection as long as I live. You must be, I guess, even more handsome than ever after the bath.

The couple even shared their intimate medical details, as lovers are wont to do: sleeplessness, diarrhea, and bouts of indigestion.

So desperately in love was the empress with Potemkin that she was willing to abase herself, at least in writing: "For you, one would do the impossible and so I'll be either your humble maid or your lowly servant or both at once." It was all part of her perpetual reassurance of her devotion to him. "I'll never forget you. . . . Darling I love you like my soul," she wrote. But after Potemkin threw another of his too-frequent temper tantrums, she was quick to defend herself. "Fool! I am not ordering you to do anything! Not deserving this coldness, I blame it on our deadly enemy, your spleen!"

Catherine was more passionately in love with Potemkin than with any previous paramour, and his intensity matched her own. They were also fiercely competitive in everything, including which of them loved the other the most. Potemkin was an exceptionally jealous and possessive paramour, requiring continual confirmation of Catherine's affections. He was a man apart, with the chutzpah to demand an inventory of Catherine's previous lovers, accusing her of having fifteen of them.

So on February 21, 1774, Catherine penned her "Sincere Confession," in which she revealed that Potemkin was her fifth paramour, insisting that she was not guilty of debauchery or wantonness, and if she had enjoyed a fulfilling marriage, she never would have felt the urge to stray. As she delineated the details of her first four liaisons in the Sincere Confession, she confided to Potemkin, "the trouble is that my heart is loath to remain even one hour without love."

When she was still Grand Duchess, her first lover, to whom she gave herself "unwillingly" was her chamberlain, Sergei Saltykov. He was twenty-six when the empress Elizabeth all but shoved him into Catherine's bed in 1752, after seven years of a celibate marriage to her husband, Grand Duke Peter. Then twenty-three, she had tried to remain faithful to Peter, but he had no interest in sex (at least with her, despite her beauty), and Russia was desperate for an heir to succeed them. Catherine later admitted that it had been difficult to resist Saltykov. "He was as handsome as the dawn. There was no one to compete with him in that, not at the Imperial Court, and still less at ours [the separate court that she and Peter kept]."

At the age of twenty-six, and a new mom for the first time, in 1755 Catherine captivated the virginal twenty-two-year-old secretary to the British ambassador. Stanislas Poniatowski, a war hero and the son of a Polish count, arrived in the nick of time, because Catherine had heard reports that not only had Saltykov indiscreetly discussed their love affair at the courts of Sweden and Dresden, but that he was flirting with other women. Poniatowski described Catherine at the time of their meeting.

". . . She was at that peak of beauty which most beautiful women experience. She was of a vivid coloring, with dark hair and a dazzlingly white complexion, large, slightly prominent and very expressive blue eyes, very long dark eyelashes, a Grecian nose, a mouth which seemed to invite kisses, perfect hands and arms, and a narrow waist. On the tall side, she moved with extreme agility yet at the same time with great nobility. She had a pleasant voice and a laugh as merry as her disposition."

Poniatowski also noticed Catherine's ability to turn on a dime from behaving playfully to becoming utterly focused on a serious matter. He found her fearless, affectionate, but a genius at pinpointing a person's weak spot. By the summer of 1756, Catherine and Poniatowski were both physically and emotionally involved. It was a sentimental attachment worthy of the Baroque period. Catherine tried to secure him a diplomatic posting that would keep him in Russia more often, so she sent him to King Augustus III of Poland with a letter of introduction. In December 1756, Poniatowski returned to Russia as the official representative of the Polish king and resumed relations with Catherine, fathering her second child, Anna Petrovna, born on November 29, 1757. The little girl never made it to her second birthday, dying on March 9, 1759.

Poniatowski was recalled to Poland in 1758. After the death of Augustus in 1763, Catherine, by then empress of Russia, made it extremely clear that she wanted Stanislas Poniatowski to be elected the next king of Poland. She got her wish in 1764.

Eleven days before Catherine's thirty-third birthday she gave birth to a son by the third lover mentioned in her Sincere Confession. This was the handsomest of the five strapping Orlov brothers, the burly and formidable Lieutenant Grigory Orlov of the elite Izmailovsky Guards. Grigory Orlov was Catherine's lover for more than eleven years, and her paramour at the time she seized control of the throne.

Lover number four was the twenty-eight-year-old Alexander Vassilchikov, who became Catherine's lover "in despair," according to the Sincere Confession. She made him a gentleman of the bedchamber on August 1, 1772. Dark, of average height, polite and unprepossessing, he seemed an unlikely candidate to topple the formidable Orlov, particularly after so many years. But on the day that Orlov left Tsarskoe Selo (the "Tsars Village" where the Catherine Palace and the Alexander Palace were situated, located some fifteen miles south of St. Petersburg), en route to a peace congress, she was reliably informed that he had been having affairs with other women. Still, after a dozen years, Catherine didn't relinquish her passion for the duplicitous Orlov so easily. As late as June 1772, she was still describing him as "without exaggeration, the most handsome man of his time." Yet as Vassilchikov notched a number of court appointments, the usual indication that an imperial paramour was in the ascendant, Orlov was finally, although generously, pensioned off.

And so, with these bold, daring, and vulnerable strokes of the pen, Potemkin was fully apprised of the empress's sexual history. But she advised him that the way for a lover to keep her was to demonstrate as much friendship as affection, to continue to love her, and to tell the truth.

New lovers often try to spend as many hours as possible together, but in the case of Catherine and Potemkin, their schedules didn't mesh. Potemkin was a night owl, often gambling at faro until the wee hours of the morning and rising late. Although she was a hedonist, Catherine's strict German discipline never deserted her; she was usually in bed by ten or ten thirty and up at seven every morning, ready to tackle the business of the empire. As a result, she and Potemkin rarely spent the night together, even at the start of their relationship. Although Catherine was a widowed autocrat and Potemkin a bachelor, it was still considered unseemly for her to be seen in his rooms, or he in hers. And the empress didn't like sneaking around like an illicit lover to tryst with him.

She also feared that her own feelings for Potemkin were so intense that they weren't reciprocated with the same ardor. Only five days after the Sincere Confession, it seemed as though he was merely toying with her affections after she had completely bared her soul to him. On February 26, she wrote to him, "As soon as I had gone to bed and the servants had withdrawn, I got up again, dressed and went to the doors in the library to wait for you, and there I stood for two hours in a draught; and not until it was nearly midnight did I return out of sadness to lie down in bed where, thanks to you, I spent the fifth sleepless night."

One can't help feeling sorry for Catherine, one of the most powerful women in the history of the world, with her hair about her shoulders, standing in her slippers, hidden in the shadows, holding her breath and anxiously waiting for the lover who never came.

Was Potemkin holding sex for ransom? Thirty-six hours later he asked to be made adjutant-general and Catherine's personal aide-de-camp, having written, "I remain unmotivated by envy toward those who, while younger than I, have nevertheless received more signs of imperial favor than I. . . ." He couldn't bear to think that she would deem him less worthy than others for the post. Although Potemkin had distinguished himself in battle, the strong emotions he inspired in people were not always positive. But the empress was so impressed by his bluntness that she had the paperwork drawn up right away, and Potemkin was confirmed as adjutant-general on March 1.

One of the keys to their romance was that Potemkin made Catherine laugh, and he could also keep her entertained for hours. For a woman who claimed that her previous lover had bored her, she was ecstatic that Potemkin had utterly bewitched her. And she admitted to him, "In order for me to make sense, when you are with me, I have to close my eyes or else I might really say what I have always found laughable: 'that my gaze is captivated by you.' An expression which I used to think was stupid, improbable and unnatural . . ." She went on to add that she was afraid *he* would become bored with *her*.

Back in March, impressed by his sex appeal, she had written to him, "I don't wonder that there are so many women attributed to you. It seems to me that you are not an ordinary person and you differ from everyone else in everything."

On her own admission, one of the smartest minds of the day lost its focus in his presence. ". . . I have given strict orders to the whole of my body, down to the last hair to stop showing you the smallest sign of love. I have locked up my love in my heart under ten locks, it is suffocating there and I think it might explode. Think about it, you are a reasonable man, is it possible to talk more nonsense in a few lines? A river of absurdities flows from my head, I do not understand how you can bear a woman with such incoherent thoughts. Oh, Monsieur Potemkin! What a trick have you played to unbalance a mind, previously thought to be one of the best in Europe. . . ."

Life was never dull with Grigory Potemkin around. He took prerogatives with the empress that no one had ever dared before, appearing in her rooms at all hours unannounced and unsummoned. Sometimes he would be the wittiest member of the party; at other times he would remain silent, in one of his sulks, barely acknowledging Catherine's presence. His appearance, when he had no need to be anywhere, was that of mountain man–meets-dandy: barefoot, with a shaggy fur cloak thrown over his enormous frame, and a pink sash tied about his head like a bandanna. Seeing him thus attired, Catherine nicknamed him *bogatyr*, the knightly Slavic hero from the mythology of Rus. And if it was too warm for the fur pelts, Potemkin would wear a dressing gown, open at the chest, and a pink shawl. He would settle his bulk on the Turkish divan he had placed in Catherine's salon, and watch her work while he munched on raw radishes or chewed his fingernails "with frenzy," a habit that gave rise to yet another one of Catherine's sobriquets: "The greatest nail biter in the Russian Empire."

"Calmness for you is a state your soul cannot bear," she once observed. If not his nails, he gnawed on whatever was at hand, prompting an affectionate warning from her that she offered as part of a list of rules to abide by in order for harmony and informality to be achieved. Rule number three stated, "You are requested to be cheerful, without however destroying, breaking or biting anything."

Potemkin's uncouth behavior scandalized the courtiers, who took pains to emulate their counterparts at the sophisticated court of Versailles. He was a slob who marked his territory in Catherine's domain by leaving his personal possessions strewn about her rooms—which she took pride in keeping neat and orderly. His slovenliness engendered another imperial scolding: "Please do not throw your handkerchiefs all over the shop in your Turkish fashion. Many thanks for your visit and I love you a lot."

Their apartments were connected by a secret spiral staircase covered in green carpeting, a lovers' color perhaps, the same shade as the carpet in the corridor connecting Madame de Pompadour's suite to Louis XV's royal apartments. It was so cold in the palace that Potemkin once caught a chill. "Sorry you're sick. It is a good lesson for you: don't go barefoot on staircases. If you want to get rid of it, take a little tobacco," nurse Catherine chided affectionately. Nevertheless, Potemkin would often pop up to visit her, munching on one of the several raw fruits or vegetables—apples, turnips, radishes, and even garlic—that he kept at his bedside, yet another of his eccentricities. His contemporaries condemned his simple gustatory tastes as "truly barbaric and Muscovite."

But Catherine took it in stride. Potemkin was one of a kind, and she adored him all the more for it. The pair of them also shared a thirst for glory, and were as well matched in that regard as Louis XIV had been with Athénaïs de Montespan. Catherine and Potemkin were both savvy political animals as well. Their romance was based on laughter, sex, intelligence, and power, in an ever-shifting order of importance.

Sir Robert Gunning, the British envoy, damned the empress's new man with faint praise. "His figure is gigantic and disproportioned, and his countenance is far from engaging. From the character I have had of him he appears to have a great knowledge of mankind, and more of the discriminating faculty than his countrymen in general possess, and as much address for intrigue and suppleness in his station as any of them; and though the profligacy of his manner is notorious, he is the only one who has formed connections with the clergy. . . ."

Within weeks of becoming Catherine's lover, Potemkin collected promotions like blooms in a bouquet. In addition to the adjutant-general post on March 1, on the fifteenth of the month he was made lieutenant-general of the Preobrazhensky Guards, a position formerly held by Grigory Orlov. Catherine herself was the colonel of the regiment. And at the end of March, he was named Governor General of New Russia, the vast expanse to the south bordered by the Crimea and the Ottoman Empire.

Yet in April, less than two months into their romance, this passionate letter to Potemkin reflects Catherine's anxiety regarding his level of commitment to her.

Fear not that one can free oneself from your webs, but from hour to hour one becomes more entangled. But should you yourself somehow lessen my passion, you would make me unhappy. And even then I would probably not stop loving you. But I pray God that I might die at that hour when it seems to me that you are not the same towards me as you have deigned to be these seven weeks! Only whatever happens, I need to think that you love me and the slightest doubt about this troubles me cruelly and makes me unspeakably sad.

On another occasion the empress rather desperately wrote to her lover, "How awful it is for someone with a mind to lose it! I want you to love me. I want to appear lovable to you. But I only show you madness and extreme weakness. Oh, how awful it is to love extraordinarily. You know, it's an illness . . . only I don't send for an apothecary and neither do I write long letters. If you like, I'll summarize this page for you in three words . . . here it is—I love you."

Even autocrats get moonstruck.

Catherine feared that such discombobulation made her feel like a "headless chicken," incapable of attending to affairs of state.

On April 21, 1774, Catherine's forty-fifth birthday, Potemkin was given a gift of fifty thousand rubles and received the Order of St. Alexander Nevsky from the empress's former paramour the king of Poland, Stanislas Poniatowski. But the honoree must have said something unpleasant during the ceremony, because the following day Catherine scolded him for reproaching her in public, writing to Potemkin, "We ask that in future you don't humiliate us, but that you cover our vices and mistakes with a stole [the vestment a priest places over a penitent's head when he grants them absolution] and don't parade them in front of people, for that cannot be pleasant for us. And anyway it's inappropriate to treat a friend, let alone your w[ife], like that. Now there's a reprimand for you, though a most affectionate one."

Catherine's reference to herself as Potemkin's wife is what immediately catches one's attention. By this stage in their relationship, he was already boasting that he would kill any successor as the empress's favorite, and although each would eventually take other lovers, Potemkin was never supplanted as her primary confidant and counselor. Catherine was also complaining in the manner of neglected wives, accusing Potemkin of being sleepy when she came to him, peeved that he visited her only "on forays," saying he couldn't spend much time with her because he was dashing off elsewhere on business. Catherine hinted that Grigory Orlov had behaved the same way.

Perhaps she had an emotional pattern of choosing strong men who would master her, and then resenting them for it, both as the sovereign and as the tenderhearted woman beneath the autocrat's protective carapace who had vulnerably exposed herself by falling so hard for them and letting them know just how dependent she was upon their love and esteem.

During the spring of 1774, Catherine consulted Potemkin on matters large and small, from affairs of state to spelling and grammatical errors in her documents, both personal and official. "If there are no mistakes, please return the letter and I will seal it. If there are some, kindly correct them. If you want to make any changes, write them out. . . . Either the ukase [a proclamation made by a Russian emperor] and the letter are perfectly clear, or else I am stupid today."

On May 5, Potemkin became a member of Catherine's council. Later in the month he was made vice president of the College of War and awarded the rank of General in Chief, a promotion that particularly offended Russia's top military brass.

And then, on June 8, 1774, came an event that historians continue to dispute; even the couple's contemporaries could not agree on what happened. That evening, Potemkin and Catherine attended a dinner at the Summer Palace in St. Petersburg. At midnight, accompanied only by her loyal maid, Catherine slipped away. Wearing a hooded cloak, she clambered into an unmarked carriage that clattered away for the jetty on the Little Nevka. From there she was rowed across the river and climbed into another coach that brought her to the Church of St. Sampson, where Potemkin was already waiting for her. He was wearing his General in Chief uniform: a red-collared green coat with gold lace trim and braid, red breeches, a regimental sword, and a hat bordered in gold trim and festooned with white plumes. Catherine had not even changed clothes for the ceremony. She'd spent the entire day in her green regimental gown trimmed in gold lace, which resembled a ladies' riding habit.

Inside the church, in addition to the unidentified priest, were two groomsmen. Potemkin's nephew Alexander Samoilov stood up for him; Catherine's chamberlain, Yevgraf Alexandrovich Chertkov, was her witness. In accordance with Russian Orthodox tradition, two crowns were held over the heads of the bridal couple. It was a lengthy ceremony, after which the wedding certificates were signed and given to the two witnesses, both of whom were sworn to secrecy.

This is the story that has passed into legend. But the reputed certificates have never come to light. And there are other versions of the "secret marriage," one of which alleges that the pair wed in Moscow in 1775. Another claims the ceremony took place in St. Petersburg in 1784 or 1791 (long after their sexual relationship had ended). Catherine's biographer Virginia Rounding doubts the veracity of a legal union, yet believes the June 8 rite may have been more of a commitment ceremony. Meanwhile, Simon Sebag Montefiore, who has written the definitive twenty-first-century biography of Potemkin, allows for the probability of a fully legitimate wedding ceremony that night and gives the legend credence.

The empress's most recent biographer, Robert K. Massie, leaves the door open for the possibility that a royal wedding did indeed occur, pointing out that Catherine never addressed any of her other lovers as "husband," nor ever referred to herself as their "wife." Only Potemkin received that distinction. Additonally, the empress allowed him vast viceregal power, even long after their sexual liaison ended—and she was not a woman who relinquished power lightly. The existence of a marriage provides the best explanation for the unique authority Potemkin wielded in the empire and the special place he retained in her heart and esteem.

What can be confirmed regarding their putative royal wedding are the dates and content of the court records that show Catherine leaving the palace on the night of June 8. The certificate that was placed in the hands of Chamberlain Chertkov passed into obscurity, but the document given to Potemkin's nephew was passed down through several generations. However, Montefiore provides conflicting information as to its denouement, saying at one point that it was buried with one of Potemkin's male descendants, but later mentioning that the certificate was tossed into the Black Sea by one of his grandnieces. Under the assumption that Potemkin and Catherine were indeed married on June 8, 1774, Montefiore does justify the suppression of the documents, stating that no one would have wanted them to come to light during the reign of Paul I, Catherine's son (who detested both his mother and Potemkin), nor during the militaristic reigns of the two subsequent tsars. And the Victorian-era Russians were embarrassed about Catherine's sex life.

Another thing that is certain is that Catherine and Potemkin behaved both publicly and privately like a married couple. They even bickered like spouses—and indeed referred to each other in their letters as husband and wife. These terms of endearment could have been statements of fact, or merely a reflection of the way the lovers perceived their relationship. If Potemkin and Catherine had indeed married (and at least in her heart she felt that way), it makes his insecurity more difficult to comprehend. However, in a misogynistic society like imperial Russia, one has to wonder why a female autocrat would legally remarry when her husband, especially one as gifted and capable as Potemkin, might be expected to seize the reins of power from her hands. Why would she risk losing the scepter? On the other hand, Potemkin, for all his eccentricities, was exceptionally devout and may have wanted to legalize their liaison. Catherine was so passionately in love with him that she was incapable of denying him anything. Perhaps the *secret* marriage was the compromise.

The empress refers to Potemkin as her husband in at least twenty-two surviving letters, and calls him her "lord" or "master" in many others. She also treated several of his relatives as generously if they were her own kin. That is still no proof of a legal marriage ceremony, but a letter from Catherine to Potemkin written most likely in early 1776 provides the strongest evidence in favor of a genuine religious wedding.

> My Lord and *Cher Epoux* [French for "dear spouse"] . . . Why do you prefer to believe your unhealthy imagination rather than the real facts, all of which confirm the words of your wife. Was she not attached to you two years ago by holy ties? I love you and I am bound to you by all possible ties. Just compare, were my acts more meaningful two years ago than they are now?

Foreign ambassadors suspected something, but didn't mention the word "marriage" in their written dispatches. Many years later, in December 1788, the French ambassador, the comte de Ségur, informed Versailles that Potemkin "takes advantage of . . . certain sacred and inviolable rights . . . The singular basis of these rights is a great mystery which is *known only to four* people in Russia; a lucky chance enabled me to discover it and when I have thoroughly sounded it, I shall, on the first occasion . . . inform the King." By October of the following year, Louis XVI was jokingly referring to the empress of Russia as "Madame Potemkin."

The British envoy, Lord Keith, as well as the Holy Roman Emperor (Joseph II, brother of Marie Antoinette) also found out what the French had been surmising.

And perhaps, although it might dilute her power, the more Catherine came to know Potemkin, the easier it was to understand that there would be no one better to rule the vast empire with her, and she really did not lose much in marrying him as long as the union remained a secret.

Unfortunately there may be some truth to Lao Tzu's adage "The flame that burns twice as bright lasts half as long." By the middle of 1775, only a year after their alleged marriage, Catherine and Potemkin's romance was on the rocks.

As early as the spring, it was rumored that Potemkin was pleading illness to avoid Catherine's bed. He was becoming even more restless than usual. Catherine complained that she wasn't able to see him often enough. "This is really too much! Even at nine o'clock I cannot find you alone. I came to your apartment and found a crowd of people who were walking about, coughing, and making a lot of noise. Yet I had come solely to tell you that I love you excessively." On another occasion she wrote, "It is a hundred years since I saw you. I do not care what you do, but please arrange that there should be nobody with you when I come. . . ."

The empress was also wearying of Potemkin's volatility. What had once seemed exciting was now draining. The pair of them were high-maintenance—"human furnaces," to quote Montefiore—and required massive amounts of stoking and stroking in their desires for affection, glory, power, and extravagance. Their gargantuan egos and tempestuous personalities were too similar for them to remain compatible in the long run.

Upon the death of his sister in May, Potemkin became the legal guardian of his five unmarried nieces. When they came to court, Catherine appointed the oldest two girls imperial maids of honor. All five were hailed as great beauties. Uncle Grigory thought so, too. Eventually, three of them would become his lovers, although it was rumored that he had seduced all five. The court was scandalized, and Potemkin's mother, Darya, wrote several letters to him, to the effect that sleeping with his late sister's children was immoral. Potemkin burned the correspondence. The empress, however, took a far more liberal view. Uncle-niece liaisons were fairly common in royal circles, (the Spanish and Austrian Hapsburgs and the Wittelsbachs of Bavaria were rife with them; Catherine and her own uncle had flirted, petted, and contemplated marriage before she was summoned to Russia), and Potemkin's nieces, who were all "of age" at the time they graced his bed, were passionately, sexually in love with him.

Also in the spring of 1775, Catherine hired a new secretary, a handsome Ukranian named Peter Zavadovsky. Around the end of July, he began regularly dining at the empress's table and accompanying her on short excursions into the countryside. After the couple returned to the capital, along with Potemkin they formed a frequent troika at dinner and at work. Both he and Potemkin had helped her implement her system of education reform. On November 26, Catherine awarded Zavadovsky the Cross of St. George, fourth class.

Even after Zavadovsky had piqued Catherine's sexual interest, Potemkin could be found weeping in her arms, desperate to find a way to make their relationship work. They would settle arguments with dialogue letters. Potemkin would write to the empress and she would comment on the same letter, referring in the right margin to specific phrases in his original correspondence. She would then return his letter to him with her notations on it.

Their daily pattern had become one of violent arguments, followed by tearful reconciliations. They needed to figure out how to salvage what was working in their relationship and jettison what was tearing their insides out. As the couple struggled to decide whether to stay together or separate, Catherine, wounded by Potemkin's increasing callousness to her ("I believe that you love me in spite of the fact that often there is no trace of love in your words" and "I am not evil and not angry with you"), ultimately conceded, "The essence of our disagreement is always the question of power and never that of love."

It's a testament to Catherine's clear-sightedness, despite her passion for and frustration with Potemkin, that she was able to cede him so much power and authority, and play to his strengths without compromising her status as empress, even when they were no longer each other's primary sexual partners. On January 1, 1776, he received command of the Petersburg troop division, and his mother was made a lady-in-waiting. But Her Imperial Majesty's bounty didn't end there. The following day Peter Zavadovsky was made adjutant-general, the code, as Potemkin himself knew so well, that the empress's private secretary had been promoted to lover.

On March 21, 1776, Potemkin was given permission to use the title Prince of the Holy Roman Empire, which Catherine had requested through her ambassador in Vienna. She also gave him sixteen thousand serfs. Denmark awarded him the Order of the White Elephant. And on April 2, Prince Henry of Prussia invested Potemkin with the Order of the Black Eagle.

Unfortunately, the promotion, along with the collection of ribbons and medals, were also a form of adieu. Potemkin realized that Zavadovsky had superseded him in Catherine's bed, and she was shoving him out the door with the equivalent of a golden parachute. However, he was also able to recognize that the nature of his relationship with the empress was such that it could survive and even thrive without the sexual element, and that it could still be possible to ensure his own favoritism even if Catherine had another lover. In fact, the new dynamic would allow him some freedom from what he had privately begun to admit was a suffocating liaison. With a standby stud in the wings, Potemkin wouldn't feel as though he always needed to be there for Catherine.

Her Imperial Majesty, too, needed the respite from Potemkin's volatile mood swings, and the time and energy she devoted to her all-consuming passion for him made it inconvenient to running an empire. Although Catherine replaced Potemkin with a less demanding but emotionally fulfilling paramour, Zavadovsky was far from ideal. Evidently, he was prone to premature ejaculation. Yet Catherine was understanding about his little problem, remarking, "You are Vesuvius itself. [W]hen you least expect it an eruption appears," then assuring him, "but no, never mind, I shall extinguish them with caresses."

Zavadovsky received no key political appointments as a mark of the empress's favor. She had no need to bestow them when Potemkin held every important post and remained as her chief adviser. By the spring of 1777, the young secretary was near collapse. It was all too much for him. Catherine always set the timetable for their assignations. He hated the scrutiny of his private life. He was a natural administrator, not a courtier, and because his French wasn't strong enough to sustain social conversation, he never fit in. He, too, had his jealous sulks, primarily because Potemkin was around all the time. The prince was always bursting in on Catherine and her boy toy of the year, a flamboyant sight in his fur wraps, pink shawls, and bandannas. And the empress always expected her young men to pay court to Potemkin. None of them could match the giant man's equally towering wit or charisma, and all of them felt inadequate by comparison, despite Catherine's protestations of affection for them.

By her own admission, Catherine could not live without love for a moment. At the beginning of each new affair, she expected it to last forever. And when she and Zavadovsky first became paramours, she assured him, "Petrusa dear, all will pass, except my passion for you." But the Zavadovsky experiment barely lasted a year. Catherine told her secretary-lover that perhaps it was best if they took a break. Potemkin, however, was convinced that the dynamic of a ménage à trois of sorts, though not in the literal sexual sense, was still the best way to preserve his relationship with the empress. It was just a matter of finding the right other man. This third wheel could not be a threat to Potemkin's political sovereignty, but he had to please the empress. Some of these studs came from the prince's own stable, in his employ as adjutants, and had therefore already been vetted, at least for character.

From then on, with her acquiescence, Potemkin approved each of Catherine's lovers to ensure their compatibility with the empress and their inability to displace him in her affections. When Her Imperial Majesty was between relationships, Potemkin resumed his role as her lover.

After Zavadovsky, Catherine spent a year (May 1777 to May 1778) in the arms of Semyon Zorich, a swarthy, curly-haired, thirty-one-year-old major of the hussars. But the rest of 1778 belonged to Ivan Rimsky-Korsakov, although he barely made it to December.

Rimsky-Korsakov, whom both Catherine and Potemkin nicknamed "the child," cheated on the empress, first with her confidante Countess Bruce (who lost her job over her foolish indiscretion), and then with another lady of the court. Both women left their husbands for him.

The empress was a magnanimous lover and always pensioned off her paramours with real estate, thousands of serfs, and lovely parting gifts of china and silver, tableware and linens. But each time one of her affairs ended, Catherine, who had expected it to last until the end of time, became despondent, and very little state business was accomplished for a few weeks until she got over it.

Catherine's next lover was Alexander Lanskoy, who warmed the empress's bed from 1780 to 1784. When the royal romance began, Lanskoy was a twenty-two-year-old officer of the Horse Guards, eager to learn, and happy to accept Potemkin's primacy and position at court. Lanskoy would die on June 25, 1784, probably from diphtheria, although it was rumored that Potemkin had poisoned him. Catherine was brokenhearted at his passing.

But in the early 1780s, with Catherine happily in love with Lanskoy, she and Potemkin could focus on politics. On December 14, 1782, Catherine secretly instructed Potemkin to annex the Crimea, in order to prevent the Turkish from doing so. Soon after he had risen to favor, Potemkin had become Governor General of New Russia, Azov, Saratov, Astrakhan, and the Caucasus. In 1778, Catherine approved his plan for a port on the Black Sea to be called Kherson. Potemkin supervised every detail of building the town, including designing the houses. The following year he gave the order to found Nikolaev, another city on the Black Sea, named for Saint Nicholas, the patron saint of seafarers.

Potemkin had nicknamed the Crimea "the wart on the end of Catherine's nose," but it became his own paradise, a lush, cosmopolitan peninsula. He or she who owned it controlled the trade routes across the Black Sea. Potemkin returned to the Black Sea as a stealthy conqueror in 1783. On May 11, he wrote to Catherine from the city of Kherson to say that he had found everything in disarray but was sorting it out. Wanting the issue resolved as soon as possible, the empress replied, most likely in early June, "Not only do I often think of you, but I also regret and often grieve over the fact that you are there and not here, for without you I feel as though I'm missing a limb. I beg you in every way: do not delay the occupation of the Crimea."

The annexation was completed in July. To thank him, Catherine created Potemkin Prince of Tauris, or Taurida. He immediately began building cities, towns, and roads to plan for the empress's eventual journey to her new territory.

By the late 1770s, and most definitely after he had annexed the Crimea in Catherine's name, Grigory Potemkin, Serenissimus (His Serene Highness), was the de facto coruler of the Russian Empire, a domain so vast that it needed rulers in both the east and west. Potemkin had the rare gift of being able to manage in microcosm, like running the College of War, and he also had the talents to govern in macrocosm—a skilled viceroy for the steppes of the south. His demesne comprised all new territories acquired in the name of the empire between 1774 and 1783, from the River Bug in the west to the Caspian Sea in the east; and from the Caucasus and the Volga River across most of Ukraine, almost as far as Kiev. It was unique for a Russian emperor to delegate so much power to a consort, or to any individual, but Catherine's relationship with Potemkin was matchless.

Her journey to the Crimea in 1787, organized by Potemkin, took several days, covering four thousand miles. The imperial convoy consisted of 14 huge coaches mounted on runners, and 124 sleighs, with 40 sleighs in reserve. Catherine's conveyance was a miniature dacha, or vacation home, on runners. It consisted of three rooms—a library, bedroom, and drawing room—all sumptuously decorated. Six windows provided panoramic views of the scenery.

They departed Kiev in opulent galleys and sailed for part of the way, a flotilla of eighty boats carrying three thousand troops, baggage, and munitions, in addition to the empress's vast entourage of laundresses, cooks, maids, valets, doctors, apothecaries, and even dishwashers and silver polishers. It was a cross between a progress of Elizabeth I and a Cleopatran journey down the Nile.

All along the riverbanks of the Dnieper the village houses were bedecked with floral garlands and triumphal arches, which may be the origin of the "Potemkin villages." The phrase, coined by a German historian, Georg von Helbig, refers to a ruse he alleged was concocted by the prince to convince Catherine that he had built a vast number of villages and towns in the south, when in fact she was merely riding past a series of painted facades outside of which thousands of peasants appeared to bustle about their daily duties. Von Helbig claimed that all of the pasteboard facades as well as thousands of peasants, livestock, and conveyances were silently transported numerous times in the dead of night, and at every new location the facades were reconstructed at breakneck speed so that Catherine saw the same town over and over again, although each time she was told it was a new place. The assertion defies common sense on a variety of levels. For one thing, the empress wasn't stupid. She'd notice. And if she didn't, some of the hundreds of others in her entourage would. For another, it would have been nigh impossible to relocate everything on dirt roads in the middle of the night, in addition to rebuilding all of it. Additionally, there is no evidence of orders given by Potemkin to create false villages or towns. The locations and edifices visited and observed by Catherine's entourage were authentic and were genuinely inhabited.

While two cities certainly did whitewash their poverty by constructing some spanking-clean false houses (a trick still being tried in the blighted Bronx during the 1970s), the Prince de Ligne, the Austrian field marshal who, along with his boss, Emperor Joseph II, did some sightseeing on his own during the empress's visit to the south, found no evidence of fraud. However, the lies about "Potemkin villages" were evidently spread immediately, because the prince refuted these allegations, based on his eyewitness experience. "Already the ridiculous story has been circulated that pasteboard villages were painted on our roads . . . that the ships and guns were painted, the cavalry horseless. . . . Even those among the Russians . . . vexed at not being with us, will pretend we have been deceived."

One of those who was so vexed was Catherine's son, Paul. But, groundless as it was, von Helbig's mud stuck. Potemkin's detractors, including Paul, were even unwilling to believe that there was water in the Crimea. Paul preferred the sham to stand and the lies to be perpetuated even after he had been proven wrong.

Not only were the vessels not oil paintings, but by 1787, Potemkin had created a formidable navy, including twenty-four ships of the line, warships carrying over forty cannon apiece. He became known as the father of the Black Sea Fleet. Another remarkable feat of the prince's was his ability to attract peasants, tradesmen, and professionals to populate his new Crimean cities by offering incentives, such as no taxes for ten years.

When Potemkin's enormous achievements in the Crimea were disbelieved, or worse, written about as shams or deceptions, he spiraled into one of his depressions, maniacally chewing his nails. During the last years of his life he lived and governed from Jassy in Dacia, Moldavia (modern-day Bucharest), enjoying a sybaritic lifestyle with a series of beautiful young mistresses.

In 1785, the year after imperial paramour Alexander Lanskoy's death, while Potemkin was in the Crimea planning for her visit, Catherine took another lover, Count Alexander Matreievech Dmitriyev-Mamonov. She nicknamed the twenty-six-year-old athletic guardsman "Monsieur Redcoat." But the empress dismissed him in 1789 when he cheated on her, impregnating one of her ladies-in-waiting. Catherine gave Mamonov and his fertile girlfriend a generous gift and even presided at their wedding.

Later that year, at the age of sixty, Catherine took a new bedfellow, a twenty-two-year-old handsome and swarthy boy toy named Platon Zubov, although the empress called him "Blackie" because of his dark complexion. Zubov was very ambitious, yet he seemed to satisfy Catherine, which kept Potemkin, now at Jassy, at least cautiously pleased. But the prince was anxious to come to St. Petersburg in order to personally check out Zubov, and to gauge the present status of his own influence with the empress.

Potemkin arrived in the capital around the end of February 1791, and Catherine pronounced him "more handsome, more lovable, wittier, more brilliant than ever, and in the happiest mood possible." But the couple argued over Prussian foreign policy, and Potemkin's visit was fraught with much door slamming and tears. On his last night in the capital Potemkin dined with his niece Tatiana. He mentioned during the meal that he was certain he would die soon. Months earlier he had remarked with equal certainty that the sixty-two-year-old empress would outlive him.

Potemkin returned to Jassy, falling ill that August 13. He convalesced by composing hymns, and was moved from the palace to a country house. The arrival of Catherine's letters both cheered him and released a flood of nostalgia. Potemkin wept bitterly, knowing that they would never see each other again. But he continued to correspond with the empress, writing on September 21, "My paroxysms continue for a third day. I've lost all strength and don't know what the end will be." Six days later he told Catherine, "Beloved matushka, my not seeing you makes it even harder for me to live." He turned fifty-two on September 30.

On October 2, he slipped into a coma for several hours, but awoke the following day and was given last rites. On October 4, he insisted on quitting Jassy, convinced that if he could reach the sea air of Nikolaev, he would recover. He penned his last letter to Catherine, signing it, "Your most loyal and grateful subject."

They set out at eight a.m. on October 5, 1791, but Grigory Potemkin, Prince of the Holy Roman Empire, died on the roadside about forty miles from Jassy in the arms of his niece Alexandra. After realizing he was too ill to continue the journey, he had asked his companions to "[t]ake me out of the carriage and put me down. I want to die in the field." A Persian carpet was unfurled to make him more comfortable; he was covered with the silken dressing gown that had been a gift from his beloved Catherine. A search was made for a gold coin to place over his (good) eye, according to Orthodox tradition, but none was to be found in such a remote location. One of the Cossacks escorting the party offered them a copper five-kopeck coin instead, which closed the eyes of His Serene Highness at midday. The cause of death was most probably bronchial pneumonia, undoubtedly exacerbated by exhaustion.

Catherine, who did not receive the news until it arrived by courier at six in the evening on October 12, was inconsolable. She fainted and had to be bled. Then she went into seclusion. At two in the morning, in a letter to her friend and correspondent of many years Friedrich Melchior Grimm, she poured out her heart and the contents of her pen in a eulogy that encapsulates why she had loved Potemkin.

. . . my pupil, my friend and almost my idol, Prince Potemkin-Tavrichesky, has died after about a month's illness in Moldavia!

You can have no idea of how afflicted I am: he joined to an excellent heart a rare understanding and an extraordinary breadth of spirit; his views were always great and magnanimous; he was very humane, full of knowledge, singularly lovable, and always with new ideas; never did a man have the gift of *bon mots* and knowing just what to say as he had; his military talents during this war must have been striking, for he did not miss a single blow on land or sea. No one in the world was less capable of being led than he; he also had a particular gift for knowing how to employ his people. In a word, he was a statesman in counsel and execution; he was attached to me with passion and zeal; he scolded and became angry when he thought one could do better; with age and experience he was correcting his faults. . . . But his most rare quality was a courage of heart, mind and soul which distinguished him completely from the rest of humankind, and which meant that we understood one another perfectly and could let those who understood less prattle away to their hearts' content. I regard Prince Potemkin as a very great man, who did not fulfill half of what was within his grasp.

Catherine spent the next several days weeping, convinced that she would never be able to survive without him. "Prince Potemkin did me a cruel turn by dying! The whole burden falls on me."

"How can I replace Potemkin?" she lamented to her secretary, Alexander Khrapovitsky. "He was a real nobleman, a clever man, no one could buy him. Everything will be wrong. . . ."

As the days passed, Khrapovitsky could only report, "Tears and despair . . . tears . . . more tears." On December 12, continuing to grieve, Catherine confided to Grimm, "I am still profoundly afflicted by it. To replace him is impossible, because someone would have to be born as he was, and the end of this century announces no geniuses. . . ."

Potemkin's funeral was held at Jassy. He had wanted to be buried in his birthplace at Chizhova, but Catherine played the empress card and decided that his final resting place should be at one of his Crimean cities. She settled on Kherson, where Potemkin's body arrived on November 23, 1791. As if he were a royal, his heart and viscera were removed and buried elsewhere: His organs, including his brain, rest beneath the floor before the Hospodor of Moldavia's red velvet medieval throne. Potemkin's heart was supposed to have been placed under the throne of St. Catherine's in Kherson, but there's no trace of it there. The villagers of Chizhova believe it was taken there in 1818 by Archbishop Ivov Potemkin.

After Catherine's death in November 1796, her son commanded the destruction of Potemkin's tomb, but apparently his orders were botched. The marble monument that Catherine had commissioned wasn't completed at the time of her demise, so the prince rested in an unmarked grave, and perhaps the emperor Paul's lackeys never found it. The grave was desecrated during the Russian Revolution of 1918, and Potemkin's corpse was as defiled as that of Madame de Maintenon during the French Revolution.

In 1930, a writer and native of Kherson, returning to his hometown for a visit, noticed Potemkin's skull and burial clothes displayed behind glass in the "Anti-Religious Museum." He sent a telegram to the ministry responsible for protecting art, and Potemkin was reburied.

On May 11, 1984, his coffin was exhumed and analyzed. Some additional items had found their way into the more modern casket, such as a British officer's Crimean War–era epaulette, but forensic tests concluded that the body was Potemkin's. In July 1986, the i's were dotted and the t's were crossed. It was confirmed that the coffin dated to 1930. It was also supposed that any icons that would have been buried with Potemkin's body had disappeared during the looting of the Russian Revolution. At St. Catherine's Cathedral in Kherson, Potemkin was reinterred for the final time, with a proper headstone.

Everything about Potemkin had been larger than life. Leonine, broad chested, well over six feet tall, the prince, known across Russia as Serenissimus, had coruled the empire with Catherine for seventeen years. They had met three decades before his death during a time of crisis, and a gallant gesture sealed their combined destiny. After their romance ended, he remained Catherine's partner, friend, adviser, minister, and confidant, and she surely loved him more deeply than she had ever loved another. Catherine called him her "Colossus," her tiger, her idol, her hero, and her greatest eccentric. They were unquestionably each other's grand passion.

Potemkin won the Second Turkish War for her, annexed the Crimea, created Russia's Black Sea Fleet, and founded the cities of Kherson, Nikolaev, Sevastopol, and Odessa. He was as intelligent, creative, and brilliant as he was arrogant, indolent, and debauched.

Perhaps the most succinct epitaph, although it was not written as one, was penned by Charles-Joseph, the Prince de Ligne. The Austrian ambassador found Potemkin to be ". . . the most extraordinary man I have ever met. He gives the appearance of laziness yet works incessantly . . . always reclining on his couch yet never sleeping, day or night, because his devotion to the sovereign he adores keeps him constantly active . . . melancholy in his pleasures, unhappy by virtue of being happy, blasé about everything, quickly wearied of anything, morose, inconstant, a profound philosopher, an able minister, a sublime politician and a child of ten . . . prodigiously wealthy without having a sou, discoursing on theology to his generals and on war to his archbishops; never reading, but probing those to whom he speaks . . . wanting everything like a child, capable of dispensing with everything like a great man . . . what then is his magic? Genius, and then genius, and then more genius!"

In addition to the numerous titles and offices that Catherine awarded Potemkin, she gave him several palaces, the most famous of which was the Tauride Palace in St. Petersburg. Tsar Paul I avenged himself on his mother and her lover after Catherine's death by turning the Tauride into the Horse Guards barracks.

And since our thoughts have turned to horses . . .

While Potemkin was Catherine's most famous and influential lover, history has all too often assigned her a more original and unusual partner—one of the equine species. The origin of this ridiculous horse tale begins long before Catherine's birth, with a courtier from Holstein named Adam Olearius. In 1647, Olearius published an account of his travels throughout Russia in 1630, writing that the Russians were fond of practicing sodomy, even with horses. In the ensuing misogynistic decades after Catherine's death, accounts of her passion for horseback riding morphed into the legend of bestiality, which was taken to its preposterous conclusion with the story that the empress met her untimely end when the harness broke as it was lowering a stallion on top of her, and the horse crushed her to death. The truth is far more prosaic, to say nothing of plausible. The great Catherine suffered a stroke in the commode.

CAROLINE MATHILDE

1751–1775

*A*s king of England, George III, who acceded to the throne in 1760, had the authority, if not also the obligation, to unite his younger siblings in marriages that would be strategically advantageous for Great Britain. Princess Caroline Matilda was the prettiest of George's sisters—the youngest child of Augusta, Princess Dowager of Wales, and Frederick, Prince of Wales—born only four months after their father died.

Even as a little girl, Caroline Matilda was made aware that no royal child could marry for love. If you wanted to stay home, then you remained a spinster. Otherwise you were sent off to another land, ostensibly forever, to cement a diplomatic alliance with a foreign entity. Caroline Matilda had known since 1765 of her connubial destiny—to wed Christian, the Crown Prince of Denmark. Walter Titley, the British envoy to Copenhagen, made sure to emphasize Christian's handsome, if slightly fey, looks as well as his many other fine qualities.

"To an amiable and manly countenance, a graceful and distinguishing figure, he joins an address full of dignity and at the same time extremely affable," observed the assistant British envoy William Cosby, who described the young crown prince with effusion after visiting Copenhagen in the spring of 1764. When he wasn't terrorized by his own fears, the small, slight, tow-haired prince was witty and charming. The problem with Christian was that he would probably be diagnosed today as a bipolar paranoid schizophrenic. Nowadays he'd be medicated to quiet the demons in his head and modify his masochism, fetishism, and other behaviors deemed outside the norm.

His mother, Queen Louise, the youngest daughter of George II of England and Caroline of Anspach (making Christian and Caroline Matilda cousins), died when Christian was only two. His father, King Frederick, consoled himself with alcohol and took a second wife, a daughter of the Duke of Brunswick-Wolfenbüttel, Juliane Marie. Christian's stepmother wasn't cruel to him, but she wasn't exactly maternal. After her own son, Prince Frederik, was born in 1753, she focused all her energy and her love on her biological child.

When Christian was six he was given his own household, and his head was crammed with mathematics and theology by his strict and humorless tutor, Count Dietlev Reventlow. The prince was a sensitive and intelligent boy but was never nurtured, and consequently began to dwell inside his mind, where his phobias grew and multiplied.

At the age of eleven in 1760, he got a new tutor, Elie Salomon François Reverdil, who realized that he had a very strange kid on his hands. Out of the blue Christian would unbutton his breeches, yank up his shirt, and press against his abdominals, telling his tutor that he was intent on achieving a perfect body. He believed that if he could make himself physically invincible, he could overpower his demons.

Sixteen days before Christian's seventeenth birthday, on January 13, 1766, Frederick of Denmark died, his body bloated with booze and dropsy. Christian was now king of Denmark, Norway, of the Goths and the Wends; Duke of Schleswig-Holstein, Stormarn, and the Dittmarsches; Count of Oldenburg and Delmenhorst.

He sounded like a good match for Caroline Matilda on paper, but the truth was far from the reality. Although many European royals considered debauchery practically an expression of noblesse oblige, Christian's behavior was over the top. He frequented the tawdriest brothels and hung out with roustabouts, engaging in street brawls and other violent activities. He practiced self-mutilation and liked to be physically dominated by his whores. But his ministers moved up the wedding date on the assumption that wedlock would domesticate him.

On the evening of October 1, 1766, Caroline Matilda was married to King Christian VII in a proxy ceremony in England. The Archbishop of Canterbury and the secretary of state officiated. The bride was in tears throughout the entire ordeal, although Lady Mary Coke observed that she looked "very pretty in the midst of her sorrow."

The new bride, who had yet to meet her groom, was still sobbing as she was conducted to the carriage that would convey her to the royal yacht at Harwich. Although she was now a queen, she was also just a sheltered teen who had never before left her homeland. She confessed to seasickness on the journey.

The Danes had refused to allow their new queen to bring even one English lady-in-waiting with her to Denmark. All that Caroline Matilda brought aboard the ship was her trousseau and a letter from her brother the king. In it, George exhorted her to take comfort in God's guidance and warned her against expecting too much from her marriage, yet urged her to use her influence with her new husband to further British interests with the Danes.

A contemporary, Elizabeth Carter, summing up not just Caroline Matilda's fate, but that of all royal brides, wrote, "The poor Queen of Demark is gone out alone into the wide world; not a creature she knows to attend her any further than Altona [a city on Denmark's southern border]. It is worse than dying; for die she must to all she has ever seen or known; but then it is only dying out of one bad world into another just like it, and where she is to have cares and fears, and dangers and sorrows, that will all yet be new to her."

At Altona, she left her English life entirely behind. German was the official language of the Danish court; from then on she would speak German or French, using English only in letters to her family. Even her name changed from the English to the Danish spelling, from Caroline Matilda to Caroline Mathilde.

Christian and Caroline Mathilde were wed on November 8, 1766, at Christiansborg Palace, the center of government and the most massive of Denmark's palaces. The queen looked plump and rosy, more zaftig than her slender groom, who was dressed in a silver suit.

Unfortunately, once they embarked on their married life, Christian saw no reason to be nice to his fifteen-year-old wife or to include her in his regular activities. She dared not confide in her brother how horribly lonely she was, telling him instead that she passed her time going to the theater drawn in sleighs across the snow, and hosting masquerades. But her real curiosity was politics, and she yearned for an active role in governance.

Although the sovereigns lived apart at Christianborg, the king at least recognized his dynastic responsibility to beget an heir. In early May 1767, the sixteen-year-old queen became pregnant. But Christian, in awe of his wife's strong personality, continued to hang around with libidinous lowlifes, surrounding himself with a raucous, decidedly unregal entourage. While she was pregnant, he took a mistress, the notorious prostitute Støvlet-Cathrine ("Boots-Catherine"), who'd earned the sobriquet either because her mother was a bootmaker or because she had especially dainty feet. Her father was reputed to be Prince George-Ludwig of Brunswick-Bevern.

But Christian's ministers deplored the liaison, and before too long they convinced him to pension her off. On January 6, 1768, he signed a document kicking Cathrine out of Copenhagen and packing her off to a cushy retirement.

The ministers had hoped that Caroline Mathilde would become a stabilizing influence on him, but she had thus far been incapable of wooing him away from the dark side. The delicate and diminutive Christian, who hated to be king, had a profound death wish—the only way he knew his sentence as king of Denmark could end. He was enamored of violent games that often involved bondage and masochistic fantasies. He would ask to be tied to a chair and, pretending to be a convicted criminal, would beg for torture. Fearing they might actually injure their employer, his servants would whack at him with a roll of paper. After dismissing his mistress, he took to producing plays in which he would perform many of the roles, including the part of Orosmane in Voltaire's tragedy Zaïre, which required him to perform an onstage murder and then to commit suicide. His ministers continued to be nervous about his state of mind and his penchant for violence.

After a difficult pregnancy, compounded by her husband's utter indifference toward her, Caroline Mathilde gave birth to an heir, Crown Prince Frederik, on January 28, 1768. The queen followed the new fashion among aristocrats, embracing Rousseau's philosophy of naturalism by breast-feeding her infant. Meanwhile, Christian made a state visit to England without her in 1768, living it up riotously on the docks and in the brothels of London when he wasn't under the watchful gaze of his royal brother-in-law. He also enjoyed all the entertainments George III planned for him, in no hurry to return to Copenhagen. Avid to escape his regal responsibilities, he even suggested to his new physician-in-ordinary, a German named Johann Struensee, that the two of them run off together and join the army. The ambitious Struensee came to believe that the only way to tire Christian's mind and keep the demons at bay was by exhausting his body, so he prescribed strenuous physical exercise, such as horseback riding.

With such a husband, it was no surprise that Caroline Mathilde's head might be turned by a viable alternative. Her romantic trajectory somewhat mimics that of Sophia Dorothea of Celle in that her extramarital affair also resulted in the loss of her children as well as her freedom. A princess of the Hanoverian dynasty by birth, Caroline Mathilde would even end up in Celle, a Hanoverian dominion. She died there of scarlet fever at the age of twenty-three, having experienced the marriage from hell, then found true love and held the kingdom of Denmark in the palm of her hand, only to lose it all within the span of a few brief years.

CAROLINE MATHILDE AND JOHANN FRIEDRICH STRUENSEE (1737–1772)

The son of a prominent Lutheran minister and grandson of a doctor who had been the physician-in-ordinary to Christian's grandfather, King Christian VI of Denmark, Johann Struensee was born in 1737 in Halle, a small town in northern Germany. Johann, who possessed the inquiring mind and temperament of a child of the Enlightenment, was among the first generation of doctors to view the mind and body as complementary entities. He understood that the infirmities of one could intensely affect the other, and that a patient's emotions could have a profound impact on his state of being. And he quickly realized that Christian had a bunch of screws loose upstairs.

Struensee began his medical practice in Altona in 1758. He was charming, tall, blond, broad-shouldered, and handsome, with soft, voluptuous lips, an aquiline nose, and, as one contemporary put it, a "merry look" in his sensitive and intelligent blue eyes. He wore his own hair in preference to wigs, in full, symmetrical curls on either side of his head, tied with a black ribbon. Sometimes he powdered it; sometimes he left it blond. His clientele included members of the nobility who helped him gain his royal appointment.

Ten years later, at the age of thirty-one, Struensee was appointed temporary physician-in-ordinary to King Christian VII while he was traveling throughout Europe. But he may not have been the perfect chaperone for such an unstable person. A contemporary writer later said of the atheistic doctor that he "carried freedom of thinking as far as any man . . . deficient in both . . . morality and religion."

Johann Struensee had arrived at court at the perfect time, because the sovereign had been looking for someone who would stay up all night with him and help chase the demons out of his head. In January 1769, Struensee's position was made permanent, and he gave up his private medical practice in Altona.

During his first few months in Copenhagen, Struensee shored up his position as the king's personal physician, making friends with the other doctors at court. He did not have political ambitions at the time, or if he did, they were carefully masked.

As Christian became more incapacitated mentally, he spent increasingly more time in his own apartments, behind closed doors with Struensee. Observers noticed that if the king and queen happened to see each other in one of Christianborg's numerous hallways, they would pass each other in a sullen, stately silence. It was common knowledge that the royal couple was living entirely separate lives.

In May 1769, Christian appointed Struensee to the rank of state councilor, which allowed him to attend official functions. With the eye of an astute student, the physician began to take note of how the kingdom was governed. While he was always in the company of the king, he had also observed that Caroline Mathilde was determined to despise anyone who had her husband's confidence. Consequently, he endeavored to remain cordial to the queen, so that she would not mistake him for an enemy.

That autumn, Christian's mental and emotional condition deteriorated even further, and he became openly hostile toward his wife. Only eighteen years old, and hopelessly depressed by the painful awareness that this was how she would be forced to spend the rest of her life, Caroline Mathilde retreated from society.

After observing Struensee's increasing influence on Christian, the British envoy to Denmark became alarmed at the notion of a power behind the throne. ". . . [T]he mainspring . . . of all the present intrigues is discovered to be another person, of whom it cannot easily be determined whether his talents are more formidable, his principles more relaxed, or his address more seducing. These qualities, combined with almost constant attendance on the King, have contributed to give him the most alarming ascendancy over His Majesty. . . . [I]t becomes hard to judge whether it be less easy to remove him or more dangerous to suffer his continuance."

But Struensee's manipulating behind the scenes had already borne fruit, and he had gained another influential fan: the queen. When she fell ill during the summer of 1769, he was the physician she asked to attend her. And in early November she sought his advice regarding her melancholia. One consultation led to another, and soon he was visiting her quarters alone and unchaperoned by her servants. A sympathetic ear and a handsome shoulder didn't hurt, and Caroline Mathilde soon fell in love with him. In January 1770, she managed to secure him lodgings in the palace at Christianborg. By February, he was making regular nocturnal pilgrimages through the corridors and back stairs to her bedchamber. Their romance became hot and heady, their exhilaration fueled by the element of danger. It was a capital crime to sleep with the queen of Denmark.

One thing that made their royal affair so unusual was the vast difference in their social stations. Struensee was a commoner, far beneath the blue-blooded Caroline Mathilde. Her choice of a man of the people reflected her general disdain and disregard for court etiquette.

According to one of her contemporaries, Caroline Mathilde was "not only clever, but had a good mind." She knew that Struensee had swiftly gained her husband's trust, and that he could levy this influence with him to increase her own political clout. Now *she* desired an active role in ruling the king. Craving an entrée into the mannish sphere of politics, which she believed to be her due as queen of Denmark, she began to dress the part in coats and breeches, and took up riding astride.

At first Caroline Mathilde tried to keep her adulterous romance under wraps. But after two of her chambermaids began to suspect something, they enlisted the aid of Her Majesty's lady-in-waiting Anna Petersen and began to gather evidence against their mistress. They asked a maid to sprinkle powder on the floor outside the queen's bedchamber; the following morning, large footprints—too large to belong to the king's dainty feet—were discovered in the powder. White powder marks were also found on the carpet inside Caroline Mathilde's bedroom. Her ladies knew that the king never visited her rooms that way.

They also put wax in the keyhole. When they found a lump of it on the floor outside her room they knew that she had unlocked her door to admit someone in the middle of the night. The maids also found Her Majesty's sheets rumpled and stained, with similar smears on the towels. And the enthusiastic lovers didn't confine themselves to the bed. The chambermaids also reported stains on the queen's upholstered sofas that "modesty" forbade "them to mention."

When the maids confronted the queen, she told them to go get Struensee (who, of course, didn't confirm anything). After he departed she scolded them for making such bold accusations about their sovereign. But the maids held firm, and then presented their evidence. At this, Caroline Mathilde realized they had ensnared her. Seeing no way out beyond bargaining, she asked them whether they believed that the gossip about her romance would die down if she and Struensee saw each other less frequently. The attendants agreed that Johann should shorten the duration of his visits to her rooms. But after a couple of weeks the lovers were back to their usual all-night stands.

Unfortunately, the queen was reckless enough to admit to her maids that the doctor was good for her; he understood her, and he "had such a good mind." But taking her maids into her confidence hardly won their sympathy, so she issued a new set of rules governing her household staff: Maidservants and ladies-in-waiting were to remain in their rooms until she rang for them.

By now, grateful to the physician for inoculating the two-and-a-half-year-old crown prince against smallpox after an epidemic had broken out in Copenhagen, Christian had elevated Struensee to the rank of *Conseiller des Conferences*, as well as reader to the king. It was a very controversial move; inoculation had been championed by Voltaire, so it was equated with godless, radical thought, not to mention the French.

By early 1770, Struensee had become the king's keeper. Christian's ability to think rationally and coherently was diminishing by the day. Sometimes he told the physician he was a changeling; on other occasions he would insist that his father was really an English nobleman, or that his birth was a mystery that would be revealed in the fullness of time—but in any event, he was advancing toward a happier state of mind. Once he attained it he would leave Copenhagen forever, for the real world—a world in which he had committed multiple murders and had been fed large quantities of opium so that he would forget his complicity in these numerous deaths.

He was preparing his body to live in this better world. He would need to be invincible, impervious to pain. So Christian would practice by rubbing whatever was at hand all over his bare skin, everything from hair powder to snow to burning embers. The details of the Danish sovereign's other world always involved pain. The doctor found it remarkable that there never was any mention of love or affection being given or received.

A true masochist, according to Struensee, Christian liked to be treated with "indignation." He enjoyed being emasculated, and his wife's appearance in male costumes excited him. Perhaps it was the riding habit, and her leather boots and whip. When he imagined the queen as a dominatrix, he liked her best.

At the bottom of it all was Christian's fervent desire not to have to be king. It also troubled his physician that the sovereign never seemed to care for or about anyone, and he also ascribed Christian's insensitivity to his wife as a nervous disorder. Although Struensee never diagnosed the king's malady as madness, by this time he had observed enough of his behavior to presume it was incurable. At first Struensee tried to convince Christian that he was only imagining things, but that only depressed the monarch. So rather than have a

gloomy Dane moping about Christiansborg, the king's closest attendants instituted a strict regimen for him, including regular walks to
contain his violent outbursts, and cold baths to combat Christian's
frequent masturbation. Meanwhile, the king's errant behavior was
kept a secret from the public and the rest of the court.

Christian was clearly an unfit ruler, and from then on he was trot-
ted out only at ceremonial occasions—which were few and far
between, because neither Christian nor Caroline Mathilde liked
them. Struensee then began issuing orders on behalf of the king.
Christian would sign the various documents and proclamations, but
they were all the brainchildren of his physician. At the time the sovereigns and the doctor were of the same opinion, so Christian didn't
seem to mind.

Struensee's first ghostwritten announcement to the people of
Denmark was an explanation of why there had been no official celebration to mark Caroline Mathilde's nineteenth birthday in July
1770. "The Queen's birthday was not celebrated this time because
she has wanted it this way herself, and because we both [meaning the
monarchs] think that the usual tedious ceremonies come less from
the heart than ought to be the case on such an occasion. I have neither handed out medals nor made appointments because I have decided only to do so in extraordinary cases for the time being, and
because of the great number I have promoted in previous years."

The king had no idea that the real reason his wife didn't want a
big formal celebration of her birthday was that it would have deprived
her of spending her special day with the one person she wanted to
share it with—the third member of this dysfunctional triumvirate:
her lover.

Both Caroline Mathilde and Struensee were strongly in favor of
progressive reform, and they began right at home, with the court.
Within a couple of months the physician had reduced Christian's
household staff and pensioned off several of his officials and courtiers. He and the queen were closing ranks around the increasingly
demented king, gradually shoring up their power base. No one was
permitted access to the royal couple, and their movements and decisions were kept a secret even from their own households.

Struensee replaced Christian's Court Marshal with one of his cronies and began to gather his own set of advisers around him. It became clear to Count von Bernstorff, the chief minister, that the physician was not content to merely take control of the king's personal life, but had intentions of pushing his way into the political arena as well.

Regardless of what the outside world thought, the members of the triumvirate were perfectly happy with the way things were. Christian didn't want the burden and responsibilities of power anyway. And Caroline Mathilde wished to be left alone to rule in tandem with her paramour. Count von Bernstorff had never seen the queen "so beautiful and cheerful." With the yoke of responsibility removed from his slim shoulders, Christian's fantasies took on a less troubled form. He traveled everywhere with his dog Gourmand, who rode in his own coach ahead of the king's carriage.

Meanwhile, Caroline Mathilde and Johann Struensee did little to conceal their romance from their tight circle of friends. According to a contemporary, "Their intimacy showed that they loved each other, searched for each other and were happy when they found one another. . . . [T]heir love showed in a way that can be noticed but not described." The paramours developed little rituals, taking tea together every morning, either in the queen's bedchamber or in her parlor with all the shades drawn. By now, the queen's maids discreetly left the couple alone.

Caroline Mathilde was in love for the first time in her life—and she was behaving like it. She bought yards and yards of feminine fripperies: lace and ribbons, silk hose. Struensee purchased a sentimental gift for her: a pair of red garters, which she wore every day. The queen called them her "ties of feeling." By then she had a collection of objects that represented their love: a pair of gold-and-enamel buttons, and a garnet cross that she wore beneath her bodice, where the king couldn't see it. She had a small portrait of Struensee that she kept hidden inside a book, later moving it to a special keepsake box made of gold-and-green enamel.

Their relationship was not only becoming more public; they flaunted it almost brazenly. The lovers enjoyed every meal together. Servants observed Struensee sneaking into Caroline Mathilde's bedroom each evening, and one night the queen accidentally awakened her son's nurse when she tiptoed through the nursery on her way to visit her paramour.

When Johann Struensee wasn't making love to Caroline Mathilde, he was ruling Denmark. He gave the chief minister his walking papers and began reorganizing the way the kingdom was governed, setting a new progressive tone and issuing decrees in Christian's name, the first of which, on September 4, 1770, declared freedom of the press. Over the next several months he reduced the authority of the Council of State to an advisory one. Apparently it was all right if Denmark remained an autocracy as long as Struensee was the autocrat.

Christian willingly signed whatever papers Johann Struensee put in front of him, content to be no more than a figurehead. On December 27, 1770, a decree was issued ostensibly from the king, abolishing the privy council, but it had been ghostwritten by Struensee. And from then on it would be Struensee who would be running the kingdom *"lui seule"* [by himself], as the queen wrote to her brother George III.

On December 18, the king had granted the thirty-three-year-old physician the post of *maître de requêtes*, which authorized him to take decrees directly to Christian for his signature. Struensee himself was the author of those decrees.

Something was rotten in Denmark, but the abuse of power by the king's physician was hardly the juiciest subject of gossip. Caroline Mathilde commissioned the portraitist Peter Als to depict her as a periwigged gentleman in the uniform of the Danish Royal Life Guards, in boots and spurs, holding a black tricorn, and wearing a ceremonial sword. The painting, completed during the summer of 1771, deliberately invites comparisons to the mannish Queen Christina of Sweden, who refused to marry, and to the formidable Catherine the Great, who also enjoyed dressing *en travestie*. Als flattered his subject by making her appear tall and slim. Caroline Mathilde's detractors, who were unnerved to see a voluptuous woman dressed like a man and behaving in a bold, assertive manner, insisted she was far too plump to pull off the look.

Meanwhile, during the early 1770s, bored and annoyed with the perpetual business of reviewing and signing papers, Christian gazed down at the dog snoozing at his feet and declared, Caligula-like, that his pet should have a government post. On another occasion he announced that he was appointing as his chamberlain the man who lit the ceramic stoves in each room.

Life at the Danish court was a combination of free spending and pragmatic restraint, noblesse oblige and bourgeois domesticity. In particular, Caroline Mathilde's conduct as queen, wife, mother, and lover scandalized people. In 1771, an astonished British visitor, arriving from the chilly formality of St. James's, remarked, "This court has not the most distant relationship to any other under the sun." Some years later another observer would opine, "Nothing could be more licentious than the court of Mathilda [sic] in 1770 and 1771. Her palace was a temple of pleasure, of which she was the high priestess. Everything was found here calculated to excite and gratify sensual desires."

At age nineteen and a half the queen was now pregnant with her second child. Very few Danes in the know assumed it was her husband's. By ostentatiously displaying her increasing belly she was advertising not only her general immorality, but her relationship with the king's physician.

Rare for a queen, Caroline Mathilde was very close to her son, the Crown Prince Frederik, now a toddler. Struensee saw that the boy was raised according to the back-to-nature precepts promulgated by the eighteenth-century philosopher Jean-Jacques Rousseau. This child-rearing technique was all the rage in England, and Caroline Mathilde's fondest girlhood memories were rural idylls, such as the months she passed at Kew. As a progressive physician, Johann Struensee would have advocated lots of fresh air and sunshine. Christian, who'd endured a nightmarish, loveless, and very strict upbringing, had no objections.

In the name of the king, Struensee instituted a raft of unprecedented reforms. Walking the Rousseau walk and talking the talk, he opened the royal gardens to all Danes. To get them to visit on Sundays as well, the atheist doctor booked military bands to entertain them.

This all-out reformation was a team effort between Struensee and Caroline Mathilde, abetted by a number of forward-thinking aristocrats whom the physician had appointed to government posts. Many of these reforms were already sweeping the world to one extent or another. It was all the fashion to espouse English liberty (i.e., freedom of the press) and the French philosophy of Rousseau and Voltaire, who advocated the notion that morality began from within one's own being, and that everyone should cultivate their own metaphorical garden.

Caroline Mathilde emulated Catherine the Great by opening a foundling hospital. Struensee's friend Enevold Brandt became the manager of the Royal Theatre, democratizing the repertoire by producing French comedies and Italian operas, and opening the venue to all. Even more scandalous than allowing the riffraff to purchase a ticket was that performances were offered on Sundays. To religious conservatives and nobles who were losing the perquisites of the aristocracy, it was a sure sign that Denmark was in the bull's-eye of the apocalypse.

Struensee also appointed another German, Adolph von der Osten, to the foreign ministry. Von der Osten was a talented career diplomat who would maintain Denmark's political neutrality, much to the consternation of Robert Gunning, Britain's ambassador to Denmark, who hoped that the queen's more active role in government would make her a partisan for her homeland. But Caroline Mathilde had no love for the country that had sent her into exile, yoked to a known psychopath in a loveless marriage. And in any case, she agreed with her paramour's politics.

Struensee instituted additional civil reforms, such as streetlamps, and addresses on houses. He also cracked down on police brutality and unlawful searches and seizures. Unsurprisingly, he abolished the punishments, including fines, for adultery. Adultery trials could now be brought only by one of the aggrieved spouses, and not by the authorities. Big Brother was no longer permitted to peep into people's bedrooms. He abolished state-sanctioned torture. Nobles would no longer be forgiven their debts. He reduced the number of civil servants and trimmed government offices and budgets, cutting waste.

Ironically, royal spending didn't diminish a jot. The queen and her lover never tightened their own belts.

But, according to Newton's Laws of Motion, to every action there is an equal and opposite reaction. Struensee, a man of science, should have realized that. He had enacted wide-reaching reforms, but had formed no plans to deal with the consequences. Unemployment (due in part to his downsizing so many bureaucrats out of a job) created homelessness, forcing people to live on the streets. The press, reveling in its newfound freedom, used the power to criticize the reforms and their architects. Scads of corrupt civil servants had been dismissed. But who would replace them? The business of government had to continue. And despite Struensee's budget cuts, spending remained out of control.

King Christian's lucidity continued to diminish throughout 1771. In April, he had another manic episode, hurling everything within reach off a palace balcony—books, sheet music, dolls, a fire poker. Because he was the sovereign, unlike other mentally unstable Danes, he was never forcibly restrained or formally confined. By the summer his depression, his schizophrenic moods, and his paranoid delusions had all increased, and he spoke of committing murder and/or suicide. In rare moments of clarity, Christian would pathetically admit that he was confused, lost, and could not seem to quiet the voices inside his head. Sometimes he almost seemed to know what was going on with his wife, informing his former tutor Elie Reverdil one day during a picnic that the queen was sleeping with the king of Prussia—and identifying Johann Struensee as Frederick the Great.

Caroline Mathilde was (incorrectly) depicted, even by the British envoy Robert Gunning's network of informers, as an innocent, caught in her lover's egalitarian web. Yet the ambassador knew full well that she was an active and willing partner in all of the reforms. The bitter Gunning refused to regard Struensee through the queen's eyes, incapable of acknowledging her admiration for his intelligence and the world vision they shared. "It is a universal matter of wonder, how he has managed to gain so entire an ascendancy over their Danish Majesties."

The fact that the royals didn't behave as such—meaning regally—was jarring and unnerving to the people. Their lifestyle, though opulent, was—in Reverdil's opinion—common. Reverdil was stunned by the way Caroline Mathilde, Johann Struensee, and their courtiers conducted themselves like a bunch of *petits bourgeois*.

The queen admitted to her maids that she envied their ability to marry the men they loved. She behaved as though she and Struensee were spouses, even though he was (shockingly, since much of his position depended upon her) unfaithful to her. In the physician's disingenuous words, "The happiness of a human consists in the freedom to express his desires." But Caroline Mathilde still adored him, endured his infidelity, walked out in public with him, dined with him, and had no shame about flaunting their relationship. According to the new British ambassador Robert Murray Keith (who replaced Gunning), Her Majesty's "partiality for Count Struensee seemed to gather strength from opposition."

In July 1771, twenty-year-old Caroline Mathilde bore Johann Struensee a daughter, Princess Louise Augusta. He remained at the queen's bedside during the birth, stroking her hair, holding her hand, soothing her during the contractions, and supporting her neck, while a male *accoucheur* delivered the baby. The queen looked into Struensee's eyes throughout the ordeal. When the proud papa left the room, Caroline Mathilde requested her purse, took out his portrait, and gazed lovingly and longingly at the image.

On July 22, the day of the little princess's christening, both Struensee and his friend Enevold Brandt were ennobled, becoming counts, fueling the rumors that the physician was Louise Augusta's father. Although only the king could bestow a title, most people assumed that the elevation of Struensee had been the queen's idea. The previous week, Christian had made Struensee a privy cabinet minister, stating (in an edict ghostwritten by the physician himself) that "all orders which I may give him orally shall be drawn up by him in accordance with my meaning, and he shall lay them before me for signature, or issue them in my name."

But the ambitious lovers had taken on far too much. The kingdom was not ready for such reforms; nor were the Danes prepared to accept the scenario of a commoner (with the foreign-born queen at his side and in his bed) as the crazy king's puppeteer. Struensee's improvements were perceived as too draconian. For example, he fired the entire staffs of all public departments without any pension or other compensation. Not only did it impoverish the workers, but it won him numerous enemies. Once the civil servants were gone, the doctor either assumed the reins of power himself or replaced the fired employees with his own cronies. The new hires were invariably fellow Germans who often lacked the necessary governmental experience of their predecessors. The bitter icing on the pastry was that Struensee didn't even speak Danish, instead conducting all business in his native tongue.

Caroline Mathilde and Johann Struensee enjoyed their new government and taste of power very briefly. Within months, unpaid Norwegian dockyard workers who had been hired to build a fleet to repel pirates marched on the palace of Hirschholm to deliver a petition to the king. Weavers protested the closure of the silk factories. Although Struensee remained convinced that everything he was doing was for the welfare of the state, fearing an insurrection the royal family decamped to their nearby estate of Sophienberg.

During the autumn of 1771, Struensee's enemies began to coalesce. They found sympathetic ears in King Christian's forty-two-year-old stepmother, Juliane Marie, and her eighteen-year-old son, Hereditary Prince Frederik (not to be confused with little Crown Prince Frederik, the son of Christian and Caroline Mathilde), who had been ostentatiously excluded from the nuclear royal family. It took very little convincing to get Juliane Marie to become the titular head of the conspiracy to oust Struensee.

The cabal met for the first time on January 13, 1772. Atop the agenda in their plans for a coup was to separate the malleable Christian from his wife and her paramour. They chose to strike on the night of January 16, because the trio would be focused on the masquerade presented in the Royal Theatre.

In the middle of the night, upon discovering that the king's bedchamber was locked from the inside, the conspirators awakened his valet and made him open the door. Juliane Marie tried to tell Christian that they had come as friends, but was too overcome with emotion to make her point, so a coconspirator named Rantzau declared that they had come to liberate him, and by extension Denmark, from the clutches of Johann Struensee and the queen. But

Christian refused to believe that his wife and best buddy meant the kingdom any harm, so the conspirators quickly invented a lie and told the confused sovereign that his wife was plotting against his life. Decrees were thrust in his face that compelled Christian to hand over control of the government to them. In the intriguers' presence he was forced to sign the documents. But in a devastating flash of clarity the monarch acknowledged, "My God, this will cost streams of blood."

Armed now with Christian's signature, the conspirators, accompanied by a number of the palace guard, broke into Struensee's lavishly decorated apartment and made straight for his bedchamber. He was permitted to dress, but because they feared his valet might help him escape, he could don only what was nearest at hand, which turned out to be the powder blue velvet ensemble he had worn to the masquerade ball.

Struensee and his governmental crony Enevold Brandt were arrested, bundled into carriages, and driven across the frozen ground to the fortress of Kastellet, where they were thrown into bare cells and shackled, hands and feet, to the wall. Meanwhile, back at Christiansborg, under duress Christian was busily signing arrest warrants for Struensee and Caroline Mathilde's circle of advisers and ministers.

He penned an ungrammatical note to his wife:

Madam, I have found it necessary to send you to Kronborg, your conduct obliges me to it. I am very sorry, I am not the cause, and I hope you will sincerely repent.

Early the following morning, when the queen was awakened and told that Rantzau, one of the intriguers, waited for her in the antechamber to her bedroom, she immediately (and correctly) suspected the worst. She jumped out of bed and tore through the rooms searching for Struensee, repeatedly shouting, "Where is the Count?" After she finally paused for breath, she was handed her husband's note.

When the guards tried to lay their hands on Caroline Mathilde, she endeavored to evade them by running around the room. If they got too close, she fought them off like a tigress. They called for backup. The foreign minister, Adolph Siegfried von der Osten, was brought in to make her see reason—explaining that she had to comply with her husband's note and be taken into custody. Finally Caroline Mathilde agreed to be incarcerated on the proviso that her children could accompany her to prison, knowing that they were her safeguard. She was permitted to bring only her infant daughter (whom she was still breast-feeding); the crown prince had to remain in Christiansborg Palace. Although Christian had acknowledged paternity of little Princess Louise Augusta, no one believed it, nicknaming the child "*la petite* Struensee."

By midmorning, the carriage transporting the queen, the baby Louise Augusta, and one lady-in-waiting reached Kronborg, a fortress bordered on three sides by the sea and moated on the fourth wall. At first Caroline Mathilde and her tiny entourage were incarcerated in the "Queen's Chamber," a tiny room with bars on the windows. They were later moved into the quarters occupied by Kronborg's commandant, whose family was displaced to an outbuilding.

Struensee was replaced as de facto prime minister of Denmark by one of the conspirators, Ove Høegh Guldberg, the former tutor to Juliane Marie's son, Hereditary Prince Frederik. Guldberg was eager to demonstrate the coup's legitimacy, which he did by parading the hapless king in front of his subjects. But the cabal had to tackle the thorny issue of incarcerating Denmark's queen. If the matter were treated as an affair of state, it would take on international significance and would be sure to rouse the ire of Britain, as Caroline Mathilde was George III's sister and an English princess. The conspirators hoped to keep the whole event a personal matter—just one guy getting rid of an adulterous wife and her scheming lover. The last thing they wanted was war with Great Britain, the world's preeminent naval superpower.

Fat chance of England brushing it aside as just a marital dustup.

Guldberg knew he required a better justification for a coup than the queen's illicit affair with the king's physician and privy cabinet minister. And he also needed actual proof that Caroline Mathilde and Johann Struensee had enjoyed a sexual relationship. Neither party was about to confess to it, and even if their servants tattled, their testimony would be worthless. An anonymous observer wrote, "As to the intimacy, the Queen had no confidants and Struensee was very close and reserved upon all points. The laws in Denmark too are very rigid as to the proofs required on that head: people of a low class are not admissible evidence, I believe, against a crowned head."

So the new government forced Christian to copy a trumped-up document they had created, which stated that he had discovered a conspiracy intended to force him to resign and thereupon declare the queen the regent for their son, the crown prince. Guldberg's staff deliberately leaked the false news, with predictable results—a backlash against immorality. Five brothels were destroyed by an angry mob, which then set upon the homes owned by known supporters of Struensee and the queen. Troops had to be brought in to quell the violence.

Fearful that the public animosity might very well turn on *them* and question *their* legitimacy to govern, and that Christian might at any time wonder what the heck was going on in his name and want his throne back, the conspirators gradually removed him from public view. They placed him under a permanent military guard, and turned him into the ultimate puppet, who was forced to sign whatever was placed in front of him.

While Guldberg and Christian's stepmother, Juliane Marie, were pulling the king's strings, it occurred to them that it had not been Caroline Mathilde's lover, but the queen herself who had been the power behind the Danish throne.

It drove the conservative opposition mad that Caroline Mathilde had dared to shape her life and destiny according to her own rules—although, admittedly, they were unique. Like so many other princesses sent abroad to wed, she was supposed to have been a mere pawn in international affairs, but she didn't know her place, because she refused to stay in the background or the bedroom.

The longer the queen remained incarcerated and unreachable at Kronborg (located at Helsingør, also known as Elsinore to those who are more familiar with Danish geography via Shakespearean tragedy), the angrier she became. On January 19, 1772, three women from her household were sent to keep her company and, more probably, to spy on her, since it was known that she actively disliked each of them.

Back in London, the British press was excited by the story of a beautiful young queen imprisoned in an inaccessible tower, the victim of a perfidious plot hatched by her Danish in-laws.

What would King George do? Would he be so embarrassed by his sister's conduct that he would try to keep things as quiet as possible from his end—a near impossibility with a free press clamoring for information and scandal? Or, with the power to declare war without first applying to Parliament for permission, would he muster the royal navy?

The British ambassador's secretary, Charles Ernst, traveled to London to deliver the news of Caroline Mathilde's imprisonment to King George. By this time His Majesty was up to his eyeballs in wayward younger siblings, having heard his brother the Duke of Cumberland confess just six weeks earlier that he'd secretly wed a commoner. George would shortly learn that another brother, the Duke of Gloucester, had done the same.

But to insult one of his relations was to insult him as well, as far as the king of England was concerned. And as the head of the family he was honor- and duty-bound to do something about it. But what? And how would it be done? And if Caroline Mathilde were indeed an adulteress, George, who ate moral fiber for breakfast, could not more strongly condemn her conduct. He would never condone or excuse it, no matter who she was.

He sent her a letter that chided her, while simultaneously assuring her of his support.

Dear Sister, I cannot omit taking the first opportunity of expressing the sorrow I feel that your enemies have so incited the King of Denmark as to remove you from his presence. You can never doubt of having a warm advocate in me whose advice if followed might have preserved you from misfortune. . . .

He then exhorted her to trust in God. But with Caroline Mathilde so remotely confined, it's doubtful the letter ever reached her.

Britain opened secret negotiations with Denmark on behalf of Caroline Mathilde as "a daughter of England." In the meantime, as George just as secretly readied a fleet to invade Denmark,

Ambassador Keith was instructed to do everything in his power to prevent Christian from divorcing Caroline Mathilde. If proceedings were commenced anyway, George also secretly intended to kick the crap out of Denmark.

Although he was prepared to take the field as his baby sister's champion, what George failed to realize, or accept, was that Caroline Mathilde had no love for her motherland; she didn't think of herself as a daughter of England. She was queen of Denmark and intended to stay that way.

On Danish shores, Guldberg's government assembled a commission of inquiry called the Inkvisitionkommissionen that would interview the incarcerated parties and determine how to proceed depending on the answers given by the prisoners.

As it became clearer to Guldberg that Caroline Mathilde and Johann Struensee had not conspired against the king, the new prime minister had to focus instead on the charge of adultery. Unsurprisingly, the Inkvisitionkommissionen decided to play dirty. On February 20, 1772, filthy, bearded, and bedraggled, Johann Struensee was dragged from his cell and interrogated. Throughout his entire incarceration and inquisition, he had no idea where his lover was. Unaware that she was also imprisoned, he assumed she was still at the palace in Copenhagen.

The commission posed 238 questions to Johann Struensee over the course of the next two days, and he persisted in denying a sexual relationship with the queen. But finally he broke. To the 239th question, he conceded that he and Caroline Mathilde "had gone as far as they could between people of two sexes."

The commissioners persisted, looking for specifics. Struensee answered in the affirmative to each of their queries, except he did not concede that he and the queen enjoyed relations during the royal family's trip to Holstein in 1770—when he knew full well that Louise Augusta was conceived. Instead, he admitted that it was entirely possible that the king had spent at least a full night with his wife, thereby skirting the issue of the girl's paternity so that she would remain a princess.

Struensee refused to sign a confession of any crime whatsoever. Nevertheless, a document dated February 2, 1772, was presented to

Caroline Mathilde with his signature at the bottom. She refused to believe it, insisting that it was a forgery.

And yet Struensee's testimony included descriptions of their passionate encounters amid rumpled bed linens, semen-stained sofas, and other furniture so soiled with their bodily fluids that they needed to be reupholstered. He mentioned the handkerchief he secretly carried as a love token, besmirched with his semen and her blood. He even admitted—shock, horror—that he and the queen made love totally and unabashedly naked, as opposed to the sort of perfunctory copulation that occurred beneath raised nightshirts.

Meanwhile, Guldberg insisted to King George and his emissaries that His Britannic Majesty's sister had brought the whole situation upon herself, and that she alone was responsible for her state.

And the English press, referring to Caroline Mathilde not by name but only as the queen of Denmark, swallowed the truth of her lover's "confession" and took bets as to what her fate would be—divorce, exile, or execution.

On March 9, she received a visit from four men associated with the new government and the Inkvisitionkommissionen. The queen had no advocate or attorney and still had no contact with the outside world. The delegation read her forty-six pages of testimony about her romance with Struensee, taken from members of her household staff and given by her lover under extreme duress.

Offered the chance to admit to the affair, Caroline Mathilde vehemently denied the relationship and insisted that the commission had no authority to question her. She further maintained that the confession she was told was Struensee's was a forgery.

Then the commissioners played their trump card and showed her the physician's signature on the back of the purported confession. Faced with this evidence, Caroline Mathilde was induced to sign her own confession admitting to an adulterous liaison with Johann Struensee.

Divorce proceedings commenced on March 13 with the creation of the Skilsmissekommissionen, the divorce commission. King Christian was not permitted to be present at the trial, because no one knew what might come out of his mouth. If in a lucid moment he were to comprehend what was going on, he might even change his mind about divorcing his wife, which would have been disastrous for the new government.

Peter Uldall, Caroline Mathilde's court-appointed advocate, was convinced that the queen had been duped by strong, corrupt, and clever men, and that the poor woman had been a victim of their machinations. He couldn't possibly wrap his brain around the idea that she was an intelligent and passionate female who had taken full command of her own life. When he went to interview her at Kronborg and was shocked to find himself confronted by an angry and contentious woman, his chivalrously misogynistic fantasies were utterly demolished.

In Uldall's presence, Caroline Mathilde retracted her confession of adultery and refused to believe that Struensee had confessed as well. According to the naive Uldall, "I tried to raise her pride by telling her how much he had done wrong against her. It seemed to have some effect, and would have had more if she had known to the full his cowardice, but she always returned to this; he must have been forced."

As for her relationship with her husband, the queen admitted to Uldall, "I always feared that he would sacrifice me if somebody put evil in him against me."

Uldall presented Caroline Mathilde's verbatim statement before the Skilsmissekommissionen: "If I have possibly acted incautiously, my age, my sex and my rank must excuse me. I never believed myself exposed to suspicion, and, even though my confession appears to confirm my guilt, I know myself to be perfectly innocent. I understand that the law requires me to be tried: my consort has granted me this and I hope he will, through the mouths of his judges, acknowledge that I have not made myself unworthy of him." For someone privy to the actual relationship between the queen and Christian, or to his mental illness, they could have read between the lines for a master stroke of legalese.

Fully aware that a guilty verdict was a foregone conclusion, Caroline Mathilde was nonetheless desperate to hang on to her children, although she realized it would be a long shot to win custody of her son, the crown prince. She then begged to keep Louise Augusta, insisting to Uldall, "I must have her with me. I will declare that she does not have anything to do with that family. Can I not then keep her?" At this outburst, the queen's lawyer delicately reminded her that if she made such a claim it would be an admission of her adultery.

After the divorce degree was pronounced, Christian, of all people, was the one who had a fit, destroying his wife's property and then falling into an even more profound depression.

The English were still threatening war if the Danes continued to incarcerate Caroline Mathilde after the divorce. So she was exiled to the Hanoverian duchy of Celle, which was also a dominion of George III.

Johann Struensee and his crony Enevold Brandt were sentenced to death—Struensee for a number of crimes, including adultery with the queen. Brandt received the sentence for abetting the affair and for embezzling royal funds.

They were executed on the morning of April 28, 1772. Each man first lost an arm to the ax, followed by their respective heads. Then the victims were stripped naked, quartered, and their entrails were scooped out and tossed into a cart. Owing to the nature of his crime, Struensee also had his genitals hacked off. The quartered bodies were chained to carts to be pecked at by birds and ogled by curious on-lookers with strong stomachs. The heads were then displayed on a pair of pikes with the hands, nailed below.

Forced to leave baby Louise Augusta behind at Elsinore, a very angry Caroline Mathilde boarded a boat for Germany. Meanwhile, Britain's ambassador to Denmark, Lord Keith, burned every one of his papers that was pertinent to the whole sordid business. Back in London all relevant documents were consigned to the flames as well.

On May 1, George III wrote to his sister at the retreat of Göhrde in Celle to advise her that he had "ordered . . . that every sort of Honour should be showed to you." But the moralist in him, knowing what stuck in her craw the most, sadistically rubbed it in:

The parting with your children is a distress in which all who have any feeling must greatly sympathise with you, but, dear sister, this would have equally attended your remaining prisoner in Denmark, and must be looked upon as the natural consequence of the whole transaction.

On October 20, 1772, the exiled Danish queen finally arrived at the moated castle that from then on would be her home. She could hold court, but only according to strict etiquette, and not in her previous egalitarian manner.

Caroline Mathilde pretended that everything was rosy and that she was enjoying herself, but she was desperate to return to Denmark and to assert her right to the throne. She began to gather a collection of sympathetic minds (among them Struensee's brother, who had been exiled to Oldenbourg), even as she insisted to her brother that her concerns were maternal and not political. Despite her ability to hold court, play music, and entertain, her every move was watched by King George's informers and reported to him.

In 1774, an ambitious, adventurous British subject named Nathaniel William Wraxall decided he would be Caroline Mathilde's white knight. He became involved with the Danish ex-pats in an (eventually unsuccessful) plot to overthrow Guldberg's government and restore the exiled queen to the Danish throne. King George's reaction was cryptic. Unwilling to incriminate himself in any way he wrote to his sister:

. . . I shall not only not prevent your going but support I hope [those] who have been accessory to it. But from what I have declared I cannot either enter further into the affair or be entrusted with the plans on which they mean to act. . . .

Unfortunately, a triumphant return to Denmark was not in the cards. On the night of May 10, 1775, Caroline Mathilde fell victim to a scarlet fever epidemic. She was only twenty-three years old. Her corpse was interred in the crypt at Celle where the bodies of the duchy's dukes were buried. Conspiracy theories later abounded. It was variously rumored that she had been poisoned or that she suffered from porphyria, the same disease that ultimately felled George

III, or that someone else had been buried in her stead and she had emigrated to America.

In accordance with her wishes, Caroline Mathilde's personal papers were burned. But back in Denmark, her children kept her memory alive. Sixteen-year-old Crown Prince Frederik was awarded a seat on the Council of State in 1784, and immediately dissolved Guldberg's government with a writ that had been signed by—you guessed it—King Christian VII. Frederik was proclaimed regent on his father's behalf, and when Christian died in 1808, the crown prince became Frederik VI. He married his cousin Maria Sophie of Hesse-Kassel, dying in 1839 with no living male heirs.

Princess Louise Augusta, who was an infant when she was taken from her mother and only four years old at her death, grew up to be impetuous and romantic, just like Caroline Mathilde, and as much a fan of political reform. She supported the French Revolution and adored Napoleon.

Louise Augusta's daughter married a grandson of Christian's stepmother, Juliane Marie. Upon the death of King Frederik VI, the crown passed to the husband of Louise Augusta's daughter, making the granddaughter of Johann Struensee and Caroline Mathilde the queen of Denmark.

MARIE ANTOINETTE

1755–1793

QUEEN OF FRANCE: 1774–1792

*M*arie Antoinette was the fifteenth of sixteen children born to the Holy Roman Empress Maria Theresa of Austria and her husband, Francis of Lorraine. France and Austria had been enemies for 950 years, and the union of the youngest Hapsburg archduchess and the heir to the Bourbon throne was intended to checkmate encroachments on the Austrian empire by Maria Theresa's closest neighbors and greatest enemies, Catherine the Great of Russia and Frederick the Great of Prussia. The children's marriage was hardly a love match; it was an international alliance that had been years in the making, originally the brainchild of the French king's late mistress Madame de Pompadour and his foreign minister the duc de Choiseul.

Marie Antoinette was not yet eleven years old in 1766 when negotiations for her hand began in earnest. Pompadour was dead by then, but Louis XV had given Choiseul his blessing. Unfortunately, the prospective dauphine required a substantial makeover before the French would formalize their offer. Beginning in 1768, an army of stylists and tutors descended on Vienna. A French dentist subjected her to an eighteenth-century form of orthodontia. A famed Parisian coiffeur reconfigured her hairline, which the Bourbons had deemed *"trop bombé"*—too prominent. Lessons in French, elocution, dance, and the walk unique to the ladies of the court, known as the Versailles Glide, came next. And then, when the adolescent archduchess's academic education was judged to be lacking, a preceptor was engaged to cram her head with the history of France and its royal families. After she got her first period in February 1770, the two courts exhaled a collective sigh of relief. Now the little girl was ripe to become a bride.

Marie Antoinette was married to Louis Auguste by proxy in Vienna on April 19, 1770. Two days later, only fourteen years old, she left her homeland forever. On May 16, she wed the fifteen-year-old dauphin in the chapel at Versailles.

What happened on their wedding night was immortalized by the dauphin in his hunting journal with a single word: *rien*. Nothing—although the reference was really a notation that the bridegroom had not killed any woodland creatures that day because he'd not gone hunting. Not only was Louis Auguste shy and uncomfortable around his new bride, but he may have suffered from a mild deformity of the penis known as phimosis, where the foreskin is too tight to retract. This condition (which also afflicted Peter, the husband of Catherine the Great) made intercourse, and even an erection, painful.

Historians' opinions are divided as to whether Louis Auguste suffered from phimosis and underwent a minor procedure (not as radical as circumcision) in late 1773 to correct the defect, or whether his inability to make love to Marie Antoinette was purely psychological or psychosomatic. The latter is harder to believe, because Louis Auguste—who became Louis XVI upon his ascension to the throne with the death of his grandfather on May 10, 1774—admitted that he both loved and respected Marie Antoinette and found her very beautiful. While a number of present-day scholars vehemently dispute the phimosis speculation as being the pet theory of Marie Antoinette's twentieth-century biographer, the Freudian Stefan Zweig, they cannot explain away the preponderance of correspondence that came out of the Bourbon court at the time. This included not merely the November 1773 dispatch from the Spanish ambassador to his sovereign graphically discussing the issue of the dauphin's penis (which could be dismissed as gossip), but a number of letters written between Marie Antoinette and her mother discussing whether or not Louis was prepared to submit to the operation, and the medical opinions of the various court physicians on the subject. The language of that correspondence most clearly refers to a physical problem. That it was compounded by psychological and emotional issues is also a possibility. Unfortunately, Louis' boyhood tutor, the duc de la Vauguyon, had instilled in him a hatred of women and a particular distrust of Austrian females. But by 1773, the dauphin and dauphine had become close friends, and presented a united front against the duc's malevolent influence.

In any event, the result was the same: The royal marriage was not consummated for more than seven years.

The course of history might have been different had the child-loving Marie Antoinette been granted her dearest wish and become a mother early in her marriage. During all those wasted years, had she given birth to at least one healthy son, the hopes of two great kingdoms would have been satisfied. She also might not have made as many enemies both inside the court and among her subjects, because she would have focused her energy on her children instead of channeling her frustration into flights of fancy, fashion, and frivolities—all-night faro games, outrageous coiffures, and masquerade balls.

True, she became an influential fashionista, and in her view stimulated the kingdom's economy, because women slavishly copied her style. But that, too, was highly criticized. Damned if she did and damned if she didn't, Marie Antoinette was condemned for dressing opulently—frankly in a manner befitting a monarch—and equally vilified for gowning herself more casually, derided for appearing to be wearing her lingerie, considered undignified for the queen of France.

The irony of it all was that her mania for acquisition and thrills was enabled by Louis. All too aware that his own deficiencies were the cause of his wife's unhappiness, he indulged her requests no matter how extravagant, seeking to satisfy her desperate attempt to stave off boredom.

Although Marie Antoinette was not a classic beauty—saddled with the prominent eyes and the pronounced Hapsburg jaw of her forebears—she had also inherited their much-prized rose-and-gold complexion, which was clear in an age when foreign princesses' faces were too often riddled with smallpox scars. Her contemporary, the writer and bureaucrat Sénac de Meilhan, remarked, "[S]he had more sparkle than beauty. There was nothing remarkable about her features taken singly but in their *ensemble* there was the greatest attraction. The word 'charming' is the exact word to describe the final effect. . . . Her movements were of an extraordinary grace and nobility. . . ." Marie Antoinette lacked the intellect and dazzling rapier wit so prized in eighteenth-century France, "but she had another quality that seemed to come to her intuitively," according to Sénac. "Somehow she always knew the exact phrase that should be used in every circumstance. These always came from her heart rather than her mind."

This statement in some measure contradicted the propaganda composed by her detractors that Marie Antoinette cared nothing for her subjects. She never uttered the infamous, tin-eared "Let them eat cake" remark in response to news that her people lacked bread. In truth she and Louis regularly gave alms. Marie Antoinette's mother had raised her to comprehend and attend to the misfortunes of her people.

The image handed down to generations of schoolchildren in their textbooks is vastly skewed. It is famously said that history is written by the winners. Marie Antoinette couldn't catch a break as queen of France, and ultimately became the greatest victim of the nation's bloodiest revolution.

She did, however, enjoy a brief "honeymoon" with her adopted country when she was dauphine, if only because by then, the people detested their sovereign, Louis XV. Even during her very early years as queen, she represented a fresh hope for the kingdom.

But when too many childless years had passed and she poured her passion and energy instead into the pursuit of pleasure, the grace period was over. Marie Antoinette was criticized for gallivanting off to Paris for the nightlife with her girlfriends and the king's younger brother the comte d'Artois, while her husband slumbered back at Versailles. She became a scapegoat. Those who had wished her ill from the start began the drumbeat. They were joined by the ostracized courtiers who disseminated their poisoned screeds among the people. It was the aristocrats who invented the character of the debauched spendthrift queen, the "Austrian bitch."

As dauphine, Marie Antoinette had had no use for the older generation of courtiers, and her open mocking of them as straitlaced fuddy-duddies continued when she was a young queen. Her behavior would come back to haunt her. Owing to their mutual dislike, instead of regally tolerating their presence, Marie Antoinette excluded these courtiers from her intimate circle of friends and from le Petit Trianon, her personal idyll at Versailles. On one level, it's understandable that the queen would not wish to surround herself with detractors. But when she shut out those whose families had for decades, if not centuries, earned privileges that brought them into close proximity with the sovereigns, Marie Antoinette reaped a heap of revenge.

The insulted and disgruntled courtiers spread rumors about her conduct at le Petit Trianon, spinning perfectly innocuous behavior behind the doors that were closed to them into tales of illicit orgies with lovers of both sexes. Even after Marie Antoinette finally became a mother in December 1778, giving birth to a daughter, the diatribes did not abate. In fact, they increased when she finally bore a son and heir to the throne in October 1781. Scurrilous pamphlets accused her of cuckolding the king with the comte d'Artois. Marie Antoinette bore Louis a total of four children, although two of them died before the French Revolution began.

In June 1789, Louis convened a meeting of representatives from France's three Estates. The clergy and nobility comprised the First and Second Estates. Everyone else was lumped into the Third Estate, the only entity that paid taxes.

By the time the Bastille was stormed by a mob of more than twenty thousand vitriolic Parisians on July 14, it was far too late for Marie Antoinette to reverse her bad press. Her demise was inevitable. The king's authority was gradually eroded, until in 1792 the National Assembly abolished the monarchy, deposed the sovereigns, and renamed Louis and Marie Antoinette, although they had been Bourbons, Citizen and Citizeness Capet, for a monarchy that had ended in 1328.

Tried and found guily of high treason and crimes against the state, Louis was sent to the guillotine in January 1793, and as French queens were never more than consorts, Marie Antoinette, now the Widow Capet, no longer had any political standing. But the most radical revolutionary element worried that after the king's execution their cause was losing steam, and the people's thirst for bloodshed was on the wane. To them, Marie Antoinette's existence still represented that of the monarchy, so they needed to present her as a treacherous and dangerous woman whose death was the only way that France could be fully cleansed and a new order reborn.

She was tried for treason, the verdict of guilty a foregone conclusion. The ultimate victim of the Revolution, Marie Antoinette was executed on October 16, 1793. Forbidden to wear black, as she was still in mourning for her husband, she dressed in white, which the revolutionaries seemed unaware was the traditional color of mourning for medieval and Renaissance queens.

Some scholars believe that on her ascent to the scaffold she accidentally stepped on the foot of the executioner, Henri Sanson, and politely asked his forgiveness. Along with several other victims of the guillotine that day, Marie Antoinette's remains were taken unceremoniously to the Cimitière de la Madeleine, where, as one story goes, the gravediggers, taking their lunch break, tossed her head between the legs of her corpse, while they casually ate their meal. As burials were costly, not until sixty bodies were accumulated was her coffin smothered with quicklime and interred with the others.

After Napoleon's exile to Elba and the restoration of the Bourbon monarchy, an effort was made to accord Louis and Marie Antoinette a proper burial. On January 15, 1815, Marie Antoinette's bones were identified by scraps of her black filoselle stockings and the garters that she customarily wore. Louis' remains were found the following day. Their bones were reinterred in the royal crypt at Saint-Denis on January 21, ironically the twenty-second anniversary of Louis' execution.

Their surviving daughter, Marie Thérèse, had been released from prison during the Revolution in an exchange of prisoners and joined her mother's family in Vienna. She eventually wed her first cousin, the duc d'Angoulême, and died in 1851.

Her younger brother, the dauphin Louis Charles, died in the Temple prison on June 8, 1795, at the age of ten, although rumors abounded that he had been smuggled out of the Temple and replaced with a changeling. However, in 2000, mitochondrial DNA testing on the child's heart, which had been preserved in a crystal urn at Saint-Denis, proved without a doubt that the DNA sequences were a match with Marie Antoinette's.

At least *la reine martyre*—the martyred queen, as she is commonly known among her adherents in France and Canada—was finally and conclusively reunited with her beloved son, a soupçon of comfort in a tale of considerable woe.

MARIE ANTOINETTE AND
COUNT AXEL VON FERSEN (1755–1810)

One of the great royal romances of all time may never have been consummated. The stakes, the risks, the temptation, and the queen's morals could not have been higher. Because so many documents were destroyed and heavily redacted, even during the couple's lifetime, there is no concrete evidence that Marie Antoinette and Axel von Fersen became lovers. On the other hand, precisely for the same reason, there remains the possibility that what began as a flirtation and blossomed into a friendship at some point passed a definable boundary into a physical relationship. Of course, not every romance involves or culminates in sex. Whether Marie Antoinette and Axel von Fersen had that kind of romance remains one of royal history's most hotly debated issues, with each side occasionally displaying intolerance for the opposite view. There are some royal couples who spark strong emotional responses and personal convictions. Fersen and Marie Antoinette crown the list.

By the time Marie Antoinette met Count Axel von Fersen on January 30, 1774, she yearned for someone to love and who would love her in return. The Opéra ball at the Palais Royal that night would change her life. At around one a.m., Count Axel von Fersen, an eighteen-year-old Swede, arrived to find the halls thronged with partiers. Among them were the dauphine (also eighteen) and her nineteen-year-old husband, up long past his bedtime, as well as Louis Auguste's brother, the portly and wily comte de Provence. Like many of the other aristocrats at the ball, the members of the royal family were masked to preserve their incognito. The count had been in the hall for a half hour or so before a fair *inconnue* approached him and struck up a conversation. Fersen spoke for about ten minutes with the masked young lady, later writing of the incident in his *Journal intime*,

"The Dauphine talked to me for a long time without me knowing who she was; at last when she was recognized, everybody pressed round her and she retired into a box at three o'clock: I left the ball."

Count von Fersen departed the Opéra exhilarated, having charmed, and been enchanted by, Marie Antoinette. And, having been formally presented at Versailles on New Year's Day, he would have many opportunities to see her again at court. Fersen had arrived in Paris in November 1773. The glamorous capital was a requisite destination on the Grand Tour embarked upon by gentlemen of the eighteenth-century nobility as a rite of passage. Having traveled the globe since the age of fifteen, Fersen, nicknamed "the richest man in Sweden," was the older son of a decorated field marshal and statesman and a countess related to the royal house of Vasa.

In addition to his native tongue, the impossibly handsome teen, tall and slender, with a narrow face, soft brown hair, strong dark brows, and hazel eyes that alternately appeared blue, green, or brown, spoke fluent French, Italian, German, and English. These qualities, combined with his melancholy aura, and later his military heroism, made him the ultimate chick magnet. Georgiana, Duchess of Devonshire, praised his "most gentleman-like air." Another female acquaintance found him "a burning soul with a shell of ice." But he had admirers among his own gender as well. The comte de Tilly considered Fersen "one of the best-looking men I ever saw," despite, or perhaps because of, his "icy countenance," which women undoubtedly hoped to melt. The duc de Lévis described Count von Fersen as looking like the hero of a novel—but not a French one, as the Swede was too serious and discreet. Nor was he foppish or fey, like so many of his English and French counterparts. And Marie Antoinette's famed *friseur*, Léonard Hautier, described the count as being like Apollo—someone who excited amorous feelings in women and jealous ones in men.

Fersen returned to Sweden at the end of his Grand Tour in May 1774, around the same time Marie Antoinette became queen of France. He expected to follow in his father's footsteps, pleasing him by entering the military and finding a rich woman to wed.

In April 1778, the count courted an English ironworks heiress, Mademoiselle Catherine Lyell, whom he'd met on his Grand Tour, traveling to London to pursue his suit, but she rejected him. Disillusioned and defeated in the marital mart, he decided to focus on his martial career instead. Fersen applied to be a mercenary in the army of Frederick the Great, king of Prussia. Later that year he returned to France to await Frederick's answer.

"It's an old friend!" Marie Antoinette exclaimed when he presented himself at the Bourbon court. Now queen, and pregnant for the first time, she welcomed him back, inviting him to her parties and making a point of honoring the count by speaking to him on each occasion. Having more experience of the world, and of the opposite sex, Fersen recognized that they were beginning to develop a *tendre* for each other.

After she learned that he had graced one of the celebrated Parisian salons in his "snappy" (according to the hostess) new military uniform, an ensemble designed by the king of Sweden himself, Marie Antoinette insisted on a personal fashion show—not at her *lever*, but in her private apartments. Fersen arrived in his "blue doublet over which was a white tunic, tight-fitting chamois breeches and a black shako topped by a blue and yellow plume." The command performance was the talk of the court, as the gossip spread throughout the palace. "All Versailles can only talk of a certain Count Fersen who came to court wearing the Swedish national outfit which the Queen examined very carefully," noted the future Bishop Lindholm.

Marie Antoinette would blush and tremble when he entered a room. Her not-so-secret nickname for him was "*le bel* Axel" (the handsome Axel). Although even her detractors admitted that charm was one of the queen's strongest assets, she was not a natural flirt, unskilled in the coquetry that came so naturally to the ladies of the court. Marie Antoinette had been married for reasons of duty and dynasty at the age of fourteen, too young to know anything of the world or understand the ways of human behavior, no matter what her mother had taught her. She had never been in love. By the time she met Axel von Fersen her only previous sexual awakening had been her crush on the duc de Choiseul's nephew, the rakish duc de Lauzun. The story goes that when he misunderstood her intentions and took her seriously, her propriety was shocked. Where Fersen was concerned, however, the queen was evidently unable to conceal the emotions he stirred inside her, and was far more ambivalent about how to handle them.

To avoid compromising the queen and endangering her situation by embarking on an illicit love affair, the count became determined to put distance between them, jumping out of the fire before it burned the pair of them. Equally ambitious for advancement in his military career, and eager to participate in France's support of America's bid for independence, with Marie Antoinette's aid, Fersen secured the brevet of colonel in the Royal Deux-Ponts regiment. He was "in a state of joy that cannot be expressed" about the position. It would be only a matter of time before his regiment would sail for North America.

Marie Antoinette's fondness for Axel von Fersen had not escaped notice at the French court, and the news was rapidly transmitted to those at the highest levels in his homeland. Fersen's bosom friend, Baron von Taube, his sister Sophie's extramarital lover, informed King Gustavus III about the pair's behavior during the early months of 1779, confiding that the queen "often walked about with Count Fersen, even entered a box alone with him and remained there talking for a long time." French courtiers soon saw what the baron had. "People spoke of meetings, of prolonged *têtes-à-têtes* at the Opéra balls, of looks exchanged in place of conversation at intimate parties at Trianon." Taube is a reliable source. He and Sophie were the only people to whom Fersen poured out the details of his travels and the contents of his heart. Sophie Fersen Piper was unhappily married, and her older brother fully supported her emotionally and enabled her adulterous romance with Baron von Taube. And when Fersen was in Sweden, he lived with the two of them.

Count Creutz, the Swedish ambassador to France, and a dispassionate witness with nothing to gain or lose politically by sharing this intelligence, wrote to King Gustavus, "I must inform Your Majesty in confidence that young Count Fersen has been so warmly received by the Queen that a number of people here have taken umbrage. I must admit that I cannot help believing that she has an inclination for him. I have seen signs that are too clear to be doubted. Young Count Fersen's behavior on this occasion was admirable in his modesty and reserve. . . . By deciding to go to America he has avoided all danger, but assuredly this decision must have taken strength of character beyond his years. During the last days the Queen has hardly been able to take her eyes from him. Whenever she looked at him her eyes would fill with tears."

The ambassador pointedly requested Gustavus not to share this intelligence with anyone other than Axel's father, Senator Fersen.

But the regiment's departure was unavoidably delayed, allowing Fersen and the besotted sovereign several more months of quality time together. In January 1780, as he still awaited orders to depart for North America, Axel wrote to his father that Marie Antoinette was "the most amiable princess I have ever met," informing the senator, "She has always treated me very kindly." The French ambassador at Vienna, the middle-aged baron de Breteuil, had also been highly influential vis-à-vis his reception at court. Axel informed his father, "Since the Baron spoke to her, she singles me out even more. She almost always walks with me at opera balls. . . ." He then added, "Her kindness has aroused the jealousy of the younger courtiers who cannot understand a foreigner being better treated than they are." Indeed, many young Frenchmen resented the promotion of a Swede to colonel of the Royal Deux-Ponts.

It was strategically intelligent for the queen to favor a foreigner, because it eliminated some of the potential for infighting among the factions at court and reduced the influence of powerful members of Marie Antoinette's coterie.

In the weeks leading up to Fersen's departure, the queen invited him to several of her supper parties. At one soiree, the duchesse de Saint-James teased, "Are you abandoning your conquest so easily?" referring to Her Majesty's *tendre* for him. The count, who was the soul of discretion, and the antithesis of the frivolous French courtiers, soberly replied, "If I had made one, I would not abandon it. Unhappily, I depart . . . without leaving any regrets behind me."

The queen, however, nursed many of them. Fersen's regiment finally left France in the spring of 1780. Marie Antoinette was said to have wept at his parting. The count distinguished himself at the Battle of Yorktown and was asked by General Rochambeau to serve as his aide-de-camp. It was Fersen who acted as the general's translator for George Washington.

In June 1783, Axel von Fersen landed at Brest with the American auxiliary corps and hastened to Versailles. Although he had corresponded with Marie Antoinette, they had not seen each other for three years. Much had changed for both of them. She had just learned she was pregnant for the fourth time (though one pregnancy had been terminated due to a miscarriage in the summer of 1779). This baby had probably been conceived in May. The count was no longer so handsome; "*le bel*" Fersen was now something of a misnomer. "He had been ill in America," wrote the comtesse de Boigne in her memoirs, "and he returned to Versailles aged by ten years, having lost the beauty of his face."

Axel's boots had scarcely made a footprint on French soil when, with the queen's enthusiastic encouragement, he applied for the command of a French regiment, the Royal Suédois. The elder Fersen, remembering the letter three years earlier from the Swedish ambassador, was suspicious, and with good reason.

Upon his return, Axel became one of the queen's intimate circle, enjoying frequent invitations to her idyll, the Petit Trianon, her private estate a mile or so from the Château de Versailles. Louis XV had commissioned the Petit Trianon as a gift for Madame de Pompadour, but she died before its completion. Instead it became his little pleasure palace, which he enjoyed with his last mistress, the comtesse du Barry; there the lovers could tryst without the necessity of servants hovering about or intruding every two seconds, thanks to clever mechanical contraptions, such as a dining table that could ascend from the subterranean kitchen, fully laden. In June 1774, a month after he became king, Louis XVI gave the Petit Trianon to Marie Antoinette, and she began to make her own improvements to the house and vast gardens.

By 1783, when Fersen returned from America, the queen's popularity was already on the wane. Gone was the delighted clamor that had greeted her a decade earlier when, as dauphine, she had made her first formal visit to Paris. Instead, childless for the first eight years of marriage, her extravagant overspending and bedecking herself like a glamorous royal mistress instead of emulating the two previous Bourbon queens—a pair of pious, milquetoasty homebodies—had turned the public mood against her.

Worst was the vicious cycle she had created by alienating the aristocrats who had routinely vilified her. The courtiers who suddenly found themselves on the outside looking in grew angrier than ever at the elimination of their age-old perquisites—most important, proximity to the queen. And so their slanders and libels began, and Marie Antoinette retreated with greater frequency to her safe haven of the Petit Trianon, sometimes with her children and their governess, or with a very small circle of friends, where, with the villa's enforced rules of informality, they waited on themselves. It was the one place on earth where the queen of France could enjoy some privacy, because no one could enter the grounds without her express permission. At Trianon, Marie Antoinette exercised her right to surround herself with only her favorite people and her beloved children, and sought to recapture some of the bucolic, untrammeled charm of her Viennese childhood. She began construction of a little working farm and dairy, the *Hameau*, or hamlet, where a dozen impoverished farmers and their families were relocated and given employment.

Le Petit Trianon had been used for amorous assignations in the past. In fact, the villa even boasted several original features that facilitated them. By this time the windows had been fitted with blinds that were mirrored on the side that faced the exterior. When the blinds were closed, the prying gaze of a would-be intruder would be his own.

The queen's biographer, historian Antonia Fraser, posits that it was during these summer months of 1783 that Marie Antoinette and Axel von Fersen consummated their romance. Fraser asserts that, as birth control was well-known to the aristocracy, and Fersen seemed to have successfully avoided impregnating his numerous lovers on all but one occasion, there was nothing to preclude the queen from sleeping with both Axel and her husband. Nothing except perhaps her faith and moral scruples.

But setting those two things aside for the moment, if Marie Antoinette was so deeply in love with Fersen that she was willing to become the very thing she had always detested—an adulteress—recalling her scorn for Madame du Barry and even for her dear departed father, who had cheated on her mother, Ms. Fraser omits a key point: *In the summer of 1783 Marie Antoinette was already pregnant.* Therefore the fear of pregnancy was eliminated, and there was no more propitious time, biologically, for her to consummate her passion for Axel von Fersen. Is that why Marie Antoinette fought temptation and lost—at the cost of everything she had been taught to value?

Fraser attributes the queen's topple off the moral wagon to human nature, citing an irrational expectation that her feelings for Fersen would be of the pure and lofty sort, like an unconsummated ardor out of the age of chivalry and the medieval Courts of Love. There is indeed no accounting for the vagaries of the human heart.

In some ways, Marie Antoinette lost the true north of her moral compass with the death of her mother in 1780. And although she came to the Bourbon court a decade earlier determined not to become one of the louche and debauched French courtiers—and for the most part she retained the values she was raised with—in time, she did end up a victim of Stockholm syndrome, as much like her captors, if not more so, when it came to certain extravagant behaviors.

But did it cross the line at adultery, in 1783, or at any other time?

In the absence of concrete proof either way, the Fersen and Marie Antoinette love story has become a matter of forensics. Based on the scant evidence remaining to us and our own values and experiences, it is inevitably colored by the hunches of whichever detective is assigned to the case, analyzing the queen's fondness for Fersen and making assumptions about whether it was a purely platonic friendship, an adulterous romance, or any one of the several shades of gray in between.

Although Marie Antoinette had innocuously flirted with other men when she was dauphine and even during her early years as queen, she was far too intimidated to act upon her desires or impulses. In addition, at that point she had yet to consummate her marriage and couldn't possibly risk pregnancy. When it came to morality, Marie Antoinette viewed adulterers as ants on a dunghill. And in royal marriages, politics always came first. If she indulged in an affair and it was discovered, she could be sent back to Austria in disgrace, destroying her mother's greatest political achievement, the Franco-Austrian alliance forged between the millennium-old enemies.

But the queen's feelings for Axel von Fersen may have forced her to reexamine everything she believed and held dear. She had fallen in love with him, experienced sensations in her heart, body, and soul that were entirely new. The game changed. It was a moment of crisis. In her late teens and twenties, with no other outlet for her energy, Marie Antoinette had demonstrated little impulse control when it came to her extravagant purchases of jewelry and clothing, her high-stakes gaming and gallivanting into Paris late at night, as well as her disregard for the feelings of some of the older courtiers. Her mother had chided her sternly and repeatedly about it. It is not a wild leap to ascribe to her similar uncontrollable behavior in acting upon her desire for Fersen. And in the summer of 1783, when she was in her first trimester of pregnancy, her hormones were already all over the place.

According to the comtesse de Boigne, "Whether or not [Fersen's lost looks due to his illness in America] was the reason, those who knew her did not doubt that she now yielded to the passion of M. de Fersen. He indemnified her sacrifice by a boundless devotion and by an affection that was as deep as it was respectful and discreet. He breathed only for her and all his habits of life were calculated to compromise her as little as possible."

This may be the only surviving account to boldly confirm consummation. The comtesse de Boigne's connection to the court, however, is only hearsay; her aunt was a lady-in-waiting to the king's maiden aunt, the tart-tongued princesse Adélaïde, who had not only moved out of Versailles into the Château de Bellevue in 1774, but detested Marie Antoinette. Yet the comtesse's mention of the event in her memoirs in 1783 indicates that people were discussing it—discreet as the relationship was alleged to have been.

However, in Fersen's own words that summer, on July 31, barely a month after his return to France, he wrote to Sophie, "No matter how much pleasure I would have in seeing you again I cannot leave Paris without regret. You will find this very natural when I tell you the reason. I will tell you because I don't want to hide anything from you." And yet the count does not tell his sister "the reason," at least not in this letter.

To his father, the count wrote asking for money to remain in Paris. "Your consent is the only thing that could make me happy forever.

There are a thousand reasons for this which I dare not put down on paper."

Fifteen years after the fact, Fersen mentioned the date of July 15, 1783, in his *Journal intime*, writing, "I remember this day. . . . I went *chez Elle* for the first time." *Chez Elle* (meaning "her house/home/place") was the count's code phrase for spending the night with a lover. Does the reference to July 15, 1783, give a date certain in Axel von Fersen's words to the first time he and Marie Antoinette made love?

Unfortunately, there's no way to be certain that *"chez Elle"* is a euphemism for sex in this context. It could simply mean that Fersen went to see the queen to discuss his potential acquisition of the Royal Suédois. But if that were the case, why not say so? The location of their meeting is not mentioned either, but was likely le Petit Trianon, Marie Antoinette's favorite place for whiling away the sultry summer days. Yet he had visited both the Château of Versailles and the Petit Trianon countless times, so why did the July 15 meeting merit a coded mention?

With Axel's father wary of his son's reasons for lingering around Versailles, the count devised a subterfuge—"to marry an heiress, Mlle. Necker, with her Swiss millions," he told the old statesman. Fortunately (and unbeknownst to the elder Fersen), Germaine Necker had her eye on fellow Swede Baron Erik Magnus Staël von Holstein. In the letter to Sophie Piper of July 31, only two weeks after he wrote of his rendezvous *"chez Elle,"* Axel confided the truth to his sister. "I have determined never to marry. It would be unnatural. . . . I cannot belong to the one woman to whom I should like to belong, and who loves me, so I will not belong to anyone."

The timing of this determination is certainly noteworthy.

Regardless of whether they believe there was a sexual relationship between Fersen and Marie Antoinette, not a single historian disputes the fact that Marie Antoinette was the woman referred to in this letter. And with all the opportunities open to him, the handsome and highly eligible Fersen, only twenty-seven years old at the time, kept his pledge to remain a bachelor.

As word would eventually reach Axel the elder in Sweden that his son had abandoned his quest for a wealthy bride, the count nipped the matter in the bud himself, writing to his father, "Unless marriage vastly increases my own wealth, it's hardly worth the trouble, with all its burdens, embarrassments, and deprivations."

Marie Antoinette worked diligently to obtain Fersen the colonelcy of the Royal Suédois. It came at a hefty price tag—a hundred thousand livres—and the count did not personally have the funds to afford it. Nor would his father bankroll the extravagance, accusing Axel of frivolity. The regiment would never earn back what it cost to buy it. The old senator viewed the Royal Suédois as a vanity purchase that would bankrupt the family at the expense of Axel's younger siblings, who had yet to make their way in the world and who deserved the same financial support that Axel had received as a youth. And he had more than a sneaking suspicion as to why his son wanted to put down roots in France.

Enduring the same sort of scolding from his father that Marie Antoinette had received from her late mother on countless occasions, Axel reminded the elder statesman that he had in fact quit the pleasures of the French capital for the hardships of the North American winter and had spent three years with Rochambeau. The military was his life.

In the end, in addition to the open purse of Marie Antoinette, it was the king of Sweden, Gustavus III, who supported his countryman's bid for the colonelcy of the Royal Suédois. In a strong character reference to Louis XVI, his fellow monarch wrote that Fersen had "served with general approval in your armies in America." Marie Antoinette wrote a similar recommendation, mentioning that Fersen had "greatly distinguished himself in the American War." A soldier in an age when soldiering was the manly thing to do and the most glamorous profession in the world, Fersen must have seemed exotic to Marie Antoinette when she was surrounded all day by idle courtiers. And she was wedded to an overweight man who (and wisely, for the most part) did not relish going to war, but his reluctance to commit to combat wasn't considered cool at the time. In an era of perpetual martial conflict, Louis had never even visited the École Militaire, had closed the military training camp at Compiègne (where he preferred to hunt instead), and never reviewed his troops or staged practice drills.

Axel's monarch demanded a quid pro quo for his support. He had never made the Grand Tour, and despite the fact that Gustavus was a reigning sovereign, he decided to leave his throne in the hands of a regent and visit the world. He asked (which meant commanded) Fersen to accompany him as his aide-de-camp.

The count left France on September 20. During the king's Grand Tour, much of Fersen's responsibilities fell into the realm of damage control, keeping his boss out of the equivalent of gay bars and his name out of the press. Gustavus was very jealous of any free time his ADC spent out of his company, and Fersen found himself stealing precious moments when he could just to write to Marie Antoinette. He also corresponded with a breeder in Sweden about getting a dog for "Joséphine" (a code name for the queen that turns up several times in his letters). "Not a small dog," it was to be like his own hound, Odin. But the process was taking much longer than anticipated, and finally, to light a fire under the breeder, Fersen admitted that it was to be a gift for the queen of France.

Marie Antoinette may have chiefly occupied his thoughts, but she was not the sole obsession of his loins. The count also snagged enough time for romantic dalliances. As with the proverbial sailor, there was a girl in practically every port. He had a fling with Emily Cowper in Florence and enjoyed nookie in Naples with Lady Elizabeth Foster, the best friend of one of Marie Antoinette's acquaintances, Georgiana, Duchess of Devonshire. But when things with Bess Foster began to get too serious, Fersen backed off. In his letter book, he noted one he wrote to Bess in which "I told her everything," those words heavily underlined in his own hand. There is such emphasis on the underscoring that one is tempted to wonder exactly what he revealed. Fersen and Lady Elizabeth Foster remained close friends for the rest of their lives, and after Marie Antoinette's execution, the queen was the chief topic of their conversation.

Marie Antoinette's pregnancy of 1783 tragically ended in a miscarriage on November 2, her twenty-eighth birthday. It took her ten days to recover her health. But she and Louis were intent on trying for a second son, conceding that with each passing year the dauphin's health was not improving. Whatever love the queen bore for Axel von Fersen, she continued to have regular marital relations.

Paris (and Versailles) were destinations on Gustavus's Grand Tour, and Axel was briefly reunited with Marie Antoinette in the early summer of 1784. He brought her the Swedish hound, which she named Odin, in honor of his own dog.

On August 18, Marie Antoinette reported the confirmation of a new pregnancy; she believed herself two months gone at the time. Rumors swirled even then, which gives credence to the theory that some people believed there was a sexual element to their attachment, and throughout the years historians have debated whether the child could have been Fersen's. If they were indeed lovers, it is *theoretically* possible for the count to have fathered the boy, who was born on March 27, 1785, and made duc de Normandie, but it is not likely. Little Louis Charles's paternity was never doubted by the king, and even Marie Antoinette's fiercest detractors concurred that her pregnancy coincided with her husband's regular conjugal visits. Although the little duc did not resemble his portly father (nor, for that matter, was he saddled with his mother's unfortunate Hapsburg jaw and bulging eyes), the beautiful boy looked like the slenderer members of the Bourbon family, including Louis XV in his childhood.

Additionally, if Fersen and the queen were sleeping together during the summer of 1784, he surely would have been careful, so that there would have been no doubts as to the legitimacy of a future heir, should she become pregnant and bear a boy. The count was an experienced lover, well versed in how to avoid pregnancies. He loved the queen, and the last thing he wanted was to compromise her.

After their charming visit to Versailles, Fersen and Gustavus resumed their Grand Tour. Marie Antoinette turned thirty on November 2, 1785, the age she had mocked when, as the newly minted eighteen-year-old queen of France, she wondered why anyone over thirty dared to show their face at court. She had become demoralized over the scandal regarding the "Affair of the Diamond Necklace," in which a female con artist descended from the Valois dynasty claimed that the queen intended to purchase an ostentatious bauble for 1.6 million livres, using the Cardinal de Rohan (whom Marie Antoinette had detested all her life) as an intermediary. Unfortunately, people believed that the covetous queen with a taste for expensive jewelry and no understanding of economy had swindled the court jewelers out of their investment, fooled the cardinal, and taken advantage of poor, tragic comtesse Jeanne de Lamotte-Valois, the impoverished aristocrat who had dared to befriend her. (Jeanne later went so far as to claim that they were lovers.)

Not a word of it was true. Before the scandal broke, Marie Antoinette had never even heard of the so-called comtesse, so she had certainly never met Madame de Lamotte-Valois, let alone bedded her! The theft of the necklace was the brainchild of Jeanne, her husband, and Jeanne's lover. The comtesse was also sleeping with the cardinal, who was their arch-dupe; they tricked him into fronting the money for the necklace, which they then pocketed and dismantled, selling the loose stones in London.

And yet, even though she was sentenced to be flogged, branded, and imprisoned (the cardinal was ultimately exonerated), Jeanne de Lamotte-Valois was a martyr in the eyes of the people, while their queen was tarred as a spendthrift foreign whore. Mortally wounded by the trial verdict, which came at a time when she was enduring her most difficult pregnancy, Marie Antoinette retreated like a wounded lioness to le Petit Trianon, sorely in need of the comfort of genuine friends.

Fersen had returned to France in 1785. Witness to the character assassinations the queen had endured during the investigations regarding the Affair of the Diamond Necklace, he wrote to his sister Sophie, "She is most unhappy, and her courage, which is admirable beyond compare, makes her yet more attractive. My only trouble is that I cannot compensate her for her sufferings and that I shall never make her as happy as she deserves." The more unfortunate Marie Antoinette became, the more she was forsaken.

When he was in France, the count visited le Petit Trianon unattended three to four times a week. He and the queen snatched what fleeting hours they could, giving rise to gossip, as would the arrival of any handsome, unchaperoned caller. A campaign of concealment was undertaken. Count von Fersen kept a meticulous diary, but he never indicated why he went to the palace, nor who had summoned him.

Fersen was in England in 1786, where he was nicknamed "the Picture" for his striking looks. By 1787, he was back on French soil.

Informally, he was Marie Antoinette's admirer; officially, he was the emissary of the Swedish sovereign, couriering correspondence between Gustavus III's court and the Bourbons. In time, Fersen's role as Gustavus's liaison would prove invaluable. The count continued to travel, notching numerous voyages between France and Sweden, and his letter book dutifully noted his absences from "Joséphine."

In the spring of 1788, Fersen returned to his homeland to participate in Gustavus's Finnish campaign against Russia. But by November 6, four days after Marie Antoinette's thirty-third birthday, he was back in Paris. Twenty-two letters mark the six-month absence from her. In the period that followed, Fersen most certainly visited Versailles, because he meticulously recorded the tips he gave to the servants in his account books.

But by this time the nature of his rendezvous was more likely political than sexual. Much had changed since the idyllic days of 1783. The May 31, 1786, verdict in the trial of the Diamond Necklace Affair had sent Marie Antoinette into paroxysms of rage, followed by a profound depression. The political landscape of France had changed as well. No one was happy with the status quo. The clergy and nobility were angry about the progressive measures Louis' ministers had proposed, because it meant they would have to pay taxes. The bourgeoisie and the poor, having been inspired by the success of the American Revolution, decided it was time for them to have a voice in their governance. The common denominator for everything was their scapegoat: the outsider; the foreign-born queen, *l'Autrichienne* [sometimes spelled *l'Autruchienne*], a pun on "the Austrian woman" and the word for a female dog. Marie Antoinette was even blamed for acts of nature such as crop failure and bad harvests.

Many of the poorer classes had no grasp of the lofty concepts of revolution; their discontent and disillusion were taken advantage of—fired up by pamphlets (mostly lampooning Marie Antoinette) that were financed from the deep pockets of the king's own cousin, the duc d'Orléans. Philippe d'Orléans hoped that the people would overthrow Louis and reform the kingdom as a constitutional monarchy, placing *him* on the throne as their new king. Oh, how wrong he was, but that's another story.

Marie Antoinette had been devastated by the most personal sorrows as well. Her daughter princesse Sophie Hélène Béatrix, born several weeks premature on July 9, 1786, never lived to see her first birthday, dying on June 14, 1787. And the dauphin, Louis Joseph, was bravely enduring the physical torments of rickets and a severely curved spine. His declining health and Sophie's demise brought Marie Antoinette closer to God, and after the mechanical devotions of the daily Masses she had been attending for years, she became more genuinely devout.

This was the emotional state of the woman Axel von Fersen greeted in 1788. It is possible that in a time of such tremendous upheaval, Marie Antoinette needed his love and comfort and his reassuring presence more than ever; that dynamic is very plausible. But it is equally conceivable that what she most desired from the count, having turned her thoughts to her husband and children, God and kingdom, was his unwavering friendship.

Of that she could be certain until she drew her final breath. Count von Fersen remained her champion even when it seemed as though everyone in France was ready to tear her to pieces. In 1789 he wrote to his father, "You cannot fail to applaud the Queen, if you do justice to her desire to do good and the goodness of her own heart."

If, by the late 1780s, Axel von Fersen was no longer Marie Antoinette's lover (or, according to some biographers, had never been her lover), it does make sense that he eventually moved on carnally, embarking on other relationships—yet they were invariably with other unattainable women, ensuring the queen's primacy at the pinnacle of his affections. However, there was one who evidently captured his heart. Eléanore Sullivan, who had arrived in Paris in 1783, was five years their senior. After enjoying a checkered romantic past, she married an Irishman whom she'd first met in Paris, but was living under the protection of a Scot, Quentin Craufurd, who had met her in Manila and brought her back to the French capital. Around April 1789, Eléanore became Fersen's lover, although she remained involved with Craufurd, who for the next several years would have no inkling of her affair.

Although Craufurd was apparently ignorant of Fersen's liaison with Eléanore, the rest of Europe learned of it quickly, thanks to the acid tongue and pen of one of the count's jilted paramours, the wife of the comte de Saint-Priest. In the crucial days that followed the royal family's aborted flight to Varennes, during the summer of 1791 Madame de Saint-Priest traveled to England, Germany, and Sweden, spreading the news of Axel von Fersen's newest conquest. Sophie Piper wrote to her brother, fretting about Marie Antoinette's reaction should the queen ever find out about the affair.

"I have not spoken to you about this or warned you about it out of respect for Her because She would be mortally wounded should this news reach her ear. Everybody is watching you and talking about you and you must think of Her and spare her this cruelest of blows."

In addition to his arrangement with Eléanore and Craufurd, the count's other triangular relationship was with the king and queen of France. As much as he adored Marie Antoinette, Axel was always respectful of Louis, paying tribute to the "goodness, honesty, frankness and loyalty of the king," and he fervently believed that the French monarchy should prevail at all costs, returning the nation to the influence she had always enjoyed across Europe. Fersen placed his life in jeopardy as much for Louis' sake as for the queen's.

He arrived in Versailles on September 27, 1789, to spend the winter in a house he had acquired in town. By that time, Marie Antoinette had buried her older son. The seven-year-old dauphin had died on June 4 during the tumultuous weeks-long convention of the three Estates General. The callous representatives were so eager to push their governmental reforms forward that they were unwilling to begrudge the king the afternoon off to mourn his heir.

Fersen had no way of knowing that just a few days after his arrival in Versailles, the life of his beloved queen would be frighteningly upended. Antonia Fraser posits that he may have passed the day of October 5, the queen's last full day at Versailles, in her company, while other historians believe he was not there, instead riding hell-for-leather for the palace when he heard the terrifying news, so that he could be with her in her hour of peril. That morning an armed mob more than six thousand strong, comprised purportedly of prostitutes from the Palais Royal and Parisian fishwives, their numbers swelled with men disguised as women, had begun to march in the pouring rain from the capital to Versailles, demanding bread. The *poissardes* later claimed that they were unfairly blamed, and that many amid the throng were in fact disgruntled members of the aristocracy in disguise.

By late afternoon on October 5, Louis was prepared to capitulate to the (now drunken) mob's demands, but rumors were spread among them that he had no intentions of honoring his pledge. The following day, they stormed the Château de Versailles, destroying priceless treasures and beheading two of Marie Antoinette's bodyguards in their frenzied search for the queen. Bursting into her bedroom, they stabbed at her mattress with pikestaffs, and would have done the same to her had she not slipped through a secret door in the nick of time and fled to Louis' apartments.

The royal family was lucky to escape with their lives, but they would be denied their freedom as they had always known it. From that moment the mob took them hostage, and they were conveyed to Paris in a slow-moving procession that afforded every citizen the opportunity to ogle and jeer at the "Baker," the "Baker's wife," and the "Baker's boy." When the Bourbons reached the disused Tuileries Palace, where they would remain essentially under house arrest, among the loyal friends waiting to meet them was Axel von Fersen. "I was witness to it all," he wrote to his father a few days later. "I returned to Paris in one of the carriages that followed the King. We were six and a half hours on the road. May God preserve me from ever again seeing so heartbreaking a spectacle as that of the last two days."

He sold the house and horses he'd bought in Versailles and purchased a house in Paris in order to visit Marie Antoinette more easily, although his official cover was as the *un*official observer of the unrest on behalf of the king of Sweden. Gustavus III worried about the effects of French revolutionary violence on the rest of Europe.

As early as January 1790, Fersen wrote that only a war, be it "exterior" or "interior," could reestablish the royal authority in France. But how could that be achieved "when the king is a prisoner in Paris?" the count asked. The solution seemed clear: Get the king out of Paris.

During the summer of 1790, the royals' energy was focused on whether they should remain in the capital or flee. Fersen was an early advocate of escape. If he was not the queen's lover, then or ever, he was certainly her closest confidant at the time, and, as he admitted to Sophie, her most zealous admirer. The count saw in Marie Antoinette a sensitive and suffering heroine who had been both misused and misjudged, a woman full of goodness at a time when any positive opinion of her was rare.

Two others who shared Fersen's sympathetic estimation of the queen were his mistress Eléanore Sullivan and her protector, Quentin Craufurd. These fervent royalists played an integral role in the royal family's escape from the Tuileries in June 1791, personally helping to bankroll their flight.

Fersen was more or less at Marie Antoinette's side during the royal family's twenty-month house arrest in the Tuileries, managing to discreetly come and go from the palace, although it bustled with guards and spies. Several times the comte de Saint-Priest states unequivocally that after the monarchs were permitted to journey to the Château de Saint-Cloud during the summer of 1790, Fersen was seen leaving the queen's room at three a.m. At this time the count was deeply involved in plotting the royal family's escape from France, and his lengthy visits with Marie Antoinette may have been devoted primarily, if not entirely, to political and strategic, rather than amorous, conversation. Fersen's journal from this period was burned soon afterward, so the truth will never be known for certain.

It is from Axel von Fersen's letters to his sister Sophie and her lover, Baron von Taube, that we know how critically and intimately involved he was with the affairs of Marie Antoinette and the French crown. The queen came to rely upon the count's efforts even more after Louis, overwhelmed by events, suffered a nervous breakdown during the winter of 1790. Confined to the Tuileries by then and denied the daily hunting that had always been his emotional and physical outlet, he collapsed under the strain. With the king inactive, Marie Antoinette assumed control of their destiny. In the past she had been falsely accused of being the power behind the throne; now the allegations became the reality. The storming of Versailles on October 6, 1789, had marked a turning point in her life.

In December 1790, in the name of the baronne de Korff, a Franco-Swede who provided her own passport for the royal family's flight, Fersen commissioned a *berline de voyage*, a capacious, heavy traveling coach of the type meant to comfortably transport a fairly large aristocratic party from Paris to St. Petersburg. The conveyance had to carry six adults and two children, and Fersen had participated in all the details involved in securing it. It was he who paid the five thousand or so livres to purchase the carriage, a vehicle "unknown" to the royal family, as it bore no resemblance to their official coaches. After the escape proved ill-fated, Monday-morning quarterbacks would criticize the carriage's size, bulk, and appearance, but there was in fact nothing unusual about it. It was not bright yellow, as some historians have erroneously stated. It was the undercarriage and wheels that were yellow, which was very common for the era. Built by Monsieur Louis, the finest coachman of his day, the body of the *berline* was green and black, and the interior was upholstered in white taffeta.

When it came time to decide on the family's ultimate destination, the king preferred to remain within the borders of France, while Marie Antoinette was in favor of emigrating to Switzerland via Alsace. However, she expected assistance from her homeland, which would mean a mustering of troops on the Austrian frontier. But the emperor, her brother Leopold II, had a vast territory to govern, and with limited resources. Leopold didn't begrudge his sister the soldiers, but someone else would have to pay them. Louis and Marie Antoinette were short of funds. Money had to be borrowed. In addition to applying to Italian banks, Count von Fersen loaned the French monarchs the money from his own pocket. The other investors included Eléanore Sullivan and Quentin Craufurd, as well as the baronne de Korff and her sister—who happened to be Craufurd's other mistress.

As the plans were hatched for the royal family's flight from the Tuileries, Fersen's role was under debate. He had expected to escort the royals all the way to the frontier town of Montmédy, but Louis forbade it. Fersen's explanation for this decision was simply that it wasn't desired. The reasons for the king's denial have long been the subject of speculation. Did he believe Fersen had already done enough for them and it was not worth risking his life to do more than drive them just a few miles out of Paris? Was he jealous of Fersen and resented the idea of being rescued by his wife's lover or, at the very least, her special confidant? Was it Gallic snobbery because the Swedish count wasn't a French nobleman? Or was it because if they got caught being aided by a foreigner things could be dire for all of them? The second possibility can be eliminated. Louis was at this point so mired in inertia and indecision that he surely didn't have the energy to be jealous of Fersen. It was the queen who at this time found herself suddenly rising to the occasion and discovering a well-spring of resourcefulness, courage, and strength she never knew she had.

After a series of glitches, the royal family managed to escape the Tuileries in the middle of the night on June 20, 1791. A disguised Count Axel von Fersen was the coachman on the box. As he waited for the royals to sneak out of the palace he played his role to the hilt, whistling and chewing tobacco. In accordance with Louis' instructions he surrendered his post at Bondy to another coachman, saddled a horse, and rode for Brussels.

Tragically, the night ended in disaster at the little town of Varennes when the king was recognized. "Do you think Fersen has escaped?" Marie Antoinette whispered to her husband. The family was bundled into their *berline* and escorted back to Paris. After their arrival, disheveled and demoralized, Marie Antoinette managed to scribble a few lines to the count: "Be reassured about us; we are alive." A second letter read, "I exist. . . . How worried I have been about you. . . . Don't write to me, that will expose us, and above all don't come here under any pretext. . . .We are in view of our guards day and night; I'm indifferent to it. . . . [B]e calm, nothing will happen to me. . . . Adieu . . . I can't write any more to you. . . ."

One of the two men who accompanied the royal family in the *berline* from Varennes to Paris was a deputy of the Revolution named Antoine Barnave. During the hot, dusty, and exceedingly cramped three-day journey, the deputies, and particularly Barnave, were charmed by the queen, who was not at all the monster they'd been taught to despise. By the time the carriage reached Paris, the twenty-nine-year-old Barnave had a little crush on Marie Antoinette, and she would soon take advantage of his sympathy to advance the royalist cause. In no time, rumors were spreading that the queen was sleeping with Barnave and had corrupted him. The rumors were absurd, but Fersen was crushed and disgusted, even though he was betraying both the queen and Quentin Craufurd with Eléanore Sullivan. During the summer of 1791, after King Gustavus had dispatched Fersen to Vienna in an effort to secure the support of both Austria and Prussia in his scheme to save the French monarchs, Marie Antoinette heard nothing from the count for two months, although she sent him several letters. It's possible, however, that the correspondence was intercepted and he never received it.

Following their attempted escape to Montmédy and the debacle in Varennes, the royal family was watched even more closely and guarded more heavily. But Fersen remained among the small, loyal circle of royalists that continued to foment escape plots. The only European sovereign willing to offer his support was Gustavus III, although he suggested that Louis be smuggled out alone. Fersen argued that such a plan would leave Marie Antoinette and the dauphin vulnerable to becoming hostages of the Revolution.

Through her old friend Count Esterházy, she sent Fersen a little gold ring, new and inexpensive. It was engraved with three lilies and bore the inscription, *"Lâche qui les abandonne"*—"Faint heart he who forsakes her." Historian Antonia Fraser translates the inscription as "Coward who abandons them."

The queen told Esterházy ". . . Should you write HIM tell him that many miles and many countries can never separate hearts. I feel this truth more strongly every day." Esterházy undoubtedly knew the identity of the "HIM" she referred to in capital letters. Her letter continued. "I am delighted to find this opportunity to send you a little ring which I am sure will give you pleasure. In the past few days they've been selling like hot cakes here and they are very hard to come by. The one that is wrapped in paper is for HIM. Send it to HIM for me. It is exactly his size. I wore it for two days before wrapping it. Tell him it comes from me. I don't know where he is. It is dreadful to have no news of those one loves and not even to know where they are living. . . ."

Scholars who insist that the relationship between Marie Antoinette and Fersen was strictly platonic are quick to point out that the sending of a ring is a common token of affection in the chivalric manner of sovereigns and their devoted servants. But this was not the

Middle Ages. It was Revolutionary France with life-and-death stakes; and with both parties already under suspicion and the queen's every movement spied upon, to believe that she took the enormous risk of dispatching such a personal item (and a cover letter revealing intimate details about it) to a man who was no more important to her than any other friend or royalist (and potentially compromising Esterházy as well, were he to be apprehended) is somewhat disingenuous. The *un*-engraved ring she sent as a gift to Esterházy may even have served as a deliberate cover for the engraved one she included in the package to be forwarded to Fersen. And the fact that she *wore* Fersen's ring *herself* for *two days* places it far above an ordinary token.

Axel had been collaborating with the king of Sweden on another escape plan and needed to speak with the French monarchs, but he had been banned from entering Paris. Essentially, there was a bounty on his head were he to be discovered there. Nevertheless, on February 13, 1792, heavily disguised, he managed not only to enter the capital, but to sneak through a side door of the palace. Marie Antoinette had not seen him since they had said farewell at Bondy in the middle of the night on June 20–21, 1791. Fersen had much to say to both sovereigns about his plans, but the notation about the night of February 13 in his *Journal intime* has been the source of vehement debate for generations of historians. Because the king and queen were so heavily guarded inside the palace as well as from without, it was just as risky for Fersen to try to sneak back *out* of the Tuileries, and so he remained the night. His journal does indicate that he did not see or meet with the king until six p.m. the following evening—many hours after his arrival—and did not leave the palace until nine thirty that night. The words he wrote were *"À 9:30 je la quittai"*—"At 9:30 I left her." As the French word for "palace" is masculine, the intimation in Fersen's diary is that he left *her*—Marie Antoinette—and all the unwritten subtext their relationship and the extremity of the monarchs' circumstances implies.

Exactly where he slept, or was hidden, on the night of February 13 remains a mystery. Fersen seems to have written two words that he, or someone else, subsequently tried to erase, so that they remain barely discernible. The two words are *"resté là,"* which was his usual shorthand for spending the night with a lover. Translated literally, the words simply mean "stayed there." And that's all that might have happened. The count sneaked into the Tuileries and found himself stuck, so he had to stay the night.

Or perhaps *resté là* does mean that on the eve of Valentine's Day, which would be almost too perfect, the royal lovers enjoyed one final night of passion with guards stationed everywhere. There are no references to the nature of Fersen's disguise. He must have dressed in a manner that fooled the guards into believing that he could plausibly visit the sovereigns for a considerable amount of time, because he was able to remain inside the Tuileries for nearly twenty-four hours and eventually meet with both of them long enough to thoroughly discuss the details of the latest escape plot.

At the Tuileries, the monarchs had separate apartments; Louis' was upstairs from Marie Antoinette's, and they were connected by a staircase. The king always retired early, his customary bedtime undisturbed by such nuisances as a revolution. And he was a heavy slumberer. Exceedingly deferential with his wife, he wasn't likely to come barging downstairs and into her room in the middle of the night; he was too solicitous of her privacy.

But even if Marie Antoinette and Fersen somehow managed to distract her maid, and the sentry outside her door, long enough to enjoy a furtive embrace, this scenario remains highly speculative, perhaps better suited to the genres of fiction or film. Were they to be caught— literally under the king's nose—the humiliation for the queen would be too great, and the price for Fersen would likely be death.

After Fersen was able to slink out of the Tuileries, he remained in Paris for another week, hiding in Eléanore Sullivan's attic, although Marie Antoinette thought he had left for Spain. He departed France for Brussels on February 21.

They lost their greatest ally on March 16, 1792, when Gustavus III was assassinated by a disgruntled Swedish nobleman, dying thirteen days later. Although Fersen's role as the king's emissary to Louis and Marie Antoinette was mooted by Gustavus's death, he never stopped trying to rescue the French royal family.

On April 22, 1792, the French Republic declared war on Marie Antoinette's native Austria.

On June 23, three days after the Tuileries were stormed on the first anniversary of the flight to Varennes, Marie Antoinette wrote to Fersen in code, "Your friend [meaning Louis] is in the gravest danger." In a metaphor for their increasingly dire situation as the wheels of the Revolution turned apace, she added, "His illness is moving with terrifying speed. . . . The doctors no longer recognize him. If you wish to see him again you must make haste. Tell his relations about his dangerous condition."

In the wake of Marie Antoinette's desperate letters to Fersen, written both in cipher and "in clear," (pretending to be the lady friend of a French émigré named Rignon whose business affairs she managed in his absence), the count became more determined than ever to rescue her.

He was instrumental in the drafting of an ill-advised proclamation issued to the people of Paris on July 25 by the Duke of Brunswick, commander of the Allied Army, comprised primarily of Prussian and Austrian forces. Known as the Brunswick Manifesto, it declared that if the French royal family were to be harmed, then the Allies would retaliate with force against the Parisian civilians. The intention of the Brunswick Manifesto was to intimidate the Parisians, but it had the opposite effect. Instead of frightening them, it fired up their revolutionary zeal all the more.

After the January 21, 1793, execution of Louis XVI, Fersen heard a rumor that the entire royal family had been put to death. Devastated over the purported loss of Marie Antoinette, he wrote to his sister Sophie, "She was once all my happiness, for whom I lived—yes, my tender Sophie, for I have never ceased loving her—the one I loved so much, for whom I would have sacrificed a thousand lives, is no more. Never will her adored image be erased from my memory. Why, oh why didn't I die by her side—for her and for them—on June 20. It would have been better so than to have to drag out my days in sorrow and remorse. . . ."

When he learned that the queen still lived, his concern for her fate remained palpable. "Sometimes I have hopes, sometimes I despair, and my compulsory inaction, the limited means there are of serving her, add even more to my sorrow. In my social circle, we speak only of her, of ways of saving her, and do nothing but grieve and cry over her fate."

At the end of March 1793, Marie Antoinette dispatched a trusted emissary, the Chevalier de Jarjayes, on two missions: He was to deliver Louis' seal and wedding ring to the late king's brother the comte de Provence in Brussels, and then Jarjayes was to bring an impression of her seal, taken from a little gold signet ring she had made up, adorned with Fersen's arms, to someone else. The queen told Jarjayes, "Toulan will give you the things that are to go to the princes. The wax impress which I include here is something else again. When you are in a safe place, I would very much appreciate it if you took it to my great friend who came to see me last winter from Brussels and you are to tell him when you give it to him *that its motto has never been more true.*"

Fersen explained the device in his *Journal intime*. "This motto was from a seal showing a pigeon in flight with the motto *Tutto a te mi guida.* ["All things lead me to you."] Her idea, in those days, had been to take my emblem and we had taken the flying fish for a bird. The impression was on a piece of paper. Unfortunately, it had been completely erased in the heat. In spite of that I keep it carefully in my casket with the note and the drawing of the seal."

For some reason, Count von Fersen did not receive Marie Antoinette's letter until January 21, 1794, a year to the day from Louis XVI's execution, a tragic memory for Fersen that would "never be effaced."

Fersen was sickened by the report of Marie Antoinette's much-altered appearance during her trial before the Revolutionary Tribunal in October 1793. Still only thirty-seven, she had evidently become old and sunken-looking. Something must be done to save her! He met with Craufurd, the comte de la Marck, and the Russian minister Jean Simolin, a royalist. Fersen asked: As a private individual, rather than in his capacity as a sovereign, shouldn't the new Austrian emperor, Francis II, Marie Antoinette's nephew, demand her release? Ultimately, the men chose not to pursue this avenue for fear of further provoking her antagonists.

Fersen was frustrated by the foot draggers and the cowards. Those who counseled caution drove him crazy. He was all in favor of riding in from the frontier at the head of the cavalry and snatching Marie Antoinette out of the Conciergerie.

She was guillotined on October 16, 1793. Fersen was in Brussels and did not hear the news until October 23. For a long while he felt utterly numb. He would see her face in his mind's eye. "It follows me wherever I go. Her suffering and death and all my feelings never leave me for a moment. I can think of nothing else. . . . That she was alone in her last moments with no one to comfort her or talk to her, with no one to whom she could give her last wishes, fills me with horror."

In the privacy of his diary he compared his devotion to Marie Antoinette to his passion for Eléanore Sullivan. "Oh, how I reproach myself for the wrongs I did Her and how deeply I now realize how much I loved Her. What kindness, what sweetness, and tenderness, what a fine and loving, sensitive and delicate heart! The other [Eléanore Sullivan] isn't like that, although I love her and she is my only comfort and without her I should be very unhappy."

From then on he kept the date of October 16, "this atrocious day," as a day of mourning for "the model of queens and women," as he told Lady Elizabeth Foster. Marie Antoinette represented an ideal in his heart, and he was flooded with memories of her goodness and sweetness, her tenderness, sensibility, and loving nature. He confided to Sophie that Eléanore Sullivan could never replace Marie Antoinette—"*Elle*"—in his heart, although he eventually asked Eléanore to marry him. But when it came to choosing between Fersen and Craufurd, Eléanore's allegiance went to the Scot who paid her rent. She finally wed the man who for all intents and purposes had been her common-law husband for years, and settled down to a life of so-called respectability.

In the years after Marie Antoinette's execution, Axel von Fersen was heaped with honors in his homeland. He was created a Knight of the Order of the Seraphim, Grand Marshal of the Court of Sweden, and Chancellor of Uppsala University, and he was made Lieutenant Governor of the kingdom in 1800, 1803, 1808, and 1809. Yet he remained haunted by the events of the failed escape of June 20, 1791, and by the death of the queen of France, commemorating the tragic anniversaries with heartrending entries in his *Journal intime*.

Seventeen years to the day after the ill-starred flight to Montmédy, Count Axel von Fersen, then Sweden's highest-ranking official after the king, would meet his own demise. He was torn to pieces by a Swedish mob that believed he had poisoned Crown Prince Christian, the heir to the Danish throne. At Christian's funeral procession on June 20, 1810, to cries of "Traitor!" and "Murderer!" Fersen was kicked, stomped, and savagely beaten with sticks and stones while a battalion of the royal guard stood by. They would later claim that they hadn't acted because they'd received no orders to stop the attack. Seriously battered, Fersen was helped to a nearby house, where he was allowed refuge in a small room. But the building's second story housed a restaurant whose patrons mercilessly attacked him again, ripping the ribbon with the Order of the Seraphim from around his neck and tossing it out of the window. A suggestion was made to similarly eject Fersen. Men began to beat him about the head with their walking sticks, and he lay crumpled on the floor of the small chamber, bleeding profusely, until General Silfversparre, no friend of his, arrived on the scene and established order. Silfversparre convinced Fersen that his only hope lay in placing himself under arrest and allowing himself to be imprisoned for his own security in Stockholm's Town Hall.

But the rabble followed Fersen and his escort inside the municipal building and dragged the count back outdoors, where the vicious pummeling continued. The fatal blow was delivered when a young man jumped on his chest, crushing his ribs.

Count von Fersen was never repaid the massive amounts of money he loaned the French crown in an effort to aid the monarchs' escape from the talons of the Revolution. His substantial generosity was yet another manifestation of his love for Marie Antoinette. While it can be argued that they were never more than good friends, time after time in her hour of peril, none of her other intimates from her days at Trianon came forward to open their purses. Not one member of her Hapsburg family lifted a finger financially, and the same can be said of the Bourbons. It was Axel von Fersen and his immediate circle of friends, the odd ménage à trois he comprised with Eléanore Sullivan and Quentin Craufurd, who stepped up to the plate.

It was Axel von Fersen who was there for Marie Antoinette as often as his own king and country and the parameters of decency allowed.

So, did they or didn't they enjoy an affair that crossed the boundaries of loyal friendship? It remains one of history's hotly debated mysteries. Marie Antoinette and Axel von Fersen's contemporaries were more certain of it than not, although after the French Revolution, to harbor the suspicion of an affair was yet another way to tarnish the late queen's reputation. A courtier at Versailles who knew them both, the comte de Saint-Priest, was convinced that Fersen and Marie Antoinette were lovers, leveling the accusation in his memoirs. But the academics who vehemently dispute the possibility of a romance between the count and the queen cite Fersen's affair with Saint-Priest's wife as the comte's rationale for flinging mud at the Swede. Fersen did indeed dally with Madame de Saint-Priest, which might, understandably, have angered the comte. But that doesn't mean the allegation wasn't true. And we must take care not to ascribe twenty-first-century North American morals to the aristocrats at the court of Versailles, for whom extramarital affairs were a matter of course. Besides, it was the queen's reputation that would take the bigger hit from the revelation of an affair with Fersen. And what did the comte de Saint-Priest have against Marie Antoinette?

Four years after Marie Antoinette and Louis XVI were guillotined, in 1797, Fersen attended the Second Congress of Rastatt as the Swedish delegate, but Napoleon refused to acknowledge him as an ambassador, pejoratively calling him "monsieur" instead of "Your Excellency," nor did he addresss him as a count, or a lord of Sweden. Bonaparte insisted that he would have nothing to do with a man who had enjoyed a love affair with the Widow Capet, as Marie Antoinette was called by the revolutionaries after the fall of the monarchy. How ironic that just thirteen years later, Napoleon would be desperately courting the Widow Capet's grandniece Marie-Louise of Austria, in an effort to solidify his imperial status by allying himself with an ancient and legitimately royal house.

It strains credulity to believe with unequivocal certainty that Marie Antoinette, so passionately in love with Axel von Fersen that she reportedly trembled in his presence, a woman famous for her lack of impulse control, prudishly kept herself for a husband to whom she had been united for purely political concerns and with whom she had never known sexual pleasure (as Louis didn't enjoy intercourse), despite her admission to finding her *bonheur essential*—essential happiness—within her marriage. The possibility exists that the queen and Fersen may have consummated their romance during the summer of 1783, although as the years progressed, they may not have remained lovers as numerous unhappy and stressful events reordered the queen's outlook on life.

In 1930, the Finnish archivist Alma Söderhjelm pieced together Fersen's diaries and correspondence and deduced that the mysterious "Joséphine" he often alluded to was Marie Antoinette. Fersen's letters to the queen are meticulously numbered, and the dates coincide with his departures from and returns to Versailles. Söderhjelm came to realize, however, that there was another Josephine (Eléanore Sullivan's maid) who was mentioned in the letters. Some of Fersen's 1787 correspondence refers to a niche in the wall for a stove. A few scholars have wondered why Fersen would write to the queen of France about such a mundane subject, reducing the import of the count's secret references to Marie Antoinette by that code name, and insisting that the "Joséphine" in question is Madame Sullivan's maid.

Au contraire. Fersen did not know Eléanore Sullivan in 1787. The stove in question was specifically a Swedish stove. And the papers of the *Directeur Général des Bâtiments* at Versailles (the man in charge of construction, building, and renovation at the palace) show work orders relating to Marie Antoinette's apartments for the month of October 1787, including one dated October 18, for a set of marble slabs to be delivered to those apartments to be used as a hearth for a Swedish stove. There is also a letter dated October 14 from a man named Loiseleur to the *Directeur Général des Bâtiments*, regarding the specific renovations and construction that would have to be undertaken for the installation of the Swedish stove.

Moreover, the room in which the Swedish stove was to be installed was to become part of a suite set aside for Fersen's use. Like many courtiers at Versailles, the count had a tiny room under the eaves should he wish to avail himself of it, but Marie Antoinette was determined that the Colonel Proprietor of the Royal Suédois should have more spacious accommodations. And so she—scandalously—carved away a couple of rooms in her ground-floor apartments for Count von Fersen.

Throughout her reign, Marie Antoinette was caricatured in pamphlets known as *libelles* that accused her of sexual indiscretions with both men and women, most often with her brother-in-law the comte d'Artois and her two favorite *dames du palais*, the princesse de Lamballe and the comtesse (later duchesse) de Polignac. The *libelles* were written by aristocrats as well as commoners, and while some of the plays, poems, and prints originated in Holland and England, others were of the homegrown variety, tumbling off presses right inside the palace of Versailles, the personal property of courtiers who wished to see the queen disgraced. Yet none of the *libelles*, as vicious as they were, named Count Axel von Fersen as one of Marie Antoinette's paramours. And even during her October 1793 trial before the Revolutionary Tribunal, where she was accused of all manner of vice, including that of incest with her eight-year-old son, never once was Fersen's name introduced, except in connection with his role in aiding the royal family's escape from the Tuileries by driving their coach out of Paris.

On the other hand, the *libelles* depicted Marie Antoinette's carnal depravity with a number of people, *none* of whom were her lovers. So should the *libelles* be relied upon as a trusted source to get it right because they didn't accuse the queen of fornicating with Fersen? Perhaps the anonymous authors of the *libelles* missed the romance because they weren't looking for it. Or because the Swede was often out of the country, they lacked the opportunities to observe him as frequently with Her Majesty. Or because his renowned discretion kept whatever relationship they enjoyed very quietly under wraps. The only one who truly seemed to know the count's heart was his beloved sister Sophie Piper.

The story of Marie Antoinette and Axel von Fersen raises far more questions than it answers. Deprived of irrefutable and conclusive evidence of a sexual relationship, or even of a romantic affair of the heart, academics and historians can only theorize, basing their analyses on the extant letters and memoirs of the parties themselves, and of their contemporaries (courtiers, friends, attendants, ambassadors, lovers, relatives), some of whom were only children during the period of a purported romance, or who had good reason to sanitize the characters of the principals.

This argument continues to be waged online and inflames the passion of readers and academics; few royal romances still excite as much spirited debate. The discussion seems deeply personal at times, because, in the absence of tangible, irrefutable proof either way, those scholars on both sides of the dispute cannot help but color their arguments with their own life experience. For example, Antonia Fraser, Vincent Cronin, Stanley Loomis, André Castelot, and Evelyne Lever all allow for the possibility that Marie Antoinette and Axel von Fersen did enjoy a romance that eventually became sexual. Fraser and Loomis give credence to the contemporary references dating its consummation to sometime during the summer of 1783. After evaluating everything about the character of both parties and the circumstances of their lives up until that point, Fraser credits human nature with the couple's ultimate inability to resist each other. Some believe (or know from experience) that it is possible to fully love, or be in love with, more than one person simultaneously, or to love two people very completely, but in two different ways. Marie Antoinette was a woman, not an icon. There were parts of her heart touched by Count von Fersen that no one else had ever reached. In time, Marie Antoinette came to love her husband very deeply, and there was never a question that she would not stand beside Louis no matter what befell them. But that does not preclude the possibility of a deep and abiding passion for someone else as well.

And it does not discredit the work of the fine biographers whose interpretation of the extant material related to Marie Antoinette's life as it pertained to her connection with Axel von Fersen led them to conclude that where there was smoke, it might be prudent to install a fire alarm.

Nor, however, is it an indication that the legion of historians, including two Brits—the eminent Simon Schama, and the Fascist party member/conspiracy theorist/anti-Semitic journalist Nesta Webster—as well as the two late-twentieth-century French biographers Simone Bertière and Philippe Delorme, whose work has not been translated into English, are off the mark when they deny the probability of a physical romance between Fersen and the queen. Their interpretation of the same material and their own life experiences shade their theories differently from those of their colleagues who are less unequivocal.

On the subject of a romance with Axel von Fersen, the memoirs of Madame Campan, an attendant of Marie Antoinette after she became queen, are often relied upon, as she was an eyewitness to history. The problem with Campan's memoirs is that they were written several years after the events took place, and she often had no personal knowledge of many of them. Madame Campan also embellished her memoirs. Not only were they larded with fictional detail, but they were slanted in order to sanitize, and therefore protect, her beloved beheaded queen's reputation. The most famous Campanism, repeated from pen to pen down through the decades, is her description of Marie Antoinette and Louis Auguste's reaction upon learning of the death of his grandfather Louis XV. She wrote in her memoirs that they knelt and prayed, "Dear God, guide us and protect us, for we are too young to reign." Historians in nearly every biography attribute this exclamation to the new king and queen. The only problem is, they never said it. Henriette Campan, who wasn't there, made it up years after the fact. So if Madame Campan could freely fictionalize that most salient historical event, it stands to reason that she liberally embroidered other aspects of her memoirs in order to create a certain portrait of Marie Antoinette, the one she wished posterity to view, and not necessarily the warts-and-frailties version of her.

The denials of Count von Fersen's descendants, his great-niece the duchesse de Fitz-James and Baron R. M. de Klinckowström, the great-nephew who published Axel's *Journal intime* and heavily censored copies of his letters as *Le Comte de Fersen Et La Cour de France* in 1877, should also not be accepted at face value merely because they were related to one of the parties. Their relationship gives them an even greater reason to remove anything they deemed to be morally repugnant. By the time Baron de Klinckowström published his substantially edited text, Marie Antoinette's replies had long since vanished, and readers were presented with only a fraction of the puzzle. It is true that Count von Fersen acted as the emissary between the Swedish court and the imprisoned Bourbon sovereigns, and that sensitive political subjects were discussed. And it is true that if the correspondence were to fall into the wrong hands, it could prove extremely compromising, if not fatal. A good deal of this political intrigue was undoubtedly contained within the letters. And it has been argued that Baron de Klinckowström judiciously pruned the text before publication, although he insisted, "The Fersen family has retained the greatest veneration for those holy and august martyrs, Louis XVI and Marie Antoinette, and that there is nothing among the papers remaining from the Comte de Fersen which can throw a shadow on the conduct of the Queen." But what did the baron need to edit nearly eighty years after the queen's demise, if not compromising material of another nature entirely? The *political* information would have long since been mooted by 1877, and all the pertinent parties were dead. What else would still be so much of an anathema to Victorian sensibilities that the good baron felt it had to be redacted with such a heavy hand? His only rationale for editing with a machete is the removal of specific passages that damaged or embarrassed the reputations of important persons—either certain figures discussed in some of the documents, or that of Count von Fersen himself.

The original letters no longer exist, so they cannot be analyzed with spectrometry or other methods. On his deathbed the baron ordered a servant to burn the correspondence in his presence. Klinckowström's willful destruction of such valuable historical material at his moment of reckoning seems curious, if not downright suspicious, leading some scholars to conclude that where there was literal smoke, there most certainly could have been romantic fire, and that the baron indeed believed Fersen's descendants had something to be ashamed of. If not, then why destroy the only evidence that could prove there was *no* love affair between Axel von Fersen and Marie Antoinette?

The duchesse de Fitz-James's vehement negation of a royal romance was printed in *La Vie Contemporaine*, a French periodical, in 1893, a full century after Marie Antoinette's death.

I desire first of all to do away with the lying legend, based on a calumny, which distorted the relations between Marie Antoinette and Fersen, relations consisting in absolute devotion, in complete abnegation on one side, and on the other in friendship, profound, trusting and grateful. People have wished to degrade to the vulgarities of a love novel, facts which were otherwise terrible, sentiments which were otherwise lofty.

It is precisely because of their connection to the count that these Victorian-era descendants may protest too much. Or perhaps not, but the possibility remains that they had every reason to whitewash their ancestor's adulterous passion for a once-unpopular queen. It was certainly not to be discussed during an age when her reputation was about to be rehabilitated, or in an era of unmitigated primness.

What is undeniable is that Marie Antoinette and Axel von Fersen loved each other, and that he risked his own life on more than one occasion in an effort to save hers, personally financed her rescue attempts, and never stopped devising plans to free her. He mourned the date of June 20 every year, because he had obeyed Louis and left Marie Antoinette to journey toward Montmédy without him. She was the woman who came first in his heart, and whose existence was more precious than his own. After her death, Fersen wrote to his sister Sophie, "I have never ceased to love her . . . how I long to have died at her side . . . the sole object of my interest has ceased to exist; she alone meant everything to me; and now for the first time do I fully grasp how passionately I was devoted to her. I can think of nothing but her. . . . I have arranged for agents in Paris to buy anything of hers which may be obtainable, for whatever I can get of this sort will be sacred to me."

What could be more romantic than that?

NAPOLEON BONAPARTE

1769–1821

RULED AS EMPEROR OF THE FRENCH: 1804–1814 AND 1815

*B*orn in Ajaccio, Corsica, to an attorney and a domineering mother a year after the island lost its fight for independence to the French, Napoleone Buonaparte was ambitious from the start. He was sent to the mainland to learn French and was enrolled at a military academy in May 1779, where his scrappy but studious demeanor caught his teachers' attention. They were impressed, but wished he wouldn't get into so many fights. Little Napoleone wished the larger boys wouldn't mock his Corsican accent or his country manners. He'd teach those arrogant kids a lesson one day. He'd succeed beyond anyone's wildest expectations.

He was intense in everything, and his dedication to his studies paid off handsomely. He Francofied his name to Napoleon Bonaparte, but at first he didn't clean up too well. His full height (measured in the Parisian foot) was 21.789 inches, or five feet, six inches, slightly shorter than average for the day. His lanky dark hair was "ill combed and ill powdered," his "complexion yellow and seemingly unhealthy," and his insistence on wearing a tattered oversize overcoat everywhere lent him a "slovenly look," said Laure Permon, a friend who knew him throughout his youth.

But appearances are deceptive. At the age of twenty-four, he successfully blockaded the British at Toulon in 1793, despite their additional aid from the Kingdom of Naples. By 1795, Napoleon was Commander of the Interior and, through the assistance of his friend Paul Barras, secured a job with the influential Committee of Public Safety in Paris. Then he fell in love with Barras' lover Rose de

Beauharnais, a widowed Creole society darling who had been married to one of the movers and shakers of the French Revolution. Passionately in love, he renamed her Josephine. They were wed on the evening of March 9, 1796, in the gloomy office of the mayor of the second arrondissement. Both Napoleon and Josephine lied about their ages on their marriage certificate.

Napoleon had just been appointed commander of the Republican Army in Italy, and a few days after his wedding he set off for headquarters. While he was off campaigning, Josephine, who found her husband's intensity overwhelming, had an affair. News of her infidelity changed Napoleon's character in one key way: From then on, as an act of revenge, he was determined to be unfaithful to her with whatever woman struck his fancy.

Politically, he behaved similarly, taking France and then adding to his list of conquests as much of the rest of the world as he could obtain. In November 1799, his bold entrance into France's legislative body, the Council of Five Hundred, and his announcement that it was time for a change, resulted in an entire reorganization of the government into a consulate of three men, one of whom was himself. Before long Napoleon became First Consul, and the most powerful man in the Republic. In 1802, he was made Consul for Life.

Two years later, his hunger for power not yet sated, he became everything the revolutionaries had fought to destroy: royalty. On May 28, 1804, the Senate bestowed upon Napoleon the incongruous title of Emperor of the French Republic. He and Josephine were crowned on December 2, in a ceremony so opulent that most kings would have envied its extravagance.

Fortuitous in having a large family, Napoleon appointed his brothers and brothers-in-law his viceroys as he continued to expand his empire. By the summer of 1808, his domain extended from the Tagus River on the Iberian Peninsula to the Russian steppes, and from Hamburg and the North Sea to the boot of Italy. The empire reached its zenith in 1810, by which time it also encompassed the Confederation of the Rhine and the Duchy of Warsaw.

More than one of Napoleon's female conquests had given him children, but throughout their marriage Josephine had never been able to conceive, though she had borne her first husband a son and daughter. Desperate for an heir, as he believed that without one Europe would ultimately revert to its previous boundaries and kingdoms, Napoleon believed the only remedy was to find a new wife. Although he professed to adore Josephine, they were divorced on January 10, 1810.

Both were emotionally distraught over the proceedings, but the emperor bounced back quickly, marrying eighteen-year-old Marie-Louise of Austria less than three months later, on April 1. She bore him the yearned-for son on March 20, 1811.

Napoleon's campaign to take Russia in 1812 would fail miserably, and after that, it was all downhill. By the Treaty of Chaumont, the forces of Russia, Prussia, Britain, and Austria allied to destroy his empire. Paris was taken by the coalition, and Napoleon was compelled to abdicate on April 11, 1814. The Treaty of Fontainebleau exiled him to the island of Elba in the Mediterranean.

But one evening the following February, Bonaparte made the abrupt decision to return to France and reclaim his empire. He arrived in Paris on March 1, and his sovereignty lasted a hundred days before he was defeated on June 18 by Lord Wellington's forces at the Battle of Waterloo in Belgium.

Napoleon was exiled for the second and final time, dispatched by British warship to the remote South Atlantic island of St. Helena, where he died at 5:49 p.m. on May 6, 1821. His autopsy revealed a grossly enlarged liver, a large gastric ulcer, and a perforated stomach.

It was said that among his last words was the faintly murmured "Josephine." But of his numerous extramarital romances, there was only one woman with whom the little corporal and great dictator truly fell in love.

Her name was Marie Walewska.

NAPOLEON BONAPARTE AND MARIE WALEWSKA (1786–1817)

When the object of Countess Marie Walewska's girlhood hero worship was presented as a romantic reality, she panicked. Yet over eight years she made a remarkable journey, both geographical and emotional, from shy though impassioned patriot to passionate paramour.

During the last third of the eighteenth century, the kingdom of Poland, lacking natural boundaries, had thrice been the victim of its bordering neighbors' greed and aggression. Partitioned in 1772, 1793, and 1795 when the imperial powers of Austria, Prussia, and Russia carved away Polish territories (either by force, by treaty, or both), Poland was subsumed into their respective empires. By the final partition in 1795, Poland, in name, was erased from the map of Europe. Her last king, Stanislas Poniatowski (a former lover of Catherine the Great, who had recommended him for the job), was compelled to abdicate. But with the example of the French Revolution right in front of them, educated Poles craved nothing more than to reclaim their independence. Little more than a decade later, they were firmly convinced that the one man who could deliver their renewed autonomy was the Emperor of the French, then on the march through Western Europe.

Back in 1794, seven-year-old Marie Łaczyńska's father, Matthias Łaczyński, was mowed down by Cossacks as he tried to aid a wounded friend in the Battle of Maciejowice, one of the Polish Volunteer Army's unsuccessful bids for independence. Her mother was left a widow with seven children to care for on her own.

Madame Łaczyńska placed Marie at a Warsaw convent shortly before her fourteenth birthday in order to complete her education. A contemporary described the petite Marie at the time as "very beautiful, with incredibly blue eyes, blond hair which she wore down to her waist and a particularly sweet expression on her face. She made me think of an angel or a wood nymph."

Marie's best friend at school was Elizabeth Grabowska, the daughter of the deposed Polish king and his morganatic wife. As teenage girls are wont to do, they mooned over their mutual hero Napoleon Bonaparte, certain that he was their savior and future liberator. The patriotic Marie's puppy love took the form of her scratching his name in the frost on the windowpanes of their dorm room.

She returned to the family estate of Kiernozia at the age of sixteen and a half, greeted with the news that as the youngest and prettiest of her sisters she would have to marry as soon as possible. The target was any suitable wealthy landowner who would be able to support the Łaczyńskis and save them from financial ruin.

Cultured, dapper, pompous, and the former chamberlain to the king of Poland, the sixty-eight-year-old, twice-widowed Count Anastase Colonna Walewski had the largest local real estate holdings. He undertook to court the teenage Marie, perhaps because he was vain enough to believe that he was still a lady-killer, or possibly because he thought that, as her family was so eager to marry her off, he'd score an adorable little wife at a bargain-basement price. The May-December pair had but one thing in common: a fierce Polish patriotism.

To a girl still in her mid-teens, the contemplation of wedlock to a man pushing seventy must have seemed like a death sentence. After Marie's mother explained that marriage to Count Walewski was the only way to help lift the family out of its financial quicksand, Marie became physically ill with a psychosomatic pneumonia. But she could not forestall the inevitable forever. Several weeks later, on June 17, 1804, she wed Count Walewski. She was seventeen years old, although the day would come when she would alter the date of the marriage documents by a year, to make herself appear underage at the time.

Almost a year to the day from her wedding to Anastase, Marie gave birth to a son, Anthony Basil Rudolph Walewski. According to the local custom of placing aristocratic babies with wet nurses, the sickly infant was immediately given to a healthy peasant woman who would undertake his care.

Trapped in a loveless marriage, Marie had nothing else to focus on but her Catholic faith and her burning zeal for Polish independence. In this, her savior was her secret soul mate. On the advice of his foreign minister, the savvy Talleyrand, who believed that liberating Poland would be good for his boss's empire as he marched eastward from Berlin to Warsaw, Napoleon declared, "It is in the interest of France, in the interest of Europe, that Poland exists."

At the time, however, it was little more than empty rhetoric. Napoleon required the Poles' help to defeat Russia, but was in a delicate situation: If they actively demonstrated for their freedom, it would push the Russians into military conflict with France prematurely, and

Napoleon's Grande Armée was not only unprepared to face Tsar Alexander's troops, but needed Austria's neutrality in a war against Russia, and could not risk antagonizing the Hapsburg empire either. And yet, when Napoleon dispatched his vanguard into Poland at the end of 1806, his marshals (among them, his brother-in-law Prince Joachim Murat, whom everyone expected to be named her next king) were given orders to enter as liberators, not as conquerors.

This was how the hopeful Poles viewed the emperor, even before his arrival. They were convinced that by defeating Austria and Prussia and uniting the former Holy Roman Empire under Napoleon's imperial eagle, and in achieving his ambitions for a new Europe, Bonaparte could also manifest their dreams of renewed autonomy.

A number of festivities were organized to welcome the emperor, but the seventy-one-year-old Count Walewski, who still regaled anyone who would listen with tales of his glory days in the Bourbon court, had not been asked to help coordinate any of them. Still, he and his twenty-year-old wife, small and dainty, with a perfect figure, her waist-length, honey-hued hair piled atop her head in the manner of married ladies, were on every guest list. One of the most stunning women in the room, Marie was introduced by Count Charles de Flahaut, a lieutenant attached to the imperial staff, to his illustrious father, Charles Maurice de Talleyrand-Périgord, the prince de Bénévent.

Both Charleses had been overheard remarking upon Marie's beauty and intelligence. Talleyrand, a product of the ancien régime, considered Bonaparte a parvenu, but he understood him well and knew how to play him. It is commonly believed that it was Talleyrand's brainchild to place her in Napoleon's bed in order to further his foreign policy scheme, as the clever statesman recognized that Countess Marie Walewska's patriotism coincided with his own ideas for Polish independence.

The emperor arrived in Warsaw on December 18, reviewed his troops, but left abruptly only four days later as tensions with Russian forces escalated into violence. Warsaw became a city on the front lines, and the unhappily married Marie, who, in her mother's words, had been suffering from melancholia (the nineteenth-century word for depression) and was sleepwalking through life, found fulfillment at the hospitals tending to the wounded soldiers.

By the end of the month, Napoleon was back in Warsaw, settling in for the winter. His wife, the empress Josephine, had wished to join him. She already harbored uncomfortable premonitions of his infidelity. In October, Napoleon's mistress Eléanore Denuelle had informed him that she was pregnant. The childless state of the imperial marriage had been a matter of great concern for some time. Josephine had given her first husband two children, but had never become enceinte by Napoleon. Eléanore's news changed everything; to Bonaparte, it was the confirmation that Josephine's infertility, and not his own issues, were to blame for their lack of an heir. The empress was devastated by this new turn of events. Terrified that her husband would make good on his intentions to divorce her for barrenness (and, in fact, she may have been going through menopause, as Napoleon claimed her physician told him that her menses had ceased), she cast a pall of doubt over the emperor's suppositions by informing him that Eléanore had been two-timing him with his brother-in-law Joachim Murat. The child she carried might instead be his.

It was Napoleon's turn to be shocked. Although he had sent Josephine passionate and erotic letters at the outset of their courtship, after she had been unfaithful to him once, early in their marriage, he never let her forget her single adulterous misstep, despite his own numerous affairs. He would continue to avenge her infidelity with another of his own.

The duplicitous Eléanore might now be yesterday's news, but Josephine worried that her husband would remain so long in Poland that he would fall in love, and hinted as much in her correspondence to him. Napoleon's provocative reply of January 7, 1807, is typical of the long-distance emotional cruelty he would inflict upon her.

I don't know what you mean by ladies I am supposed to be involved with. I love only my dear little Josephine who is so good, though sulky and capricious . . . and lovable except when she is jealous and becomes a little devil. . . . As for these ladies, if I needed to occupy my time with one of them I assure you I would want her to have pretty rosebud nipples. Is this so with the ladies you write to me about?

The truth was, however, that by the time she received the letter, Josephine's prescient fears had borne fruit, and the gray-eyed, broad-chested, sallow-complected emperor was already smitten by one of these beauties: Countess Marie Walewska. They had been introduced at a soiree on the night of January 7, presumably just hours after Napoleon had written that note.

When Talleyrand first met the Walewskis at the welcome reception for Prince Joachim Murat in late December, he flattered the old count by pretending to remember him from the court of Louis XVI. But he immediately sensed that the luscious Marie would be a tempting morsel for the thirty-seven-year-old Napoleon. And after Talleyrand had heavily buttered up Count Walewski, wild horses could not have kept Anastase from meeting His Imperial Majesty.

Excited beyond measure at the prospect, he asked Marie to have a new evening gown made up and to wear the Walewski sapphires, which would complement the color of her eyes. The count then engaged Henriette de Vauban, an old friend from his Versailles days, to give Marie some pointers on court etiquette.

Perhaps it was due to the doubtful paternity of Eléanore Denuelle's fetus, but Napoleon's valet Louis Constant Wairy, known as Constant, had noted that lately his employer's opinion of the fair sex had grown even more bitter. "They belong to the highest bidder. Power is what they like—it is the greatest of all aphrodisiacs. . . . I take them and forget them."

Did Napoleon conveniently forget that the reason he'd scored so often was because he *played* the power card?

On the evening of January 7, wearing a new velvet gown, Marie stood in the receiving line waiting to meet the emperor. According to the memoirs of another guest, Madame Anna Nakwaska,

[A]s he looked around, his face gradually softened, the powerful brow relaxed . . . as he surveyed us with evident approval. *"Ah, qu'il y a des jolies femmes à Varsovie!"* ["Ah, there are such pretty women in Warsaw!"] I heard him say as he stopped in front of Madame Walewska, the young wife of the old Chamberlain Anastase, who happened to be standing next to me.

No doubt her "skin of dazzling whiteness" and "beautifully proportioned figure" (in Constant's words) grabbed his attention. What a couple they would make, the emperor might have thought—and the diminutive blonde wouldn't even tower over his five-foot-six-inch frame. Guests noticed Napoleon pausing as he met Marie and gazing at her later in the evening as Talleyrand gave him the lowdown on her background. His comment about the beautiful women of Warsaw zinged about the ballroom, though gossips were quick to add that it had been directed straight at the Countess Walewska.

A few days later, Talleyrand hosted another ball, ostensibly to inaugurate the carnival season, but his true aim was to throw Napoleon and Marie together again.

Too overcome with excitement at the prospect of seeing and speaking with her hero so soon, Marie tried to beg off. But Count Walewski, who knew nothing of the backstory, and evidently had no clue that the emperor had become smitten with his wife, wouldn't hear of it.

Napoleon had given his staff orders to find Marie as soon as she arrived and to escort her to him so that she could be his partner in the contra dance. In an eightsome formed of three other Warsaw belles, the emperor's chief of staff, and two of his brothers-in-law (the princes Borghese and Murat), Marie danced the night away. This time, instead of being jealous of all the attention his wife was garnering from other men, Count Walewski beamed with proprietary delight. All eyes were upon Marie as they watched the emperor watch her. She was gowned in white tulle over white satin lined with pink and gold. A coronet of laurel leaves wreathed her honey blond curls as though she herself were a prize, the spoils of war awarded to the conquering hero. Even the shell-like colors of her evening dress could have been an erotic metaphor for the vestal sacrifice she was poised to become.

But the emperor, making one of his customarily brusque, even rude remarks to women, derided Marie's sartorial decision that evening. "White on white is no way to dress, Madame," he told her, evidently finding the color unbecoming against her already alabaster skin. As this was his opening salvo, it's clear that he was more comfortable on the battlefield than in the boudoir. But according to Constant, Napoleon "immediately began a conversation which she sustained with much grace and intelligence, showing that she had received a fine education, and the slight shade of melancholy diffused over her whole person rendered her still more seductive."

Throughout the night she pointedly declined his invitations to dance, but the pair of French officers who had the gall to flirt with her were immediately posted elsewhere by their jealous commander.

In the aftermath of Talleyrand's soiree, Napoleon began to pursue Marie, ardently begging her to submit to his advances—his modus operandi with other women, as he'd deluged Josephine with billets-doux after they'd first met as well. "I saw only you at the ball," he wrote to Marie. "I desired only you, I admired only you." Napoleon deputized the Master of the Imperial Household, Géraud Duroc, to deliver the letter to his new crush, along with a massive corsage, and became insulted when Marie refused to accept the flowers or to reply to his barrage of correspondence. According to Constant, the notion that she was miserably wed and had sacrificed herself to Count Walewski inspired him to be "more interested in her than he had ever been in any woman."

Receiving no response to his initial floral and epistolary entreaty, the emperor followed up with a second one:

Did I displease you, Madame? Your interest in me seems to have waned, while mine is growing every moment. . . . You have destroyed my peace. . . . I beg you to give a little joy to my poor heart, so ready to adore you. Is it so difficult to send a reply? You owe me two.

He signed the note with the intimate nickname "Napole."

The Walewskis were invited to dinner in the emperor's honor on the night after Talleyrand's ball. The soiree had been planned days earlier, so there was no thought of canceling at the last minute, although Marie wished she could devise a way to worm out of it. Napoleon's persistent attentions made her frightfully uncomfortable; the reality had all but spoiled the fantasy.

She was seated opposite the emperor at the table, and while he pointedly declined to speak to her, his gaze never left her, even as he conversed with his neighbors. He seemed to be communicating in a pantomimed code with Marshal Duroc, and at one point during the evening, when Napoleon placed his hand on his heart, the Master of the Imperial Household inquired of Marie why she was not wearing the flowers the emperor had sent her. Chafing, the countess replied that she had given them to her little son. After dinner, however, it was observed by one guest that Napoleon spoke to Marie "with an almost tender expression on his face."

The following morning, another letter arrived from her imperial admirer:

> There are moments in life when to be in an elevated position constitutes a real burden, and I feel it now most acutely. How can a heart, so very much in love, be satisfied? All it wants is to throw itself at your feet; but it is being restrained . . . my deepest longings are paralyzed. . . . Oh, if only you wanted it! You and you alone can remove the obstacles that separate us. My friend Duroc will tell you what to do. Oh, come, come . . . all your desires will be granted. *Your country will be so much dearer to me if you take pity on my poor heart. . . .*

Assuming an even greater familiarity than in his previous correspondence, the emperor signed the letter with only the initial "N."

A subsequent missive read: "I want to force you to love me. . . . Yes, force you. I have revived your country's name. I shall do much for you. . . . Whenever I have thought a thing impossible to obtain, I have wanted it all the more. Nothing discourages me. . . . I am accustomed to having my wishes met. . . ." Then he applied political guilt. "I have brought back to life your country's name. I will do much more. Send an immediate answer to calm the impatient passion of N."

"N" also received no reply to this barrage of letters. Nor did Marie respond to his numerous invitations to dine with him. Appealing to her patriotism was too much. She closeted herself in her rooms, at sea about what to do next—for not only had the emperor inundated *her* with demands to become his lover, he had sent full copies of these entreaties to Marie's husband and to her brother Benedict! The text of one missive made it clear that the fate of Poland rested in her hands.

Napoleon's valet observed his employer's discombobulation by Marie's rejection. "The Emperor was in a state of unusual agitation. . . . He could not remain still for a moment. . . . He got up, walked about, sat down, got up again. . . . He did not say a word to me, though he usually talked in an easy way while dressing. . . . He still had had no answer to his letters and could not understand it. He considered himself irresistible to women."

Napoleon Bonaparte had developed a number of philosophies about the opposite sex. As a young man, he had written, "Woman is indispensable to a man's animal organization; but she is even more essential to the satisfaction of his sensibilities." Love had no place in the equation. "I regard love as injurious to society and as destructive to the individual's personal happiness," he had once pontificated. "I believe that it does more harm than good. We could thank the gods if the world were quit of it!"

And although they were "indispensable," the serial adulterer and staunch misogynist didn't trust women. They "misuse certain advantages in order to lead us astray and to dominate us. For one who inspires us to do good things, there are hundreds who bring us to folly." Napoleon's paramours held no political sway, as many royal mistresses of the past had done with their respective sovereigns. "States are lost as soon as women interfere in public affairs. . . . If a woman were to advocate some political move, that would seem to me sufficient reason for taking the opposite course."

Love and politics, like oil and water, aren't supposed to mix. The eventual romance between Napoleon Bonaparte and Marie Walewska would prove the rarest of exceptions. But acquiescence on Marie's part was still a way off; she remained one of his most difficult conquests.

Ultimately the decision to go to the emperor (or not), to play a role in Poland's liberation (or not) was hers—with the unusual blessing of her spouse and siblings. Count Walewski claimed to be willing to sacrifice his marital honor in order to save his country. There were others pushing Marie's tush toward Napoleon as well. Their contemporaries refer to a raft of letters from Polish dignitaries, including one written by Prince Joseph Poniatowski, the nephew of the kingdom's last monarch, urging Marie to surrender herself, despite her religious and moral scruples. The correspondence compares her role to that of the Old Testament's Esther who "gave herself for the salvation of her people; for that reason her sacrifice was glorious."

But Marie was not yet ready to become their vestal, their lamb, or their political pawn. So reinforcements were brought in to convince her. Henriette de Vauban, Prince Poniatowski's grande dame of mistresses, who more or less presided over a harem of younger beauties, reminded Marie of the great compliment the emperor had paid her—and Poland—by falling head over heels for a local lady. Henriette, who had coached Marie on the etiquette of Versailles, also informed the innocent countess that back in the day, the only thing that was considered objectionable at the Bourbon court was bad manners! And to refuse to at least *visit* His Imperial Majesty would constitute the height of rudeness.

As Marie still appeared to be hesitating, Henriette then deputized one of Prince Poniatowski's other mistresses, who was also a friend of the countess, to tag-team her into submission. Raven-haired Emily Cichoka managed to persuade Marie that she didn't have to have sex with Napoleon. "Nothing need happen," Emily assured her; Marie could just *talk* to the emperor—talk to him about Poland.

To make sure she didn't chicken out, on the chosen day both Henriette and Emily remained with Marie until dark, when Marshal Duroc came to fetch her in a carriage. Heavily veiled, the countess was conveyed to a side entrance of the castle. She arrived "in a terrible state," according to Duroc. "Pale, trembling, her eyes full of tears . . . she could hardly walk unaided. . . . Later, while she was with the emperor, I heard her sobbing . . . my heart ached for her." Duroc formed the impression that Napoleon didn't get "any satisfaction" from Marie that night, meaning that she didn't succumb.

Evidently, all they did, to the emperor's frustration, was converse, as he called Marie *"ma douce colombe"*—"my sweet dove"—and endeavored to put her at ease.

Napoleon allowed the distraught countess to depart unmolested, but her hysteria had only fueled, rather than cooled, his ardor for her. Tears "tug at my heart-strings," he admitted. He'd extracted her promise to return, and the following day a red leather jewelry case arrived for her accompanied by this letter:

> Marie, my sweet Marie—my first thought is for you—my first desire of the day is to see you again. You will return, won't you? If not, the eagle will fly to the dove. . . . I will be seeing you at dinner tonight—I am told. Please accept this bouquet, as a se-cret link between us among the surrounding crowd. Whenever my hand touches my heart, you will know what I mean, and I want you to reciprocate the gesture at once. Love me, my sweet Marie, and don't let your hand ever leave your heart.

The "bouquet" was a cluster of diamonds. Marie refused the gift, hurling the jewelry box to the floor with the words, "He treats me like a prostitute." The hero of her adolescent fantasies was in real life revealing himself to be a pushy creep.

Marie was livid; after their discussion the night before, all the man still wanted from her was sex! She refused to wear his diamond brooch at the dinner party, but when she read the choler in his face, her hand flew to her breast in fear.

Later that night, too afraid to refuse the emperor again, Countess Marie Walewska finally went to him. Historians disagree on what occurred, just as the players themselves gave divergent accounts of the event.

According to Marie's memoirs, penned many years later, which is the version given credence by the prolific biographer Christopher Hibbert, angry at being thwarted again in his efforts to seduce her, and mortally insulted that she did not desire him, Napoleon threw a spectacularly unsexy temper tantrum in front of the countess, vow-ing as he fumed and spumed, to utterly *demolish* Poland rather than save the former kingdom! "If you persist in refusing me your love I'll grind your people into dust, like this!" To illustrate his point he threw his pocket watch to the floor and crushed it beneath his heel. Marie fainted at the violence of his temper. When she revived, she realized he had raped her and wept copiously over the loss of her honor.

The emperor told a different story in which Marie remained compos mentis during their first sexual encounter, didn't cry or "struggle overmuch," and that after she dried her few tears he promised to do all he could for Poland.

From this point on, Countess Marie Walewska became Napoleon's mistress, her indifferent sexual submission eventually metamorphosing into genuine love. In time she became as enthusiastic and ardent a lover as he was. For her part, this married mom in some respects nearly domesticated the great conqueror, as he fantasized about a cozy relationship with her (though in truth it was anything but that), and affectionately referred to her as his "little Polish wife."

Meanwhile, his real wife continued to write, anxiously suggesting that she join him. Josephine had already come as far as Mainz, in Germany, when she received the following letter:

> *Mon amie*, I am touched by all that you tell me; but this is no time of year to travel. It is cold and the roads are bad and unsafe. . . . Go back to Paris. . . . Believe me, it is more painful for me than for you, to have to postpone for several weeks my happiness in seeing you.

Josephine did not know that Napoleon was by then spending as much time as possible in the soft white arms of Marie Walewska. Wife and new mistress could not have been more temperamentally different. Where the slender, dusky Josephine was extravagant, the petite, pink, and golden Marie was modest, declining to accept expensive gifts from her lover. She was cautious, intellectual, and reserved to the point of shyness, while the empress was barely educated but streetwise, headstrong, and flirtatious.

Marie was not coy; nor was she a designing woman. In fact, she fled from Napoleon's advances, anxious to remain a faithful wife, even though she was not in love with her husband. She took her religion seriously, unlike some of the jaded ladies of the era who kept lovers with impunity. Contemporary accounts refer to Marie's lack of sophistication, but in a complimentary way. Also praised were her innocent and unspoiled nature and her sweetness of expression. And while Countess Walewska was not exceptionally intelligent, she had received an excellent education for a Polish woman of her era and was passionately political, capable of arguing articulately and convincingly. Napoleon had become captivated not only by her fragile, pale beauty, but by the fire in her deep blue eyes when she expounded upon her one true love—the liberation of her homeland. If anyone understood the passion for conquest (or reconquest), it was Bonaparte.

On January 17, 1807, Napoleon created a provisional government for Poland, naming Prince Joseph Poniatowski Minister of War. It was a drop in the bucket compared to the hyperbole he had promised Marie if she became his mistress. The countess was now at the emperor's side as often as practicable; he never wanted her to leave his sight. She would often join the midmorning crowds that watched him review his troops. Now that they were paramours, the tone of his frequent love notes had softened, from intense (if not outright threatening) to tender and romantic. Not since the early days of his courtship with Josephine had Napoleon been such a sentimental sap.

> You were so beautiful yesterday, that for long in the night I could still see you in my mind. . . . I reproached myself for having insisted you come to the parade . . . it was so cold.

Naturally shy, Marie took a while to grow accustomed to having people gawk at her, and to the instant notoriety she had achieved. Distinguished visitors came to call on her—to the astonishment and delight of Count Walewski, who now behaved toward Marie more like a benevolent old uncle than a spouse. And every night, she would visit Napoleon at the castle where he was in residence.

Though she drew respect wherever she went, it seemed that the only one who still struggled with the moral dilemmas of her doubly adulterous romance was herself.

In early April, just weeks after France had scored a "memorable victory" (in Napoleon's words to Josephine) at the bloody Battle of Eylau between France and the Russo-Prussian army on February 8, 1807, Marie moved into an apartment in the emperor's new military headquarters at Schloss (castle) Finckenstein in East Prussia (part of modern-day Poland). Aware of the scandal it would engender for a respectable Polish woman, the mother of the old chamberlain Walewski's son, to be seen slinking about an army HQ, Marie discreetly arrived and departed from a side entrance so that she would not be seen by Napoleon's officers and troops. Nor, she was cautioned, could Josephine learn of her presence there. But the empress, who by now was receiving letters from her husband addressing her with the formal *vous*, rather than the familiar *tu* for "you," had a sixth sense for Napoleon's infidelities and had already surmised that he was having an affaire de coeur. Her supposition was confirmed as she headed back to Paris from Mainz. Two Polish women she encountered in Strasbourg boasted of the emperor's new mistress. Painfully aware that Napoleon was contemplating divorce, and mourning the death of her grandson (and her husband's potential heir), Josephine's one consolation was that at least the Polish charmer had yet to give Boney a baby.

Years later, Marie's older brother Benedict would claim that his sister viewed her sojourn to Finckenstein as yet another patriotic mission. But was he just blowing smoke to mask her reputation—or was Marie herself using that as a cover story so she could rush into the arms of her lover? Because by this time, the pair *were* deeply in love. When Napoleon sat down to cards in the evenings, even though Marie did not play, "he always wanted her in the room within his sight," according to her friend Anna Potocka. Call it true love, or his overweening desire to micromanage her life, taking care to keep other men out of the picture. This, too, was part of Napoleon's megalomania.

The lovers passed an idyllic six weeks together at Schloss Finckenstein, although Marie—kept like Rapunzel in the tower to preserve her honor and reputation—saw no one but her lover; Constant Wairy the valet; and Napoleon's private secretary, the Baron de Méneval. Constant would bring the couple breakfast in their canopied bed, and later in the morning Marie would watch from the window, half-hidden behind the red damask drapes, while the emperor reviewed his troops. When he returned to the room to work she'd sit and embroider or read in front of the fireplace or the tiled porcelain stove until Constant delivered the dinner tray at eleven. Supper was served at seven in the evening; the lovebirds ate at a cozy table before the fire, because Napoleon was always cold.

Ever the tyrant when it came to the subject of women's fashion, he once scolded her for wearing black. "When you have restored Poland, I promise I'll always wear pink," she assured him, still waiting for him to keep *his* pledge.

"Politics is a slow business, it is not as easy as winning a battle. . . . You must give me more time," he pleaded.

But as the days of their whirlwind spring romance progressed, Marie gradually grew less of a martyr to Polish liberation and increasingly more of a lover. "Her noble character, her serenity and her amazing lack of self-interest enchanted the Emperor. . . . Each day he became more and more attached to her," Constant observed.

Winning the reluctant Marie had restored Napoleon's confidence in his virility—although it was hardly his manly charms that had seduced her in the first place. Ambivalent at first, then shy in her return of his intense affections as well as in her lovemaking (after all, her only experience had been with an elderly man), she charmed the emperor with her hesitant, one-toe-at-a-time-in-the-water submission to him.

During the weeks at Schloss Finckenstein, Napoleon and Marie created an alternate reality for themselves, a domestic partnership devoid of any sordid connotations, in which the ugly facts of spouses and children or stepchildren evidently didn't intrude. Marie had her husband's blessing, and Napoleon had often declared himself a man apart from others, meaning that he could indulge in extramarital affairs with impunity. "I really felt I was married to him," the countess later told her friend Elizabeth Grabowska. Marie sensed that beneath Napoleon's bluster and bravado was a man yearning for a little tenderness and, well, perhaps a bit of stroking. And as his need for her grew, so did Marie's love for him.

Marie Walewska was Napoleon's ideal woman: beautiful, graceful, feminine, intelligent and educated, but not a pushy, intellectual blue-stocking. Most important, she made him her number one priority, which was essential for a man with such a massive ego. He boasted to his brother Lucien, "She is an angel. . . . Her soul is as beautiful as her features." And to his older brother Joseph, the emperor kvelled, "My health has never been better. . . . I have become a very good lover . . . these days."

But a lover sans results. Only one issue troubled the emperor about their romance: Marie had conceived almost immediately after wedding a senior citizen, yet in the nearly half year or so that she had been his paramour, she had failed to become pregnant. Unfortunately, their vernal honeymoon had to end before Napoleon's motility, in a manner of speaking, could be definitively confirmed. Under cloak of darkness Marie departed Schloss Finckenstein in mid-May and returned to her childhood home of Kiernozia, while Napoleon prepared to return to the front.

In June, he conducted diplomatic negotiations in Tilsit with the strapping blond Tsar Alexander (the grandson of Catherine the Great) in an effort to avoid military conflict. Napoleon became so infatuated with the tsar, he declared that had Alexander been a woman, he'd have made him his mistress! Back in Poland, Marie feared for her countrymen and -women. What concessions might Bonaparte, enamored now not of her, but of the handsome blond giant Alexander, make with Russia? Would Napoleon sell out the Poles for the sake of his own empire? Sure enough, the emperor gave Alexander the prosperous Polish province of Bialystok as a peace offering. The Poles, whose fathers, sons, and brothers had enlisted in Napoleon's Grande Armée upon the assurance that he would restore their independence, received only a semi-independent state to be called the Duchy of Warsaw. On this point the emperor never even consulted with the Polish provisional government he had set up just a half year earlier. Talleyrand was furious.

Back at Kiernozia, Marie felt wounded, too. She had forfeited her honor for a false promise. Yet she willingly accepted the present of a sapphire bracelet and a locket containing his portrait that Napoleon sent her in honor of her name day, August 15, which was also his birthday. Less than three weeks earlier, on July 27, he had given himself an early birthday present, the title of Napoleon the Great. At the time, his empire stretched over most of Western Europe, and he ruled a population of seventy million people.

After the Tilsit summit Napoleon returned to Paris. Marie, who had expected Count Walewksi to demand a divorce when she came home from Schloss Finckenstein, waited for a summons to join her lover. To save face, Anastase had made sure not to be there when his wife arrived; he had left their son with Marie's mother in Kiernozia and then took off for a spa cure. All that Marie received from Napoleon were endearing notes from the emperor addressing her as his "little patriot." "The thought of you is always in my heart and your name is often on my lips," he assured her. Finally, around Christmas 1807, she was asked to join the emperor in Paris in February.

Marshal Duroc rented a town home at 2 rue de la Houssaye for the twenty-one-year-old Marie; he even staffed it for her. The sartorially picky Napoleon wished his *maîtresse en titre* to be glamorously attired. Marie was outfitted by the finicky Parisian couturier Leroy, who even provided her with hair and makeup stylists.

Unfortunately, His Imperial Majesty had little time for her, and the countess found herself squired about the French capital instead by the tall, elegant Duroc. Nor would Napoleon have much of an opportunity for romance for the next several months; his war with Spain had been going so poorly that he had to head to the front himself. With her lover absent, Paris held no allure for Marie, and she returned to Poland.

She would not see the emperor again until July 11, 1809, arriving in Vienna (which had capitulated to the French) four days after Napoleon defeated the Austrians at Wagram. He had set up headquarters at the Hapsburg summer palace of Schönbrunn and sent her a letter insisting, "I want to give you new proofs of the warm affection I have for you. . . . Many tender kisses on your lovely hands and just one on your beautiful mouth. Napole."

The emperor was now thirty-nine, stouter and grayer than when they'd parted sixteen months earlier, and his skin had a pallid cast to it, but Marie's presence in Vienna seemed to take years off him. She was set up in a house in suburban Mödling, but after her carriage overturned one day, Napoleon sought excuses to keep her with him at Schönbrunn as often as possible.

Aware that Marie was canoodling in Austria with her husband, back in Paris, Josephine was still holding her breath and crossing her fingers, always anxious for news as to whether the countess was pregnant.

And then it finally happened

Marie realized she was enceinte in September, and Napoleon was over the moon with joy; this was the confirmation he had been seeking that he wasn't sterile, and he was one hundred percent positive that the child she carried was his. According to Constant, "I could not even begin to describe the loving care the Emperor lavished on Madame W., now he knew she was pregnant. . . . He was reluctant to let her out of his sight, even for a short time."

"I belong to him now," Marie told the emperor's valet, "my thoughts, my inspiration, all come from him and return to him . . . always."

Napoleon's doctor had suggested that she return to Paris with His Imperial Majesty, and Marie was eager to be near the father of her child, although it had already been some time since she had seen Count Walewski and their son, Anthony. Anastase's reaction to his wife's condition has not survived, but she was clearly thinking of a future with Napoleon that did not include him. She was secretly delighted to hear that her lover had given orders to wall up the private staircase connecting his rooms to Josephine's and that he intended to commence divorce proceedings as soon as he reached Paris.

During these early months of her pregnancy it surely did not occur to her that her fertile womb would end up merely a test case. She may have proven Napoleon's virility, but ultimately she only provided him with the final impetus to definitively break from Josephine and set about siring the dynasty he'd always dreamed of.

"Yes, I am in love [with Marie]," Bonaparte admitted to his brother Lucien, "but always subordinate to my policy. And though I would like to crown my mistress, I must look for ways to further the interests of France." Keeping his intentions from Countess Walewska, he secretly began scouting for potential brides. "I want to marry a womb. It matters not what she looks like, as long as she comes from royal stock."

This declaration obviously placed Marie, with child or not, out of the running.

Cheerfully increasing, she left for Paris in mid-October, blissfully oblivious of Napoleon's plans—except perhaps, for the prescient inscription on a ring she gave him entwined with strands of her golden hair. The engraving read, *"When you cease to love me, remember that I love you still."*

Napoleon was at Fontainebleau, too busy to see her; unbeknownst to her, he was wife shopping. At the top of his list of empress replacements (though he had yet to divorce Josephine) was Grand Duchess Anna Pavlovna, the fourteen-year-old sister of the Russian tsar. To sweeten the deal, he was prepared to offer Alexander . . . Poland!

Marshal Duroc gently confirmed Marie's fears; yes, it was true that her lover intended to make a dynastic marriage. Realizing that the presence of his pregnant *maîtresse en titre* presented an embarrassment to a man seeking to remarry, the countess quietly returned to her homeland. Ironically, the miracle of conceiving a child together, which under ordinary circumstances would more closely bond a couple, sundered their liaison and cost Marie the emperor's love.

Much as Tsar Alexander would have liked to have annexed Poland, Anna Pavlovna was taken off the marriage market by their mother, who not only disliked the parvenu Napoleon, but thought her daughter far too young to wed. Anna would have to wait two years before any thoughts of marriage could be entertained. Napoleon couldn't wait *three* years for an heir, so he set his sights elsewhere. On April 2, 1810, he married Archduchess Marie-Louise of Austria, the daughter of the deposed Hapsburg emperor Francis II.

Napoleon kept in touch with Marie Walewska, inquiring after her health and encouraging her to "chase away the black thoughts—you must not worry about the future." But if she had any hope of resuming their love affair, he quashed it by addressing her formally as "madame," confirming his intention to put more than geographical distance between them.

With the future of her child on his mind, Bonaparte asked his minister in Warsaw to urge Count Walewski to grant "a personal request from the Emperor" by giving Marie's unborn child his name. Appropriately flattered, the seventy-three-year-old Anastase invited his wife to return to his home in Walewice so they could all be a family again. On May 4, 1810, she gave birth to Napoleon's son, who was christened Alexander-Florian-Joseph Colonna Walewski. Throughout his life, although he may have learned otherwise, Alexander insisted that the old count was his biological father. At the very least, in so doing, he publicly preserved his mother's dignity.

In September 1810, Napoleon invited the Walewski family to join him at Schönbrunn.

Marie was presented at court in November. Napoleon had her town home in Paris redecorated in the latest Empire decor and purchased a country villa for her near Boulogne, not far from the palace of Saint-Cloud. Now twenty-three and at the height of her beauty, Marie would have preferred to rekindle her royal romance, but it was not to be. Napoleon was intent on remaining faithful to his new (and now pregnant) empress, who was wildly envious of any woman ever connected with her husband. Countess Walewska would have to content herself with remaining His Imperial Majesty's good friend. However, Napoleon awarded Marie an annuity of ten thousand francs from the Privy Purse.

During 1811–1812, she became a leading light of Parisian society, and her home on the rue de la Houssaye was a haven for Polish expatriates and tourists as well as the crème de la crème of the French *haut ton*, including Napoleon's sisters, who liked Marie and admired her honesty and modesty.

Marie's old friend Anna Potocka, who was also living in Paris at the time, observed, "Madame Walewska has become an accomplished woman of the world. She possesses rare tact and an unerring feel of proprieties. She has acquired self-assurance but has remained discreet, a combination not easily arrived at in her sensitive situation. Conscious of Marie-Louise's jealousy, she somehow managed to conduct her social life in such a way that, even in this gossipy capital, few suspect that she still remains in close touch with the emperor. It does not surprise me at all that she is the only one of his loves that so far has survived the test of time and of the Emperor's recent marriage."

One day, during her sojourn in Paris, Marie brought their son to see Napoleon in his study at the Tuileries Palace. The emperor would develop no ongoing relationship with Alexander, but he was far from a deadbeat dad. "Don't worry about the little boy. He is a child of Wagram and one day he will become King of Poland," Napoleon told one of Count Walewski's nieces.

It had to have been little more than empty badinage, but Marie found reassurance in his words. Napoleon's hyperbole was never manifested, but he did provide most specifically and generously for Alexander's future and for Marie's welfare as well. During the spring of 1812, war with Russia seemed inevitable. Their alliance had proven disastrous for the Russian economy, as the enforced blockade of England prohibited them from importing affordable goods from Britain. Additionally, some of the progressive ideas that were part and parcel of the Napoleonic Code (vis-à-vis civil rights and divorce laws, just to name two) had seeped across the Polish border into Russia. These radical reforms angered the Russian boyars, and the nobles threatened Tsar Alexander with his father's fate (assassination) if he didn't do something about it.

Recognizing that he might not survive another military campaign, Napoleon wanted to make sure that his son by Marie would be fully provided for. In her presence, on May 5 at Saint-Cloud he signed a twelve-clause legal document agreeing to set aside a substantial legacy for her and young Alexander. The boy would inherit sixty-nine farms in Naples that would yield an annual income of approximately 170,000 francs. Until he came of age, the money would be Marie's to spend as she wished. After Alexander reached his majority and assumed the inheritance, he was to pay his mother 50,000 francs a year from it. The estates were to be entailed to his male descendants, and Napoleon made contingencies should the boy die without issue. In June, he signed letters patent creating Alexander Walewski a hereditary Count of the Empire. His coat of arms combined the crests of the Walewskis and Marie's family, the Łasczyńskis.

At the end of the month, although the war had already begun, Marie left her family in Paris and returned to Poland. Her intention was to demand a divorce from Anastase Walewski, and her rationale was not emotional, but economic. Thanks to the Napoleonic Code, Poland's new laws rendered a wife equally responsible for her husband's debts, and the count's property was hemorrhaging them. If she were compelled to pay off Anastase's encumbrances, the only money she had was Alexander's inheritance.

Count Walewski was not pleased by this turn of events. He agreed to the divorce only on the proviso that Marie assumed the support of *their* son, Anthony, and set up a trust fund for him from their marriage settlement. Although the count was nearly senile by then, he was lucid enough to know what he was signing—a document attesting to the fact that Marie had been coerced into marrying him when she was not only underage, but ill, and therefore presumably not in a coherent frame of mind to make a sound decision about her future. This was a fiction, since Marie had recovered from her hysterical ailment by the time the church bells were rung. She was also seventeen on her wedding day, which took place in 1804, and not in 1803, as the paper falsely stated.

Anastase also set his signature to a second document confirming that he'd had an understanding with Marie that absolved her from marital fidelity. Since he had practically pushed her into Napoleon's arms back in 1807, at least this was more or less true. This paper was intended to buff away the adulterous tarnish from Marie's honor.

Six weeks after the documents were submitted to the Polish law courts, the Walewskis' marriage was sundered.

After the Grande Armée's devastating defeat in Russia, as the enemy advanced on Warsaw, Marie received instructions to leave immediately for Paris, to prevent the possibility that Napoleon's former mistress might be taken as a prisoner of war and her captivity used as a bargaining chip. Countess Walewska's last act as a Polish patriot was to grant the severely wounded war minister Prince Joseph Poniatowski a substantial advance from Alexander's inheritance to be used for reoutfitting the decimated Polish army. Fewer than one thousand of the forty thousand troops who had begun the disastrous Russian campaign had returned home. Poniatowski was killed at the Battle of Leipzig on October 14, 1813; years later his estate repaid Marie's loan.

After Leipzig, Napoleon's empire began to crumble. Alexander Walewski's inheritance in Naples was now in jeopardy. Napoleon summoned Marie to discuss an alternate financial arrangement. In January 1814, he purchased a Parisian villa for his son at what is now 48 rue de la Victoire and prepared a document awarding the boy an income of fifty thousand francs derived from his personal property and gilt shares.

Napoleon departed Paris for the front on January 25. Writing to one of her frequent chaperones, his Corsican cousin and aide-de-camp General Philippe Antoine d'Ornano, Marie said, "The Emperor left this morning. I did not have a chance to say goodbye to him. . . . I wonder whether he noticed . . . my nerves are in a very bad state." Her intuition told her that his luck was running out.

Napoleon was compelled to abdicate on April 11, 1814, signing the treaty at Fontainebleau renouncing his empire in exchange for exile on the Mediterranean island of Elba. Three days later, Marie secretly visited him at the château, conducted straight to his library door by the ever-discreet Constant. She did not know that on the night before her arrival, Napoleon had tried to kill himself with a mixture of opium, belladonna, and white hellebore, but the poison, which he had carried on his person throughout the Russian campaign, must have lost some of its potency, because it only gave him a case of violent cramps and vomiting.

Marie sat outside the closed door of Napoleon's library for the remainder of the day and throughout the night, awaiting the emperor's summons to enter. Constant Wairy, who had advised his master of her arrival, recalled, "I could not bear to watch her grief, so I went away and walked in the gallery." When the door never opened, she returned to Paris as quietly as she had come, not wishing to be discovered lurking about unwanted.

Less than an hour after her departure Napoleon emerged, asking for Marie, and Constant informed him of her patient, silent vigil. The emperor was visibly upset that he had missed her. "Poor woman, she must have felt humiliated. I must tell her how sorry I am. I have so many problems here," he added, rubbing his forehead.

Marie wrote to him that day. The following reply survives:

Marie—I have received your letter of the fifteenth and I am deeply touched by your sentiments. They are worthy of your lovely soul and the goodness of your heart. When you have settled your affairs in Paris and decide to take the waters at Lucca or Pisa, it would give me the greatest pleasure to see you and your son again [on Elba]. My feelings for you both remain unchanged. Keep well; don't worry. Think affectionately of me and never doubt me.

Marie did travel to Italy that summer, and received a letter from Napoleon dated August 9 while she was in Florence.

I will see you here with the same pleasure as always—either now or on your return from Naples. I will be very glad to see the little boy, of whom I hear many nice things, and look forward to giving him a good kiss. Adieu Marie.

He signed it, "Your affectionate Napoleon."

Meanwhile, her former lover was also encouraging his wife, Empress Marie-Louise, to visit him on Elba and to bring *their* son with her.

Traveling with her sister Antonia and brother Theodore as chaperones, Marie and Alexander embarked for Elba from the port of Livorno on August 31, planning to remain on the island for as long as Napoleon would have her. Whatever intentions of fidelity the ex-emperor might have had toward his wife may have melted away when he beheld Countess Walewska again, because others detected the chemistry between them. They were fairly certain that if the couple hadn't already resumed their love affair, they were about to do so as soon as they had the opportunity. Alexander called Napoleon *Papa l'Empereur* and the pair of them romped and roughhoused on the lawns like a typical boy and his dad. Napoleon's chef, Louis-Etienne Saint-Denis, observed, "The young boy looked a bit pale and his features were very like the Emperor's; he was rather serious for his age."

That night Napoleon visited Marie's room. The following day he received word that the whole island was talking about the arrival of a heavily veiled blond woman and an equally towheaded little boy. Napoleon's local doctor, Fourreau de Beauregard, donned his Sunday best to pay a special call on the imperial family and found Napoleon sitting with a little blond child on his knee, who the doctor assumed was his son by Marie-Louise. Beauregard paid his compliments to the little boy and asked Napoleon to please convey his respects to the empress. Napoleon, who had given the impression to the islanders of Elba that he was a fine, upstanding family man, had to do some swift damage control before the rumors continued to fly and the gossip spread over the waters and reached the real Marie-Louise. Obviously, Countess Walewska and Alexander had to depart immediately. Brokenhearted, Marie packed her things. She offered Napoleon her jewelry in case he should need money, but he refused it. The weather provided a dramatic backdrop for a truly Napoleonic farewell; the lovers said adieu before Marie and Alexander boarded their boat as the wind whipped about them in a gathering storm.

Marie-Louise would never arrive. Her father had forbidden her all further contact with her husband. By this time she had embarked on an extramarital affair of her own with the man her papa had sent to prevent her from reuniting with Napoleon, the one-eyed Adam Adalbert, Graf von Neipperg.

Marie Walewska remained in Naples for the rest of 1814. In January 1815, she learned of Count Walewski's death. By April she was back in Paris. She saw Napoleon on June 11, one week before the Battle of Waterloo, when he summoned her to the Elysée Palace to give her some financial advice. The next time she entered the palace, a few days after the fateful battle, it was to help with the pack-out. On June 22, Napoleon abdicated for the second time.

At Malmaison on June 28, he and Marie said their final farewells. "[T]he atmosphere was very sad. I can still see the Emperor. . . . He took me in his arms and I remember a tear ran down his face," Marie later recalled. She spent an hour with Napoleon, and when it was time for her to depart she collapsed into his arms and remained there for several moments.

His refusal of Marie's offer to join him in his second exile on St.

Helena devastated her. The man who had been the center of her world for more than eight years was now exiting it forever.

Marie continued to live quietly in Paris. Napoleon's dashing cousin General d'Ornano wanted to marry her, but she needed time for her emotional wounds to heal before moving on. They were finally wed on September 7, 1816, in Brussels. On June 9, 1817, she bore d'Ornano a son, Rodolphe Auguste. The infant was strong and healthy, but Marie remained frail. Although she didn't know it, she had already been suffering from advanced kidney problems for a few years.

Her acute toxemia grew worse during the autumn of 1817. On December 11, at the age of thirty-one, she died with all three of her sons at her side. When Napoleon learned of her passing he was still wearing the ring she had given him bearing the inscription, *"When you cease to love me, I will love you still."*

Napoleon died in 1821. His will stipulated that Alexander Walewski join the French army. Alexander did both of his parents proud; he became the French ambassador to the Court of St. James's and served as foreign minister under his half cousin Napoleon III.

Marie's romance with Napoleon was born out of her Polish patriotism. He had promised her that he would do much for her homeland, but despite his florid pledges made in the urgent heat of desire, Poland got very little out of the liaison. And Napoleon's policies were not at all influenced by her.

However, their royal romance may have changed the course of history. Marie's pregnancy proved Napoleon capable of siring a son. It precipitated his divorce from Josephine and led to his marriage with Marie-Louise of Austria. Countess Walewska undoubtedly meant much to the emperor during their love affair, but politics always came first.

"[T]he hero, in order to be interesting, must be neither completely guilty nor completely innocent." This was Napoleon's view of the protagonist in a classic drama, and he applied the formula to himself as well. Marie also qualifies. She knew she was violating Church doctrine by committing adultery, and yet she was then, and is still, viewed as a Polish patriot. Her face even graced a postage stamp in the last quarter of the twentieth century.

Marie Walewska had worshiped Napoleon Bonaparte since girl-hood and carried her genuine passion for him to her grave. Throughout her life, her destiny, it seems, was to be a sacrifice: as a teenage bride to save her family's estate; as a young wife and mother to save Poland; and finally, as the test womb that proved her lover's virility, sacrificed on the altar of his dynastic and political ambitions.

LUDWIG I OF BAVARIA

1786–1868

RULED: 1825–1848

*T*hough a monarch of the progressive nineteenth century, Ludwig seemed to be a man of another place and time, looking backward for inspiration. Perhaps it's because his godparents were Marie Antoinette and Louis XVI, for whom he had been named. Born into a minor branch of the Wittelsbach dynasty, which ruled Bavaria for a thousand years, Ludwig was the oldest son of the count palatine Maximilian at the Zweibrücken court in Strasbourg and the princess Wilhelmine Auguste of Hesse-Darmstadt. He eventually became king of Munich upon the death of his father in 1825. Having traveled extensively throughout Greece and Rome, Ludwig was enamored of classicism, art, and antiquities, and it was his ambition to transform Munich into the Athens of Bavaria.

Ludwig had soft features, wide-set blue eyes, and a proud mouth, but his face bore several marks as a result of his having survived smallpox at the age of eleven. He was also profoundly deaf and spoke with a stammer, which may have been related to his loss of hearing. Despite his aural deficiency he fought with distinction and courage, though not with passion, for Napoleon—whom he intensely disliked. Ludwig was delighted when the tide eventually turned against the emperor in 1814 and Napoleon lost Germany, even though Ludwig's sister, Princess Augusta of Bavaria, had married the emperor's stepson, Eugène de Beauharnais. Ludwig's joy in Napoleon's defeat was dampened only by the fact that because of their family connection to the emperor, his father had prohibited him from actively taking up the sword for the enemy allied forces.

The Roman Catholic Ludwig's October 12, 1810, wedding to the

Protestant princess Therese of Saxe-Hildburghausen had marked
the occasion of the first Oktoberfest. It was a political alliance, although Therese, a tall, fresh-faced, serious-minded brunette, was
said at the time to be the prettiest catch in Europe. She bore Ludwig
nine children, one of whom died in infancy. Determined to preserve
the lifestyle he had enjoyed as a bachelor, Ludwig, then crown prince,
maintained a separate bedroom, sleeping apart from Therese unless
he made conjugal visits to her boudoir. He continued to take his daily
constitutionals alone, frustrated that he could no longer enjoy a conversation with every pretty woman he chanced to meet during his
strolls.

A poet long before he was a king, Ludwig had the acquisitive collector's eye for beauty, which encompassed everything from art and
architecture to gorgeous women. His wife was a popular queen who
endeavored to turn a blind eye to Ludwig's numerous extramarital
infidelities, although she displayed her displeasure in discreet ways,
once leaving town during one of his affairs. Therese would, however,
draw the line at his infatuation with Lola Montez.

As a sovereign, Ludwig was an eccentric workaholic. He would
often rise by five a.m., and his was always the first lamp to be lit in
the palace as he tackled the pile of official documents awaiting his
perusal, comfortably attired in the green banyan, or dressing gown,
that he had worn for the past forty years. Ludwig went out among
his subjects, which was unusual for a ruler of his day, shopping and
strolling, visiting museums and enjoying concerts, dressed like a
rumpled professor and always carrying an umbrella.

Despite his sartorial oddities, he was an able administrator, rescuing
Bavaria from the financial disarray in which his father had left it. Not
only did he turn the kingdom around, but he transformed it into one
of the most fiscally sound monarchies in Europe by micromanaging its
cash flow—which often involved a good deal of penny-pinching.

He was a good steward, using that money to make Munich a
showpiece of culture, art, and design. Although Ludwig's aesthetics
were rooted in the classical antiquities of the past, his pragmatic eye
was firmly on the future. He built Bavaria's first railway, launched
her first steamship, and constructed a canal that linked the beautiful
blue Danube with the Main River, which allowed for access to both

the North and the Black seas, extensively broadening Bavaria's trade possibilities.

But a pair of flashing blue eyes proved to be Ludwig's undoing when his penchant for pretty women allowed other parts of his anatomy to cloud his judgment. His affair with the Spanish dancer Lola Montez, a self-made Irish-born adventuress who passed herself off as an exotic Iberian of noble birth and a victim of the Carlist civil war, brought down his monarchy, forcing his humiliating abdication in favor of his son, the crown prince Maximilian.

At the age of eighty in 1866, Ludwig acted as an adviser for his grandson, who by then had assumed the throne as Ludwig II. The second Ludwig was the "Mad King" who built Neuschwanstein Castle and whose crush on the composer Richard Wagner earned the latter the nickname "Lolus," a direct reference to Ludwig I's royal favorite, Lola Montez.

On February 29, 1868, Ludwig I died at the age of eighty-one after a leg infection became gangrenous. His will stipulated the wish to be buried beside Queen Therese, who had passed away thirteen and a half years earlier.

LUDWIG I OF BAVARIA AND LOLA MONTEZ (1821–1861)

The maxim "Whatever Lola wants, Lola gets" did not originate with the Broadway musical *Damn Yankees*. It was the angry protest of a group of nineteenth-century Munich university students against the malignant influence of a seductive foreigner upon their sovereign.

Lola Montez—her greed, her immorality, and her anti-Jesuitical ideas—were, in their view, the ruination of the nation, and they wanted her gone.

But King Ludwig I, who was old enough to be Lola's grandfather, was smitten, so blinded by his infatuation that he refused to believe his "Lolitta," with her sultry looks, fiery temper, and passion for politics, was perhaps the finest grifter of the age. "Lola Montez" was her greatest role—one that she lived so well and so fully that she began to believe her own lies.

By the time the woman born as Elizabeth Rosanna Gilbert met the sixty-year-old king of Bavaria in October 1846, she had already lived a wildly colorful life. She was born in 1821 in County Sligo, Ireland, to an infantryman and his sixteen-year-old wife, who were almost immediately posted to India. Gilbert died soon after their arrival, and his widow wed one of his fellow officers, an upright Scot named Craigie. As soon as she learned to walk, little Eliza ran about India nearly unsupervised, an ungovernable hoyden even then, soaking up the exotic sights, sounds, and scents.

In 1826, she was packed off to Montrose, Scotland, to live with her stepfather's family. Five years later she was sent south, first to Durham, to the home of Captain Craigie's former commanding officer, Major General Sir Jasper Nicolls. The gruff major general had eight school-age daughters of his own, and from the other side of the world Eliza's stepfather relied on his judgment to superintend her education, placing the girl in an appropriate school after she left the Nicolls household. In 1832, Nicolls enrolled Eliza in a boarding school in Bath.

Her mother came to collect her in 1837, because she had arranged a good marriage for Eliza with Craigie's current commanding officer in India, a man in his mid-sixties. Mrs. Craigie was accompanied by thirty-year-old Lieutenant Thomas James, whom she had met on the voyage from India; it seemed clear from their body language that the pair had enjoyed a shipboard romance.

By then, Eliza was a stunning sixteen-year-old with raven hair and gentian blue eyes. Lieutenant James fell for his paramour's daughter and the couple eloped to Ireland, wedding on July 23, 1837. They eventually went to India, but the marriage was a complete fiasco. The couple called it a day in 1840, but was never legally divorced. With the equivalent of ten thousand dollars from her stepfather, Lola sailed for England. While at sea she had an affair with the nephew of the Duke of Richmond. When Thomas James learned about it, he sued his wife for divorce. The decree was granted on December 15, 1842, but prohibited either of them from remarrying during the other's lifetime.

With limited options available to her socially, Eliza Gilbert James decided to reinvent herself as an actress. She enrolled at Fanny Kelly's renowned drama school in London, but was told that her talents would be better employed in other artistic pursuits—perhaps as a dancer. She was far too old to begin ballet lessons, but Spanish dancing had become the rage of the age. Mrs. Kelly suggested that Eliza might have better luck learning the popular ethnic dances.

She spent four months in Spain taking lessons in their language and dance. The woman who left the country was not Mrs. Eliza Gilbert James, but Doña Maria Dolores de Porris y Montez, complete with a biographical backstory that she told to people so often, she grew convinced of it herself, even though she adjusted the details (of birth dates, parents' professions, marital status, and persecuted relatives) to fit her audience. Playing upon their sympathies, she would even win letters of introduction to highly influential people. In truth, she had pirated the moniker of a famous matador, Francisco "Paquito" Montez, whose own surname wasn't even Montez.

Lola embarked upon her European career, speaking with a thick accent that was assessed as a hybrid of Irish and Spanish. As she'd had only four months of lessons in her "native" tongue, it's remarkable that she was able to fool so many people with her broken Spanglish and Sprench, depending on the country she was performing in.

As a dancer, Lola received mixed reviews, mostly along the lines of: Looks 10, Dance 3. Her blue-black hair, huge blue eyes, and the "splendor of her breasts . . . made madmen everywhere," according to her German biographer Edward Fuchs. But as a performer, she appeared to have more passion than talent, and she had a lot of competition, as this was the age of Carlotta Grisi, Marie Taglioni, and other exceptional ballerinas. Although her act was unique, audiences still expected strong technique.

But Lola was in dangerous territory in more ways than one. In London, the press "outed" her as Mrs. Thomas James, and she fought back, in character, stepping down to the footlights to defend herself in her thick-as-salsa accent. And every time Lola opened her mouth, she usually compounded her troubles. Her biggest detractor, the Englishman Albert Vandam, observed, "Her gait and carriage were those of a duchess for she was naturally graceful but the moment she opened her lips the illusion vanished—at least to me . . . her wit was that of a pot-house, which would not have been tolerated in the smoking room of a club in the small hours."

Audiences became increasingly hostile with each performance. After only a few shows in London, Lola's contract was not renewed; it was time to move on. Her career and personal life were crowded with incident everywhere she went. She took lovers with impunity, but had a few ground rules: They had to be gorgeous and, if possible, royal. One of them was the emotionally tormented composer Franz Liszt. Unable to countenance any ridicule of her dancing or challenges to her Spanish identity, she traveled with a full complement of knives, whips, and pistols, and employed them if necessary. It was part and parcel of Lola's volatile personality, but often got her into trouble. After only one or two performances Lola was kicked out of city after city as a result of violent incidents.

A member of her Australian touring troupe many years later described her as "frivolous, naughty as a little child; can charm with a wink; woe to him who falls into her disfavor. She has a very excitable nature and for the slightest reason her whole body will tremble and her eyes flash lightning. For this reason one has to treat her very carefully because she is the most courageous and foolhardy woman who ever walked this earth."

Although Lola's affair with Lizst ended unhappily, he provided her with letters of introduction to several of his friends in France, many of whom were among the literary lights of Paris, including Alexandre Dumas *père* and *fils*, the respective authors of *The Three Musketeers* and *La Dame aux Camélias*; and Lola's idol of female independence, George Sand. Lola had been in the capital for barely a month when her connections led to a booking at the prestigious Opéra. Once again, the crowd went wild for her beauty, but did not rave about her terpsichorean talents. She fell in love with Alexandre Henri Dujarier, editor of the Parisian newspaper *La Presse*, and the two planned to marry. Lola, always denying that she had ever been married to a Lieutenant Thomas James, considered herself a bachelorette.

But after Dujarier, whom she called her one great passion, was killed in a duel, a contretemps that for once had nothing to do with her, Lola left France, done with love forever. Dumas *père* purportedly said of Lola, "She has the evil eye. She is sure to bring bad luck to anyone who closely links his destiny with hers, for however short a time. You see what happened to Dujarier. If ever she is heard of again it will be in connection with some terrible calamity that has befallen a lover of hers."

On October 5, 1846, Lola arrived in Munich with her pug Zampa and her lover of the moment, the junior Robert Peel, son of the former British prime minister. Two days later she was trolling for an engagement at the Royal Theatre. But she may also have been looking to trade up in the romance department.

Munich and Lola were perfect for each other. William Bennett, who wrote for the *New York Herald*, claimed, "The number of illegitimate children born in Bavaria is almost the same number as those born in wedlock. The beer is particularly excellent in Bavaria but their morals from the king down to the codger are as bad as they can be."

The king was nothing to look at by the time Lola Montez was prepared to seduce the capital with her most famous number, the "Spider Dance," which, to some, more closely resembled an epileptic fit than a cousin of the tarantella. A vivacious sixty-year-old, with eyes that still twinkled for pretty women, Ludwig nonetheless suffered from a recurring skin rash, and the beholder's gaze could not avoid being drawn to a prominent cyst on his forehead.

On October 8, Lola presented herself to Ludwig. How she was able to secure an introduction to the Bavarian sovereign is unknown. It may have come through a mutual acquaintance, a thrice-married German lothario named Heinrich von Maltzahn whom Lola had encountered during her travels in London or Paris.

Ludwig not only had a passion for dancers in general, but he had fallen victim to the popular mania for all things Spanish and had taught himself the language, there being no native speakers in Bavaria. Consequently, he was eager to meet this exotic woman he had heard so much about. A lurid description of Lola and Ludwig's first encounter, written years after her death, has Ludwig ogling Lola's famous chest and inquiring, "Nature or art?" Lola allegedly answered by producing her omnipresent dagger (or grabbing the scissors from Ludwig's desk) and slicing through her laces, revealing her stunning, and completely natural, bosom. The tall tale is in keeping with the sort of outrageous drama Lola was known for—but it never happened. For one thing, although Ludwig may indeed have been curious about Lola's *poitrine*, he was also a cultured gentleman and would not have behaved like a lager lout. Additionally, for anyone who knows about the structure of Victorian-era women's garments and underpinnings, it would have been nigh impossible, not to mention anticlimactic, for Lola to have tried to saw through (or worse, snip) a tight bodice, a heavily boned corset—that laced in the back—and her chemise before her bare flesh was revealed.

She made her dancing debut in Munich on October 10, Ludwig's thirty-sixth wedding anniversary, performing to polite applause during the entr'actes of a comedy prophetically titled *Der Verwunschene Prinz—The Enchanted Prince*. Although critics spared their praise for her talent and technique, she received high marks for her sultry looks and fiery passion. But only one member of the audience really mattered, and he had indeed become enchanted.

Ludwig owned a portrait collection of gorgeous women, his *Schönheits*, or Gallery of Beauties, several of whom, such as the English adventuress Jane Digby, had been his lovers. As soon as the king saw Lola dance, he commissioned the court painter, Joseph Stieler, to immortalize her for his gallery.

Lola Montez was in Munich for barely a week before she attracted a coterie of admirers, most of whom were young army officers. Maltzahn, too, was hanging about, although young Robert Peel seems to have disappeared altogether. Now she was about to land the biggest fish in Bavaria. Ludwig began visiting her hotel every afternoon or evening, sometimes calling on Lola twice a day, and often remaining so late into the evening that the hotel staff had already locked the doors. When Maltzahn was present, the three of them conversed in French. If Lola and Ludwig were the only ones in the room, they spoke in rudimentary Spanish. It was lucky for Lola that the monarch was just a beginner, because her fluency wasn't significantly better. When the pair corresponded, the letters were written in fractured Spanish. If Lola didn't know a word, she wrote it in French. If Ludwig got stuck, aware that Lola spoke no German, he would write it in Italian or Latin.

Lola danced again on October 14. This time her performance engendered a good deal of hissing. After the leader of the detractors was identified, Ludwig exiled him from Munich, banished to the city of Regensburg.

Five days after this performance, Lola began to sit for her portrait. Naturally, Ludwig insisted on visiting Stieler's studio to watch paint dry. During the sitting Lola gave the king a rose, and when he accidentally left it at the atelier, Ludwig sent the artist a note asking for the flower to be couriered to him in a protective bag. By this time the king was composing lovestruck poetry in Spanish to his new flame. "I love you with my life, my eyes, my soul, my body, my heart, all of me. Black hair, blue eyes, graceful form."

Lola had scheduled a booking in Augsburg on October 24, but Ludwig, already head over heels in love, pleaded with her not to leave him. Realizing she had the monarch practically eating out of her hand, "*No puedo dejar Munic,*" she confessed. "I can't leave Munich." She canceled her upcoming engagement in Augsburg; her poorly received performance of October 14 was the last time she danced for five years.

As rumors of Ludwig and Lola's improper relationship began to swirl, the king confessed his passion to his old friend Heinrich von der Tann.

What does my dear Tann have to say when I tell him that the sixty-year-old has awakened a passion in a beautiful, intelligent, spirited, good-hearted twenty-two-year-old [Lola had shaved four years off her age] nobly-born woman of the South! . . . I thought I could no longer feel the passion of love, thought my heart was burned out, thought I was no longer what I had been. . . . Now I'm not like a man of forty or even . . . like an amorous boy of twenty; I'm in the grip of passion like never before. Sometimes I couldn't eat, couldn't sleep, my blood boiled feverishly, I was lifted to heaven's heights, my thoughts became purer, I became a better person. I was happy, I am happy. My life has a new vitality, I'm young again, the world smiles on me.

On November 1, within a month of Lola's arrival, Ludwig awarded her an annual pension of a hundred thousand florins (at a time when a university professor's salary was two thousand florins a year, and a cabinet minister earned six thousand florins). But Lola also availed herself of the king's wallet to grant financial favors for friends who were down on their luck, including a pair of starving dancers who lacked the money for new ballet slippers.

However, she made enemies as swiftly as she collected adherents, due to her massive ego and overweening sense of entitlement. The first indication that Lola was becoming too self-important came during the intermission of a concert, when the entire audience saw the king leave his wife sitting in the royal box while he quit it to visit his new paramour. As though she were the sovereign and Ludwig the commoner, Lola did not deign to rise from her chair.

One of the young men who had attached himself to Lola during her early days in Munich was Artillery Lieutenant Friedrich Nüssbammer. Several people suspected that while she was greedily taking advantage of Ludwig, tantalizing, yet denying him her body, she was bestowing it elsewhere, and Nüssbammer was the likely candidate. Two nights running Lola came looking for the lieutenant at his residence, ringing every doorbell and awakening all the tenants. On the second night, she was told to cease and desist by Nüssbammer's landlady. The woman shouted, "I'm not deaf, Miss," and Lola retorted, "I'm not 'Miss,' but the King's mistress."

After this incident, the pupils at a Munich girls' school were exhorted to pray for their "mad king," so that God would make him see the light and banish his lover.

Public disturbances such as the one with the landlady did not endear Lola to the local police. And before she came under the king's protection she had refused to register with the authorities, a policy required of all foreign visitors. When Lola finally agreed to comply, in the box marked "accompanied by," she wrote "*un chien*" (a dog), referring to her pug, Zampa. The thirty-seven-year-old chief of police, Johann Nepomuk, Baron von Pechmann, was not amused. After making some inquiries about Lola, he discovered that she had been asked to leave a number of cities, including Berlin, Warsaw, Dresden, and Baden-Baden, as a result of volatile incidents.

Although Lola's hair-trigger temper had already instigated several disruptive episodes in Munich, the besotted Ludwig, convinced that his beloved was being unjustly persecuted, ordered Pechmann to cease his inquiries into the doorbell affair. Writing to Baron von der Tann, the monarch confided:

> Lolitta (that's what I call her) is slandered terribly, has been and will be. A foreign woman who wants to settle in Munich, who's pretty, whom the king loves, who's spirited, what more does it take to arouse hatred, lies, and persecution. All that will be defeated, too, firmness will triumph in the end. She is not simply someone who loves me, she is my friend, too. She's told me that she'll always speak the truth to me, and she's already told me a number of things I didn't enjoy hearing. . . . She loves me so much. I'm providing for her, but she's not my kept woman.

The same day Ludwig had sent Lola to see Pechmann to smooth over the doorbell business, he had added a codicil to his will. Lola would receive the Stieler portrait, one hundred thousand florins as long as she did not marry (Ludwig didn't know about Lieutenant Thomas James or it would surely have nullified the contract), and an income of twenty-four thousand florins for life, or until she subsequently wed.

> I would not be a man of honor, would be unfeeling if I made no provision for her who gave up everything for me, who has no parents [he obviously didn't know her mother lived], no brothers or sisters, who has no one in the wide world except me; nonetheless she has made no effort to have me remember her in my last wishes, and I do so totally on my own initiative. . . . Her friendship has made me purer, better. Therese, my dear, good, noble wife, do not condemn me unjustly.

All of this largesse came within six weeks of meeting Lola.

But rumors circulated throughout Bavaria that made Ludwig appear the fool and Lola a whore. It was said that she intended to marry Nüssbammer in order to secure her citizenship. And it was reputed that she was measured for her corsets and other lingerie stark naked, often with her shutters open. The king appeared unconcerned by the gossip. He also ignored the advice dispensed by a previous mistress, Jane Digby, warning him to be more discreet about the contents of his letters to his paramours. But on November 12, 1846, Ludwig was addressing himself to "My dearest Lola" and signing, "Heart of my heart, your Luis." He wrote often and floridly, sending not only letters, but a daily poem, his modus operandi with previous paramours as well.

On December 1, Ludwig bought a town home for Lola at Barerstrasse 7, providing the property with its own guard of gendarmes. The purchase was made in Lola's name, in part to conceal the origin of the money, and in part because as a property owner she could apply for Bavarian citizenship. The generous king also considered buying the house where Lola was staying, plus another plot of land on which to build her a third house. Nothing could be enough for his Lolitta. As far as Lola was concerned, the Barerstrasse house needed a considerable amount of refurbishing. But it took a year to complete the renovation (which included the loan, or gift, of several priceless treasures from the Pinakothek Museum), because of Lola's willful but typical disregard for the requisite building permits.

Money slipped through Lola's hands like sand. No sooner had Ludwig given her an allowance than it was spent and she was in debt, exceeding her hundred-thousand-florin annual income almost immediately. On Christmas Eve, 1846, Ludwig drew up a plan for her monthly expenditure, but it was impossible to tether her. Instead, he fueled the financial fire, lavishing even more money on Lola, with extravagant gifts such as a coach with all the extras, including a pair of blue harnesses for her horses.

Lola's new nickname, "the German Pompadour," which she took as a compliment, only sparked her imagination; how else might she emulate Louis XV's notorious paramour? A request for her own private chapel and confessor was denied, as no cleric would accept the post. There would be no whitewashing of Lola's virtue.

Ludwig deputized their mutual friend Baron von Heideck to keep an eye on Lola's expenses, and Lola sent him all her bills. However, the baron soon found himself more involved in the couple's life than he had bargained for, when they began using his regular tea parties as a convenient location for their trysts.

Bavaria had a constitution, but Ludwig was one of the last true Western European autocrats. Nonetheless, his primary interests were aesthetic and cultural, not political. By the 1840s the king had all but ceded control of his government to a repressive Catholic faction of Jesuits called the Ultramontane, because their primary allegiance was "over the mountains," to the pope in Rome, rather than to their local sovereign. This party was led by Bavaria's Minister for the Interior, Karl August von Abel. Though a staunch conservative working for a socially liberal king, Abel, who had held his post for a decade, was Ludwig's ablest minister.

Abel and Lola would become bitter enemies, and their mutual hatred would change the fate of the kingdom. As the autumn of 1846 faded into winter, Minister von Abel began to mount an opposition to Lola's influence on the king. But Ludwig was deaf, both literally and figuratively, to Abel's warnings that his Lolitta was a temptress who was ruining both him and the monarchy.

Lola's other major nemesis, Munich's chief of police, Baron von Pechmann, also confronted Ludwig directly to inform him that his mistress was generating no end of ill will. Her tantrums and outbursts alienated shopkeepers and citizens. Compelled to do damage control when a confectioner lost much of his Christmas business due to a Lola-engendered incident, the king promoted the man to the post of court chocolatier.

But even when Lola was inspired to do something beneficial, it backfired. She used her substantial influence with Ludwig to get schoolteachers a pay raise, but before the increase was formally announced, she leaked it to the press, taking credit for it. A backlash ensued when people complained that she wielded *too much* power over the king.

Baron von Pechmann had become the indefatigable Inspector Javert to Lola's Jean Valjean. Determined to unmask her as a fraud, he planted a spy inside her household. Crescentia Ganser wasn't totally reliable, but she was credible enough, reporting to the chief of police that Lola entertained young men at her home at all hours. Among them was Nüssbammer, whom Lola had repeatedly assured the king was just a good friend.

Ludwig was devastated by the secret reports the baron had collected. Although he was advised never to see Lola again, he could not bear the prospect. He scribbled a dramatic note to Baron von Heideck.

> Happiness is not for this earth. I was happy here, but now I am thrown down from my heaven. *The unbelievable has happened.* The years I have yet to live I had hoped to pass in exalted love. It was a dream. . . . *It is over now.* . . . The bearer of this, the wife of the sculptor Ganser, will show you the evidence. . . . I intend to come to your home about 1:30 today. I think it would be best for Lolitta to meet me there. If I must break with her forever (I fear nothing else is possible), still I want to see her one more time. . . . The king is ashamed, but the 60-year-old man is not, that tears fill his eyes as he writes this.

> Just one hour ago, happy yet was
> Ludwig

Heideck had scarcely received the note when Ludwig breathlessly arrived, launching himself into the baron's arms and weeping, "So there is no more joy for me. I thought I had found a woman to be a friend to me for the rest of my days, someone to fill the empty hours with intimate, spiritual joy and make me forget the troubles of state with quiet inspiration and companionship. I honor and love the queen, but her conversation is simply not adequate for my spirit, and my heart needs feminine society. I'm used to it. I had hoped that I'd found such a woman in Lola, and she betrayed me."

At this point in their romance, Ludwig and Lola had yet to consummate their relationship. Lola tantalized; Ludwig pined and worshiped. What the pair had been enjoying were indeed long sessions of stimulating discourse, rather than intercourse. And there is a great deal to be said for the fact that even in broken Spanish, Lola was witty, intelligent, intellectual, and clever enough to keep as cosmopolitan and sexual a man as Ludwig utterly infatuated.

Heideck supported a clean break with Lola, because seeing her again would only cause the king additional stress. But Ludwig insisted, "I . . . can't condemn her without a hearing. I couldn't live with myself if I did that. . . . She may be innocent, or at least not so guilty as this woman claims. . . . Think how persecuted she is, how she and I have already been slandered. . . . [H]er faithlessness has caused enough pain in the depths of my soul that I don't want to compound it with self-recrimination because I was unjust to her."

So Ludwig called on Lola, and a scene of denials, tears, and recriminations followed. And she was forgiven. Triumphant, she wrote to her friend Pier-Angelo Fiorentino,

> I left Paris at the beginning of June as a lady errant and raced about the world and *today* I'm on the point of receiving the title of *countess*! I have a lovely property, horses, servants, in sum everything that could surround the official mistress of the King of Bavaria.

Adding that the king loved her passionately, in typical Lola fashion, she then launched into a mixture of hyperbole and blatant lies.

> I am surrounded by the homage of great ladies, I go everywhere. All of Munich waits upon me, ministers of state, generals, great ladies and I no longer recognize myself as Lola Montez. I do everything here. The king shows his great love for me. He walks with me. Goes out with me. Every week I have a great party for ministers etc. which he attends and where he can't do me enough homage.

The great ladies and ministers were waiting, all right. Waiting for her to leave.

The confrontation between king and royal mistress was replayed in Lola's drawing room after Crescentia Ganser went to the king herself, at Pechmann's prompting. Once again, Lola wept and swore on her father's grave that the allegations against her were false. Even Ludwig would later write that, had Lola confessed to nocturnal rendezvous with Lieutenant Nüssbammer, he would have forgiven her, so great was his passion. Nonetheless, he decided that Lola was in need of a minder and hired Lola's old friend Maltzahn, who returned from Paris to take the job. But Maltzahn had his price: a government appointment. So Ludwig made him an adjutant at court.

Public opinion of Lola continued to sink. Count Karl Sensheim, the finance minister, endeavored to convince Ludwig that Lola was manipulating him. She, of course, denied it, but the monarch wasn't entirely unaware of her behavior, writing in his diary that she was meddling in affairs of state, and that his concessions to her only ended up with demands for additional concessions. He worried about where it would all end.

Nonetheless, on December 8, 1846, he wrote, "I hope I may never suffer again what my poor heart suffered last Saturday the 5th (a day which I will never forget to the end of my life) and what my darling Lola suffered. They tried to tear us asunder forever."

In a burst of passionate enthusiasm, Ludwig had offered to make Lola a countess, an event she alluded to in her letter to Pier-Angelo Fiorentino. Now, realizing he might have been too rash, the king tried to backpedal, offering to make her a baroness instead. But the horse was already out of the barn. It was countess or nothing for Lola. If not, she would quit Munich forever and never see Ludwig again!

Sigh.

Countess it would be. But first Lola would have to become a citizen.

Unfortunately, having made a sworn enemy of the chief of police, she hardly aided her cause. An incident at the post office in Munich had turned violent when she was unable to retrieve an ill-advised letter she'd just dropped in the mail to Nüssbammer. Her confrontation with Baron von Pechmann grew ugly; she told him that Ludwig would certainly inform him to lay off her. Pechmann ignored her threats and sent Lola a summons to appear in court for "excessive behavior in the postal building." She tore the summons to pieces, insisting that she didn't understand German. Get a translator, growled Pechmann. Finally, Ludwig demanded that the baron cease his deliberate persecution—and prosecution—of Lola, and ordered his transfer to Landshut.

The chief of police may have been the most prominent of Lola's victims, but he was far from the only one. This would become the pattern with anyone who displeased, crossed, or somehow insulted her. They would find themselves fined, imprisoned, transferred, or exiled by the king. On December 26, 1846, a young man who "lorgnetted" Lola (the rude term for someone ogling another through their opera glasses at the theater), was sentenced to three days' house arrest.

Stephen Henry Sulivan, nephew of England's prime minister, Lord Palmerston, had also been keeping a watchful eye on her, presumably on his uncle's behalf, providing the prime minister with updates on Lola's behavior and her influence with the Bavarian king. Evidently, Lola was denied admission to an arts club in Munich where she wished to become a member. As an explanation for why she had been blackballed, the club's president showed the following paper to Sulivan. It was signed by the king, who overrode the vote of the admissions committee, instructing them to treat Lola with the deepest respect.

The number of people thrown into prison for one, two, and even three months for having affronted Lola, or for not having taken their hats off when she passed, is extraordinary. The nobility is disgusted, the burghers are angry, and even the protestant party, who hope to profit by the present state of things [Lola was vehemently anti-Jesuit, and the Jesuits were running the government], agree that the King of Bavaria has "lost his senses."

Exactly why the English were so keen to keep tabs on Lola has never come to light or been made fully clear. Rumors have always circulated that she may have been a spy, most probably for the British, and who better to gain intelligence from foreign courts than someone in a position to travel the world, such as a performer, with the looks and talent to gain entrée into such lofty circles? It was also rumored that Lola was a polyglot.

None of these rumors was very plausible. The truth was that she was not at all conversant in several foreign languages. The French critic Théophile Gautier, who never much liked her, wrote that "she *hablas* very mediocre Spanish, barely speaks French, English passably." And she didn't speak German at all, which could hardly be handy for a spy in Bavaria. English was, of course, Lola's native tongue, which she needed to mangle deliberately in order to stay in character for most of her life. Indiscreet, with an ungovernable temper, she called attention to herself, when a good spy needs to blend in. She got fired from engagements and exiled from cities where it might have been politically beneficial for an actual agent to remain until the necessary intelligence was obtained. She also lived a lie every day of her life; already "outed" more than once as Mrs. James, Lola Montez was too easily blackmailed or compromised to be an effective spy. Yet the Jesuits, whom she detested with an irrational hatred, believed she was a tool of the Freemasons. The French thought she was a British agent while she was in Paris, but she wouldn't have been all but penniless and trolling for protectors if Queen Victoria had been secretly footing the bill. Moreover, no concrete evidence of who Lola might have been working for, and why, has ever come to light.

So the Lola-as-professional-spy-on-someone's-payroll story should be pretty well debunked. Most likely, the British were interested in her because they knew she was one of their own and were keen on obtaining whatever information she happened to passively glean.

But the only thing more dangerous in a king's court than a spy is a powerful royal mistress. Stephen Henry Sulivan's letter to Lord Palmerston in December 1846 assessed Lola quite critically, comparing her to the most famous of her ilk.

She is handsome, ambitious to act the part of Madame de Maintenon, and with talent enough to gain ascendancy over the King who, instigated by her, is committing a series of arbitrary and unjust acts which will destroy the little popularity which the King has enjoyed. The King's ruling passion has always been to be an absolute sovereign, and anyone who encourages him is sure to gain great influence over him. This is the secret of the immense influence which Abel has acquired. As Lola proves to the King that he ought to be an absolute monarch and shows him how to be so, she is sure to gain and maintain her power, even if the King gets tired of her as a mistress.

Even Lola's friends couldn't rein her in. On December 31, 1846, Maltzahn wrote to Ludwig that he was resigning his job as her keeper. It was far more than he'd bargained for, and even his position at court wasn't enough of an inducement to stay. Not only were people accusing him of pimping Lola to the king, but "unfortunately during my absence Lolita [sic] has insulted all classes of society, offended everyone, and the city and the nation are so up in arms that with the best will it is too late, impossible, to improve her position. At least I am too feeble to manage it."

Maltzahn personally offered Lola an annual pension of fifty thousand francs to quit Bavaria forever, prompting Ludwig to wonder how the baron could be so wealthy. He later learned that Maltzahn had taken a lengthy meeting with Archbishop Reisach. It was the Catholic Church that was offering to permanently sponsor Lola's exile.

On January 1, 1847, Ludwig announced that the departments of religious affairs and education would henceforth become independent of the Ministry of the Interior, Abel's home turf, and the oversight of those two departments would be transferred to the less conservative Minister of Justice. The decision happened to have been a long time in the making, but to Abel and his cronies it seemed to have Lola's anti-Jesuitical fingerprints all over it. Ludwig surmised correctly when he assumed they would blame her. What he failed to recognize, even as he endeavored to reform his government, was that by and large the Bavarians were content with the Ultramontanes and believed that Abel was doing a fine job. Alienating the Interior Minister and his adherents sowed the seeds of discontent in yet another previously healthy pasture.

And then the other poisoned fields began to yield their crops.

Additional incidents of Lola-related violence occurred. A flurry of insults during a pre-Lenten party at her hotel resulted in a melee. Three days later, her bull mastiff, Turk, bit a deliveryman. When the messenger raised a stick to beat the dog, Lola slapped the man around.

The woman was a walking time bomb. During the month of January she was hissed and booed in the streets and was even pelted with horse manure. Police were dispatched to tear down posters proclaiming, "Montez, you great whore / your time will come soon," and, "To the devil with the royal house / Our loyalty is at an end / It brings us only shame and ridicule / God help us."

Ludwig, looking stressed and ill, fainted several times that month, and congregations were exhorted in their respective churches to "pray for the redemption of the great, gray man." He hoped to rush Lola's citizenship process through, because if she were to be arrested, as a foreign national she could be imprisoned awaiting trial. There was a good deal of behind-the-scenes wrangling. The lone Protestant council member voted in Lola's favor, but had demanded a quid pro quo for his assent: a law professorial post for his son at the university, a house in town, and a sinecure in the legislature, the Reichsrat. The man's son got the university position.

In any event, the council could only *advise*, and they had refused Lola Bavarian citizenship on the grounds that she lacked the proper papers. So on Monday, February 10, 1847, Ludwig signed the decree granting citizenship to Lola Montez "with retention of her current citizenship."

In response, Interior Minister Abel announced that he would resign, and his colleagues in the cabinet followed suit. They drafted a letter to the king, warning him that the loyalty of the army was in doubt as well. One paragraph read, "At the same time, national pride is deeply offended because Bavaria believes itself governed by a foreigner whom the public regards as a branded woman and any number of opposing facts could not slake this belief."

The letter was given to Ludwig on February 11. He gave Abel and his colleagues two days to reconsider. When they refused to do so, the government was immediately dissolved. The stranglehold of the conservative Jesuits was broken, but Ludwig found it difficult to replace his ministers, because people were afraid of clashing swords with Lola.

Yet not everyone vilified the royal mistress after the reorganization of the government following Abel's downfall. In some circles she was viewed as the standard-bearer for liberalism, although Lola didn't support a free press because they printed insulting things about her and Ludwig; and she also believed he should have a secret police force to crack down on dissenters. Nonetheless, after the ouster of the Ultramontanes the king was hailed as the most enlightened monarch of his age, and the cry of "Lola and Liberty!" was heard in some parts of Bavaria.

Even with the dissolution of Ludwig's government, politics seemed to take a backseat to art, and there was leisure time enough to immortalize Lola in marble and oils. On January 26, 1847, she gave the king a cast of her foot made by the prominent sculptor Leeb, receiving a thank-you note from Ludwig on a piece of paper embellished with a serenade.

Corazon di mi corazon, mia Lolitta
[Heart of my heart, my Lolitta]

You gave me great pleasure by the lovely surprise of sending me your foot in marble—your foot has no equal—it appears to be an antique ideal—when Leeb had left, I covered it with ardent kisses. . . . I want you to receive my lively thanks, which I will express to you at noon.

Tu fiel Luis.
[Your faithful Luis]

Over time, Ludwig would develop a fetish for Lola's feet, whether in flesh or marble, perhaps because she routinely denied him access to most of the rest of her, conveniently pleading headaches, her period, some other ailment or indisposition, or fear of pregnancy.

In the early months of 1847, the king commissioned a second Stieler portrait of Lola and engaged another, edgier painter, Wilhelm von Kaulbach, to immortalize her as well. Depicting her a bit too dramatically for Ludwig's taste, the artist made his disgust abundantly apparent. Her hair wild and loose as she mounts a scaffold, Lola carries a riding whip as a serpent winds itself about her waist. The clasp of her belt is a skull. Ludwig rejected the portrait and it remained in von Kaulbach's studio for decades.

In February, Lord Palmerston's nephew, Stephen Henry Sulivan, dispatched the following update to the prime minister.

> The influence and power of Lola Montez over the mind of the King of Bavaria is so great that everyone is alarmed.
>
> She has beauty, talent and so violent a character that the King, partly from love and partly from fear, is sunk into the position of a simple register of the acts of his mistress. . . . The exasperation of all classes is so great that the idea of dethroning the King is daily gaining ground, and if the Prince Royal [Ludwig's eldest son, Maximilian] was in Munich, instead of being at Palermo, some serious riots would have already taken place.

Maltzahn informed Ludwig of a plot to kidnap Lola. He had just been offered fifty thousand francs to lure her into a trap. Lola would believe she was meeting Maltzahn, but would ultimately be taken to a remote castle a day's drive from Munich, where she would be thrown into an underground dungeon for the remainder of her days. The following day, Ludwig received an anonymous tip warning that Lola would be abducted and taken to Vienna. Lola, too, had discovered a similar plan to the one Maltzahn had described to Ludwig, writing about it to a friend. She claimed to have been warned by one of the conspirators "to whom I had done a kind action on the morning of the very day" of a plot to convey her to the Spielberg prison at Brno, Czechoslovakia, "where I would have been immured to this day, lost and unheard of."

Lola's anecdotes were always riddled with untruths and exaggerations, but the fact that both she and Maltzahn independently described a nearly identical plot lends the story credence. It's also conceivable that there may have been more than one plan to abduct Lola and remove her from Bavaria.

Lola also maintained that her archenemies, the Jesuits, had poisoned her with arsenic; that she'd twice been shot at; and that they had placed "a fanatic upon my stairs at midnight, with a poignard [a type of dagger] in his coat. . . . These are truths and facts." It may be safe to assume that as soon as Lola makes outright claims to veracity, at the very least they are exaggerations, but it was certainly true that the mood in the street was ugly, and vehemently anti-Lola. On March 1, 1847, a riot erupted outside her home after a gifted Catholic professor was dismissed from the university for meddling in politics, by suggesting that Abel and his fellow former ministers be given a vote of thanks for their service to the kingdom. After he was sacked, as a parting shot, the professor posted a protest on the students' message board, blaming Lola for Bavaria's ills.

The mob of angry scholars set off for Lola's residence, arriving around three thirty in the afternoon. They shouted at her from the street and she returned the favor, taunting them from her window. In retaliation, the students began throwing stones, as Lola continued to bait them. Wondering what the commotion was all about, Ludwig went outside to investigate, making his way to Lola's house. It took two hours for troops to clear the streets. Then the students moved down Ludwigstrasse and began stoning the palace, daring to jeer at their own sovereign. At eleven p.m. they awakened the neighborhood with cries of "Down with Lola! Long live the queen!" Ludwig told his wife, "If ever I have sinned against you, you now have your revenge, for never has a King been so pilloried or dragged through the mud."

He bravely and angrily pursued the mob of students, but they turned on him. After several hours, order was restored, and the following day the riot act was read.

On March 9, Ludwig's skin erupted into a rash. He also suffered from bone pain and headaches at night. His illness was not diagnosed at the time, but the condition did resolve itself after several weeks. Some of his biographers have posited that it was a manifestation of syphilis, which he perhaps gave to Lola, or she to him, at some point. But they had not yet consummated their romance; beyond whatever mild kissing and caressing Lola had permitted Ludwig, there had been no penetration. The king had been exceptionally overstressed by recent and current events, and by his volatile relationship with Lola. Given these circumstances, in addition to his age, it seems more likely from the description of his symptoms that he was suffering an attack of shingles.

Being "greatly disfigured" by his illness and confined to his room for some time, Ludwig was unable to visit Lola, but she came to see him. Apart from an incident when she was refused some items of silver because she never paid for a previous purchase, and became so enraged that she smashed the glass door of a display cabinet, requiring a doctor to tend to her hand, she began to behave more rationally, working diligently to improve her image. She wrote to the press to explain that she was not responsible for the change in government—that it had all been Ludwig's doing.

But then the *Pictorial Times* blew the cover off her lifelong disguise on March 20, accompanied by a cartoon of Lola brandishing a whip. She felt she had to set the record straight with the truth—her version of it—in a letter to the editor that began by shaving two years off her age. She was already deceiving Ludwig, who had thought she was only twenty-two at the time they met, when she was really twenty-six.

My father was a Spanish officer in the service of Don Carlos, my mother a lady of Irish extraction, born at the Havannah, and married for a second time to an Irish gentleman, which I suppose is the cause of my being called Irish and sometimes English, "Betsy Watson, Mrs. James, &, &."

I beg leave to say that my name is Maria Dolores Porris Montez and I have never changed that name.

Having tantalized Ludwig for months, Lola knew that the king's desire for her could never be sated if she continued to string him along. But she was also canny enough to recognize when it was time to surrender. The queen left for Franzensbad on June 15, 1847, and on June 17, Ludwig and Lola spent their first, and possibly only, full night together. It may also have been the one time Lola permitted Ludwig to enjoy full sexual intercourse with her.

The very next day, a new man entered her life. On June 18, Lola met a handsome student, twenty-one-year-old Elias "Fritz" Peissner, the son of a bureaucrat. In time, her relationship with Peissner would humiliate the king. But first she embarrassed Ludwig by insisting, as they embarked on their minivacation, that they pay a call on Lieutenant Nüssbammer, who was recuperating after a riding accident. It was an ill-starred holiday all around. At Bad Brückenau, Ludwig's eldest son, Crown Prince Maximilian, refused to meet Lola, who pitched a fit, crying that it was no way to treat a countess-in-waiting.

After he had enjoyed a taste of paradise, Ludwig found himself on an even tighter leash. Lola continued to tease him, but wriggled her way out of having intercourse with him again. So Ludwig directed his focus elsewhere. By now he had developed a full-blown fetish for her feet, and Lola graciously allowed him to kiss them and to suck on her toes. She also gave the king pieces of flannel that she claimed she had worn beneath her lingerie and instructed Ludwig to wear them next to his own skin.

But on July 20, the couple had a furious argument. Ludwig, having had enough of Lola's outrageous behavior and incessant demands, walked out on her. Seeing her world crumble before her eyes, Lola became hysterical.

It was Ludwig who caved first, writing a pathetically humble note, conceding that he should not have spoken harshly to Lola and pleading with her to treat him as a friend, as someone who loved her, and not as a servant. He hated always coming last in her world, when he always put her first, and he resented the fact that she reached out to him only when she wanted something.

In Munich, Stieler's second portrait of Lola went on display, and Ludwig's fourth volume of poetry was published. It included a poem dedicated

To L***
I believe thee, and when appearances deceive,
Thou art faithful and ever true,
The inner voice betrays me not,
It says: Your loving feeling is right.

Lola continued to hold for ransom her desire to be made a countess, threatening to leave Munich forever if it were not granted, and dramatically packing her coach with (empty) boxes as she prepared to depart. Unaware that she was bluffing, Ludwig panicked and pleaded with her to stay.

Although the king's confidants insisted that it was not a politically propitious time to ennoble his mistress, on August 25, 1847, Ludwig's sixty-first birthday, it was Lola who received the present she'd been craving: the title of Countess of Landsfeld. The certificate was mounted in blue velvet with a blue-and-white braided cord leading to the metal box that contained the wax impression of Ludwig's seal. Opposite the page that bore his signature was Lola's coat of arms. A different image was depicted in each of the four quadrants of the shield: a sword on a red field; a crowned lion, rampant, on an azure field; also on azure, a silver dolphin; and a pink rose on a white field. The coat of arms was crested with the nine-pointed crown of a countess.

The package was couriered to Lola that morning with a note from Ludwig:

> Countess of Landsfeld, for me, my ever dear Lolitta, on my birthday I give myself the gift of giving you your diploma as a countess. I hope it has a good effect on your social situation, but it can't change the government. Lolitta can't love, much less esteem a king who doesn't himself govern, and your Luis wants to be loved by his Lolitta. Enemies, especially your female enemies, will be furious to see you a countess, and it will be that much more *necessary* for you to be modest and prudent and to avoid all occasions for tumult, to avoid places where there are a lot of people. It's possible enemies will try to cause disturbances in order to make attempts on your life. Be careful!

Unfortunately, Lola's ennoblement wasn't valid until the announcement was published in the *Regierungsblatt*, the equivalent of the *London Gazette* (Great Britain's official newspaper of record), and it was another week before the news was made public. Unaware of this formality, Lola ungratefully laced into Ludwig, accusing him of being ashamed of her. It was hardly the case. The king kissed her portrait twice daily, first thing in the morning and before getting into bed at night. But more important, upon her elevation he immediately increased her monthly allowance to twenty thousand florins, a sum commensurate with being a countess.

Some people believe that once you reach your goals it's time to set new ones. So the newly minted Countess of Landsfeld turned her sights on Bavaria's highest honor, the Order of Theresa, which she would later claim was personally presented to her by the queen. Not only did this never happen, but Her Majesty had no interest in ever clapping eyes on Lola. On October 13, 1847, the usually mild-mannered queen wrote to inform her husband that she never could have imagined he would have ennobled his mistress.

I owe it to my honor as a woman—which is dearer to me than life itself—she whom you have raised in rank never—under any circumstances, to see face to face; should she seek to gain admission at court through a promise of yours, you can tell her as a fact—yes, from my mouth: the Queen, the mother of your children, would never receive her.

With typical Victorian-era primness she added,

And now, not one more word written or spoken, of this difficult matter. You will find me as before, cheerful, grateful for every joy you give me, and ever watchfully endeavoring to maintain for you, my Ludwig, the untroubled tranquillity of our home.

Lola nonetheless continued to press her advantage with the king, parlaying her influence into royal appointments for friends, both at court and in the army. Individually they were insignificant, but as an aggregate they made her appear to be the power behind the throne.

Surrounding herself with university students, she now had the gall to take not one, but two young lovers, the twenty-two-year-old Peissner, and a Polish man calling himself Count Eustace Karwowski, who turned out to be a tailor.

Ludwig discovered Lola's infidelities and had Karwowski deported. When he confronted her about Peissner, she unleashed the full force of her wrath upon him, chasing the king into the street under a hail of curses. The following day, recognizing that she'd gone too far, she sent Ludwig a contrite apology, urging him to return that afternoon "to your always faithful and devoted Lolitta."

But in January 1848, he learned that Peissner had not left the romantic picture at all and was visiting Lola at all hours. Another quarrel ensued and Ludwig retreated, both physically and emotionally. Lola recklessly added another lover to her collection, a student named Leibinger.

Her coterie formed a loyal opposition, true to Lola and the country. They called themselves the "Alemannia," and her cadre of Alemannen became her bodyguards and her private spies. But they were creating a rift at the university. Nineteenth-century German university students were extremely conservative and rigid, the opposite of the radical, progressive thinkers at similar academies elsewhere in the world. The Catholics and all non-Alemannen at the university called Lola a foreign whore. If a member of the Alemannia showed up for class, the other students would stage a walkout, and the professors refused to teach to an empty lecture hall.

On February 7, the Alemannen were set upon by the other students. Ludwig ordered the bullies to stop and the boys promised to behave, but fighting broke out again that afternoon as well as on the following day. On February 9, 1848, the king dismissed a number of officers whom Lola disliked. Afterward, she was set upon by an outraged mob and found herself in genuine danger. She raced into a church, seeking sanctuary, but the rabble followed her. She was finally rescued by mounted gendarmes who escorted her to the palace.

On February 10, Ludwig shut down the university, which led to further student protests. Two thousand of them marched on the palace, and there were demonstrations outside Lola's home as well. She stood on her balcony and watched as the police charged into the crowd with bayonets, crying, *"Très bien! Très bien!"* The burgomaster sent word to the king that the only way that peace could be restored was for Ludwig to order Lola to leave Munich.

At two p.m., Lola sent her own message to her royal paramour to stand firm, but as the afternoon wore on, it became clear that the protestors outnumbered the police three to one. There were now six hundred of them—a citizens' army.

That evening, the rector of the university handed Ludwig a list of Lola's felonies. The king's family and his ministers pleaded with him to dismiss her. For the sake of their children, Queen Therese even went on bended knee before her husband.

That night Ludwig sent Lola a letter urging her to leave until things cooled down.

> . . . *I implore you* if you ever loved me and if you love me now, leave for *one day.* . . . Better that you leave tonight. . . . I'm afraid for you, and if blood is shed on your behalf, the hatred will increase enormously and your situation will become worse. . . . *The world, you know, is not capable of separating you from me.* . . . Lolitta will always love
>
> Her faithful Luis

Lola returned the note with the messenger: She wasn't budging.

Finally, within the palace, a compromise was reached. The university would be reopened, because the burghers had appealed to Ludwig.

But on Barerstrasse, Lola remained defiant, even as her exile was being demanded, stepping onto her balcony and shouting, "Here I am! Kill me if you dare!" to the rabble below. They answered her with a barrage of stones. When they missed her, she shouted, "Bad shot!" and, pointing to her heart, shrieked hysterically, "If you want to kill me, here's where you have to hit!"

Ludwig refused to formally order Lola's exile, but it was clear that she would have to leave of her own accord in order to avoid any further escalation of unrest. She climbed into her carriage and set out for the palace, but found the garden door locked and a mob surrounding the building. Her coachman then drove her five miles away, and she sent word to Ludwig that she was safe.

After Lola had gone, the crowd that had gathered in front of her house stormed it and began looting until the king arrived and informed them that it was *his* property they were destroying, and he demanded that they disperse.

Ludwig's plan was for Lola to flee to Switzerland, where he would eventually meet her. But she tore up the deportation order, and her

Alemannen had to calm her down and usher her into the coach for the rail station, where they would board the train for Lindau, the first leg of the journey. Lola scribbled a note to the king en route, telling him her heart was broken, adding that she had no clothes, and had been forced to leave Munich in her pajamas. She assured Ludwig that she was faithful to him until death. She omitted the fact that Peissner was one of her traveling companions.

Rather than continue to Switzerland, Lola remained in Lindau for two weeks, hoping for a reprieve from Ludwig. Meanwhile, he attempted to placate the demonstrators, even as the Prince de Wallerstein, the head of the university, maintained that Lola had been deceiving him. The king claimed that Lola wasn't responsible for her actions, and that anyone who was against Lola was against *him*. Ludwig was now convinced, as was Lola, that they were indeed being brought down by a Jesuit conspiracy. He told Wallerstein that if the students went on holiday en masse, he'd be fired.

Ludwig and Lola continued to correspond, and maintained their plans to meet in Lausanne on April 12, but when the king learned that Lola had slept with Peissner on the night of her flight from Munich, he was utterly crushed, writing, ". . . you have betrayed my love in public and made an enemy of it. Your infidelities have deceived my heart but it forgives you and I repeat: the world is not capable of making me break with you, you alone can do that." Lola was now a "faithful friend but a faithless lover."

With a passport issued by Ludwig in the name of Mrs. Bolton, Lola finally departed for Lausanne, as she swore to him that "*not one of them is or will be my lover* . . . If you could read my heart, you would see that love without you is no love at all."

But the king was no longer so quick to believe her, writing the same day,

Very dear Lolitta,

    . . . *The decisive moment has arrived*. If a student travels with you, or joins you, *you will never see me again, you have broken with me*. Lolitta, you inspire a love in me as no one ever has before in my life. Never have I done for another what I have done for you. With your love, it would mean nothing to me to break with everything. Much beloved, think of the past 16 months, how your Luis has conducted himself in this time we have known each other. You will never find a heart like mine. Lolitta has the decision.

Unfortunately, he never sent the letter.

Back in England, her stepfather's former commanding officer Sir Jasper Nicolls, who had been largely responsible for Lola's upbringing there, gloated over the newspaper clipping from the *Times* announcing her deportation from Bavaria. He pasted the article in his scrapbook, scribbling beneath it, "What a hold this miserable witch has obtained over this old, adulterous idiot Sovereign. Wretched country to be ruled by such a shameless rogue—but I must remember that Munich is the most abandoned capital in Europe."

On February 25, Lola arrived in Switzerland. Instead of going to Lausanne, she traveled to Berne after receiving a letter from former flame Robert Peel to rendezvous with him there. In early March, while Ludwig was still pathetically focused on meeting Lola across the border and avenging themselves on their enemies, his advisers were informing him that his position on the throne was fatally weak. The subject of abdication was on the table.

Troops were called into Munich on March 6. The mob warned Ludwig that if he continued to resist their demands, the palace would be torched. At eleven a.m., he capitulated to every request, leading to a two-day period of law and order.

But on March 8, the foolhardy Lola was apprehended in Munich, having sneaked back into the capital disguised as a man. She was taken to police headquarters, where she insisted on seeing the king. On Ludwig's arrival she once again urged him to flee with her to Switzerland. Instead, she was ushered into a carriage, which departed the city at dawn. The Bavarians lost track of her after the conveyance reached Landsburg.

Ludwig returned to the palace and spent the next few days penning lovesick notes to his mistress. "These three hours talking together with you were worth a year," and, "I picked out your vest to put on and in the presence of my servants couldn't resist giving it a kiss."

On March 15, he was compelled to revoke Lola's Bavarian citizenship, although she was permitted to retain her title as Countess of Landsfeld. How humiliating it was to write to his beloved Lolitta with the unhappy news, beneath his dignity for an autocrat to have to capitulate to his ministers. Ludwig felt he had betrayed her.

He told the queen on March 16 that he was against abdicating, and wrote as much to Lola the following day. On the eighteenth, it was proposed that he appoint the crown prince as coregent, but the idea fell flat.

On March 19, 1858, Ludwig I of Bavaria abdicated his throne in the presence of his sons, although, to save face, he had negotiated a palatable deal. He would still retain the form of address "His Majesty, King Ludwig of Bavaria," as well as his real estate, and he would have an annual income of five hundred thousand florins. But he would have to endure a temporary exile.

He penned his farewell speech and then wrote to Lola to tell her he could meet her in April in Vevey. "God knows when I would have been able to see my Lolitta without this. . . . I put down the crown, but Lola I could not leave."

Lola Montez may not have been entirely responsible for the downfall of King Ludwig, but for eighteen months she was the perceived power behind the throne, inspiring him to carry out long-overdue reforms. If he had not given her his heart, soul, and the keys to the kingdom, Ludwig I might have ruled Bavaria until his death, content with the status quo Ultramontane policies of his Jesuit ministers. But the unpalatable combination of the unpopular reforms, the grasping and volatile Lola, and the king's obsession with her proved fatal for his sovereignty.

Munich's burghers had threatened that Ludwig would lose his income and risk permanent exile if he visited Lola. The year 1848 had already seen revolutions in other parts of central Europe. He had forfeited his reign, but his kingdom remained. If Ludwig were to quit Bavaria to visit his mistress, his monarchy, too, might be the next to fall.

From Switzerland, where she swanned about with her coterie of male admirers, Lola wrote to Ludwig, asking for money. But the king himself was in financial straits. When he offered her the interest on a bank deposit instead of hard cash, Lola accused him of punishing her. "[I]f you don't help me I will kill myself and go mad [in that order]," she threatened. "This is what I get for my sacrifices in Munich. I hope this letter will touch your heart."

Her infatuated ex-monarch sent her enough to live on for another few weeks, even as Lola added more men to her collection. But Ludwig had grown jealous, and she had to tantalize him with the promise that she would give herself to him when next they met. He asked if she would *besar* him [which literally means "to kiss," but he intended it more crudely], admitting that for the time being he had to content himself with dreams of sucking her toes.

All through the summer the couple corresponded, their plans to rendezvous always changing, as Lola played a game of round-robin with her lovers—former, current, and some new flames—all the while demanding funds from Ludwig like a child asking for her allowance. After passing an unhappy sixty-second birthday on August 25, he enclosed some money with the following note:

The drawing in your letter that is meant to represent your mouth (each time I give it a kiss), I took at first to represent your *cuño*, and my *jarajo* began to get erect. As much pleasure as your mouth has given me, your *cuño* would have pleased me greatly. I give kisses to the one and to the other.

In her reply, Lola ignored his sex talk and instead complained that his family was conspiring to keep them apart. She fretted that he had not forwarded her diamonds to her, per a previous request, and she didn't even have the grace to acknowledge his birthday.

On November 28, she set out for England, after sending Ludwig yet another request for money. By this time the story of her royal romance was being dramatized on the London stage. Written by some British hack, it was probably not half as sensational as the actual events.

In 1849, a con man named Papon whom Lola had met in Switzerland began to blackmail Ludwig, threatening to publish his memoirs that allegedly contained the deposed king's correspondence with Lola. Ludwig tried to retrieve the letters and paid Papon ten thousand francs, but the swindler published the volumes anyway.

That July, Lola obtained a false French passport under the name of Mademoiselle Marie Marie, with the intention of traveling to Seville. Instead, within four days she met and married twenty-one-year-old George Trafford Heald, a handsome, slightly effete cornet in the 2nd Life Guards, after convincing Heald that she was not Mrs. James. The name she inscribed in the parish register was Maria de los Dolores de Landsfeld. She was still receiving her allowance from Ludwig.

When the long arm of the law caught up with her for bigamy, Lola insisted that she had been granted a divorce by Lord Brougham, the former lord chancellor (who may also have been a lover). She jumped bail and fled to the continent, writing to her *"querido Luis"* in despair over her marital mistake.

> . . . How after knowing you, can I give my love to another, and this other man is without spirit, ignorant, a quasi-lunatic who is incapable of taking a step by himself. . . . My soul is yours forever and ever—I can love no other but you—believe my words they are written in affliction far from you—if I have one wish, it is to see you again *mi querido* Louis—once more I beg you to write to me—it is my consolation—I love you more in my unhappiness than when I was happy—Goodbye dear Louis, I am still the same Lolitta of heart and soul, loving you more than ever—Your Lolitta, yours unto death.

By Christmas of 1849, the marriage was over. Heald returned to England, while Lola went to Boulogne and reproached Ludwig for abandoning her while she was in ill health. For the next half year he paid her monthly allowance, but felt that Lola was blackmailing him over their love letters. She appeared to be threatening, just as Pabon had done, to publish their correspondence if Ludwig did not continue to subsidize her, as he as promised to do, "with the little pension you swore to give me all my life."

On June 1, 1851, Ludwig sent her three thousand francs, the last Lola ever got from him. The aging former monarch had finally had enough of the fickle, hot-tempered gold digger. He subsequently learned that she had never been ailing, and the intermediary she had dispatched to negotiate for their love letters was her latest conquest.

Lola traveled through Western Europe, securing engagements because of her notoriety, rather than her talent. On December 5, 1851, having heard there was money to be made in America, she sailed for New York, where she made her debut on the twenty-ninth of the month. By 1853, in addition to the dances that had brought her renown, she was performing in a repertoire of plays: classics, new works, and those she claimed to have written or translated herself, some of which were autobiographical. Her notices as an actress were fairly passable, and she was even lauded for her interpretation of Lady Teazle in Sheridan's comedy of manners *The School for Scandal*.

On July 2, 1853, although Heald and James still lived, Lola wed a thirty-three-year-old San Francisco newspaperman, Patrick Purdy Hull, because she claimed he was the best raconteur she'd ever known. They moved to the gold-mining town of Grass Valley, California. By mid-September, it was rumored that Lola had filed for divorce.

In 1855, she formed a theatrical troupe and set off on a tour of Australia. Predictably, there were a number of violent incidents, just as there had been during the 1840s, when she traveled through Europe. While she was in Australia, she learned that George Trafford Heald had died at the age of twenty-eight, after a long illness. During her return voyage in May 1856, her costar and lover, Frank Folland, either committed suicide or was pushed over the side of the ship.

Folland's death marked a literal sea change in Lola's life. She cleaned up her act, jettisoning "narcotics and stimulants," as well as her lifelong habit of chain-smoking cigars and cigarettes. In 1858, her autobiography was published to great acclaim in the United States. By then she had reinvented herself one more time, as an articulate and entertaining lecturer on such subjects as "The Arts of Beauty," "Fashion," and "Heroines and strong-minded women of history." She spoke to packed houses about American culture in Europe, and

English and continental culture in America. Her faux Spanish accent was almost entirely gone. She became a critical and financial success until her plans to open a boardinghouse in London bankrupted her.

Later that year she turned another corner and found God, embracing the Episcopalian beliefs of New York clergyman Reverend Ralph Hoyt, whom she met after his church was destroyed by fire. A New York City resident during the final two years of her life, Lola was genuinely devout. A stroke on June 30, 1860, left her legs partially paralyzed; after she learned how to walk again, Lola volunteered at the Magdalen Hospital for repentant prostitutes.

While she was out walking on Christmas Day, Lola caught a cold that developed into pneumonia. She died on January 17, 1861, at the age of forty, and was buried two days later in the Green-Wood Cemetery in Brooklyn under the name Eliza Gilbert. After shaving years off her age all her life, she would have been mortified had she known that her original headstone claimed she was forty-two. Her biographer Bruce Seymour, whose winnings on the game show *Jeopardy!* afforded him the opportunity to spend several years researching Lola's life, funded a new headstone that was unveiled on April 25, 1999. It reads, ELIZA GILBERT, on one side and, LOLA MONTEZ, COUNTESS OF LANDSFELD, on the other.

Ludwig died in Nice at the age of eighty-one. He had been permitted to return to Munich following his abdication, although he admitted, "It needs a great deal of endurance to stay in this capital where my word was law for twenty-three years . . . to be a nonentity, and at the same time to keep cheerful."

George VI

1895–1952

Ruled England: 1936–1952

$\mathscr{B}$orn Albert Frederick Arthur George (and known within the family as Bertie), the second son of King George V and younger brother of Edward VIII grew up overshadowed by his glamorous and outgoing sibling, and cowed by a gruff, hypercritical father and a cruel nanny, who were insensitive to the painfully shy little prince. They were so dictatorial that the medical issues Bertie suffered as a youth (his knock-knees and rickety legs, his intestinal problems, and a profound stammer) manifested themselves emotionally as well as physically. Being a younger son, he was expected to be a sailor prince like his father (who was himself a second son), but his naval career was curtailed by his physical woes, including an operation for a duodenal ulcer.

He did, however, grow up to be a good-looking man. Bertie was short, sandy haired, and blue eyed, with chiseled features and a slight, although athletically trim, build.

When he was twenty-two years old, the royal family changed its name. Because of rampant anti-German sentiment during the First World War, his father jettisoned the house's name of Saxe-Coburg-Gotha inherited from Prince Albert, the consort of Bertie's grandmother Queen Victoria. In its stead the family created a new identity that sounded one hundred percent English, and on July 17, 1917, after a massive brainstorming session to rebrand the dynasty, George V's Privy Council announced that henceforth the royal family would be known as the House of Windsor.

In the early 1920s, Bertie, then Duke of York, fell in love with a pretty young Scottish aristocrat, Elizabeth Bowes Lyon, the vivacious daughter of the 14th Earl of Strathmore and Kinghorne. They were wed in Westminster Abbey on April 26, 1923. Elizabeth was the first commoner (meaning anyone of nonroyal blood) to marry into the House of Windsor, but she was hardly "common," boasting a noble lineage that descended from Irish and Scots monarchs.

The Duchess of York became Bertie's ultimate helpmeet. In 1926, she suggested that her husband schedule an appointment with an Australian speech therapist, Lionel Logue, who might help the duke overcome his stammer. Logue and Bertie worked together for years at his Harley Street office in London; at first the duke attended sessions almost daily, where he learned a variety of techniques that would enable him to surmount his stuttering.

After Bertie ascended the throne in 1936, his ability to confidently speak in public became a matter of international importance, because the radio was a primary means of communication. Bertie's speech therapy was arduous, and ultimately successful, although he was never entirely "cured" of his stammer.

His other physical issues resulted in problems in the boudoir. The Duchess of York conceived their daughters, Elizabeth (born in 1926) and Margaret Rose (born in 1930), by artificial insemination.

Nicknamed "Betty and Bert," the close-knit Yorks, who called themselves "Us Four," were viewed as the model modern royal family—the polar opposite of the Prince of Wales, with his wild house parties, his nightclubbing, and his married paramours. As the two brothers rarely socialized, especially after Edward VIII became king, Bertie was unaware of the possibility that his older sibling might abdicate the throne if he were unable to wed his girlfriend, the American Wallis Simpson, until just a few weeks before the event.

Back in 1934, when Edward was still Prince of Wales, he had fallen in love with Wallis Warfield Simpson, a divorced Baltimore native who was still married to her second husband, Ernest Simpson. The pair shamelessly paraded their romance, a rather tawdry and dysfunctional relationship, which I profiled fully in both *Royal Affairs* and *Notorious Royal Marriages*. After Edward became king upon the death of George V in January 1936, he made it quite clear that he intended to wed Wallis as soon as she divorced Simpson. The royal family was appalled, and for numerous reasons, the British government was not about to let this happen. As Wallis's morality was questionable, she was hardly queen material (it had nothing to do with her being an American). She had two husbands still living, and Britain's monarch is also the Supreme Governor of the Church of England, which, like the Catholic Church, did not recognize divorce. The king could not wed a divorcée as long as her ex-husbands remained alive. Had she been a widow, things might have been different. Additionally, the British had amassed copious dossiers on both Wallis and Edward and had learned of their sympathies toward fascism and the Third Reich.

Edward compromised by suggesting a morganatic marriage in which Wallis would not be styled as queen of England; nor would any children of theirs have rights of succession. But the prime minister, Stanley Baldwin, ultimately made it clear to Edward that he would have to choose between Wallis and his crown, as neither England's Parliament nor the British Empire's Dominion governments supported the morganatic option. They refused to consent to his marriage with Wallis and would not accept her as queen of England in any way, shape, or form. Apart from the fact that no one could stand her personality, it was her politics that caused the most concern. She was roundly believed to be a friend of the Nazis and fascists, and her power over the king was so influential—in part because he was so madly in love with her—that the dynamic of their relationship bordered on sadomasochism.

Baldwin informed Edward that if he insisted on wedding Wallis *and* remaining king, his government would resign en masse, a disaster for the nation. The prime minister offered Edward two clear choices: the lady or the crown. Edward chose Wallis.

So, on a technicality (which in fact was a big deal), by refusing to countenance Edward's marriage with Wallis if he were to insist on defying both religious and civil law, Parliament was able to rid England of a monarch with problematic political views that could have proved disastrous for the country at a time when Hitler was on the rise.

On December 10, 1936, Edward VIII renounced his throne,

the only English sovereign to voluntarily abdicate. A reluctant monarch who stepped up to the plate to do his duty when his brother abrogated it, Bertie succeeded him. He reigned under the last of his four names, becoming George VI in order to give his subjects a sense of stability and continuity after the terrible flux of the Abdication Crisis.

George V had prepared both of his sons to become rulers by deputizing them to make appearances for him during his own reign. When Bertie ascended the throne he was able to ensure a smooth transition, as assiduous and diligent as Edward had been irresponsible.

During the Second World War, Bertie overcame his fear of public speaking, surmounting his stammer thanks to Lionel Logue's tireless, if unorthodox, coaching; the king's Sunday radio broadcasts became a source of comfort to his subjects. In the aftermath of the Blitz in 1940 the monarchs toured the areas ravaged by the bombing. Buckingham Palace itself was struck nine times by German bombs.

When George VI ascended the throne at the age of forty-one, the British Empire covered twenty-five percent of the globe. By the time World War II was over, the landscape had changed dramatically. On August 15, 1947, India declared her independence. On Easter Monday, 1949, thirty years after the famed Easter Uprising that began at the Dublin General Post Office, the Republic of Ireland was declared. That January, a new Indian Constitution no longer recognized the king of England as their sovereign, but agreed to acknowledge him as "Head of the Commonwealth." Ceylon, Pakistan, and South Africa still recognized him as king, but no longer as "Defender of the Faith." Only Canada, New Zealand, and Australia still acknowledged him as both their king and Defender of the Faith, yet all of these former "kingdoms" had become "realms."

A heavy smoker throughout his life, George VI was operated on for arteriosclerosis in 1949 and for lung cancer two years later. His health remained fragile and he died on February 6, 1952, at the age of fifty-six. His eldest daughter, the twenty-five-year-old Princess Elizabeth, learned that she had become queen while on a state visit to Africa with her husband, Prince Philip, the Duke of Edinburgh.

Elizabeth II celebrated her diamond jubilee—sixty years on the throne—in June 2012.

GEORGE VI AND
ELIZABETH BOWES LYON (1900–2002)

Baptized Elizabeth Angela Marguerite Bowes Lyon on September 23, 1900, the ninth child of Lord and Lady Glamis (later the 14th Earl and Countess of Strathmore), the future queen of England enjoyed an idyllic Edwardian childhood in England and Scotland. She divided her time between the stately (and purportedly haunted) Glamis Castle and the charming St. Paul's Walden Bury in Hertfordshire.

In the summer of 1905, Lady Elizabeth met her future husband—although neither of them knew it—at a house party hosted by the Duchess of Buccleuch, the mistress of the robes to the queen. The royal children were present, and as usual, the king's eleven-year-old grandson, Edward, was the life of the party. His next-youngest brother, nine-year-old Albert, known as Bertie, already self-consciously hampered by a stammer, was silent and withdrawn, standing off to one side, removed from the gaiety. For a long time, he found himself beside a tiny girl nearly dwarfed by the enormous blue bow in her hair. She plucked the crystallized cherries from her cake and solicitously transferred them to his plate.

The pair of them would not recall this first encounter, but when they finally fulfilled their destiny, the dynamic between them would always remain the same.

Five summers later, at a garden party at Glamis, the subject of young Elizabeth's fate was literally at hand, when a palmist hired to entertain the guests made a startling prediction. Elizabeth's French governess, Mademoiselle Lang, asked if she'd gotten her palm read. The little girl replied, "Yes, I did. But she was silly. She says I'm going to be a queen when I grow up."

"That you can't be, unless they change the laws of England for you," said her French teacher.

Elizabeth tossed her straw hat on a chair. "Who wants to be a queen anyway?" She never did aspire to the role that was marked out for her. But when called to fulfill it, she rose to the occasion and inspired her subjects during their darkest hours.

The First World War, which broke out on Elizabeth's fourteenth birthday, delayed her entry into society, yet made her grow up fast. She saw her older brothers volunteer to fight, and pitched in herself on the home front when Glamis Castle was converted for five years into a convalescent hospital for wounded soldiers. She knitted her fingers to the bone making shirts for their local battalion, the Black Watch. She shredded paper to make the lining of sleeping bags, served tea to the men, and played secretary by writing letters home on behalf of those unable to do so on their own.

On April 2, 1916, at a tea party at Spencer House, Elizabeth and Bertie, who was then a twenty-year-old naval lieutenant home on sick leave, crossed paths once again. The event was so forgettable on both sides that four years later he would think they'd never met.

Elizabeth Bowes Lyon made her society debut in 1919, a year after the armistice. She was immediately popular, although she was the very antithesis of a flapper. Lady Airlie, a lady-in-waiting to Queen Mary, who was also a friend of the Strathmores, described her as "very unlike the cocktail-drinking, chain-smoking girls who came to be regarded as typical of the nineteen-twenties. Her radiant vitality and a blending of gaiety, kindness and sincerity made her irresistible to men."

One of those men had no way of knowing she was already getting astral nudges toward Westminster Abbey.

At Ascot in June 1919, as Elizabeth was walking toward the royal enclosure, Mrs. Donald Forbes, a clairvoyant who went by the nom de guerre of Gypsy Lee, stopped her and echoed the prediction of the Glamis palmist a decade earlier: "One day you will be Queen—and the mother of a queen."

That year, perhaps in an effort to emulate his brother, the Prince of Wales, Bertie became infatuated with a married woman, Lady Loughborough, née Sheila Chisholm, a gorgeous Australian unhappily wed to an alcoholic aristocrat. The monarchs were not amused, greatly displeased to now have *two* sons who were bounders and cads. In April 1920, the king cut a deal with Bertie: George V intended to provide him with his own establishment and make him Duke of York, but if this was an example of how he intended to conduct himself, then all bets were off. If he wanted his independence and his dukedom, he would have to dump his married paramour. Bertie obliged and was created Duke of York, as well as Earl of Inverness and Baron Killarney, on June 5.

In awarding his son the venerated dukedom, George V wrote, ". . . I feel that this splendid old title will be safe in your hands & that you will never do anything which could in any way tarnish it. . . ."

That year (historians can't seem to agree as to whether the event was the May 20 or June 10 ball hosted by the king's friend Lord Farquhar, or the July 8 Royal Air Force Ball), Bertie said to his equerry, the Honorable James Stuart, "That's a lovely girl you've been dancing with. Who is she?"

Soon, Elizabeth Bowes Lyon was in the arms of the Duke of York. "I danced with Prince Albert who I hadn't known before. He is quite a nice youth," Elizabeth wrote to her friend Beryl Poignand. But Lady Airlie wrote, "The Duke told me long afterwards that he had fallen in love that evening, although he did not realize it until later."

Bertie also didn't realize that he had competition. James Stuart was a genuine contender for Elizabeth's hand, and among her suitors was the only one she had feelings for.

In August, Bertie's sister, Princess Mary, visited Glamis. She and Elizabeth formed a warm friendship, and it provided an excuse for the duke to come a-courting, inviting himself up from Balmoral to join a house party. Elizabeth was nervous about being left alone with him, especially when their friends contrived to allow them a long stroll à deux, taking a break from the noisy hijinks—practical jokes and parlor games, and the frenetic dancing and loud piano music.

By November, Bertie had begun to correspond with Elizabeth, and she always replied to his letters with charm and enthusiasm, yet kept him at arm's length because she remained uncomfortable with his romantic interest in her. The duke sent her a box for Christmas in 1920, and by January he was cautiously courting her. Elizabeth invited him to lunch at St. Paul's Walden Bury on January 17, but cautioned that her mother was very ill, and so the party would have to be small. Her epistolary style is full of animated, winsome self-deprecation, even as she gives Bertie driving directions.

[K]eep to the right all the way, till you come to a tumbledown old white gate on the left. Then you go up a bumpy road full of holes, and eventually reach an even more tumbledown old house, and a tumbledown little person waiting on the doorstep—which will be *ME*!!! . . . I am Sir, Yours sincerely, Elizabeth Lyon.

Bertie informed his parents that he intended to ask Elizabeth to marry him. "You'll be a lucky fellow if she accepts you," said his blunt-spoken father.

Bertie proposed on February 27. And she didn't accept him. "She was frankly doubtful, uncertain of her feelings, and afraid of the public life which would lie ahead of her as the King's daughter-in-law," recalled Lady Airlie.

The following day, Elizabeth wrote to her rejected suitor.

Dear Prince Bertie, I must write one line to say how *dreadfully* sorry I am about yesterday. It makes me miserable to think of it—you have been so *very* nice about it all—*please* do forgive me. Also please don't worry about it—, I do understand so well what you feel, and sympathise so much, & I hate to think that I am the cause of it. I honestly can't explain to you how terribly sorry I am—, it worries me *so* much to think you may be unhappy—I do hope you won't be. *Anyway* we can be good friends can't we? Please do look on me as one. I shall *never* say anything about our talks I promise you—and nobody need ever know. . . . Yours very sincerely, Elizabeth.

Bertie must have responded, but the letter doesn't survive. Her reply, however, does.

Dear Prince Bertie, Thank you so much for your letter, which much relieved my mind. I feel just the same as you do about it, and am so glad. . . . Yes, I feel I know you so much better this last few weeks—I think it is so much easier to get to know people in the country—even if it's only for an hour or two—don't you? One is more natural I expect.

Bertie was inconsolable. The disappointed mother-in-law-who-might-have-been, Lady Strathmore, wrote to the matchmaking Lady Airlie,

> I have written to the young man as you advised—& told him how truly grieved we are that this little romance has come to an end. . . .
>
> I do hope that the Queen is not very much annoyed with E. & me, altho' it wd be quite natural that she shd be, but I shd be so unhappy to cause her (the Queen) any worry in her strenuous life. I hope "he" will find a very nice wife, who will make him happy—as between you & me, I feel he will be "made or marred" by his wife.

Queen Mary herself arrived at Glamis on September 5. According to Mabell Airlie, "Lady Elizabeth filled her mother's place as hostess so charmingly that the Queen was more than ever convinced that this was 'the one girl who could make Bertie happy.'" Lady Airlie wrote, "I always felt that the visit . . . was inspired by her desire to help him, although she was much too tactful to let it be apparent." But the queen herself insisted, "I shall say nothing to either of them. Mothers should never meddle in their children's love affairs."

On September 24, Bertie told his mother, "It is delightful here and Elizabeth is very kind to me. The more I see her the more I like her." She in turn appreciated his solicitousness when it came to her mother's grave illness. "It is *such* a help to have the sympathy of one's friends on these occasions," Elizabeth wrote the duke. Recognizing that she could both count on and confide in Bertie was an important step in the development of their tentative relationship. So many royal unions, and myriad postwar romances, were rushed affairs, cemented for either dynastic or desperate reasons. It was a huge gamble for Elizabeth to take a step back and seek a friendship first; she risked losing the prince altogether, but she had to know for certain whether she wanted the man, his family, and their lifestyle before committing to him. She had too much integrity to break his heart and too much practicality to apply for a job with The Firm, as England's royal family is known, a career she already knew she didn't want.

The courtship still remained lopsided at Christmas 1921, when Bertie gave Elizabeth a little clock—perhaps because she was perpetually tardy—along with a photo of himself. He received a charming thank-you note, with the apologetic "I wish I had got something to send you too."

Over the New Year holiday James Stuart came to say good-bye to Elizabeth, having accepted a job in America. Years later he would claim that Queen Mary intervened to remove him as a rival for Elizabeth's affections. There is nothing in the royal archives to substantiate this allegation—which doesn't necessarily mean it isn't true. Many years later when he was king, George VI told Princess Margaret that her mother had almost married Stuart, but he'd gone abroad. While there is no indication that Stuart ever proposed marriage to Elizabeth Bowes Lyon, by her own admission many years later, she viewed him as a "very serious" suitor.

On February 28, 1922, Elizabeth had her first taste of what it was like to participate in an extravagant royal event when she was a bridesmaid at Princess Mary's wedding. Unfortunately for Bertie, it didn't change her mind about wanting to become a member of the family. However, he remained both optimistic and persistent, catching Elizabeth off guard when he popped the question again on March 7. As she had assumed that her first no, given the previous year, had sufficed, she refused the duke again, writing to Bertie the following day to apologize for rejecting him a second time.

Dear Prince Bertie,

I am so terribly sorry about what happened yesterday, & feel it is all my fault, as I ought to have known [that he still felt the same way about her as before]. Will you please forgive me? You are one of my best & most faithful friends, & have always been so nice to me—that makes it doubly worse. . . . If you ever feel you want a talk about things in general—I hope you will come and

see me, as I understand you know. I do wish this hadn't
happened. Yours, Elizabeth.

Bertie replied that afternoon, informing Elizabeth that her note
had depressed him.

I have been thinking over what happened yesterday all today &
I feel that you must think so badly of me. . . . I was entirely in
the wrong to bring up the question in the way I did without
giving you any warning as to my intentions. Ever since last year
I have always been hoping to get to know you better & to let
you know my thoughts, but I see that I failed to enlighten you.
How were you to guess what they were when we never really
had any good talks like we did yesterday? I see it all now and
blame myself entirely for what happened.

. . . When shall I have a hope of seeing you again as I feel we
cannot leave things in this uncertain state. It is so bad & unset-
tling for us both, & whatever you decide will I know be best for
both.

The pair of them were falling over themselves to accept the blame
for misunderstanding each other's intentions and level of affection,
but their frank discussions about it and the fact that they were able
to take the time to get to know each other at all depicts one of the
first modern royal romances developing in real time. Theirs was
hardly an arranged union, and Elizabeth was not a foreign princess,
the traditional go-to gals for the British royal family. Most important
of all, it was a love match, even if, in the spring of 1922, it was primarily one-sided.

A few days after she received Bertie's letter, Elizabeth told him that
she was heading up to Scotland. "So we shall not meet for several
weeks I expect. Please do try & forget about this," she urged him.

He worried that she was fleeing because he was urging his suit
once more.

I do hope I was not the cause . . . but I feel I must tell you that
I have always cared for you & had the hope that you would one

day care for me. . . . But I know you will keep it a secret from everyone else in this world as I shall. This letter as you may imagine is one which I have found very difficult to write & I only hope that you will always look upon me as more than an ordinary friend. If you will do this I shall feel much happier after what has happened. Ever, Yours very sincerely, Albert.

Elizabeth had confided in her mother, but Bertie had not told his parents about the second proposal. The queen managed to learn of it nonetheless, writing in May 1922 to Lady Strathmore to tell her that both she and the king were

> . . . much disappointed that the little "romance" has come to an end as we should so much have liked the connection with your family. My son feels very sad about it but he is quite good and sensible and they are to remain friends. I hope you and E. will not reproach yourselves in any way, no one can help their feelings & it was far better to be honest. . . . With my love to you and E. and <u>many</u> regrets.

By the middle of the year, much to Bertie's consternation, while he hadn't entirely given up courting Elizabeth, hoping that her invitation to discuss the matter still might mean "maybe," he heard that she had received no fewer than five other marriage proposals, some from highly eligible prospects. The only comfort he could derive from this news was that she had rejected these suitors as well. On July 22, he sailed for Dunkirk to perform a royal naval duty and was introduced by his friend the naval doctor Louis Greig to John Campbell Davidson, a member of the Parliamentary delegation to Dunkirk.

The future Viscount Davidson noticed how unhappy the duke appeared. "He seemed to have reached a crisis in his life and wanted someone to whom he could unburden himself without reserve." After discussing with Davidson his distaste for the stuffiness and formality at court (both parents were tremendous sticklers), the prince finally came to the point. "He declared that he was desperately in love, but . . . it seemed quite certain that he had lost the only woman he would ever marry. I told him that however black the situation looked, he must not give up hope; that my wife had refused me consistently before she finally said 'yes,' and that like him, if she had persisted in her refusal, I would never have married anyone else."

Davidson despaired for his friend. "The question was, what was he to do? He could not live without her, and certainly he would never marry anyone else."

Bertie kept himself busy with royal engagements throughout the autumn of 1922, but he spent time with Elizabeth during the weekend of November 24, when her father invited the duke to come shooting at St. Paul's Walden Bury. The young couple had a marvelous time, but Elizabeth grew concerned that their continued friendship might give rise to gossip of something more between them, even though she had quashed that possibility. Elizabeth and Bertie crossed paths a few times that December at parties and dances and continued to correspond, which concerned the queen. Her Majesty worried that all this togetherness only set her son up for further heartbreak.

Poor Lady Airlie was deputized as a go-between once more, pointedly asking Elizabeth to stay away from the upcoming Pytchley Ball because her presence would only upset the duke—though the request was expressed so tactfully and discreetly that Elizabeth wondered what she had done to upset him. So she wrote to Bertie and the couple commiserated about how the older generation just didn't understand that not only could they still socialize as friends, but they enjoyed doing so.

At the end of the year, writing to her friend Beryl Poignand, Elizabeth conceded, "I don't seem to be able to like anybody enough to marry them! Isn't it odd? I *love* my friends but somehow can't do more. . . ."

The Prince of Wales urged her to accept Bertie. David, as he was known inside the royal family, told Elizabeth that "she had better go ahead and marry him, and eventually 'go to Buck House,'" referring to Buckingham Palace. This comment from the heir to the throne as early as 1922, when his father, George V, was still very much alive, and a good dozen years before he fell madly in love with Wallis Simpson, offers a telling insight into David's frame of mind regarding the succession. Although it was his birthright, the playboy bon vivant never wanted the responsibilities and burdens of kingship.

On January 3, 1923, Bertie took Elizabeth on a lovely date: dinner at Claridge's, followed by the theater, then a return to the hotel for a bit of dancing, during which, having taken to heart John Campbell Davidson's advice on persistence, he proposed marriage for a third time. The following day, Elizabeth discussed the matter with Lady Airlie, then wrote to the prince, explaining why she continued to remain so ambivalent. For most women, an offer of marriage from a handsome prince, and the married life of a duchess, with crowns and castles, would be a dream come true. But it was not a decision to be taken lightly, even if Elizabeth were madly in love with Bertie, for she would not be getting the man alone, but a lifetime in the public eye: all privacy and spontaneity forever sacrificed to a schedule of never-ending obligations and responsibilities. She wrote to the duke:

> It is so angelic of you to allow me plenty of time to think it over—I really do need it, as it takes so long to ponder these things, & this is so *very* [she double underscored] important for us both. If in the end I come to the conclusion that it will be alright, well & good, but Prince Bertie, *if* I feel that I can't (& I will not marry you unless I am quite certain, for your own sake) then I shall go away & try not to see you again. . . . I do hope you understand my feelings—I am more than grateful to you for not hurrying me, and I am determined not to spoil your life by just drifting on like this. You are so thoughtful for me always—oh I do want to do what is right for you. I have thought of nothing else all today—last night seems like a dream. Was it? . . .
>
> Perhaps you had better not say anything just yet to *anybody*—what do you think? Do as you think best.

Intriguingly, although she kept a diary, even within it, she spelled her *most* private thoughts backward. After airing her reasons for refusing Bertie yet again to Lady Airlie, Elizabeth wrote in her diary, "I ma tsom dexelprep"—"I am most perplexed." And on Friday January 5, awakening already tired and overwhelmed, she penned, "Ma gnikniht oot hcum. I hsiw I wenk."—"Am thinking too much. I wish I knew."

That day, London's *Daily News* printed the announcement of her engagement. But they had the wrong prince! SCOTTISH BRIDE FOR PRINCE OF WALES, read the headline. The *Star* followed suit that evening, blasting, LOVE MATCH FOR THE PRINCE. The next day the palace issued a denial.

On the afternoon of January 11, Bertie and Elizabeth spent a few hours deep in conversation—from tea time until seven thirty. But their discussion seemed to raise more issues than it resolved. "I ma yrev deirrow oot"—"I am very worried too"—Elizabeth wrote in her diary. By now their respective families were losing patience with what they viewed as Elizabeth's dithering. On January 9, Her Majesty had penned an apologetic note to the poor, harried Mabell Airlie, thanking her for her assistance "in this tiresome matter. The King & I quite understand from yr & [Bertie's aide-de-camp] Com: Greig's letters what is going on. I confess now we hope nothing will come of it as we both feel ruffled at E.'s behaviour!"

And one of Elizabeth's brothers told her, "Look here. You know you must either say yes or no. It's not fair."

Bertie apologized to his parents for having given them the impression that the courtship was over. "I know she would have said no, had I pressed her for an answer before now."

On Saturday January 13, he drove alone to St. Paul's Walden Bury and took a quiet stroll with Elizabeth. There, in the bucolic idyll where she had played as a child, enamored of fairies and owls, Bertie proposed marriage for a fourth time. Elizabeth hesitated yet again. The duke went off to saw wood with her father; then after tea, he and Elizabeth talked for hours. She asked if she could sleep on it, then wrote in her diary, "dediced ot tiaw a elttil—epoh I ma ton gnivaheb yldab"—"decided to wait a little—hope I am not behaving badly."

After breakfast the following day, and another long walk, plus a second lengthy stroll after lunch, and a third one after supper, Elizabeth finally accepted Bertie's marriage proposal late in the evening of Sunday, January 14. Historians disagree on whether the prearranged three-word coded telegram, "All Right. Bertie," which signified a yes, was, in the excitement of the moment, ever dispatched to the monarchs. Everyone in the Strathmore household had been sworn to silence until Their Majesties received the magic words.

Lady Strathmore wrote, "He came down to St. P.W. suddenly on *Friday*, & proposed continuously until Sunday night, when she said yes at 11:30!! My head is completely bewildered, as all those days E was hesitating & miserable, but now she is absolutely happy—& he is *radiant*."

Delighted that things were finally settled, and relieved that the duke had not only gotten the girl of his dreams, but that he could not have made a better choice, the king wrote to tell Elizabeth that "... I most gladly give my consent to your marriage with him. I know you will do all you can to help him in his many duties. ..." Her Majesty urged Elizabeth to look upon her as a "second mother."

On Monday, January 15, the newly affianced couple took tea with the king and queen at Sandringham. The following day, the duke wrote to his mother, "I am very very happy and I can only hope that Elizabeth feels the same as I do. I know I am very lucky to have won her over at last."

When the felicitous event was officially announced in the Court Circular on January 16, their friend Chips Channon observed, "... we had begun to despair that she would ever accept him. ... He is the luckiest of men, and there's not a man in England today that doesn't envy him."

That same day the *Dundee Advertiser* in Scotland proudly claimed inside knowledge of events.

Today's announcement of the betrothal of the Duke of York and Lady Elizabeth Bowes Lyon, youngest daughter of the Earl of Strathmore, will be received with great gratification throughout the Kingdom and with very special emotions of pleasure in Forfarshire. But, in Forfarshire, at any rate, the news will contain little of the element of surprise. Rumour, which does not always lie, has prepared the public to hear that a very charming romance was maturing which would link the Royal House with the ancient and historic family of romantic Glamis. It is just the kind of wedding which the British public would like—a wedding of free choice yet in every way charmingly right. The Duke, if nobody else, has reason to thank his stars that the war has been fought. Otherwise a dread convention of pre-war Royalty might have sent him to meet his fate in Germany instead of Strathmore.

Elizabeth wrote to tell the king how much she was anticipating meeting him at Sandringham the following Saturday, adding, ". . . and I do hope you will think I shall make Bertie a good wife, we are both so happy, and it is all wonderful."

At Buckingham Palace, a selection of engagement rings was presented to them by the jeweler Bert of Vigo Street. Elizabeth chose a large sapphire flanked by diamonds in a platinum setting, a description that sounds quite similar to the ring chosen by Lady Diana Spencer on her engagement to Prince Charles in 1981—and for which Diana was purportedly criticized by the royal family (what, not a diamond?!). How soon they forget!

After they became engaged, the couple's letters took on a more affectionate and relaxed tone; neither was afraid of using endearments for the other. Elizabeth sent "Her dear Darling" a letter on January 25, just to say she was thinking of him, adding that "I *do* [underlined several times] love you Bertie & feel certain that I shall *more & more*." She signed it, "From your always & forever loving E."

The duke's letter crossed with hers. He began:

My own little darling one,

How I hated leaving you this evening after our delightful little tete a tete dinner. . . . This is my first letter to you since you made me such a very happy person that Sunday at St. Paul's Walden & you don't know what a wonderful difference it has made to me darling, in all ways. I think I must always have loved you darling but could never make you realise it without telling you actually that I did & thank God I told you at the right moment.

Their clear affection for each other is quite different from the chilly and remote interpersonal relationships that come to mind when one thinks of the Windsors. It's far closer to the rapture that the young Victoria and Albert derived from each other's company. Even Elizabeth's initial reluctance to accept Bertie's suit bears echoes of Victoria's ambivalence about proposing to *her* Albert.

On February 11, 1923, the duke wrote to Elizabeth, "I loved the weekend with you & hated leaving you this evening, just a month tonight isn't it darling when you told me you loved me. What a day that was for me!!! & for you too."

Throughout the month of February, Elizabeth began the assimilation process into the royal family. Her name appeared in the Court Circular for the first time on February 21, when she and her fiancé accompanied the monarchs to a horse show in Islington. Photographers lay in wait when she made her excursions to select china, crystal, and millinery. All was pomp, circumstance, and tradition. Queen Mary presented her with a piece of antique lace in the same room at Buckingham Palace where Queen Victoria had given Mary a present before she wed *her* Duke of York.

The couple's marital home was to be White Lodge within Windsor Great Park, but neither Bertie nor Elizabeth was too keen on the queen's micromanaging of their future lifestyle. Her Majesty even insisted on choosing the furnishings. Elizabeth pronounced the decor in her bedroom "HIDEOUS." Bertie was annoyed by his mother's unwanted intrusion, telling Elizabeth, "All I want is that you should have what you want & that you should get the benefit & pleasure of going round & finding them for yourself & not having things thrust at you by other people."

Ironically, it was Elizabeth who had to mollify the duke. She wrote reassuringly, "Don't worry about White Lodge and furniture. I am quite certain we shall make it enchanting—you and I. . . . You are such an angel to me always, and I hate to think of you worrying about anything. 'Keep calm and don't be bullied. . . .'"

Their wedding day, April 26, 1923, dawned chilly, damp, and blustery. As Queen Mary put it, "[T]he sun came out between showers." Elizabeth's wedding gift from the king was a tiara and a suite of diamonds and turquoises, and she received a sapphire necklace from Her Majesty. Lord Strathmore gave his daughter a diamond tiara and a rope necklace of diamonds and pearls. Elizabeth's mother gave her a diamond-and-pearl necklace and bracelet with a matching pendant. The bride's gift to her groom was a platinum-and-pearl watch chain. The glamorous Prince of Wales presented the couple with a fur wrap and a luxurious motorcar.

The wedding of the Duke of York and Elizabeth Bowes Lyon was the first marriage of a king's son in Westminster Abbey, and only the third royal marriage since the union of Richard II and Anne of Bohemia to be performed there. It was also the first time that a commoner had wed a sovereign's son since Anne Hyde had wed the Duke of York in 1660—and theirs had been a clandestine ceremony.

Bertie was the first royal groom to wed in the dress uniform of the newest branch of the armed services, the Royal Air Force. He glittered with his war medals, and his tunic was also decorated with the gold ribbons and star of the Order of the Thistle, which his father had bestowed upon him in honor of his Scottish bride. The duke's supporters (best men, in America) were his brothers, the Prince of Wales and Prince Henry.

Elizabeth's eight bridesmaids wore ivory crepe de chine gowns embellished with Nottingham lace covered in white chiffon. Leaf-green tulle sashes accentuated their waists, the belts secured with a white rose (the emblem of York) and a silver thistle. A bandeau of myrtle leaves and white roses encircled their hair, and like the bride they wore long white veils. The attendants also sported their gift from the bridegroom: a carved crystal brooch in the shape of a Yorkist rose with the initials E and A in diamonds in the center.

Elizabeth was uncharacteristically punctual, arriving at the Abbey just as the sun fittingly broke through the clouds. Her bridal gown was constructed of cream chiffon moiré with appliquéd bars of silver lamé, embroidered with gold threads and pearls as well as paste beads. The dress had a slim silhouette with a deep square neckline, short sleeves, and a slightly gathered skirt with a modest train set into the waist seam. Her shoes were ivory silk moiré. Over the dress she wore a longer train made of silk net edged with lace and a *point de Flandres* lace veil, both of which were "something borrowed" from Queen Mary. With the veil drawn low over Elizabeth's forehead and held in place by a wreath of white heather, white roses, and myrtle leaves— the floral symbol of love and constancy that had graced every royal bridal headdress since Victoria's—the headdress lent her the appearance of a twelfth-century Norman princess. The wedding gown, featured in magazines of the day, inspired popular fashion trends.

As Elizabeth entered the Abbey on her father's arm and began her long processional toward the altar, she spontaneously halted to lay her bouquet of roses and lily-of-the-valley upon the Tomb of the Unknown Warrior. Her gesture has since become a tradition. Catherine Middleton did the same at her April 29, 2011, wedding to Prince William of Wales.

As Elizabeth walked down the aisle, "The Duke of York faced with shining eyes and a look of happiness the girl who, hand in hand with her father, was advancing in her lovely old fashioned dress, gleaming with silver and veiled in old lace . . . they seemed to think of no one but each other," reported the *Times*.

Approximately 1,780 people witnessed the service, conducted by the Archbishop of Canterbury as well as the Archbishop of York, the Most Reverend Cosmo Lang (who as Archbishop of Canterbury in 1936 would weigh in heavily on the event that would come to be known as the Abdication Crisis). Elizabeth had asked Lang to deliver the address. One point in particular encapsulated the image that the Yorks would strive to project after the birth of their daughters, and later as king and queen of England: ". . . The nations and classes which make up our Commonwealth too often live their lives apart. It is . . . a great thing that there should be in our midst one family which, regarded by all as in a true sense their own, makes the whole Empire kin and helps to give it the spirit of family life."

Elizabeth and Bertie were Victoria and Albert for the modern century, a postwar world in which too many British families had been torn asunder by the tragedy.

Although she had entered Westminster Abbey as a commoner, Elizabeth exited as Her Royal Highness The Duchess of York, a princess of the United Kingdom, and the fourth-highest-ranking woman in the realm. After the ceremony, their scarlet-and-gold coach took a circuitous route back to Buckingham Palace in order to allow the maximum number of spectators a chance to catch a glimpse of the newlyweds. By the evening, silent film clips of the processions to and from the Abbey could be viewed throughout the nation. And across the pond, the interest in the young royals was just as high. The following morning, the headline of the *New York Times* proclaimed with a combination of wild understatement and pure invention, DUKE OF YORK WEDS SIMPLE SCOTCH MAID—LITTLE BRIDE APPEARS OVERWHELMED.

Although the wedding had been filmed, it was not broadcast, because the Archbishop of Canterbury feared that people would listen to it in public houses (which indeed would do a booming business on April 29, 2011, during the wedding of their great-grandson William). So the only people sitting down to a celebratory wedding breakfast were the royals and their guests, who dined on a menu of Frenchified courses for this most consummate of British occasions: *Consommé à la Windsor, Supreme de Saumon Reine Mary, Chapons à la Strathmore, Côtelette d'Agneau Prince Albert,* and *Duchess Elizabeth Strawberries.* The nine-foot-tall wedding cake was donated by a friend of Bertie's, Sir Alexander Grant.

The bridal couple had very practical wishes when it came to their wedding registry. They had asked for furniture.

The day after the wedding, as the newlyweds embarked upon their honeymoon in Surrey and Scotland, they telegrammed their parents to say how delighted they were with their new spouses. The king replied to Bertie, ". . . Elizabeth will be a splendid partner in your work & share with you & help you in all you have to do."

Several years later, George VI's biographer John Wheeler Bennett commented on George V's prescience. "No prophecy could have been more completely fulfilled, no expression of confidence more entirely justified. The Duchess was not only to be the partner of his happiness but his inspiration of encouragement in the face of adversity, his enduring source of strength in joy and sadness."

George V and Queen Mary were delighted with their son's choice. A commoner modernized and humanized the monarchy. They hoped that Elizabeth's levelheaded pragmatism, combined with her pluck and can-do attitude, would draw out Bertie and instill in him the confidence he so sorely needed. Indeed, as partners they were well suited; both were raised with a strong sense of duty. But Elizabeth soon discovered the restraints of life as a royal, which went far beyond her misgivings about the "HIDEOUS" boudoir at White Lodge, whose Windsor location was too suburban for a young couple who spent most of their time in London. The new duchess had limitations placed on her freedom and couldn't go out as she used to do, or do anything spontaneous, or even socialize with her friends in the manner she once had, a lament voiced by royal brides ever since. After she had enjoyed a relaxed upbringing, the rigidity of the court took a good deal of readjustment, beginning with the dress code. The royals at the top of the food chain changed clothes for dinner every night, no matter whether they had guests, and dressed formally at all times.

At least she was appreciated. The king and queen utterly adored their new daughter-in-law. "The better I know and the more I see of your dear little wife, the more charming I think she is and everyone falls in love with her," the king told Bertie. George V was notoriously brusque and blunt and had a tense relationship with his children. But Elizabeth had thoroughly enchanted him from the start, and she never found herself at the receiving end of the criticism that had so undermined her husband's confidence.

One of their contemporaries, Henry "Chips" Channon, observed of Bertie, "He had few friends and was almost entirely dependent on her, whom he worshipped. She was his will power, his all." Before their marriage the duke had never been self-possessed. He was always nervous in public, particularly about his stammer. His anxiety exacerbated the problem, and the problem exacerbated his anxiety. It was a vicious cycle of perpetual torment.

As an adolescent, Bertie had serious gastric problems, attributed to his being badly fed by his nurse during his infancy. And his acute stammer could have been a result of his father's gruff insistence on breaking Bertie of his left-handedness. The duke also had an ungovernable temper, suffering fits or outbursts that his family called "gnashes." These tantrums alternated with periods of introspection and profound melancholy. Unfortunately, his various afflictions may have had repercussions in the marital bed.

The duchess's archnemesis, Wallis Simpson, upon being asked why she had no children with her third husband, the former Edward VIII, replied with her typical brittle wit, "The Duke is not heir-conditioned." His younger brother evidently suffered the same or similar medical, emotional, psychological, or psychosomatic issues.

In February 1911, when they were boys at the Royal Naval College, Bertie and David both succumbed to back-to-back epidemics of measles and mumps that were so severe that two of their classmates died. The adolescent princes were at the age where a rare complication from mumps, known as orchitis, which affects the testicles and can impair procreative capacity, may have resulted in a profound effect on their virility.

Elizabeth and Bertie were very much in love but, after two childless years, turned to a radical option: manual fertilization. Only through this process of artificial insemination was the duchess able to conceive their two daughters, the Princess Elizabeth Alexandra Mary, born on April 21, 1926, and Princess Margaret Rose, born on August 21, 1930. Both infants were delivered by Caesarean section. A family friend whose mother was a goddaughter of Queen Victoria claimed that the method of the princesses' conception was an open secret within their circle, although the press protectively and euphemistically reported only that "a certain line of treatment was successfully adopted." But according to the Yorks' family friend, "My mother and the Duchess . . . talked about it because they shared the same gynecologist. . . . The Duke had a slight . . . problem . . . with . . . a . . . his 'willy. . . .' "

Treating Bertie's speech problem was the next step. In this, Elizabeth's influence was profound; she persuaded him to visit speech therapist Lionel Logue's Harley Street clinic. Logue had heard Bertie deliver his maiden radio speech at Wembley Stadium on May 9, 1925, inaugurating the opening of the British Empire Exhibition. Bertie had been terrified, aware that he would have to perform before a live audience that included his severest critic—his father. Not only that, the speech would also be broadcast to millions of listeners over the wireless.

According to Elizabeth's diary, Bertie set out for Wembley that morning "very downhearted." His legs trembled throughout the speech, and he had trouble articulating some of the words. The duchess listened over the wireless from White Lodge. "It was marvelously clear & no hesitation. I was *so* relieved," she wrote. Bertie admitted after it was over that he thought it was "easily the best I have ever done. Papa seemed pleased which was kind of him." However, His Majesty told the duke's brother George, "Bertie got through his speech all right, but there were some rather long pauses."

Bertie's first appointment with Lionel Logue did not take place until October 19, 1926. The Australian, who had trained as an engineer but took up speech pathology to help soldiers traumatized during World War I, wrote of his first session with the Duke of York, "He entered my consulting room at three o'clock in the afternoon, a slim, quiet man, with tired eyes and all the outward symptoms of the man whom habitual speech defect had begun to set the sign. When he left at five o'clock you could see that there was hope once more in his heart."

Elizabeth, who accompanied Bertie to nearly every session, encouraged her husband each step of the way during his course of therapy, supporting him through the rigorous battery of exercises, from rapid-fire tongue twisters to diaphragmatic breathing exercises on the floor. Together with Logue, she gave him the confidence to deliver his speeches, where previously he'd been a self-conscious embarrassment—to the royal family, to the kingdom, and to himself.

Logue later stated that the Duke of York was "the pluckiest and most determined patient I ever had," largely, and most likely, because his plucky and most determined duchess refused to let him become defeated.

The duke still remained anxious about public appearances, however. Laura, Duchess of Marlborough, recalled how Elizabeth would take charge of her bashful husband. After attending a public function in Leicester, the Yorks boarded a Pullman car. A crowd had gathered outside the train and "The Duke was very shy and rushed along the carriage, pulling down the blinds. I was very impressed by the way that the Duchess snapped them up again immediately, saying to her husband, 'Bertie, you must wave.'"

Nicknamed "the smiling duchess," Elizabeth managed to balance a pitch-perfect ear for public relations with her genuine adoration for her husband. Theirs was clearly a love match, as Duff Cooper, a contemporary who later became Secretary of State for War, wrote to his wife, Diana, after seeing the Yorks at the theater one night in 1926. "They are such a sweet little couple and so fond of each other.

They reminded me of us, sitting together in the box having private jokes, and in the interval when we were all sitting in the room behind the box they slipped out, and I found them standing together in a dark corner of the passage talking happily as we might. She affects no shadow of airs or graces."

In the 1920s the British Empire reached its geographical zenith, covering a quarter of the world. And ever since the Prince of Wales's successful state visit to Australia in 1920, the Duke of York had longed to follow in his footsteps. Now that he had the exceptionally popular Elizabeth at his side, the monarchs finally agreed. So in 1927, the Yorks embarked on their first official state visit: a comprehensive tour of Australia that would keep them away from their infant daughter for half a year or so, given the additional ports of call that would take them around the world. The duchess was heartbroken, but soon learned that one's royal duties always trumped domestic yearnings.

The Yorks departed England on January 6, and did not return until June 27, 1927. After sailing thirty thousand miles and traveling many more on land, the duke and duchess came away with a few valuable lessons from their lengthy journey. With his wife at his side, Bertie had a newfound confidence; he felt respected, rather than mocked, by the world. And Elizabeth discovered that her personality was currency. Wherever they went, she could use it to win people's hearts, not just for herself, but for her husband and his kingdom.

The state visit had also been priceless practice for what lay ahead.

At the end of 1928, George V caught a chill and nearly died. Not daring to believe that his father was as ill as the doctors feared him to be, the Prince of Wales refused to quit his African safari with Denys Finch Hatton. The king's assistant private secretary, Alan "Tommy" Lascelles, cabled the heir to the throne. "Sir, the King of England is dying, and if that means nothing to you, it means a great deal to us." The prince's behavior was a foreshadowing of the future, when, eight years later, David, thinking of no one but himself and Wallis Simpson, would relinquish the throne.

In December 1928, and again in July 1929, the king needed an operation to drain an abscess just behind his diaphragm. In each case a rib had to be removed. As discussions were privately undertaken about the inevitable succession, the royal household even then de-spaired of David. His charm and popularity were undeniable, but palace insiders agreed that he lacked the seriousness to do the job.

Many years later, Elizabeth recalled that during his convales-cence the ailing king told Bertie, " 'You'll see, your brother will never become King.' He must have seen something we didn't, because I remember we thought 'how ridiculous,' because then everybody thought he was going to be a wonderful King. . . . I remember we both looked at each other and thought 'nonsense.' "

In 1935, George V celebrated his jubilee: twenty-five years on the throne. But he was not a well man. During the last weeks of his life the ailing king passionately exclaimed to Lady Algernon Gordon-Lennox, "I pray to God that my eldest son will never marry and have children, and that nothing will come between Bertie and Lilibet [the family's nickname for Princess Elizabeth] and the throne." He wor-ried that the café society in which his heir traveled, with its easy virtue, was a bad influence on the manners and morality of the mon-archy. David and Bertie could not have been more different, the for-mer a glib bon vivant, and the latter a stammering family man. Their father took a dim view of the Prince of Wales's character. "He has not a single friend who is a gentleman. He does not see any decent society. And he is 41."

The king's condition worsened throughout the month of January 1936. On the sixteenth, Queen Mary sent for the Duke of York. Four days later, the public was informed about the grave condition of His Majesty's health, as the BBC announced, "The King's life is moving peacefully to its close."

Just before the end, the Prince of Wales "became hysterical, cried loudly and kept on embracing the Queen," according to Lord Wi-gram. Helen Hardinge, wife of the king's private secretary, judged Edward's display of emotion to be "frantic and unreasonable." And yet, if one is losing one's father and inheriting the responsibility of governing an empire where the sun never sets when one isn't particu-larly keen on doing so, one might cry hysterically, too.

The royal physician Lord Dawson scandalously gave the dying king a lethal injection of cocaine and morphine to help him sleep, hastening the process so that His Majesty would pass in time for his demise to be recorded in the more respectable morning papers, rather than the evening tabloids. His time of death was recorded as 11:55 p.m. on January 20. George V's body lay in state at Westminster Hall and was interred in St. George's Chapel at Windsor on January 28.

The Prince of Wales, now Edward VIII, came to the throne on a tide of popularity. He had served in World War I, so it was expected that the veterans would like him. He was affable and charming and not hampered by a stammer. Yet George V had predicted, "After I am dead the boy will ruin himself in twelve months," and he was not far off the mark. Edward made it clear early in his reign that he found his royal duties irksome and had no intentions of giving up his fast set of friends for a more staid circle of associates. There were greater concerns as well. Winston Churchill was troubled about the rise of fascism across Europe, and the king's sympathy for Mussolini and the Third Reich. According to Lord Wigram, senior officials at Whitehall believed he was in the pocket of the German ambassador, Lord Ribbentrop. Insiders at Buckingham palace used the words "irresponsible" and "impractical" to describe the new king.

The most heinous crime of all, in the eyes of his government and his family, was Edward's romance with Wallis Simpson, who was still married to her second husband when their affair began in 1934. Appalled that this brash American upstart was sleeping in Queen Mary's bed at Balmoral and loudly discussing how the royal gardens should be rearranged, Elizabeth refused to accept her as Edward's hostess. She resented the king's shirking of his royal duties and responsibilities to accommodate "That Woman" instead. The duchess also resented seeing Wallis's name at the top of the Court Circular with the Yorks'. From then on, whenever Mrs. Simpson's name was mentioned, Elizabeth's ordinarily twinkly blue eyes would harden and her smiling mouth would become tight.

But Edward was head over heels in love with Wallis. She was the one nonnegotiable element in the king's life. On November 16, 1936, he summoned his prime minister, Stanley Baldwin, and informed him that he intended to wed Mrs. Simpson and make her his queen— just as soon as her divorce proceedings were concluded and she received her *decree nisi*. Duff Cooper, the Secretary of State for War, recalled Baldwin saying, as he passed the news to his colleagues, that "he was not at all sure that the Yorks would not prove the best solution. The King had many good qualities but not those which best fitted him for his post, whereas the Duke of York would be just like his father."

The childless Edward's accession had made Bertie the heir presumptive to the throne, yet the king never took the duke into his confidence throughout the debacle known as the Abdication Crisis. The Yorks did not know what was on Edward's mind until October 20, 1936, when his private secretary, Alec Hardinge, visited them at 145 Piccadilly, their London residence, to officially inform them of the possibility of Edward's abdication and their succession to the throne. Elizabeth was incredulous at the news; Bertie was aghast. When the duchess saw her husband's ashen face she grew even angrier at his irresponsible brother and *her*—his married floozy. How dared Edward consider abandoning his duty and leaving Bertie, clearly overwhelmed by the mere thought of it, to pick up the pieces?

On November 17, the king finally told the Duke of York of his intentions to abdicate if he could not marry Mrs. Simpson. After this bombshell, there was radio silence from Edward.

Panicked, Bertie tried to communicate with his older brother, but the king did not reply to his letters or return phone calls. "I do *so* [he double underscored the word] long for you to be happy with the one person you adore," Bertie wrote to the king on November 23. "I feel sure that whatever you decide to do will be in the best interests of this Country and Empire."

Always the angel on her husband's shoulder, protective and supportive, Elizabeth took up the pen and wrote to the king herself on the same day.

Darling David,

Please read this. Please be kind to Bertie when you see him, because he loves you, and minds terribly all that happens to you. I wish that you could realize how loyal & true he is to you, and you have no idea how hard it has been for him lately . . . & as his wife, I must write & tell you this. I am terrified for him—so DO help him. And *for God's sake* don't tell him that I have written—we both uphold you always. E.

Across the top of the page, she added, "We want you to be happy, more than anything else, but it's awfully difficult for Bertie to say what he thinks, you know how shy he is—so do help him."

On November 25, Bertie wrote to Sir Godfrey Thomas, "If the worst happens and I have to take over, you can be assured that I will do my best to clear up the inevitable mess, if the whole fabric does not crumble under the shock and strain of it all."

Elizabeth channeled her contempt for Edward and hatred for Wallis into keeping the Duke of York calm in the face of his increasing anxiety about the terrifying prospect ahead. On November 29, as the Yorks left to fulfill a royal engagement in Edinburgh, Bertie commented that he hated to leave London, because he was so anxious about the imminent future. "I feel like the proverbial 'sheep being led to the slaughter,' which is not a comfortable feeling."

Elizabeth was appalled by the way Edward had been treating his family throughout the Abdication Crisis. Seventy-year-old Queen Mary, so recently widowed, had become seriously depressed. The Yorks, who had the most at stake, could not fathom that the king had left them entirely out of his discussions with the government. "Everyone knows more than we do. We know nothing. Nothing!" Elizabeth exclaimed.

Edward announced his intentions to their mother on December 3, then dropped off the planet when Bertie tried to reach him. The duke humiliated himself by phoning him at Fort Belvedere nonstop for four days. Elizabeth never forgave Edward for the agony he put her husband through during those ninety-six hours. She also never forgot the humiliating rumors that serious consideration was being given to bypassing Bertie for the crown in favor of one of his younger brothers—who were not hampered by an embarrassing speech defect.

However, the Duke of Gloucester was an uninspiring boozer, and the Duke of Kent was notoriously bisexual. At least the Duke of York had a secret weapon: his extremely popular wife—and the British adored their two little daughters. Additionally, Bertie had more experience than his younger brothers, and so it was determined that the order of succession would stand. "The Yorks will do it very well," averred Stanley Baldwin.

Yet when Bertie saw the Instrument of Abdication on December 9, he broke down and sobbed on his mother's shoulder for an hour. Elizabeth was so stressed that she came down with the flu. On December 10 at ten a.m., Edward VIII signed the Instrument of Abdication, and a few hours later, Prime Minister Baldwin informed Parliament and the rest of the world.

The Yorks were together as a family when a mob converged outside 145 Piccadilly. Elizabeth rose from her sickbed to see what the commotion was all about, then told Bertie he should show himself to his new subjects. "But what on earth am I to say to them?" he asked shyly.

At three p.m., Queen Mary came to see them. Her face was wet with tears after speaking privately with Elizabeth. The new queen told their daughters' governess, "I'm afraid there are going to be great changes in our lives, Crawfie. We must take what is coming to us and make the best of it."

On Friday, December 11, at 1:36 p.m., His Majesty's Declaration of Abdication Act received Edward VIII's own royal assent in the House of Lords. At that moment "Bert and Betty" were no longer Duke and Duchess of York but Their Royal Majesties, as well as Emperor and Empress of India. (The latter titles were relinquished on June 22, 1947, when India was granted independence.)

That night the former king took to the airwaves and made a radio broadcast to the nation, referring to his successor's "one matchless blessing, enjoyed by so many of you and not bestowed on me—a happy home with his wife and children."

The following day, Edward departed Britain's shores aboard the *HMS Fury.* Bertie's first act as king of England was to confer a dukedom on his elder brother, who was henceforth to be known as His Royal Highness the Duke of Windsor. The royal family's—and Parliament's—denial of HRH status to Wallis as his duchess after they wed on June 3, 1937, would become a source of tension for the rest of the Windsors' lives.

Nine hours after Edward's departure, Bertie, now George VI, looking (in the words of his biographer John Wheeler-Bennett) "pale and haggard, yet with an innate dignity and integrity which compelled the respect and reverence, as well as the protective instinct of his hearers . . . in a low, clear voice, but with many hesitations," addressed his Accession Council at St. James's Palace. He told them, "With my wife and helpmeet by my side, I take up the heavy task which lies before me. In it I look for the support of all my peoples."

Three days after their accession, on December 14, George VI's forty-first birthday, he conferred the Order of the Garter on his queen. It was clear from the start of his reign that Elizabeth was to be a full partner. Although there was no traditional Christmas broadcast that year, Bertie released a New Year's Eve message, dedicating himself to his subjects; and, referring to the burdens of kingship, he intoned, "I shoulder them with all the more confidence in the knowledge that the Queen and my mother Queen Mary are at my side," adding, "[M]y wife and I dedicate ourselves for all time to your service, and we pray that God may give us guidance and strength to follow the path that lies before us." The new sovereigns hoped their subjects would accept them with open arms, fearing that the popular and glamorous Edward VIII would be a tough act to follow. Elizabeth knew perfectly well that the über-svelte Wallis Simpson had mocked her unfashionably plump figure and nicknamed her "the dowdy duchess," and that her husband's stammer was a source of derision. Now, more than ever, a country that had been torn asunder by public opinion needed to be healed.

Mother knew best. A proud Queen Mary wrote to Lady Strathmore, "[D]ear Bertie and Elizabeth will carry out things in the same way that George V did. . . . Elizabeth is such a darling and is such a help to Bertie."

And Bertie knew it. The Regency Act of 1937 made Elizabeth the first Queen Consort in English history to be eligible to serve as a Counsellor of State and to transact royal business in the sovereign's name. It was proof of the king's trust in her competence. His pride in

Elizabeth was further demonstrated when he insisted that she precede him on all but the most formal state occasions. It was the queen who would emerge from a car first, smiling and waving regally, acknowledging the cheers of the crowd, while at a respectful distance the diffident king followed as if he were the consort.

After their accession the royal couple also bonded more closely in other ways. The country had been riven by the Abdication Crisis. Politicians and subjects taking sides created a toxic situation that was bad for the kingdom. Elizabeth and Bertie socially ostracized the courtiers who had worked for Edward VIII and those who had been among the former king's tight circle of friends, especially the individuals who had championed Wallis. From the continent, the newly minted Duke of Windsor remained a thorn in his brother's side, perpetually offering unsolicited political advice that often ran counter to the guidance of Bertie's ministers. Edward was always ringing up Buckingham Palace to ask Bertie for money and to pressure him to grant Wallis the styling of a Royal Highness. His blasé indifference to the havoc he had wreaked on the kingdom and upon his brother's health, engendering no end of "gnashes," infuriated Elizabeth. Her husband's nerves became exceptionally frayed during the first year of his reign, no thanks to Edward's antagonizing him. Elizabeth urged Bertie to tell his brother not to phone him anymore—and that the reason for it should be clear: That Woman.

On May 12, 1937, George VI and Elizabeth were crowned in Westminster Abbey as their two daughters watched in awe. Queen Mary broke with the tradition of a surviving monarch not attending the coronation of a subsequent sovereign, to see her second son crowned. At the moment the consort's crown was placed upon the head of the diminutive Elizabeth, swathed in the purple and ermine trappings of queenship, a misty-eyed Winston Churchill turned to his wife, Clementine, and, referring to Mrs. Simpson, admitted, "You were right. I see now the 'other one' wouldn't have done."

Bertie had been anxious for weeks about the impending coronation, fearful of stammering during his public responses in the Abbey and even more so during the live broadcast he would make from Buckingham Palace after the ceremony. But the queen and Lionel Logue were on hand to see him through, as well as a BBC sound engineer named Robert Wood, who coached the king on how to use the microphone to best advantage. "It is with a very full heart that I speak to you tonight. Never before has a newly crowned King been able to talk to all his peoples in their own homes on the day of his Coronation . . . the Queen and I will always keep in our hearts the inspiration of this day. . . ."

Edward VIII had been a rock star to his subjects, and even though he had chosen to quit the throne (Wallis would have been perfectly happy to remain his mistress as long as he didn't marry anyone else), he hated his new nonentity status. As a way of drawing attention to himself, he acted in ways that were not only dangerous to England's foreign policy but, in the queen's view, were deliberately calculated to steal her husband's thunder. In 1937 the Duke and Duchess of Windsor announced a visit to Hitler's Germany—for which Edward had received no permission from His Majesty's government, and which ran counter to British interests. Bertie and Elizabeth supported Prime Minister Neville Chamberlain's policy of appeasement but privately had their misgivings about the fascist dictatorships of Germany and Italy. And in 1939, on the eve of Elizabeth and Bertie's departure for Canada and America, marking the first visit ever of a reigning king and queen of England to the USA, the Duke of Windsor announced his arrangement with NBC to give a radio address to their primarily American audience.

Bert and Betty were a huge hit in Canada. The veterans exclaimed, "Ay, man, if Hitler could just see this," when the queen insisted on mingling with them during the unveiling of the World War I War Memorial. The American journalists covering that event were duly impressed, hailing George VI as "a people's king." And in June 1939, when the monarchs visited Washington, D.C., to meet with President and Mrs. Roosevelt, a senator on Capitol Hill reached out and grabbed Bertie's hand to tell him, "My, you're a great Queen-picker."

A local newspaper headline read, THE BRITISH RE-TAKE WASHINGTON, and called Elizabeth "the perfect Queen." In New York City she was deemed "spell-binding." Elizabeth was nominated "Woman of the Year" "because, arriving in an aloof, critical country, she completely conquered it and accomplished this conquest by being her natural self." Decades later, people who had never seen Elizabeth in action would think that the magic of Diana, Princess of Wales, was unique to the House of Windsor.

The queen would later say, "That tour made us! I mean it made us, the King and I. It came at just the right time, particularly for us." No longer were they the reluctant understudies of Edward VIII. And they were about to be sorely tested.

On September 1, 1939, Germany invaded Poland. Two days later, Britain and France declared war on Germany, because they had a treaty with Poland in which they agreed to aid her if her independence were threatened by force.

During the first four months of the war Elizabeth projected an aura of calm reassurance to her subjects. Bertie's first Christmas radio broadcast (coauthored with the queen, as all of his Christmas broadcasts would be) was profoundly moving, reciting a stanza from Marie Louise Haskins's poem "The Gate of the Year."

"I said to the man who stood at the Gate of the Year, 'Give me a light that I may tread safely into the unknown.' And he replied, 'Go out into the darkness, and put your hand into the Hand of God. That shall be to you better than light, and safer than a known way.'"

Functioning as a team, the monarchs bolstered their subjects' morale. In January 1940, they began hosting Monday-night dinners for the War Cabinet and other government ministers. During the early months of the year, Elizabeth spent a considerable amount of time at Bertie's side as he perused the daily reports, telegrams, and assessments. Consequently, she acquired firsthand knowledge of the war effort and the ongoing affairs and daily activities of the government.

On May 10, Germany invaded Holland, Luxembourg, and Belgium, and began their final assault on France. That day, Winston Churchill succeeded the discredited Neville Chamberlain—he of the appalling appeasement policy—as prime minister.

Germany's air force, the Luftwaffe, began systematic attacks over England on August 12, bombing airfields and aircraft factories. The Battle of Britain was under way. On the night of September 7–8 the Blitz began in London, with the release of more than two hundred bombs over the capital. Although the initial damage was in the poorer neighborhoods, such as the capital's East End, no target was immune, including the monarchs' old residence at 145 Piccadilly,

Westminster Abbey, and Buckingham Palace, which was struck nine times during the Blitz.

On September 13, the king and queen were nearly killed during an air raid. In a letter to Queen Mary, Elizabeth described the event. She had gone to find Bertie to see whether he was coming down to the palace's bomb shelter when:

> He asked me to take an eyelash out of his eye, and while I was battling with this task, Alec [Hardinge, the king's private secretary] came into the room with a batch of papers in his hand. At this moment we heard the unmistakable whirr-whirr of a German plane. We said, "ah, a German," and before anything else could be said, there was the noise of aircraft diving at great speed, and then the scream of a bomb. It all happened so quickly, that we had only time to look foolishly at each other, when the scream hurtled past us, and exploded with a tremendous crash in the quadrangle.

Churchill later wrote in his memoirs, "Had the windows been closed instead of open, the whole of the glass would have splintered into the faces of the King and Queen, causing terrible injuries. So little did they make of it that even I . . . never realised until long afterwards . . . what had actually happened."

The following day the monarchs toured the bombed-out East End of London. Elizabeth wrote to Queen Mary:

> I really felt as if I was walking in a dead city, when we walked down a little empty street. . . . It does affect me seeing this terrible and senseless destruction—I think that really I mind it much more than being bombed myself. . . .

Elizabeth famously remarked that she was glad the palace had been bombed, because it enabled her to look the East End in the face. The disaster forged an even closer bond between the sovereigns and their subjects. In fact, the queen was so effective at boosting British morale that Hitler referred to her as the most dangerous woman in Europe.

When Bertie and Elizabeth toured the war-torn parts of the city, she would emerge from her car in muted pastels—dusky rose, lilac, and powder blue. She was always impeccably groomed and coiffed, with high heels and dyed-to-match feathers in her hats, looking every inch the queen, but tastefully so, inspiring the people with a dash of glamour and a glimmer of hope.

Many years later, Elizabeth was asked whether she had shared the war's burdens with the king, and whether he had revealed much in the way of state affairs at the time. She replied, "Oh, yes, he told me everything. Well, one had to, you see, because you couldn't not, in a way. There was only us there. So obviously he had to tell one things. But one was so dreadfully discreet, that even now I feel nervous sometimes, about talking about things. . . ."

Yet even though the queen was Bertie's ultimate partner, she saw her duty as being his protector and gatekeeper, managing his temper and making the burden of his immense responsibilities as bearable as possible under the circumstances, and not to initiate or suggest policy. She may have known about the political side of his affairs, but she did not interfere in them. Nor did she create or maintain her own coterie of courtiers with an alternate agenda from the king's, or endeavor to corrupt the opinions of her husband's servants and ministers to suit her own ends. Elizabeth's ends were Bertie's.

After the war ended, the monarchs tried to resume a normal family life around their two daughters. They undertook victory tours, including a visit to the Channel Islands, the only British Crown Dependency to be occupied by the Germans. In 1947, "Us Four" embarked on a state visit to South Africa. It would be the last time they would travel as a family unit, as Princess Elizabeth had fallen in love with—and hoped to marry—her fourth cousin Lieutenant Philip Mountbatten, son of the late Prince Andrew of Greece and the former Princess Alice of Battenberg.

But the king was tired and testy throughout the trip, exhausted by the demands of travel and the incessant crowds. Aware that his visible irritation would not play well to their subjects, Elizabeth would stroke his arm to soothe him. The royal household's Chief Clerk, Ted Grove, remarked that he didn't think Bertie "could have got through it all without the love and devotion of the Queen. We admired the way she cared and watched over him during the tour when some-times the continued heat and travel in the confined space of the Royal Train did nothing to improve his occasional bouts of temper."

During the African tour Bertie lost seventeen pounds. He fought a persistent cough and suffered severe cramping in both legs. It her-alded the beginning of a long, slow decline.

The royal family returned home, announcing the engagement of the Princess Elizabeth to Philip Mountbatten in July. The couple was married on November 20. The Duke and Duchess of Windsor were conspicuously not invited to the wedding.

On April 26, 1948, George VI and Elizabeth rode in an open horse-drawn landau past throngs of cheering crowds to a service of Thanksgiving at St. Paul's Cathedral, marking their silver wedding anniversary. Although their reign had begun with apprehension (in-cluding their own), the monarchs were now vastly popular. That night the king delivered a broadcast to the nation over the wire-less, his speech faltering from time to time. He discussed the years "full of difficulty, of anxiety, and often of sorrow. On me, in my endeavor to fulfill my appointed task, they have laid a heavy burden. I make no secret of the fact that there have been times when it would have been almost too heavy but for the strength and comfort which I have always found in my home."

That autumn, Bertie's leg cramps grew progressively worse, and he was in discomfort most of the time. By October his left foot was numb all day, and the pain kept him awake all night. Sir James Lear-month, the chair of clinical surgery at Edinburgh, confirmed on No-vember 12 that His Majesty was suffering from arteriosclerosis. He also risked gangrene and, as a result, might lose his right leg. Bertie refused to allow any word of the severity of his condition to be leaked to the extremely pregnant Princess Elizabeth, whose son, Prince Charles, was born two days later, on November 14.

An official bulletin, larded with understatement and euphemisms, was released on November 23. Omitted entirely were references to the king's heavy smoking and alcohol consumption, which were as-suredly contributing factors to his condition. There was, however, a thinly veiled accusation leveled at the Duke of Windsor. "There is no doubt that the strain of the last twelve years has appreciably affected his resistance to physical fatigue." In other words, if Edward VIII had done his duty and remained on the throne, Bertie never would have become so stressed out.

Additional strains on Bertie's health were to follow, for which Elizabeth would never forgive the perpetrators. The princesses' former governess, Marion Crawford, received payment from an American publisher for a tell-all memoir about her life with the royal family, which was serialized in 1950, first in the *Ladies' Home Journal* and later in a UK periodical. It was also published in book form on both sides of the Atlantic. Then the Duke of Windsor sold a series of autobiographical articles to *Life* magazine, his second such betrayal in three years.

The stress made Bertie even more haggard and strained. One spectator at the Epsom Derby in June 1950 noticed His Majesty heavily made up and rouged to give the appearance of health.

The Duke of Windsor's autobiography, *A King's Story*, was published in New York City in April 1951, earning Edward the equivalent of close to $1 million at the time. The British edition debuted later that year, coinciding with the final collapse of Bertie's health. Lady Donaldson wrote, "Behind the scenes the book caused unrestrained anger and concern. Those who had taken part in the events the Duke described were often astonished to read a version of them which bore no relation to their own memories. . . ."

While at Balmoral in August, Bertie developed a chill and a sore throat. His doctors insisted that he travel down to London for X-rays and further medical exams. On September 15, a bronchoscopy was performed to remove tissue from his lung for examination. After a biopsy, lung cancer was found, but the C-word was never used, either to the king or anyone else. Instead, the doctors referred to "structural changes" in the lung. The only remedy was to remove Bertie's lung, an operation that the doctors warned Elizabeth was extremely dangerous, as there was a high risk of her husband's suffering a fatal thrombosis, either during or after the procedure. A thrombosis is a clot in the blood that either fully or partially blocks a blood vessel; this leads to the destruction of tissue, owing to an insufficient supply of blood, and can cause a heart attack. But if the operation were not performed, the danger could be worse. So on September 23, the king's lung was removed along with some of the nerves of his larynx. This meant that from then on his speech could be compromised as well, and he might not be able to talk above a whisper. To a man for whom public speaking already presented a monumental challenge, this was an added obstacle.

The doctors were not optimistic. After meeting with Bertie's physician, Lord Moran, the editor of the *Spectator* asked the king's official biographer, Harold Nicolson, to prepare an obituary. And the former royal radiologist Sir Harold Graham Hodgson confided in a friend, "The King is not likely to live more than eighteen months. The end will probably come suddenly. The operation was six months too late."

Elizabeth knew the whole truth. But she went about her public duties stoically and calmly, performing her responsibilities as Senior Counsellor of State on Bertie's behalf.

On October 7, after a six-day delay, the Princess Elizabeth departed for a prearranged state visit to Canada and the United States. She carried a sealed envelope to be opened in the event of her father's death. Inside it were her accession documents. She and the Duke of Edinburgh were made members of the Privy Council on December 4. Six days later, His Majesty was deemed well enough to revoke the mandate of the Counsellors of State and resume the duties of sovereign.

A hatless Bertie stood on the tarmac at Heathrow and waved good-bye to his daughter and son-in-law on January 31, 1952, as they boarded their flight for the first leg of a state visit to Africa. News cameras zoomed in for a close-up of the king's face. He was gaunt and frail, his cheeks sunken and hollow. The public was shocked when they saw the images on television. Only seven weeks earlier he had celebrated his fifty-sixth birthday. Bertie would never see the Princess Elizabeth again.

On February 5, the king went out shooting hare at Sandringham. He was in a good mood that day, looking in on his grandchildren, Charles and Anne, in their nursery, and enjoying Princess Margaret's piano playing that evening. He completed a crossword puzzle and strode out to the royal kennels to check on the condition of his Golden Retriever, whose paw had been injured by a thorn. When he returned indoors, the family listened to the wireless reports of Princess Elizabeth and Philip's safe arrival in Kenya.

At ten thirty p.m., Bertie picked up a magazine and announced to the queen, "I'll see you in the morning." He left her sitting by the fireplace and returned to his ground-floor bedroom, where he had slept ever since his illness had precluded him from climbing stairs. After enjoying a cup of cocoa, he perused his periodical until about midnight. A night watchman in the garden observed the king fastening the latch of his bedroom window.

Bertie passed away in his sleep that night. At seven fifteen on the morning of February 6, 1952, his valet, James MacDonald, found him in his bed. The cause of death was coronary thrombosis.

Elizabeth's maid brought her tea at around the same hour. Moments later she received a message from the equerry on duty, Commander Sir Harold Campbell, who had known the royal couple for thirty years. She read the hesitation in his face and knew it could not be good news. Saving him the pain of telling her, she guessed the purpose of his errand.

"I was sent a message that his servant couldn't wake him. I flew to his room, & thought that he was in a deep sleep, he looked so peaceful—and then I realized what had happened," Elizabeth wrote to Queen Mary, disclosing the sorrowful news. From his study she issued the orders of the day just as Bertie would have done, and requested that a vigil be kept outside her husband's room, stating, "The King must not be left."

Sir Harold told his wife, "I never knew a woman could be so brave." But when the queen went to the nursery and three-year-old Prince Charles asked her when Grandpa was going to come back to play soldiers with him, she completely lost control of her emotions, hugging the little boy tightly, unable to reply.

The proclamation of the ascension of Queen Elizabeth II was delayed for twenty-four hours due to very unusual and private circumstances. The fifty-one-year-old Queen Mother had missed two consecutive menstrual cycles, and there was a slim possibility that she was pregnant. If this were confirmed, the succession would be in abeyance until she gave birth, because a boy would have displaced the Princess Elizabeth in the line of succession. However, it was quickly established that the Queen Mother was not pregnant, but perimenopausal.

The reign of George VI had begun with misgivings, but he was much mourned. A crowd of more than 305,000 waited in the frosty air for the opportunity to file past the coffin of their departed sovereign, "a good man," in the words of the *Daily Mirror*. Even more people lined the streets on February 15 to bid farewell as the funeral cortege passed. Later that day, the king was laid to rest in St. George's Chapel, Windsor. Memorial cards and floral tributes came from the great and the humble, ministers and tradesmen. But the most poignant of all was the wreath of white orchids, white lilies, and white carnations that rested atop his coffin, accompanied by a card that read, "For darling Bertie, from his always loving Elizabeth."

Two days after the funeral, Queen Elizabeth The Queen Mother, as she was to be styled from then on, released a statement to the kingdom and its Dominions: ". . . I want you to know how your concern for me has upheld me in my sorrow, and how proud you have made me by your wonderful tributes to my dear husband, a great and noble King. . . .

"Throughout our married life we have tried, the King and I, to fulfill with all our hearts and all our strength the great task of service that was laid upon us. My only wish now is that I may be allowed to continue the work we sought to do together. . . ."

Did Elizabeth blame the Duke and Duchess of Windsor for leaving her a widow at the age of fifty-one? Would Bertie have been such a heavy smoker if the stress of kingship hadn't been so overwhelming? As she prepared to recede somewhat from public life, it became clear that Elizabeth still harbored plenty of malice toward Wallis. For several weeks after the king's death people walked on eggshells around the new widow. Finally, someone had the temerity to mention the duchess's name in her presence. "Oh yes. The woman who killed my husband," the Queen Mother retorted in a brisk staccato.

Elizabeth wished for an active constitutional role after her husband died, but she was now the second lady in the land, and it was up to her daughter to determine the role she would play from now on. Fortunately the new queen understood what a valuable asset her mother was—not only experienced, but beloved—and took full advantage of it. For the next five decades, until just a few months before her death on March 30, 2002, the Queen Mother had a full calendar of public engagements. Meanwhile, she overcame colon cancer, and in the last decade of her life endured a hip replacement, another broken hip, failing eyesight, obstructions in her throat, and lesions on her legs.

On Wednesday, July 19, 2000, Britain celebrated her one hundredth birthday with great fanfare. On her actual centennial, August 4, Prince Charles escorted his grandmother from Clarence House to Buckingham Palace as the Mall was thronged with well-wishers surrounding her, in his words, "with love, devotion, and gratitude for all that you mean to people."

Elizabeth later told a friend that she didn't understand why everyone was making such a fuss out of it. "I was just doing my job."

On November 3, 2000, she fell in her bedroom at Clarence House and broke her collarbone, requiring a six-week convalescence. She slipped again just before Christmas but refused to admit she was in pain and stoically greeted people on her feet during the holiday party for the staff at St. James's Palace.

The queen telephoned her mother on February 9, 2002, to relay the sad news that Princess Margaret had died after suffering a stroke the previous afternoon. She was seventy-one. Three days earlier the family had marked another milestone: the fiftieth anniversary of Queen Elizabeth II's accession to the throne. The Queen Mother had survived Bertie by as many years.

By late March, her health was very fragile. She was barely eating anything, usually having scrambled eggs and a small glass of champagne in the evening and saying it reminded her of the late-night suppers she enjoyed with Bertie when they were newlyweds. The queen, and Princess Margaret's children, David Linley and Sarah Chatto, were at her bedside on Holy Saturday, March 30, 2002, when she died peacefully.

Elizabeth had organized the events of her own state funeral. On April 2, her body was taken to St. James's Palace, where the family could privately pay their respects. Three days later, a public procession featuring more than sixteen hundred servicemen escorted her coffin to Westminster Hall. Elizabeth's personal standard was draped over it, and atop the standard rested the crown that had been made for her coronation as Queen Consort of England and Empress Consort of India in 1937, the Koh-i-Noor diamond given to Queen Victoria, the first Empress of India, sparkling at its center. A single wreath rested on the coffin. The card beside it read, "In Loving Memory, Lilibet."

Elizabeth's coffin was placed on a catafalque in the exact spot where her husband's bier had rested fifty years earlier. So many people wished to pay their respects that the government had to keep the viewing areas open twenty-two hours a day.

After her April 9 funeral in Westminster Abbey, she was interred in St. George's Chapel at Windsor beside her husband, together with the casket containing the ashes of their daughter Princess Margaret.

The marriage of Albert Frederick Arthur George and Elizabeth Angela Marguerite Bowes Lyon—"Bert and Betty"—was not only the rare royal love match, but one of equal partners who respected and complemented each other, balancing their strengths and weaknesses. Each was possessed of a strong faith and a keen sense of duty. Reluctant monarchs at first, instead of shirking the awesome responsibility that was literally thrust upon them, they rose to the occasion with dignity, integrity, and a sense of humor. They delighted in each other and in their children, providing Britain with the image of a stable, devoted, modern family that was not merely a publicist's dream; it was their happy reality. Elizabeth dedicated herself to Bertie, and by bolstering him with the courage to succeed she helped transform him, first into an active and effective member of the royal family when his own father didn't believe in him, and later into a monarch with the strength to turn his back on his ungrateful brother and to look the real enemy squarely in the face.

And yet, the benefits were hardly one-sided. On the surface of things it had always seemed to be the bubbly, smiling queen who had instilled confidence in the bashful king. But as Lady Cynthia Colville observed, "[F]ew people realized how much she had relied on *him*—on his capacity for wise and detached judgment, for sound advice, and how lost she now felt without him. . . . That was the measure of her greatness as a woman. She drew him out and made him a man so strong that she could lean upon him."

Edward VIII was a disastrously unsuitable monarch, and had he remained on the throne, Britain's fate, and that of Western Europe, might have been wildly different during and after the Second World War. Noël Coward once quipped that every town in England should erect a statue to Wallis Simpson "for the blessing she had bestowed upon the country."

And Lady Diana Cooper observed, "We were lucky to get George VI and Elizabeth—they were by far the better loved in the end. . . . Yes, in the end it was a blessing that Wallis came along and took him away."

In 1968, the Queen Mother viewed a Cecil Beaton retrospective at the National Portrait Gallery in London. She paused in front of some of the photographs, reminiscing about the sitters. When she came to a picture of the Duke and Duchess of Windsor, she stopped and stood very still. What did she think as she gazed at the image? Had time softened the edges of her enmity? Finally Elizabeth spoke. "They're so happy, and really a great deal of good came out of it. We have much to be thankful for."

We do, indeed.

Prince William of Wales

(1982–)

Duke of Cambridge, Earl of Strathearn, and Baron Carrickfergus (2011–)

*T*he older son of Prince Charles and Princess Diana spent the first week of his life as "Baby Wales" while his parents argued over what to name him. They settled on William Arthur Philip Louis—for the Conqueror, the king of Camelot, the infant's paternal grandfather, and for Charles's mentor Earl Mountbatten, who was assassinated by an IRA bomb in the summer of 1979. Diana's empathetic comment to Charles about the earl's funeral as the pair of them sat on a hay bale made the prince view the rosy-cheeked teenager as marriage material in the first place. Theirs was one of the great mismatches of royal history—but socially it was nearly a marriage of equals. Although Diana was a commoner, she was the youngest daughter of the eighth Earl Spencer, the descendant of an aristocratic house whose English lineage stretches back farther back than the Windsors' does.

As a brief aside, during the coverage of William's engagement and wedding, American journalists, particularly the television broadcasters, appeared completely confused by the word "commoner"; most couldn't comprehend how someone who had a title could still be referred to as a commoner, and for some reason, they thought the word was pejorative, uncomfortable about applying it to Catherine Middleton, fearing they were somehow insulting her. The word is not derogatory, but it is a class distinction, and one that is extremely easy to remember. A commoner is anyone who is not of royal blood, whether he or she hails from the aristocracy, the middle classes, or the working class. Diana and the Queen Mother were commoners, even though their fathers were earls. These women became royal only by virtue of their marriages.

Diana was keen to afford her sons, Prince William, born in June 1982, and Prince Harry, born in September 1984, the most "normal" upbringing two royal boys could have. She took them to McDonald's and insisted that they be given pocket money for sweets (royals traditionally never carry cash). But most crucial to experiencing life in the real world was going to school with other children. Their lives would be uncommon as it was, and royal obligations would come all too soon; she wanted them to have the chance to be kids. Sadly, William and Harry's first official engagement would be to walk behind the gun carriage that bore the coffin of their mother on September 6, 1997. While 750 million people worldwide had watched Diana marry Charles in St. Paul's Cathedral on July 29, 1981, an estimated 2.5 billion were glued to their televisions for her funeral.

One of those people was fifteen-year-old Kate Middleton, a half year older than Prince William. In the days following Diana's death, like millions of others across the globe, she found herself shaking her head at the apparent indifference of the royal family toward the passing of the woman who had been their greatest asset, difficult at times, to be sure, but nonetheless the mother of a future king. "It's too little, too late," Kate murmured, in response to the queen's taking to the airwaves, under increasing pressure from the people, the press, and her new prime minister, Tony Blair. "The Queen really doesn't get it, does she?" the teen commiserated with one of her schoolmates. "None of them seem to get it. The Royal Family is a pretty heartless bunch. But I feel so sorry for Prince William and Prince Harry." Her empathy for the young prince began early. Who knew then that the "heartless bunch" she criticized for their callousness and cluelessness would someday become her in-laws?

Diana had died as a result of a horrific car accident in a Paris tunnel as the sedan in which she was riding with her boyfriend, Emad "Dodi" Al Fayed, was chased by a hellish cavalcade of paparazzi. Several inquests blamed the incident on the blood alcohol level of their chauffeur, Henri Paul. Prince William would always blame the paparazzi, whom he called the "hounds of hell." Very early in his childhood Diana had noticed her older son's sensitivity and vulnerability, referring to William as a male version of herself, and a "very old soul," even at the age of nine. "We are like two peas in a pod," she observed. "He feels everything too much. He needs to be protected."

From himself, perhaps. William was such a rambunctious toddler, and so destructive around the house (which happened to be Kensington Palace), that he earned the nickname "the basher." And at Mrs. Mynor's Nursery School, where he was enrolled in September 1985, the little prince was quite the tyrannical tyke. He tormented his teachers and fellow classmates, drawing his make-believe sword and threatening to lop off their heads if they didn't let him have his way, shouting, "My daddy's a real prince and my daddy can beat up your daddy!"

Appalled by the general chilliness of the Windsors, both in the specific and the abstract, Princess Diana made certain that her sons learned how to be kind. William's "basher" behavior and rude treatment of the staff and students at Mrs. Mynor's had been deemed intolerable, and a new nanny was hired, charged with making sure the spoiled brat ceased being a royal pain. Using Diana herself as a model of the necessary virtues of kindness and compassion, Ruth Wallace, or "Nanny Roof," as William called her, instilled in him a sense of empathy that replaced his anger. It worked, and in just a few months the little boy had become his mother's chief protector. In no time at all he was a changed child—almost too sensitive and vulnerable.

The Waleses' marital discord at the time caused palace staffers to become concerned about the emotional stability of William and his younger brother, Harry. William was often caught in the cross fire of his parents' screaming matches as the royal marriage disintegrated before his eyes. According to his biographer Christopher Andersen, during one skirmish he saw his father lob a riding boot across the room at his mother. And it became a habit for him to pass tissues through the closed door to his sobbing mummy, insisting, "I hate to see you sad."

If his beloved papa wasn't tormenting Mummy enough, the paparazzi made it worse. Years later, William endured recurring nightmares in which a beautiful woman was trapped in a speeding car, chased down by members of the media, but in his dreams the river wasn't the Seine; it was the Thames. And the woman was his girlfriend, Kate Middleton.

Prince William of Wales (1982–) and Catherine Elizabeth Middleton (1982–)

They affectionately call each other "Big Willy" and "Babykins."

Although his parents' royal marriage was both arranged and unhappy, Prince William chose his own bride, a woman who appears to be his best friend, perhaps even his soul mate. However, in a country founded, and still grounded, in class structure, Kate Middleton is the most common of any royal consort in British history. While William's four-times-great-grandmother Queen Victoria was transforming England into an empire, his fiancée's maternal ancestors endured a Dickensian existence in the coal mines of Newcastle.

Catherine, as Buckingham Palace reminds us that her name is from now on, is the first woman not born of aristocratic blood to wed an heir presumptive to Britain's throne since the clandestine wedding in 1660 of James, Duke of York, to Anne Hyde, whose scandalous relationship was profiled in *Royal Affairs*. But even Anne was not from such humble stock as Catherine. Anne was the daughter of a Wiltshire lawyer, but at the time of her secret wedding, her father was the Chancellor of the Realm.

Kate Middleton's lineage is significantly less grand than Anne Hyde's, although her father's ancestors included upwardly mobile businessmen and industrialists whose investments enabled their children to enjoy the privileges of the upper middle class. Over the generations, by dint of hard work, ambition, and entrepreneurship, her family became what we might call nouveau riche. Kate's mother, the vivacious Carole Goldsmith, was an air hostess at British Airways when she met the quiet, self-effacing Michael Middleton, a flight dispatcher. They married on June 21, 1980, with Carole arriving at the picturesque village church princess-style, in a horse-drawn carriage. Catherine was born on January 9, 1982, and her sister, Philippa, known as Pippa, followed in 1983. After having two children, Carole decided to become more earthbound and immersed herself in village life.

Around the time of her son James's birth in 1987, Carole established a business selling unique grab bags for children's birthday parties. Business expanded with demand, and then, with the advent of the Internet, what had begun as a local business took off. Michael quit his job to work for Party Pieces full-time. The venture soon became England's premier party-planning company, enabling the Middletons to move to a £2 million home in Bucklebury, a posh suburb of West Berkshire, and to send Kate and her siblings to expensive schools, where they could hobnob with the offspring of the aristocracy. Kate was a miniature princess even then; she and Pippa modeled sparkly tulle dresses, girly tiaras, and plastic jewelry for the Party Pieces catalog.

Fate brought William and Catherine together like the plot of a Jane Austen novel. They met during their first, or "freshers," year of college at the University of St. Andrews, but Kate almost didn't enroll there. Her excellent grades and test scores enabled to her attend any school she wished, and her initial choice was the University of Edinburgh, which had the best art history curriculum (her chosen major) in the UK. However, as far as her extracurricular activities went, in addition to captaining her high school's field hockey team and playing in the first pair at tennis, the teenage Catherine had also been an assiduous scholar of William Wales. As a lanky, geeky schoolgirl, one of the tallest in her class at the tony Marlborough College, a public (in the United States it would be called "private") prep school in Wiltshire, eighty miles west of London, she made a hobby out of clipping every news article she could find about the young prince. She followed William's schedule by logging into the Court Calendar to see where the members of the royal family were slated to appear. She studied his photographs and imagined the personality that lay beneath the rosy cheeks, fair complexion, and blue eyes, all of which earned her the nickname "Princess in Waiting" from her friends. "She was besotted," said her classmate Jessica Hay, whose boyfriend at the time was Nicholas Knatchbull, one of Prince Charles's godsons and William's cousin and mentor at Eton. From Jessica, who had met

William, Kate got a bit of an inside scoop on the heir, which served to solidify the positive opinions she'd already formed about him. "He was shyer than I ever thought. I got the feeling he wasn't used to normal girls being around him," Jessica observed.

In an interview with *The Mail on Sunday* Jessica Hay confided, "We would sit around talking about all the boys at school we fancied, but Catherine would always say, 'I don't like any of them. They're all a bit of rough.' Then she would joke, 'There's no one quite like William. . . .' She always used to say, 'I bet he's really kind. You can tell just by looking at him.'"

When the prince's coat of arms was revealed on his eighteenth birthday, Catherine was both touched and impressed that William had incorporated into it the three red scallop shells from Diana's crest that Charles had erased upon their divorce. "It's wonderful that he is paying tribute to his mother like that. It shows he's still his own man," Kate (who had still never met William) proudly told her classmates. She was also impressed that he had insisted on being addressed simply as William, rather than as Your Royal Highness, or "Sir." It was modern, yet showed the common touch without being common.

Even then, and even if it was only in jest, she felt oddly proprietary about the prince, and grew very introspective when the television blared stories about his latest potential romance, such as the time when the gorgeous blond heiress Mili d'Erlanger was invited to joined the Waleses' family cruise. One school chum observed of Kate, "She's very sweet and reserved, so it's hard to tell what she's thinking, really. But she always turned very quiet when people started talking about Mili and Prince William."

Still, their paths almost never crossed. English students typically take a gap year between the end of high school and the start of college. While William (under an alias) participated in the grueling Raleigh International program, an educational development charity located in Chile, Kate spent her gap year in Florence, learning Italian and immersing herself in Renaissance art. She happened to catch a televised press conference with princes Charles and William after Diana's former press secretary P. D. Jephson had published a tell-all memoir, pegging the late Princess of Wales as neurotic and manipulative. William was expressing the family's sense of sorrow and be-trayal. Glued to the TV, empathy exuding from every pore, she exclaimed to her friends, "My God, that voice! Isn't he sexy?" A Columbia University student who knew Kate in Florence noticed that she was "maybe a little more enthusiastic about Prince William than the rest of us. She kept saying, 'He's mine, you know.' Joking, of course, since she'd never even met him."

When Kate's ambitious mother learned that William planned to attend St. Andrews, Carole, who has been compared to Jane Austen's Mrs. Bennet, urged Kate to change her mind about Edinburgh and switch schools. Kate needed a bit of convincing. It wasn't such a sure thing as sending Jane off in a rainstorm to meet the wealthy Mr. Bingley. But by Christmas of 2000, Kate had ditched her plans for Edinburgh and had been accepted to the university on the windy coast of Fife, a Scottish town most famous for being the birthplace of golf.

William Wales met tall, willowy Catherine Middleton in Septem-ber 2001, during their first term at St. Andrews, slyly known as the top matchmaking university in Britain. They were both history of art majors and both assigned to St. Salvator's residence hall. Romance blossomed slowly and organically, born out of genuine friendship and a shared interest in sports, dramatics, literature, and the arts—very much the antithesis of William's parents' manufactured, whirl-wind courtship. In fact, both William and Kate were dating other classmates before they began to fall for each other. William was see-ing another fresher in St. Salvator's: the dark-haired, voluptuous Carly Massy-Birch, an aspiring actress who was voted "best derri-ere" at the school (though Kate had been voted prettiest in their dorm). Kate, meanwhile, was dating the athletic Rupert Finch, a six-foot-two senior. Unlike William, whose name seemed to be linked with numerous society beauties, and whose pickup line had once been positively Hanoverian ("I'm a prince, wanna pull?"), Kate had limited romantic experience. She was popular and preppy, had been sporty and studious in high school, and although she enjoyed a good time and was a little bit of a prankster, she was never a wild child, hating to lose control. A Marlborough biology classmate, Kathryn Solari, described her as "always really sweet and lovely. She was a good girl and . . . she always did the right thing. . . . I wouldn't say she was the brightest button, but she was very hard-working. I don't think you would find anyone to say a bad word about her."

Kate had seen William once when they were prep school students. His Eton hockey team had come to Marlborough College to play Kate's school. As captain of the girls' team she was permitted a close view of the players, and was impressed with the way the tall prince took charge. She had studied the way Camilla Parker Bowles first captured Prince Charles's attention in 1970 by standing apart from the crowd. It was indeed an effective way to get noticed, so Kate remained apart from her team, but the best she got that day was an exchanged glance.

By the time Kate properly met William, he had fortunately ditched the smarmy pickup line. He arrived at St. Andrews to find a throng of several thousand people waiting to greet him, most of whom were coeds. Among them was Catherine Middleton, eager to be there, but nonetheless embarrassed about it, so she hung back, blending into the crowd. Predictably, she had read about the sort of people the prince would be interested in befriending at St. Andrews. He was not looking to find chums among his own social class. "It's about their character and who they are and whether we get on. I just hope I meet people I get on with."

"I turned bright red and sort of scuttled off, feeling very shy about meeting him," Kate confessed about their first encounter. "[H]e takes your breath away," she confided to a friend. William was certainly an imposing presence: six-foot-three to her five-ten, making him the tallest (future) king in England's history, topping Henry VIII by an inch. But the heir soon proved himself to be charmingly human, spilling a drink on himself. "That's the idea," said Kate, after she grew to know him well. "Will can be clumsy, actually, but most of the time it's really just an act. Otherwise people would just keep gawping at him."

William and Kate made an impression on each other, even if it wasn't a romantic one at the time. Still, the prince recalled, "When I first met Kate, I knew there was something special about her. I knew there was something I wanted to explore there. . . ."

However, during William's gap year he had made inroads into

other uncharted territory that it seemed he had an interest in explor-
ing as well. He journeyed to the Lewa Wildlife Conservancy, an African preserve run by the parents of then-nineteen-year-old Jessica
(Jecca) Craig. Enchanted by the beauty of Africa, William developed
a special affinity for the continent. He also became enchanted by the
beauty of Jecca Craig, and during that trip he proposed to her on
bended knee beside a lake on Mount Kenya, 12,500 feet above sea
level. As William was still a teen, a student, and a commitment-
phobe at the time, and had pretty much convinced himself that he
wouldn't wed before he turned thirty, neither of them took their engagement very seriously. But in the years to come Jecca Craig would
remain on the media's short list of potential girlfriends and brides for
William as he kept his relationship with Kate under wraps, maintaining the subterfuge that he was still available.

Both Jecca and William's first college girlfriend, Carly Massy-
Birch, were unprepared to deal with the constant media attention
and the perpetual invasions of privacy that came with being his
sweetheart. Other family friends to whom he was linked, society
belles with hyphenated names, felt the same way.

The first semester at St. Andrews was a daunting one for William.
He didn't like the art history curriculum after all, and wasn't doing
well in it academically. He'd made a concerted effort not to become
involved with the social whirl either on or off campus, so he had
made only a few trusted friends from his residence hall. Fife was
rainy and geographically remote from London. He was almost ready
to drop out of school. But after a family meeting, it was decided that
William should stick it out at least for another year, so as not to embarrass crown and country, not to mention relations with Scotland.

Over the Christmas holidays he'd stayed in touch with Kate. She
was a wee bit homesick and wasn't sure she wanted to remain at St.
Andrews either. But she urged the prince to stick with it, making a
pact that if they were both unhappy after another year of school,
they'd depart together. Catherine was also instrumental in encouraging William to switch majors to geography in the second term, a
course in which he'd received an A at Eton. After that, he became
much happier and began to settle in.

William's relationship with Carly Massy-Birch had lasted only about seven weeks. And the nature of his friendship with Kate began to shift after the "Don't Walk" charity fashion show held at the St. Andrews Bay Hotel on March 27, 2002. The prince, who had paid £200 for a front-row seat, went gaga when Kate, a volunteer model, strutted the catwalk in (among other things) a diaphanous black knit dress that revealed her lingerie (and her athletic body) beneath. Her hair was a mass of tangled curls. She'd always been self-conscious about her legs, thinking they were too short, but that night she was all confidence. William turned to his friend Fergus Boyd and exclaimed, "Wow, Fergus, Kate's hot!"

As a brief aside, the most famous LBD in history has a denouement of its own. The black silk dress designed by St. Andrews textile student Charlotte Todd, and fittingly titled "The Art of Seduction," was sold to an anonymous male bidder at a charity auction on March 17, 2011, for $125,871. Todd originally conceived the garment as a skirt; it was Kate's idea to boldly restyle it as a minidress.

At the "Don't Walk" fashion show's after party the prince made his move. One of the guests recalled, "It was clear to us that William was smitten with Kate. He actually told her she was a knockout that night, which caused her to blush. There was definitely chemistry between them, and Kate had really made an impression on William. She played it very cool, and at one point when William seemed to lean in to kiss her, she pulled away. She didn't want to give off the wrong impression or make it too easy for Will."

In fact, Kate was still dating Rupert Finch at the time. Rupert graduated after Kate's and William's first year, and had a law trainee job lined up in London. She wished him the best of luck, sure that he had a successful future ahead of him. William was glad to see Finch moving out of Kate's life, because he was about to ask her to move off campus with him and their friend Fergus Boyd. Kate hesitated, unsure about being the only female in the arrangement. She laid the burden at her mother's doorstep, as in "My mother wouldn't approve. . . ." But (to the chagrin of her daughter) Carole Middleton, à la Mrs. Bennet, couldn't have been more delighted. Ultimately, another St. Salvator's coed, Olivia Bleasdale, became the fourth housemate.

Kate's modeling debut had caused something of a sensation, and the heir's reaction had been duly noted. Although the palace had brokered a media moratorium on William's college experience, the newspapers couldn't resist such headlines as, WILLIAM AND HIS UNDIE-GRADUATE FRIEND KATE TO SHARE A STUDENT FLAT (*The Mail on Sunday*), and, WILLIAM SHACKS UP WITH STUNNING UNDIES MODEL (*The Sun*).

Despite the headlines, the palace was quick to point out that because William and Kate had separate bedrooms, they were not sleeping together.

The students enjoyed dinner parties at friends' houses and made the rounds of local pubs and nightclubs. When it came to entertaining at home, the girls did the cooking while the boys headed to Tesco to shop for groceries. William admitted to being "absolutely useless" in the kitchen, but found food shopping therapeutic. Often, however, they ordered pizza or takeaway, and nestled in to watch DVDs or play drinking games.

One night, Kate's rival Carly Massy-Birch was present. The drinking game was "I've Never," where one player has to admit something he or she has never done, but if someone else in the room has done it, he or she has to down a shot. "I've never dated two people in this room," Carly declared. The whole room went silent. "I can't believe you just said that," William muttered to her before he took his drink. She had outed the burgeoning relationship with Kate that the prince and their other friends had managed to discreetly keep under wraps.

In June, the housemates went their separate ways for the summer. Catherine and William remained in touch while she worked off her student loan as a barmaid for a posh catering firm with the unfortunate name of Snatch. "[Y]ou could see her face light up every time he called. She was walking on air," observed one of her coworkers.

William spent a good deal of the summer boozily cruising aboard a friend's yacht, the *Alexander*, in the company of a gaggle of tanned and toned beauties. If he was trying to put the media off the scent of his relationship with Kate, he was doing a good job. The photos of her beau cozying up to any number of gorgeous girls amid press speculation that they were his girlfriend must have been hurtful.

William's friends thought highly of Kate. Jules Knight, a classmate and founder of the band Blake, said of the two of them, "Kate's a sweet, unassuming kind of girl. She felt something for Will straight-away, and he was all in for her, completely. . . . Kate always offered a sympathetic ear. She is very compassionate, very kind."

Another mutual acquaintance observed that she had what "none of the other girls had. Take a close look at Kate. There is a serenity about her, a kind of calm. It's hard to put your finger on it, but so many of these other beautiful girls don't know when to shut up and listen, and she did."

Kate also went out of her way to befriend William's protection officers, a gesture that was gratefully appreciated. "She is a delightful girl. Very down-to-earth, very considerate. She says hello and treats you like a person, never acting like you're not there," one of them commented. It makes one wonder how they are treated by the Windsors.

During the fall term of 2002, William and Kate's romance blossomed tentatively and discreetly. But the prince asked Kate not to tell her family about their relationship, even as Carole Middleton kept prodding her daughter for information, suspecting that Kate and His Royal Highness were more than housemates. Sensing that Kate's social life might be expanding and improving in the near future, to ensure that she had a London base of operations, in November 2002 the Middletons purchased a $2 million pied-à-terre in Chelsea.

That month, Catherine got a taste of what life would be like amid the royal family. William invited a group of school friends to go shooting at Sandringham (the Windsors' family pile in Norfolk), her first visit to a royal home, although the senior members of the royal family were not in residence at the time. Kate had not been accustomed to killing things for sport. As a little girl, when she read about William bagging rabbits or pheasants, she was certain that he was too kind to kill defenseless woodland creatures and would reassure herself by saying, "It's all part of his training to be king. . . . He's too kind a person to enjoy shooting animals," or, "The Queen must have made him do it." In fact, William is the best shot in the family.

Being an athletic and outdoorsy girl, Kate acclimated well, both to Sandringham and to Balmoral in Scotland, where she and William stayed in a cozy cabin that the Queen Mum set aside for her great-grandsons' use. The staff was impressed; as far as they were concerned, Kate was a "keeper." According to one of them, "Princess

Diana looked like she could hardly wait to leave when she came, but Miss Middleton is a perfect fit. We said to ourselves, 'The Queen is going to like this one.'"

It was William who didn't seem so certain. Like many relationships, theirs was experiencing growing pains. To Kate's delight, William would take one step forward, only, to her dismay, to fall two steps back. On January 9, 2003, Kate was at home with her family celebrating her twenty-first birthday when the prince surprised her by showing up on their doorstep. "I wouldn't have missed the chance to sing 'Happy Birthday' to Kate for the world," he told the dazed but delighted Michael and Carole Middleton.

Yet the couple had a tacit agreement to keep their romance under wraps. Even at St. Andrews, William and Kate rarely indulged in public displays of affection unless they were physically surrounded by a protective circle of friends. They left their residence separately and never held hands in public. So when Michael Middleton was asked about his daughter's relationship with William, he coyly replied, "We are very amused at the thought of being in-laws to Prince William, but I don't think it is going to happen."

At that point, an engagement was not on the front burner. It was difficult enough to stave off the inquiries as to whether William had a girlfriend. Speculation that an engagement announcement would be made on his coming-of-age was deftly deflected. William's twenty-first birthday party was quite the bash. Owing to his affinity for Africa, at Catherine's suggestion Windsor Castle was turned into a sub-Saharan wonderland. Guests arrived in costume, and were advised ahead of time not to wear anything that could be construed as ethnically insulting and might create a media incident.

However, an incident of another sort was sparked that night: the attendance of Jecca Craig, all the way from Kenya. It was a two-steps-back moment for William, who went so far out of his way to deny a relationship with her that he disavowed being involved with anyone.

"There's been a lot of speculation about every single girl I'm with, and it actually does quite irritate me after a while, more so because it's a complete pain for the girls. These poor girls, whom I've either just met or are friends of mine, suddenly get thrown into the limelight and their parents get rung up and so on. I think it's a little unfair on them, really. I'm used to it, because it happens quite a lot now. But it's very difficult for them and I don't like that at all.

"If I fancy a girl and she fancies me back, which is rare, I ask her out. But at the same time, I don't want to put them in an awkward situation, because a lot of people don't understand what comes with knowing me, for one—and secondly, if they were my girlfriend, the excitement it would probably cause."

By the end of the summer of 2003, the royal romance was an open secret at St. Andrews, but William and Kate had managed to keep it from the world, maintaining a low profile. The couple moved into Balgove House, a four-bedroom cottage a quarter mile outside town. William installed a champagne fridge; Kate put up gingham curtains.

In the early spring of 2004, the couple went riding in the Middleton Hunt (no relation to Catherine's family) in North Yorkshire, and William introduced her as his "girlfriend" for the first time. But it wasn't until a paparazzo from the *Sun* photographed them skiing at Klosters in Switzerland and published the tabloid headline on April 1, FINALLY . . . WILLS GETS A GIRL, that people clamored to know everything about the shy, gorgeous brunette.

Naturally, the next question was, When would the prince propose? But William is his own man, and when he feels pressured to do something, he either pushes back or walks away from it.

That summer, it seemed as though the prince went out of his way to show the world that he was unattached. He partied hard at pubs and nightclubs in the company of male friends or his brother, and there were witnesses aplenty who saw him getting drunk and cuddling, groping, or fondling various and sundry girls who later sold their stories to the media.

William's excessive attempts to hide his genuine romance or appear to redirect public attention from it with a little flirtatious sleight of hand smacks of a Hanoverian ancestor's conduct 217 years earlier. In 1785 the Prince of Wales (the future George IV) illegally wed a Catholic widow, Maria Fitzherbert. He then behaved like a cad in public, resuming his liaisons with previous mistresses and embarking on affairs with new ones, to discredit any stories that he had married Mrs. Fitzherbert.

Kate, who was heartbroken by William's behavior, wasn't so sure that it was just "harmless flirting," as her mother hastened to assure her. "I believe William loves me and would never do anything to intentionally hurt me," she told Carole. Yet the Windsor men and the Hanovers before them were notorious womanizers; she feared it was in his genes. "But it's that family. . . ."

For the third year in a row William wished to return to the Craigs' wildlife preserve in Kenya, giving rise to speculation that Jecca Craig remained in the romantic picture. The media brouhaha was not fair either to Jecca or to Kate. Ordinarily patient and discreet, Kate lost her customary cool; their arguments over it spilled out-of-doors. According to a mutual friend, Catherine "felt threatened and humiliated. It was one thing to never be publicly acknowledged, but quite another to have someone else bandied about in the press as the woman in his life. She knew that would happen all over again if he went to see Jecca Craig."

But William is as stubborn as his father, and when it came to women, no one told him what to do. He insisted that he no longer had feelings for Jecca, but Kate reminded him that this wasn't how it would appear to an outsider or how it would be spun by the media. She ultimately won what the press dubbed "the Battle of the Babes" when Charles and the palace agreed with her point of view. By then the Prince of Wales saw Kate as a daughter-in-law, even if William wasn't quite there yet.

Every time his raunchily romantic antics made tabloid headlines, William would apologize to Kate with a posh vacation or a cozy retreat with the royals. Yet for every indication that William took their relationship seriously, old flames kept leaping out of the woodwork. He was seen partying with some of them, and flew to Tennessee to visit an American heiress, Anna Sloan. Another of his summer 2004 excursions was an all-male cruise featuring an all-girl crew. "Kate was speechless," said a friend. "He saw nothing wrong with it, of course. But she was definitely humiliated. It was getting harder and harder for her to read him."

Journalist Katie Nicholl reported their split that summer, although Clarence House, where Prince Charles lives and works in London, and where princes William and Harry resided at the time, issued a denial. Nonetheless, according to Nicholl, William had been unhappy in the relationship for some time, and felt claustrophobic.

As they entered their senior year at St. Andrews in the autumn of 2004, Catherine and William remained on the outs. Although they still lived together, on Carole Middleton's advice Kate gave William breathing space and went home to Bucklebury on weekends. By Christmas 2004 they were back together, but she had issued William an ultimatum: If he was serious about their relationship, he was not to contact his heiress pals again—and one in particular: a stunning blond with the tongue-twisting name of Isabella Anstruther-Gough-Calthorpe.

Yet not all of William's acting out was attributable to a fear of commitment. The release of a second revealing book by Princess Diana's former press secretary in October 2004 had sent him on a babes-and-booze bender. In the spring of 2005, with final exams looming, his nerves were again sorely tested. The prince wasn't particularly studious to begin with, and he found himself cramming for his finals while Operation Paget, Scotland Yard's inquest on Diana's death, was lobbing one bombshell after another at the royal family, even suggesting that her body might have to be exhumed because of problematic issues with the toxicology report.

According to one of their classmates, "If it wasn't for Kate, Will would have crumbled with all that was going on. She quizzed him, went over notes with him, just did whatever it took to keep his mind on what was important." True to form, Kate remained steady and steadfast, keeping him on an even keel. The prince had once told his friend Guy Pelly (now a nightclub impresario), "I can rely on her totally. She is completely there for me. I've never had anyone in my life like Kate."

On June 23, 2005, Kate received her degree in history of art, and William received his in geography. As Vice Chancellor Brian Lang told their graduating class, "You will have made lifelong friends. . . . You may have met your husband or wife. Our title as the top matchmaking university in Britain signifies so much that is good about St. Andrews, so we rely on you to go forth and multiply. . . ."

The queen, Prince Philip, Prince Charles, and Camilla, Duchess of Cornwall, attended the graduation ceremony. Her Majesty approved of Catherine, though they were not formally introduced at the time. Her mother was already so revved up about being in the same place with the royal family that Kate took a pass. "She is good for him, I think," the queen said to Prince Charles. "But where do we go from here?"

Where, indeed? Kate herself seemed kind and pleasant. But the "men in gray," as Princess Diana had called the palace courtiers, were concerned that the Middletons were not aristocratic enough to be Windsor in-laws, or that some crazy relative would emerge who would embarrass everyone. According to an unnamed courtier, "The Queen was sick of all the scandal and the drama. She wanted a nice, obedient girl from a lovely, hopefully rather boring, family." In time, Kate's uncle Gary Goldsmith, who calls his Ibiza residence the "Maison de Bang Bang," would boast—to Prince William—of his own drug and prostitution connections.

After graduation William and Kate enjoyed a romantic holiday in Kenya. Then the prince began preparing for the Royal Military Academy Sandhurst, where he would follow in his brother's footsteps. Because Harry hadn't gone to university first, he was already ahead of William. Kate moved to London and submitted her résumé to art galleries. On January 8, 2006, William began his military training. Four days earlier, he and Kate had shared their first public kiss, dispelling rumors that their romance was on the rocks. The media took note as well when Kate and her parents attended William's graduation from Sandhurst that November. ITN hired a lip-reader to discern what Kate was saying to her mother as she watched William march past. The verdict: "I love the uniform. It's so sexy!"

Two weeks earlier, Catherine had been invited to spend a weekend with the royal family at Sandringham in Norfolk. The Windsors seemed very comfortable with her, and the feeling was mutual. After the disastrous marriages of three of her four children (Anne, Charles, and Andrew), the queen had become a fan of long courtships, and now favored a relationship of at least five years before she approved of the resounding clang of wedding bells. How much had changed in a generation! Charles already considered Kate one of the family, but it took Camilla some time to come around. At first, she found Kate "pretty, but rather dim" and went out of her way to say something snide about her, even as Charles complimented her. Ironically, as she had the least patrician birthright in the room, Camilla felt that the Middletons weren't blue-blooded enough and that William should marry a girl from an old aristocratic house, meddling in the heir's affairs the same way she had in Charles's marriage to Diana.

Mindful of Diana's trial by fire during her engagement and of the chilly reception the royal family had given her, William was already taking pains to ease Catherine into The Firm. He had even requested that she be advised by family members and palace staffers on how to cope with the barrage of paparazzi and the media scrutiny, as well as how to handle the loneliness and isolation that his mother had endured. But unless Kate was in William's company, or until they got engaged, she would not be entitled to a protection officer of her own.

And yet she was a princess-in-training with no assurance that William would propose. Purportedly, she was instructed to study footage of Princess Diana for lessons in everything from how to handle the press and work a crowd to gracefully getting in and out of a car without flashing any thigh. A target for every camera, Kate was always perfectly groomed and impeccably dressed when she stepped outside. Well coached, she never spoke to the press, nor posed, but smiled and kept going about her business.

According to *Tatler*'s Geordie Greig, Kate was "perfect princess material. She is the epitome of an effortlessly stylish English rose. She has qualities you can't create or manufacture. Her unaffectedness makes her particularly attractive."

While William had begun to learn the royal ropes, taking brief internships at Chatsworth, HSBC, and the Bank of England, and then embarking on a military career, Catherine had become a dabbler. Although she showed talent as a photographer, instead she enjoyed a brief stint as an accessories buyer, built a Web site for her parents' business, and curated an art show, as she placed her royal relationship above all else.

Woolworth's started manufacturing china tchotchkes with the couple's images and initials on them in 2006. Kate was amused; William not so much. The press had expected he might pop the question on her twenty-fifth birthday, January 9, 2007, mobbing her when she left her London flat. She had hoped he would get down on bended knee on Valentine's Day, 2007, but William gave her a diamond-encrusted antique compact instead of a ring. A former St. Andrews classmate described Kate as "crushed" by the disappointment.

During those early months of 2007, Catherine and William found themselves at a crossroads. The Middleton mantra was "Grin and bear it," and Kate had to do a lot of both, because William was visibly pulling away. The relationship began to crumble when William was down in Dorset for a ten-week tank commander's course at the Royal Army's training camp in Bovington. The couple was separated by a distance of 130 miles, and William preferred to spend weekends with his fellow officers instead of going up to London to be with Kate. On March 22, 2007, at a nightclub in Bournemouth, he was caught in the flashbulbs with his arm around a pretty eighteen-year-old Brazilian student, Ana Ferreira, who was quite certain that William groped her breast, and she cheerfully told the press about it. Later in the evening the prince steamed up the dance floor with nineteen-year-old Lisa Agar, and then invited her back to his barracks to hang out with him and his friends. When the story hit the tabloids, Kate predictably became infuriated.

William defended himself, insisting, at least to his friends, "I'm not 36 and I'm not married. I'm 24 and just want to have some fun."

Kate had reached the point where she wanted a commitment but dared not ask for one. In fact, the more she yearned for William to get closer, the farther he pulled away. But instead of facing his insecurity or immaturity, the prince neatly deflected attention onto the perennial adversary, the media, blaming them for the problems in their relationship. "The press will make your life unbearable as long as we're together," he told Kate. "I don't want you suffering the way my mother did." But in trying to protect Kate, William was wounding her deeply. She reminded him how much they had invested in the relationship and how much they had already shared. According to one of Kate's friends from Bucklebury, "She told him that he made her happy and that she believed she made him happy, and that was all that mattered in the end."

But William demurred, insisting that for a man in his position, things weren't that simple. Now twenty-five, he was under too much pressure to propose. He felt uncomfortable echoes of his mother's marriage jitters as well as the pressure his father was given by *his* father to marry Diana because Charles had reached a certain age. William was also determined not to let Fleet Street turn him into a fiancé just because it sold newspapers. Kate assured him that she was in no hurry to settle down, but the truth was, she wanted security.

Citing claustrophobia, over several agonizing phone calls in which he insisted, "I can't. . . . It just isn't going to work. It isn't fair to you," he ended their romance on April 11, 2007. News of the royal breakup leaked out three days later.

As soon as Catherine was no longer a royal girlfriend, she and her family seemed fair game for the press. Stories surfaced about some of William's class-bound friends who would mock Kate's roots by mimicking a flight attendant's doors-to-manual command. Then the footage was broadcast of Carole Middleton chewing gum during William's graduation from Sandhurst (it turned out to be nicotine gum to help her kick a thirty-year smoking habit). It suddenly became news that in the presence of the queen she used the words "toilet" (instead of "lavatory") and "pardon?" (rather than "what?")—perhaps "pardon" is what the royal family does to traitors. The stories turned out to be spurious inventions; Mrs. Middleton and HRM had never been introduced. But the media wondered whether the ambitious, enterprising, social-climbing Carole was too common to be William's mother-in-law and had damaged her daughter's chances of becoming a princess.

Not wishing to lose the goodwill of her middle-class subjects, the queen was quick to ensure that Kate didn't think the criticism came from her. "What rubbish. I have absolutely nothing against gum. *I* chew gum!" she exclaimed when she read the headlines. And William phoned Kate to assure her that none of his family or friends had spoken to the press about the Middletons.

William and Kate spent the next ten weeks partying separately, if frantically, as if to show the other that they could get on well enough alone. A few nights after their breakup, William racked up a bar tab of more than $17,000 with his friends at Mahiki, one of his favorite watering holes. While the Rolling Stones' "You Can't Always Get What You Want" blasted through the speakers, he raised his arms high above his head and shouted, "I'm *freeee!*"

Meanwhile, Kate stepped out in a miniskirt, as if to remind William what he was missing. She flirted up a storm on the same dance floors they had frequented together, and William's once-snooty friends rallied around her.

But by July 1, and the concert to commemorate the tenth anniversary of his mother's death, the couple was covertly reunited, having made tentative steps to rekindle their romance since the end of May. They sat separately at the concert, but at the after party, as they danced to the Bodyrockers' "I Like the Way (You Move)" (which they'd always called "their" song), guests noted that the couple was practically making out on the dance floor.

"I'm glad to hear it. She's a nice girl," the queen told her grandson when William informed her that he and Kate had reconciled. Nevertheless, an engagement announcement remained forthcoming.

But that August, during a romantic holiday in the Seychelles, William made Kate a promise. As one of their friends later divulged, "They didn't agree to get married there and then; what they made was a pact. William told Kate she was the one, but he was not ready to get married. He promised her his commitment and said he would not let her down, and she in turn agreed to wait for him."

The prince needed to be certain Catherine fully understood that his royal duty would always come first, and what it would mean to marry him—what came with the job on her end as well as his. First of all, he would be committing the next few years to training with the RAF, and if Kate thought that being a royal girlfriend was difficult, being the sweetheart of a serviceman was even harder.

On January 7, 2008, William arrived at RAF Cranwell in Lincolnshire, the oldest air force college in the world. This time he made a concerted effort to return to London on weekends. Kate would be waiting for him at Clarence House, having been cheerfully waved in like a member of the family, according to journalist and royal biographer Katie Nicholl. Kate would have a hot bath and a home-cooked meal waiting for her weary pilot-in-training. "She was almost motherly to him," a mutual friend recalled. The couple enjoyed puttering about the kitchen, just like the old days at St. Andrews. Friends observed their natural, easy intimacy and their cozy domesticity. William could (and did) finish Kate's sentences; she could read his body language and the look in his eyes, a keen judge of when he wanted to continue the party or kick the guests out.

On April 11, he qualified as a pilot. Kate attended his RAF graduation in a much-photographed white military-style coat and tall black boots. By that time, however, she had quit her job as a junior accessories buyer and been dubbed "Waity Katie" by the press. It seemed that all she was doing was waiting for her boyfriend to propose while he was busy with his military commitments, having embarked on a stint with the Royal Navy. His heavy schedule only spotlighted her own career of little consequence.

Catherine finally met the queen at the May 2008 wedding of another of Her Majesty's grandsons, Peter Phillips, son of Anne, the Princess Royal. "It was in amongst a lot of other guests," Kate later recalled, adding that the queen was "very friendly and welcoming." Phillips's marriage to Canadian Autumn Kelly marked a milestone in William and Kate's relationship, because Kate attended the event without him. William had a competing wedding to attend in Kenya— that of Jecca Craig's brother, Batian. Kate's solo presence—without an engagement ring on her finger—was also a mark of acceptance into the royal family.

Her Majesty was concerned, however, that Catherine was not doing anything useful with her time. According to news reports, William had the same thoughts. It was admirable for her to be at his beck and call, but while he was occupied with his military training, it did not look well for a princess-in-waiting to do little but shop, take posh vacations, and go nightclubbing, even if she did most of those things on William's arm. The queen is fond of career women. Kate had been working for Party Pieces, and she upped her presence at her parents' company by including her photo on the Web site, but the move backfired, seen as self-serving for the Middletons. After the queen suggested that Catherine do some charity work, in September 2008 she became involved with the Starlight Children's Foundation, which helps seriously ill children.

And yet Kate was damned if she did and damned if she didn't. Ungainly photos of her in a fun but tarty little costume, taken the moment after she landed flat on her back during the foundation's Day-Glo Midnight Roller Disco fund-raiser, made it into the papers, and the palace expressed displeasure. A courtier told Richard Kay of the *Daily Mail*, "The Queen already thinks that Kate is something of a show-off" [which seems to contradict HRM's other quoted opinions of her], and they were "appalled at what they saw as a most unladylike display," a comment that was extremely unfair to the ordinarily elegant, athletic, and discreet Kate, who'd been snapped the moment she'd lost her balance. Splattering the crotch shot of the potential future queen all over the tabloids had surely been deliberate. In any case, the roller disco event, undoubtedly aided by Kate's presence, raised more than $200,000 for the Starlight Children's Foundation, and Kate increased her involvement with the charity.

On September 15, 2008, Clarence House announced that William would devote himself to flying, rather than to royal duties, fulfilling his dream of becoming a search-and-rescue pilot. Initially, he had wished to be deployed overseas when his unit was called up, but this was deemed too risky, not to mention the fact that he represented the future of the English monarchy and its best hope. However, the prince didn't want his military training to be wasted and had discovered a way to serve his country that both fulfilled him and kept him out of combat areas. Nonetheless, even the palace was stunned by the announcement. So, too, was Catherine. By joining the RAF at age twenty-six, William could postpone his royal duties for up to five years, because the air force would occupy him full-time. What would that bode for a royal wedding? How long could Waity Katie wait?

According to biographer Christopher Andersen, after securing the blessing of the queen and Prince Charles, William finally proposed during a candlelit dinner in a cozy fishing cabin at Balmoral in January 2009. The royal family whipped out their calendars, hatching secret plans to announce both the royal engagement and a wedding date. The year 2012 was already crowded, with the queen's Diamond Jubilee and the Summer Olympics, and 2013 was deemed too far away by William. The groom would be spending the better part of 2010 earning his RAF wings, so that was eliminated as well—leaving 2011 as the best option. As Prince Philip would turn ninety on June 10, 2011, "What a lovely birthday present for your grandfather," the queen told William.

Andersen's contention about this proposal date, coming

approximately twenty months before William's formal proposal in Kenya (which evidently took Kate by surprise), seems confusing. Did William reassure Kate that he intended to marry her in January 2009, and the royal family penciled in a wedding date—another step toward the altar—but the prince didn't actually pop the question on bended knee with a ring in hand for many months? Why? Was he waiting for the right moment to surprise Kate so the proposal would feel romantic and spontaneous and all about just the two of them, rather than like a massive troop maneuver?

Meanwhile, Kate continued to be an avid student of her royal beau, determined to understand, if not fully share, his passions, the better to ensure a more seamless transition from plebian to princess. Only a completely devoted girlfriend would sit apart from the champagne drinkers during her sweetheart's polo matches, closely observing the action instead of socializing, and explaining to a guest, "I've got to pay attention to every second. I'll be discussing the game in minute detail later on." Asked why she didn't play polo herself, Kate replied, "I'm allergic to horses."

A member of the Beaufort Polo Club observed, "You certainly get the feeling that she works very hard at making Prince William happy. To the rest of us it might seem a little desperate, but then consider what's at stake."

Title, position, wealth—and love—were at stake, as well as all the energy and passion invested in a romance that had endured nearly a decade of ups, downs, and growing pains, and all in the public eye.

According to Christopher Andersen, somewhat contradicting his own anecdote about the events of January 2009 at Balmoral, in September 2010, William told his father that the time was finally right to pop the question. The Prince of Wales replied, "Well, you've certainly practiced long enough." William secured the queen's blessing as well, later remarking that she was "as happy and excited" as he'd ever seen her, adding, with tongue firmly in cheek, except possibly when "one of her horses is racing at Ascot."

Whatever may have happened between them at Balmoral in January of 2009, William formally proposed to Kate in Kenya. They had gone to visit Lewa Downs, the Craigs' game preserve. One morning the prince borrowed a helicopter and whisked Kate up to a lake nestled into the slope of Mount Kenya, about 12,500 feet above sea level—the same spot where he and Jecca Craig had plighted their troth when he was eighteen.

William knelt and offered Catherine his mother's eighteen-carat sapphire engagement ring. Caught off guard, she burst into tears. "It was very romantic. There is a true romantic in there," she later told the media. Of the ring, it was "my way of making sure my mother didn't miss out on today," William said.

On November 16, 2010, William and Kate, both twenty-eight years old, held a press conference and announced their engagement. The couple then sat down with ITV's Tom Bradby and gave their first public interview. When asked whether they were nervous about getting married and everything that now lay before them, William admitted to being "like little ducks, very calm on the surface, but little feet going like crazy under the water."

It was the first time that most people heard Catherine Elizabeth Middleton speak. Her voice was soft and breathy, with the same high-pitched upper-class diction that marks the vocal quality of the Windsor women. Regarding their ten-week split in 2007, Kate confessed, "I, at the time, wasn't very happy about it, but actually it made me a stronger person. You find out things about yourself that maybe you hadn't realized." After William released a dramatic "Whew!" Kate added that the separation ended up being "all about finding a bit of space and finding ourselves, about growing up—and it all worked out for the better."

William concurred, adding that their relationship now was "incredibly easy, because we took the time."

And Kate admitted that the prospect of filling the shoes of the previous Princess of Wales is a daunting one, and fitting into the royal family "nerve-wracking. I don't know the ropes . . . but I'm willing to learn quickly and work hard. I really hope I can make a difference."

And one day the modest girl from Bucklebury will call Buckingham Palace home. She and William were married in 2011 on St. Catherine's Day—April 29—in Westminster Abbey. They had approximately nineteen hundred invited guests, who represented the vast spectrum of society on both a state and a personal level, encompassing members of

Britain's royal family, foreign dignitaries and heads of state, representatives from charities with which William has had a long relationship, and locals from the Middletons' hometown in Berkshire, including the butcher, the publican, and the convenience store proprietors. According to tradition, the Archbishop of Canterbury officiated over the vows with the participation of the Very Reverend Dr. John Hall, Dean of Westminster.

Catherine, who did her own makeup, was radiant in an ivory gown with a nine-foot train designed by Sarah Burton, of the house of Alexander McQueen. The long lace sleeves and corseted bodice with its nipped-in waist were reminiscent of the wedding gown worn by the late Princess of Monaco Grace Kelly, although in a nod to the bride's personal sense of style, Kate's dress sported a plunging neckline. The dress had been successfully kept a secret from everyone, even William, who was seen to murmur, "You look beautiful" to his bride when she met him at the altar.

The most-speculated-about garment in three decades was created by Sarah Burton, the lead designer for the atelier of the late English couturier Alexander McQueen. According to the palace's official statement, "Miss Middleton wished for her dress to combine tradition and modernity" and "worked closely with Sarah Burton in formulating the design of her dress."

The seamstresses from the Royal School of Needlework, based at Hampton Court Palace, ranging in age from nineteen to seventy, did not know whose garment they were creating. They had been told they were building a dress for a period movie and were not even informed of the identity of the designer. In order to keep the fabric pristine, the women had to wash their hands every thirty minutes and switch to new needles every three hours in order to ensure the appropriate level of sharpness for such meticulous work.

The dress was constructed from ivory and white satin gazar, intended to resemble an opening flower, with white satin gazar arches and pleats. In keeping with Alexander McQueen's looking-back-yet-fashion-forward signature approach to couture, the gown's ivory satin bodice was narrowed at the waist and padded at the hips. It echoed both the Victorian tradition of corsetry as well as a very modern interpretation of sixteenth-century court fashion. The train measured two meters, seventy centimeters—nearly seven feet long—but was modest in comparison to Princess Diana's dramatic twenty-five-foot train. The back of Kate's wedding gown was finished with fifty-eight gazar-and-organza-covered buttons fastened in the traditional way, with Rouleau loops. The underskirt was constructed of silk tulle trimmed with Cluny lace.

Every bit of the lace appliqué for the bodice and skirt was hand-made and then appliquéd onto the gown using the Carrickmacross lace-making technique, which originated in Ireland in the 1820s. The individual flowers incorporated emblems from across the United Kingdom: the English rose, Scottish thistle, Welsh daffodil, and Irish shamrock. They were hand-cut from lace, then painstakingly stitched onto ivory silk tulle to create a one-of-a-kind design, although bridal couturiers everywhere sought to emulate the gown's silhouette as soon as Kate stepped out of the Rolls-Royce.

The vee-necked bodice and A-line skirt, as well as the trim on the underskirt of Kate's gown, utilized hand-cut English lace as well as French Chantilly lace. Sarah Burton's team vigilantly ensured that all of the floral lace embellishment, coming as it did from multiple sources, was the same shade of white.

There had also been much speculation as to whether Kate would wear a tiara, or, because it was assumed that she would enter the Abbey as a commoner, whether she might wear a wreath of flowers in her hair (even though it was Queen Victoria who set the fashion for orange blossoms). Catherine opted for the former. She wore a modest tiara with a delicate scroll-shaped design loaned to her by the queen. According to the palace's official press release, Catherine's

> . . . veil [was] made of layers of soft ivory silk tulle with a trim of hand embroidered flowers . . . held in place by a Cartier "halo" tiara, lent to Miss Middleton by The Queen. The "halo" tiara was made by Cartier in 1936 and was purchased by The Duke of York (later King George VI) for his Duchess (later Queen Elizabeth The Queen Mother) three weeks before he succeeded his brother as King. The tiara was presented to Princess Elizabeth (now The Queen) by her mother on the occasion of her 18th birthday.

Yet Kate did not enter Westminster Abbey as a commoner after all. On the morning of the wedding, Queen Elizabeth made Prince William and Catherine the Duke and Duchess of Cambridge. William's full title until the death of his father is Duke of Cambridge, Earl of Strathearn, and Baron Carrickfergus. His wife cannot officially be called Princess Catherine until she becomes Princess of Wales, owing to the passing of Prince Charles or the death of Queen Elizabeth and Charles's immediate ascension to the throne.

William, who wore the scarlet tunic of a colonel of the Irish Guards, displayed some of his late mother's charm and wicked sense of humor. Even at the altar, he put his visibly nervous bride at ease (after all, two billion people were watching them on television from around the world). "This was supposed to be a small family affair," he whispered to Kate just before the wedding ceremony began, eliciting a grin from her, even as she gripped her father Michael's hand.

During the recitation of the vows, William and Catherine maintained eye contact, the love between them abundantly evident. Meanwhile, Prince Harry, William's best man, or "supporter," as the English call it, looked straight ahead, or cast his eyes downward, pondering the solemnity of the occasion. He would coo, "You're next," to longtime girlfriend Chelsy Davy during the evening bash, but the couple has since split yet again.

As Catherine recited her vows in a soft, audibly nervous soprano, the look in William's eyes seemed to provide his silent reassurance that not only was he there for her in that moment and that everything was going to be all right, but that he would *always* be there for her all the days of their lives. There was visible relief all around once the vows had been spoken and the couple was seated to listen to the address given by the Right Reverend and Right Honourable Dr. Richard Chartres, Lord Bishop of London and Dean of Her Majesty's Chapels Royal. At one point during the sermon, William appeared to give Catherine a little wink.

Mindful of the current economic climate, the royal wedding was toned down from the lavish pageantry of William's parents' nuptials, but there were a number of modern twists. Catherine, who had mined her closet for the modestly priced dresses she wore in her engagement photos and at her first press conference with William, arrived at the Abbey in a car—albeit a Rolls-Royce Phantom IV—rather than in a coach. The couple had asked all but their immediate relations to give charitable donations in lieu of gifts. Fulfilling William's desire to hold the first-ever "people's wedding," in addition to inviting the requisite heads of state, the bridal couple peppered their guest list with charity workers. On the night before the ceremony, William and Prince Harry went out to greet the fans who had been camping on the street outside Clarence House, securing a prime location to view the royal procession. These hard-core royal watchers, many of whom were sporting silly hats and faces painted with the Union Jack, were over the moon with delight.

The traditional kiss on the balcony of Buckingham Palace after the wedding ceremony turned out to be two smooches—and they meant it. "Oh, wow," Kate breathed when the newlyweds first stepped out onto the balcony and saw a million well-wishers gathered below, stretching from the Victoria monument all the way down the Mall.

And in an extra treat for the public, the newly minted Duke and Duchess of Cambridge tootled from the palace down the Mall to Clarence House for a few hours of R & R between the queen's three p.m. reception and Prince Charles's evening bash, in the navy blue Aston Martin Volante convertible that the Prince of Wales had given to his oldest son as a twenty-first birthday present. William was behind the wheel, with his bride smiling and waving beside him. He had changed into a navy military tunic, but Catherine was still wearing her gown. Tin cans had been tied to the bumper, and the license plate read, JUST WED.

In another modern shocker, Kate and William didn't even jet off on an expensive honeymoon following the wedding reception. They enjoyed a private weekend at an undisclosed location before the new Duke of Cambridge returned to his RAF duties the following Tuesday morning. Although the twenty-room, four-story apartment in Kensington Palace once occupied by William's great-aunt Princess Margaret is being renovated for the Cambridges, the refurbishment is not expected to be completed until 2013. Kate and William will be spending much of their first few years of married life in less-than-glamorous Anglesey, Wales, where the duke is completing his RAF training. There they reside in a modest rented cottage without a staff of servants, and as newlyweds they had not initially intended to make any changes to that routine. According to royal biographer Katie Nicholl, Kate "loves cooking. They like to make British dinner parties. Their favorite dish is 'toad in the hole'—[a] very fattening—keep-you-warm-in-the-winter" English comfort-food staple.

The young couple's very normal lifestyle couldn't be more different from William's father's standard of living. Prince Charles has a staff of 149, including a butler just to squeeze the toothpaste onto the royal brush.

All too aware of the media circus that surrounded Diana's lonely and painful transition into The Firm, William remains highly protective of Catherine, and always expressed his intention to ease her conversion from commoner to princess as gently as possible. In this exercise of good old-fashioned chivalry, he has behaved like a prince, his birthright notwithstanding. But more than that, William once said, "My mother was the People's Princess. I want to be the People's King." As he and Catherine are determined to be a very modern royal couple, how he manages to strike the balance between centuries of tradition and his own vision of modernity remains to be seen. The future of England's monarchy is in their hands.

Acknowledgments

Perennial thanks to my agent, Irene Goodman, and my editor, Claire Zion, for their unflagging support for this fourth title in my nonfiction series of books on royal scandals and scandalous royals. As ever, I am also indebted to the most understanding husband on earth for accepting without a word of complaint the long hours and late nights it took to complete this opus, and for his ultimate display of support: He not only accompanied me to London for the royal wedding of Prince William to Catherine Middleton, but eased the journey with the purchase of extra frequent-flyer miles so that we could travel business class and arrive rested, knowing that I would be giving a number of media interviews that week. And, most gallantly of all, he awakened with me in the predawn hours on April 29, 2011, so that we could secure a prime spot on the Mall—and then, despite an aching back, remained standing beside me amid a fantastic, joyous sea of die-hard royal wedding watchers for eight hours straight so that I could derive the maximum enjoyment from the atmosphere as the events of the day unfolded.

This, dear readers, is a true romance.

Selected Bibliography

Abbott, Elizabeth. *Mistresses: A History of the Other Woman*. New York: The Overlook Press, 2010.

Algrant, Christine Pevitt. *Madame de Pompadour: Mistress of France*. New York: Grove/Atlantic, 2002.

Andersen, Christopher. *William and Kate: A Royal Love Story*. New York: Gallery Books, 2011.

Bernier, Olivier. *Louis the Beloved: The Life of Louis XV; A Reexamination of the Misjudged Monarch of the Civilized Century*. Garden City, New York: Doubleday, 1984.

———. *Louis XIV: A Royal Life*. New York: Doubleday, 1987.

Bradford, Sarah. *George VI*. London: Penguin Books, Ltd., 2011.

Brand, Emily. *Royal Weddings*. Great Britain: Shire Publications, 2011.

Buckley, Veronica. *The Secret Wife of Louis XIV: Françoise d'Aubigné, Madame de Maintenon*. New York: Picador, 2008.

Capefigue, M. (trans. Edmund Goldsmid). *A King's Mistress; Or Charles VII and Agnes Sorel, and Chivalry in the Fifteenth Century*. Edinburgh: Privately printed, 1887 [modern facsimile edition].

Castelot, André (trans. Denise Folliot). *Queen of France: A Biography of Marie Antoinette*. New York: Harper & Brothers, 1957.

Count Corti (trans. Evelyn B. Graham Stamper). *Ludwig I of Bavaria*. London: Eyre & Spottiswoode, 1943.

Cruttwell, Maud. *Madame de Maintenon*. London and Toronto: J. M. Dent & Sons Ltd., 1930.

Fraser, Antonia. *Love and Louis XIV: The Women in the Life of the Sun King*. New York: Doubleday, 2006.

———. *Marie Antoinette: The Journey*. New York: Doubleday, 2001.

Frieda, Leonie. *Catherine de Medici: Renaissance Queen of France*. New York: HarperCollins Publishers, Inc., 2003.

Haslip, Joan. *Madame DuBarry: The Wages of Beauty*. London and New York: Tauris Parke Paperbacks, 2005.

Hatton, Ragnild. *George I*. New Haven: Yale University Press, 2001.

Herman, Eleanor. *Sex with Kings: Five Hundred Years of Adultery, Power, Rivalry, and Revenge*. New York: Harper Perennial, 2004.

———. *Sex with the Queen: 900 Years of Vile Kings, Virile Lovers, and Passionate Politics*. New York: William Morrow, 2006.

Herold, J. Christopher. *The Age of Napoleon*. New York: First Mariner Books, 2002.

Hibbert, Christopher. *Napoleon's Women*. New York: W. W. Norton & Company, 2004.

Hilton, Lisa. *Athénaïs: The Life of Louis XIV's Mistress, the Real Queen of France*. New York: Back Bay Books, 2002.

Joseph, Claudia. *Kate: Kate Middleton: Princess in Waiting*. New York: Avon Books, 2009.

Lever, Evelyne [trans. Catherine Temerson]. *Madame de Pompadour: A Life*. New York: St. Martin's Griffin, 2000.

———. *Marie Antoinette: The Last Queen of France*. New York: Farrar, Straus & Giroux, 2000.

Loomis, Stanley. *Du Barry: A Biography*. Philadelphia & New York: J. B. Lippincott Company, 1959.

———.*The Fatal Friendship: Marie Antoinette, Count Fersen, and the Flight to Varennes*. New York: Avon Books, 1972.

Mangan, J. J. *The King's Favour: Three Eighteenth-century Monarchs and the Favourites Who Ruled Them*. Phoenix Mill, Far Thrupp, Stroud, Gloucestershire: Alan Sutton Publishing, Ltd. 1993.

Massie, Robert K. *Catherine the Great: Portrait of a Woman*. New York: Random House, 2011.

Mitford, Nancy. *Madame de Pompadour*. New York: New York Review of Books, 2001 (title originally copyrighted 1953).

———. *The Sun King*. New York: Penguin Books, 1994.

Montefiore, Simon Sebag. *Potemkin: Catherine the Great's Imperial Partner*. New York: Vintage Books, 2005.

Morand, Paul. *The Captive Princess: Sophia Dorothea of Celle*. New York: American Heritage Press, 1972.

Morton, James. *Lola Montez: Her Life and Conquests*. London: Piatkus-Books Ltd., 2007.

Nicholl, Katie. *William and Harry: Behind the Palace Walls*. New York: Weinstein Books, 2010.

Palmer, Alan. *Napoleon & Marie Louise: The Emperor's Second Wife*. New York: St. Martin's Press, 2001.

Princess Michael of Kent. *Cupid and the King: Five Royal Paramours*. New York: Touchstone, 2005.

———. *The Serpent and the Moon: Two Rivals for the Love of a Renaissance King*. New York: Touchstone, 2004.

Rounding, Virginia. *Catherine the Great: Love, Sex, and Power*. New York: St. Martin's Press, 2006.

Seymour, Bruce. *Lola Montez: A Life*. New Haven: Yale University Press, 1996.

Shawcross, William. *The Queen Mother: The Official Biography*. New York: Vintage Books, 2010.

Sutherland, Christine. *Marie Walewska: Napoleon's Great Love*. London: Robin Clark Ltd., 1986.

Thomson, Oliver. *The Impossible Bourbons: Europe's Most Ambitious Dynasty*. Stroud, Gloucestershire: Amberley Publishing, 2009.

Thornton, Michael. *Royal Feud: The Dark Side of the Love Story of the Century*. New York: Simon and Schuster, 1985.

Tillyard, Stella. *A Royal Affair: George III and His Scandalous Siblings*. New York: Random House, 2006.

Webster, Nesta. *Louis XVI and Marie Antoinette During the Revolution*. New York: Gordon Press, 1976.

Zweig, Stefan. *Marie Antoinette: The Portrait of an Average Woman*. New York: Grove Press, 1933.

ARTICLES

Aldridge, D. D. "Caroline Matilda, Princess (1751–1775)." In *Oxford Dictionary of National Biography*, edited by H. C. G. Matthew and Brian Harrison. Oxford: OUP, 2004. Online ed., edited by Lawrence Goldman, January 2008. http://www.oxforddnb.com/view/article/4721

Goldman, Lawrence. "Elizabeth (1900–2002)." In *Oxford Dictionary of National Biography*, online ed., edited by Lawrence Goldman. Oxford: OUP, January 2006. Online ed., edited by Lawrence Goldman, January 2011. http://www.oxforddnb.com/view/article/76927

Matthew, H. C. G. "George VI (1895–1952)." In *Oxford Dictionary of National Biography*, edited by H. C. G. Matthew and Brian Harrison.

Oxford: OUP, 2004. Online ed., edited by Lawrence Goldman, January 2011. http://www.oxforddnb.com/view/article/33370

Seymour, Bruce. "Montez, Lola (1821–1861)." In *Oxford Dictionary of National Biography*, edited by H. C. G. Matthew and Brian Harrison. Oxford: OUP, 2004. Online ed., edited by Lawrence Goldman, May 2008. http://www.oxforddnb.com/view/article/10697

WEB SITES

The American Heritage® Dictionary of the English Language, Fourth Edition. S.v. "romance." Retrieved November 14, 2010, from http://www.thefreedictionary.com/romance

http://www.officialroyalwedding2011.org/tag/homepage/page/3

Photo by Ron Rinaldi

LESLIE CARROLL is the author of several works of women's fiction and, under the pen names Juliet Grey and Amanda Elyot, is a multi-published author of historical fiction. *Royal Romances* is her fourth foray into the field of historical nonfiction for NAL. She is also the author of *The Royals: The Lives and Loves of the British Monarchs*, a Barnes & Noble publication featuring facsimiles of historical memorabilia. A frequent commentator on royal romances and relationships, Leslie has been interviewed by MSNBC.com, *USA Today*, the Australian Broadcasting Company, and NPR, and was a featured royalty expert on the *CBS Evening News* broadcast from London during the royal wedding coverage of Prince William and Catherine Middleton. She also appears as an expert on the lives of Queen Victoria, Marie Antoinette, Catherine the Great, and Napoleon on Canada's Proper Television documentary series *The Secret Life of. . . .* Leslie and her husband, Scott, divide their time between New York City and southern Vermont.

CONNECT ONLINE

www.lesliecarroll.com